THE NATIONAL HISTORY OF FRANCE

THE RESTORATION AND THE JULY MONARCHY

BY

J. LUCAS-DUBRETON

TRANSLATED FROM THE FRENCH BY

E. F. BUCKLEY

NEW YORK

G. P. PUTNAM'S SONS

MCMXXIX

Printed in Great Britain

CONTENTS

THE RESTORATION

THE JULY MONARCHY

THE RESTORATION

CHAPTER I

THE RETURN FROM GHENT

The 19th of March, 1815, at the Tuileries. The sojourn at Ghent. The Life of Louis XVIII before the Restoration. Waterloo. The King's difficulties on his return to France. Fouché the man of the hour. The entry into Paris. The Allies' hatred of France: the incident of the Pont d'Iéna. Fall of Fouché and of Talleyrand. The Duc de Richelieu. The Treaty of the 20th of November 1815, and the Holy Alliance. France in leading-strings. The birth of the Napoleonic legend. The state of the country on the accession of Louis XVIII.

ABOUT eleven o'clock on the night of March the 19th, 1815, the Tuileries presented a curious spectacle. Lifeguardsmen, courtisans and servants were all hustling each other on the stairs leading to the private apartments. Suddenly a door was thrown open, an usher appeared, bearing a torch, and behind came the King, Louis XVIII, leaning on the arm of the Duc d'Havré.

On seeing the sovereign who, having returned from exile only in the previous year, was now being driven out again at the approach of Napoleon, the crowd gave vent to loud cries and lamentations. "My children," said Louis XVIII, "spare me! I have need of all my courage." And heavily, step by step, he descended the stairs surrounded by his prostrate people. A few seconds later the carriage of the King of France was rattling towards the northern frontier.

The Sojourn at Ghent.

The Belgians, whom conscription and the liquor tax had inspired with but little love for the Empire, welcomed the exiled monarch with open arms. In Ghent a fine mansion with a façade adorned with Corinthian pilasters, belonging to Comte d'Hane de Steenhuyse, had been held in readiness for him, and as soon as he had been installed, Louis' first thought was to re-establish his Court and his household. Seven hundred officers and soldiers had joined him, thus providing a retinue worthy of his rank, and every day he used to summon his council of Ministers—Ministers *in partibus*, that is to say, for what territory had they to govern? He even had an official journal, the *Moniteur de Gand*, in which his ordinances were published. All this was not due to mere vanity, but arose from a desire to prove that where the King was in residence, there too was the monarchy installed.

Meanwhile the French troops, under the leadership of generals, many of whom had rallied to the cause of the Bourbons a few months previously, were concentrating in the north and marching to meet the Allied armies, the Anglo-Dutch army under Wellington, and the Prussian army under Blücher, who were stationed south of Brussels and west of Namur respectively.

On the evening of the 16th of June the roar of the cannon was heard in Ghent at the King's Court, and gave rise to a sort of panic. But Louis XVIII for his part remained perfectly calm, and said, "Let anybody who is afraid go away." Nevertheless when the news of the Emperor's victory at Quatre-Bras reached him, he had his carriages made ready. On the 18th, when rumours of a French victory had spread through the town, he continued to hide his anxiety beneath a mask of intrepidity, but, as a matter of fact, as Chateaubriand, who was an eye-witness, observed, "the legitimate monarch was stored away in d'Hane de Steenhuyse's mansion like a dilapidated old wagon." An official bulletin was awaited at the gates of the town, but none came; and that evening, contrary to the etiquette which he usually observed with punctilious care, Louis XVIII refused to go to bed. Although he was fat and crippled with gout, he walked alone from his armchair to the window, all his senses agog, and during this vigil on alien soil he recapitulated the various stages of his life.

Louis XVIII's Past Life.

A fugitive from France in 1791, having escaped the scaffold and the fate of his brother Louis XVI by the skin of his teeth, he became King on the death of the little Dauphin Louis XVII. Obliged to seek refuge in Italy, he found himself driven out by the victorious Bonaparte, and tried to find shelter in the ranks of the *émigrés*, only to be hunted out once more, to wander in Germany. In answer to his prayers, he was received in Courland by the Tsar Paul I, a strange creature, who, after heaping favours upon him, suddenly ordered him to "clear out of the country." Crossing Germany again, he arrived in Warsaw, whence, at the command of Bonaparte, who had become Napoleon, he was again driven forth, and found a refuge through the generosity of the Tsar Alexander. Fleeing before the advance of the victorious Usurper, he crossed over to England, and there, at Hartwell, he sank into oblivion and into semi-destitution. He ate the bitter bread of exile and humiliated himself to the extent of begging for help from sovereigns who were really his inferiors; for was he not by right divine the first monarch of Europe? More often than not he was met only with promises, and, scouted and scorned, was gradually deserted even by his servants. As the star of Napoleon rose to the ascendant, so did his own line of life descend irrevocably to the depths.

In 1814 the situation was suddenly reversed. On the defeat of the Usurper, Louis XVIII, who was then almost sixty, saw delegates from France bearing the white flag presenting themselves before him in his solitary retreat at Hartwell, and soon afterwards he ascended the throne amid the acclamations of the people. Wisdom and policy had led him to grant certain liberties to his subjects, a charter whereby he had hoped to win their hearts. Had he been wrong? Had he made mistakes himself or allowed others to do so? Leaving the Isle of Elba on the 1st of March, 1815, Napoleon had invaded France without striking a blow; the army, the people, the provinces and Paris had thrown themselves at his feet. And now the last act was being played on the plains of Belgium, a few miles from Ghent, and Louis XVIII was wondering whether he had gone into exile for the second time only to see the final overthrow of all his hopes.

Were all his patience and tenacity and all the concessions he had made to that new world, which his traditions and upbringing taught him to hold in detestation, only to end in this catastrophe? Yes, this war, as Pitt, the English Prime Minister, had said, was a war to the death—Napoleon or Louis. Had the Bourbons been condemned by France and by Providence? And was he, in the evening of his life, to start once more upon his wanderings and become the plaything of Fate? And then the idea that he might perhaps have misunderstood public opinion and acted unwisely towards those who should have been his main support gradually insinuated itself into his mind, and possibly without confessing it to himself, a sense of his responsibilities slowly stole over him.

In the courtyard of the mansion the horses were neighing, the footmen were jostling each other in their haste, and in the shadows the adherents of the monarchy were whispering words of despair. . . . But about two o'clock in the morning a courier from General Wellington announced the rout of the French army at Waterloo (18th of June). Whereupon the King went to bed.

The Hundred Days—that is to say, the interregnum of Napoleon—once more raised the question of the dynasty, which had been regarded as settled in 1814. The Tsar Alexander I disliked the Bourbons, and was of opinion that if they were allowed to return to the throne they had been unable to keep, France and all Europe would be exposed to fresh complications; he accordingly supported the candidature of a member of the junior branch of the House of Bourbon, the Duc d'Orléans, who had not sought refuge in Ghent, and might play a great part, since he had not compromised himself. Metternich, the Austrian Minister for Foreign Affairs, was in almost complete agreement with him; but Wellington, the victor of Waterloo, pointed out that the Duc d'Orléans, who would be regarded as a usurper, would endeavour to obliterate the illegality of his title by means of foreign wars and conquests, and that the younger branch thus presented the same menace as the elder. In the end Paris, through the Chambers, pronounced in favour of the little King of Rome, Napoleon II, who had become Emperor on the abdication of his father. Louis XVIII, the Duc d'Orléans, Napoleon II—which of the three was to be the future master?

Fouché.

The man who at this juncture was directing the home as well as the foreign policy of France had once been an Oratory Brother and had voted for the execution of Louis XVI. He had also been a Minister under Napoleon, and had returned to office during the Hundred Days. Fouché in fact had his finger in every pie and aimed at securing a place in any combination, keeping in active touch with Louis XVIII, sending envoys to Austria to plead the cause of the King of Rome, and writing to Talleyrand, the French representative in Vienna, to sound diplomatic circles regarding the candidature of the Duc d'Orléans.

Louis XVIII, who was endowed with a fine sensitiveness, was perfectly well aware of these intrigues, and, to cut a long story short, returned to France immediately after Waterloo, hoping thereby to establish his claim and "to steal his throne." At le Cateau he issued a proclamation announcing that "the powerful efforts of his allies had dispersed the tyrant's satellites" and that he was going to bring the existing laws into execution against the culprits. But when Wellington pointed out to him that to address the country with threats on his lips was not exactly the means best calculated to restore confidence, he issued a second proclamation from Cambrai couched in wise paternal terms, in which he confessed that his Government had no doubt been guilty of mistakes, and promised to pardon all those Frenchmen who had been misguided, with the exception of those whom the Chambers should appoint to be excluded from his clemency. Thus he left the painful duties to others, arrogating to himself those that would bring him popularity. But these were not the only results of Waterloo.

Paris had just capitulated to the Allied armies. There was no executive or legislative body left, and thirty soldiers had been sufficient to disperse the Chamber of Deputies, amid the ruins of which Fouché alone remained untouched. As he had protected the Royalists and the old revolutionaries, the Jacobins, during the Hundred Days, he was master of the situation. Was it then incumbent to come to terms with him? Talleyrand had already advised the King to do so; but the latter, thumping the arms of his chair, had replied with a "Never!" which had the appearance of finality. But he was obliged in the end to give way, and, what was worse, it was not Fouché who had to humble himself, but the King.

All parties, even the most extreme Royalists who appealed to the Duc d'Artois, the King's brother, were agreed in regarding him as indispensable, a necessary evil. He alone had the power to preserve the Bourbons from a second fall, to chain down "the hydra of revolution" which was perpetually raising its head, to come to terms with the victorious Allies and ensure the King's safe return to the capital. The Jacobins, on the other hand, and the Liberal bourgeois saw in him a bulwark against further reaction and the *émigré* spirit, from which they had suffered in 1814, at the time of the first Restoration. But the King would not consent. They put the alternative before him—he must accept either Fouché or the tricoloured cockade. And if the Minister was absolutely repugnant to him, what harm was there in hoisting the colours he had once worn? It was a clever way of putting the question; when it was a matter of emblems, Louis XVIII did not hesitate; the idea of abandoning the traditional symbol of royalty was not to be thought of. When he took to flight in 1791, in order to save his life he might, it is true, have worn the "revolutionary bauble"; but now nothing in the world would induce him to appear in the colours of a rebellious people. In vain did Army men like Masséna, who had rallied to the cause of the Bourbons, insist that "his colours were very old"; supported by the Comte d'Artois, he only replied, "I would prefer to pick up a lump of mud and stick it in my hat."

The affair was settled. The King thought it would be easier to get rid of a Minister than of a flag; but when the order for Fouché's nomination was put in front of him the blood rose to his temples. After having for years posed as the avenger of Louis XVI, to choose one of his executioners as Minister—what an affront to the memory of the martyr! He remained silent for a few moments, then sighing, "Alas, my poor brother!" he signed his name. Soon afterwards Talleyrand entered the King's cabinet at Saint Denis, and on his arm was a tall man, with white hair and blood-shot eyes and a certain ferocious elegance and agility reminiscent of a panther. It was Fouché, Duc d'Otrante, "the erstwhile monk and executioner, now the maker of Kings."

The new Minister soon made his presence felt; he enveloped Louis XVIII with terror. According to him the entry into Paris was going to be no easy matter. The white cockade and the acclamations of the Life-Guards might give rise to disturbances. The vanquished Bonapartists might make a move.

He was of opinion that the choice of route was bad; the Faubourg Saint Denis, with its narrow streets and working-class houses, would be dangerous; the Rue de Clichy would be better. But the King did not agree with him. "I have not the misfortune to stand in fear of my people," he said, "and I shall enter by way of the Faubourg Saint Denis." Whereupon, feeling that he had kept his sovereign waiting long enough at the gates of the capital, Fouché "let him have his head."

It was July, and from fear of the heat, or possibly from a belated sense of prudence, Louis XVIII did not drive in an open carriage. On horseback beside him rode his brother, the Comte d'Artois, and his nephew, the Duc de Berry, accompanied by the Marshals who had remained loyal—Marmont, Gouvion Saint-Cyr, Oudinot, and Victor. The cheering, which at first was faint, grew louder on the Boulevard and the Place Vendôme. The crowd sang *Vive Henri IV* and *Rendez-nous notre père de Gand*, the popular songs of the day; and when Louis XVIII appeared on the balcony of the Tuileries, and a sergeant of the National Guard came forward to kiss his hand, and the actor Huet presented him with a banner bearing the device *Vive notre père de Gand!* the crowd went mad with enthusiasm. The King tried to speak, but whether from theatricality or moved by genuine feeling, he was only able to say, "My friends . . ." In the evening the streets were illuminated as it were by the touch of a magic wand, and while the Life-Guards were breaking up the furniture and mirrors in the Café Montasier, the meeting-place of the Bonapartists, where the Bourbons were lampooned, the people of Paris "were dancing before the arch" on the lawn of the Tuileries. A few days later, the Duchesse d'Angoulême, the daughter of Louis XVI, arrived. The people had nicknamed her *l'Orpheline du Temple*, in memory of her sufferings at the time of the Revolution. The popular enthusiasm had in no way abated, and women dressed in white, with a lily embroidered on their bodices, held out their children to the princess as if to beg her blessing.

The Entry into Paris.

"I cannot believe that the French are so happy over their defeat," wrote a certain Englishman, disconcerted by such sights. But it was impossible for the foreigner to understand that Paris stood in dire need of rest after the shocks she had received, that the bourgeoisie, feeling that their hour had come, hoped by means of the Bourbons and the re-establishment of peace to improve their own position and gradually to supersede in the social hierarchy "the military caste" which had been paramount since the Empire, and that, lastly, the merchants saw in the return of Louis XVIII the prospect of a period of tranquillity in which to return to their avocations. But the presence of the victors was destined to disillusion this mob which had been just as eager to welcome the Emperor as they were to acclaim the King.

The Allies' Hatred of France.

The flowers had not faded and the white flags and candles were still to be seen all along the avenues, when the three foreign monarchs, the Russian, the Austrian and the Prussian, armed, helmeted, booted and spurred, made their entry into Paris. They were no longer "the generous Allies of 1814," but veterans weary of fighting an indomitable people, intent on vengeance and "breathing hate." The Prussians above all were conspicuous for their violence. Napoleon's brigands were to be wiped out—the Waterloo army which had been relegated to the other side of the Loire—the impious country must be dismembered and sacked; this would be the task of the brave Teutons! Russia was not so brutal, but she was angry with the Bourbons, who never learnt from experience and whose mistakes would no doubt give rise to fresh crises. The Englishman, for his part, took up a high moral tone; he was of opinion that the crushing of Bonaparte was nothing; the spirit displayed by France during the Hundred Days was sufficient proof that her pride had been in no way humbled; and when Talleyrand protested against the spoliation of the French museums and monuments, Wellington replied, "The day of reckoning has come. The Allied monarchs must not lose this opportunity of giving the French a severe moral lesson."

From the Tuileries Louis XVIII could see the Cossacks bivouacking in the courtyard and drying their clothes on the railings, the white cloaks of the Austrians blocking the entrance to the Carrousel, and further on the guns levelled, with their teams in attendance, the matches ready lighted. "Who are they angry with?" he inquired. "I shall never believe that the monarchs have authorised any such thing." It was the whole of France that they were angry with, the France of Napoleon, who had been victorious too long; and the demands of the Prussians were exaggerated to the point of insolence.

Field-Marshal Blücher gave the order for the Pont d'Iéna, which commemorated a Prussian defeat, to be blown up.

The Pont d'Iéna.

When Talleyrand informed Louis XVIII of this, the latter, moved by a natural impulse, immediately wrote, "If necessary I shall have myself conveyed to the bridge, and you can blow me up if you like." This threat had not the slightest effect upon Blücher, who regarded the destruction of the bridge as a matter of his country's honour. Wellington and the Tsar were obliged to intervene. Prussian sappers were already digging the mine galleries; three explosions were heard, but they caused no damage; it was as if this relic of the Empire were resisting the work of the invaders. Louis XVIII persisted in offering his life, repeating that the action was an odious violation of the rights of nations and of the sanctity of treaties. And indeed the capitulation of Paris should have ensured the safety of public property. He even came out from the Tuileries, but found no soldiers on the bridge —the King of Prussia had commanded Blücher to stop the work. That day Louis XVIII really got into touch again with his people, and the cheers which met him when he returned without ceremony to the palace had a peculiar ring of sincerity.

The trials which were to strengthen the bonds between him and his subjects and gradually raise him to the rank of a national King, were not yet ended. Russia declared that France was too rich, and the poorer she was made the greater would be the prospects of peace. Somebody else objected that it was scandalous to see French women covered with diamonds. If monuments were not to be blown up, the people at least could be ruined. In the face of this avalanche of hatred the advanced Royalists, the *Ultras*, as they were called, lost their heads, and openly attacked the King who had dared to include in his Ministry the agents of the Revolution and of the Empire— Talleyrand and Fouché. The former, who had once been Bishop of Autun, had just defended the rights of France in

Vienna, with great pertinacity and skill, backed by extraordinary intelligence and pride and even a certain arrogance which it was astonishing to find in this lame man, "with his dull complexion, lack-lustre eyes, and loose, flabby skin." But the *Ultras* saw in him only a married priest who dragged behind him not only his leg, but also a past heavy with crime. As for Fouché, he was no longer the indispensable Minister, whom the Comte d'Artois had recommended to the better judgment of his brother, but merely "an odious creature."

In choosing Talleyrand, and resigning himself to Fouché, Louis XVIII had been prompted by the desire to form a strong Government, capable of securing law and order, which, whilst it inspired confidence in the Allies, also made it possible to resist their pretensions. France was in the hands of the invaders, treated "as No Man's Land," and the army of the Loire had been disbanded; it was accordingly through diplomatic channels alone that a treaty that was neither too humiliating nor too onerous could be obtained from the victors. The negotiations dragged on indefinitely; and Talleyrand decided once more to have recourse to the tactics he had found so successful in Vienna. He tried to divide the Powers in order to wrest concessions from them. But on this occasion the enemies of France maintained a united front, and the Tsar did not intervene on her behalf as he had done in 1814.

The position of the King was extremely difficult. Not only had he to hold his own against the Allies, but he was also faced by the *Ultra* party, who, after the elections of August 1815, had secured a majority in the Chamber. This party demanded, in the first place, the dismissal of Fouché, and, thanks to the officious care of Talleyrand, Fouché was indeed "executed." "I wrung his neck," declared the former. But Talleyrand himself, the sacrifice of whom the *Ultras* demanded with equal insistence and to whom, since his repulse by the Powers, the King no longer clung, was not long in following his victim. He was asked to resign, in the English fashion—"the corpse dragging the dying man in its wake."

Fall of Fouché and Talleyrand.

Thus the situation was cleared; but who was to defend France against the Allies? The King would not allow himself to be influenced, but summoned the Duc de Richelieu, an old *émigré*, Governor of Odessa and a personal friend of the Tsar. "An excellent choice," observed Talleyrand. "Monsieur de Richelieu is the one man in France who has the most profound knowledge of the Crimea." Whether this were so or not, the fallen diplomat was right—the King's choice was indeed excellent.

The Duc de Richelieu.

Among the figures of the Restoration, one of the most distinguished was without a doubt that of the Duc de Richelieu. This *grand seigneur*, always carelessly dressed, wearing Russian boots and with a black cravat round his neck, exuding the odour of a foul pipe wherever he went, was possessed of a native and inborn nobility, "which seemed to owe its origin entirely to the instincts of his soul and of his blood." Although he had lived away from his native land, there was nothing of the *émigré* about him; he had remained entirely French at heart, with all the best qualities of the Frenchman. He had the supremest contempt for wealth, and was endowed with a kind of candid simplicity and the most perfect goodness of heart.

Strong in the support afforded by the friendship of the Tsar, as well as in his own patriotism and probity, he fought the foreign diplomats inch by inch. The Allies were demanding from France the surrender of a piece of territory which had belonged to her since before 1790, that part of Savoy which had remained French, the dismantling of Huningue, an indemnity of 800 million francs and a military occupation for seven years. Prussia had demanded even more—the whole of Alsace-Lorraine. Richelieu succeeded in softening the terms of this savage treaty, saving Condé, Givet and Charlemont and the fortresses of Joux and l'Ecluse; the indemnity was reduced to 700 millions, and the occupation to five years, which under certain conditions was to be further reduced to three.

"Who will do me justice?" asked Richelieu, when the ratifications had been exchanged, "who will ever know the misfortunes I have spared my country, the scourges made ready to beat her with, which I have turned aside by signing this treaty, deplorable though it is?" His conscientiousness and anxiety made him feel dishonoured in acquiescing in the loss by France of places which had belonged to her since the time of Louis XIV, and in allowing Prussia, after having made an opening at Landau, to spread into the Rhine provinces and become her neighbour; and in self-defence he showed his intimates a German map, upon which had been traced a line depriving France of Metz, Lille and Strassburg. But now "it was all over." It only remained to raise France from the dust.

Treaty of November 20th, 1815.

But the Treaty of the 20th of November, 1815, which despoiled France of 500,000 inhabitants, was not enough for the Allies; they wanted moral guarantees. And this was the object of the Holy Alliance, the idea of which first occurred to the Tsar Alexander. A handsome man, with noble and melancholy features, the Tsar had long been an admirer of Napoleon, but all understanding of the age in which he lived and the capacity to take a realistic view of things were lacking in him. Following will-o'-the-wisps and "abandoning himself to wild infatuations," he had gradually fallen, under the influence of Madame de Krüdener, into a sort of Illuminism. Enamoured of solitude, and sometimes falling on his knees to pray in the depths of a cemetery, chewing the cud of melancholy reflections on his walks, he felt himself called upon to make good the harm done by the Emperor, and conceived "the idea of a holy European League of which he would be more than the Agamemnon." The Treaty, establishing this League, known as the League of the Most Holy and Undivided Trinity, was concluded on the 26th of September, 1815, between the Tsar, the Emperor of Austria and the King of Prussia. Louis XVIII became a member later on.

The Holy Alliance.

The first article ran as follows: "In accordance with the words of the Holy Scriptures which bid all men to regard each other as brothers, the three monarchs who sign this treaty will be bound by the ties of true and indissoluble fraternity and, regarding each other as fellow countrymen, they will on every occasion and in every place render help, aid and succour to one another; looking upon their relationship to their subjects and their armies as that of the father of a family, they will direct them in the same spirit of fraternity as inspires them to protect religion, peace and justice."

This was not a political transaction so much as a religious manifesto, a family contract made "between the members of one single Christian nation," a stepping-stone as it were towards a United States of Europe. The Tsar had tried to make a grandiose gesture after the manner of Napoleon. But the statesmen realised how unsatisfactory "this ludicrous contract," as Talleyrand called it, was; and the Austrian Minister, Metternich, who believed himself "to be God's lieutenant on earth entrusted with the task of resisting new ideas," succeeded in extracting from the Holy Alliance a perfectly practical reality—he turned it into a weapon of war against the Revolution, into a bond of union between the monarchical interests as opposed to the rebellious nations. A contract, inspired by him and signed on the 21st of November, 1815, lay down the mode of procedure for the Holy Alliance. At periodical conferences the Powers were to examine the measures "best calculated to secure the tranquillity and prosperity of the nations and to safeguard the peace of Europe." Thus the right to interfere in the domestic concerns of the various countries was elevated to the rank of a doctrine, and France, who had just given proofs of "her wickedness of spirit," was the first to be attacked. She was, as it were, put into leading-strings, or at all events placed under the supervision of a European Directorate represented by Metternich, "the man of the past," the living symbol of the *ancien régime*.

France in Leading-strings.

France bitterly resented this humiliation and the fact that she was being treated as a minor, or, worse still, as a suspect, after having won glory on the field of battle and laid down the law to the conquered nations. It was at this moment that the Legend of Napoleon, as the man who carried on the work of the Revolution, first saw the light of day.

On his return from the isle of Elba, the Emperor had remarked to Benjamin Constant, "The taste for constitutions, debates and speechifying has revived. Authority is questioned." And realising that it was impossible to put the clock back, he, in his turn, had granted certain constitutional reforms. To the simplistic minds of a large number of Frenchmen this action had sufficed to give him the trappings of a liberal monarch, and from this to argue that a coalition of the reactionary Powers had tried to destroy in him a soldier of Liberty was but a short step. It was quickly taken. Henceforward those who admired Béranger's poetry and made it a sort of creed regarded it as a self-evident truth that the principles of '89 had been destroyed at Waterloo through the combined efforts of the Crowned Heads and the clergy. And thus the cult of the Emperor spread not only in the country districts where the disbanded soldiers had retired, but also in the towns among the ex-officers and the Liberal bourgeoisie.

The Napoleonic Legend.

The Comte de Ségur, for instance, carried with him into his retirement "an inconsolable spirit at loggerheads with the present, renouncing the future, and turned entirely to the past, which it endeavoured to reconstruct—in short, like Prometheus on his rock, chained to the summit of the lost glory of his country." In family circles the same thing happened. Victor Hugo as a young man was a Royalist, but his father observed, "Give him time; the child has the opinions of his mother; the man will have the opinions of his father." And, indeed, if the mothers saw in the Emperor the man who robbed them of their sons, the fathers remembered that it was he who gave them their epaulettes. Glory or Liberty, it was all the same for the Bonapartists, for those officers on half-pay—they numbered more than 15,000—who, with barely enough to live upon (a Captain only received 73 francs a month), found themselves tied down to a fixed abode from which they were not allowed to move without permission from the authorities. It was chiefly in these circles, among the men who wore the broad-brimmed Bolivar hats, long blue frock-coats and hussar's trousers, and frequented the Liberal cafés of the Palais Royal, that the fire of memory burnt most brightly. It was here that past victories were discussed and schemes of vengeance outlined; it was here that the opposition to the monarchy fermented as in a sealed vessel. The opposition was still in embryo, but it was destined soon to take shape, and the Restoration was to be faced by an alliance between Liberalism and Bonapartism.

The Treaty of the 20th of November and the compact of the Holy Alliance crystallised, as it were, the widespread hatred against the *ancien régime* and the Bourbons. Later on General Lamarque observed that 1815 had been "a halt in the mud," and it was a general belief that France, in submitting to be ruled by Kings, had suffered irreparable disgrace, and that on that ill-omened day "the Revolution had delivered up her sword."

Thus, even before the end of 1815, the results of the Hundred Days, and the terrible heritage of political and military conflicts, became fully apparent. France was in the hands of the invaders; 800,000 foreigners were occupying fifty-eight departments, supplied by means of requisitions (1,750,000 francs a day). The inhabitants of the towns and country districts were ground down and oppressed—"the skin of our backs covers the drums of their lordships the Cossacks," said one eye-witness; "they have cut off the manes and tails of our horses to trim their helmets." The conquered soldiers were returning to their homes with rage in their hearts at having seen Paris capitulate while they were still able to fight—had not Exelmans wiped out two Prussian regiments after a rash manœuvre on the part of Blücher on the left bank of the Seine? The *Ultras*, exasperated, demanded vengeance upon the conspirators of the Hundred Days and upon the Jacobins; the Bonapartists were dreaming of revenge; civil war was breaking out in the south, the exchequer was exhausted, and finally the country had been humiliated in the eyes of Europe.

The State of France.

Such was the situation when Louis XVIII took up the reins of power. It is impossible to forget this when it comes to criticising his reign and the work of the Restoration generally.

A Short Bibliography of General Histories of the Restoration.

Capefigue, *Histoire de la Restauration et des causes qui ont amené la chute de la branche aînée des Bourbons* (3rd ed., 4 vols., 1841). Dareste, *Histoire de la Restauration* (2 vols., 1871). Daudet, E., *Histoire de la Restauration* (1882). Duvergier de Hauranne, *Histoire du gouvernement parlementaire en France de* 1814 *à* 1848 (10 vols., 1857–72). Hamel, *Histoire de la Restauration* (2 vols., 1887). Lamartine, *Histoire de la Restauration* (8 vols., 1851). Lubis, *Histoire de la Restauration* (6 vols., 1848). Nettement, *Histoire de la Restauration* (8 vols., 1860). Vaulabelle, *Histoire de deux Restaurations* (8 vols., 1857). Verdier, *Histoire politique et littéraire de la Restauration* (1863). Viel-Castel, *Histoire de la Restauration* (20 vols., 1860–78). Weill, G., *La France sous la Monarchie constitutionelle* (1912). The most recent work on the subject, which is most important and to which we have frequently had recourse, is *La Restauration* by S. Charléty (fourth volume of *l'Histoire de la France Contemporaine*, published under the editorship of E. Lavisse).

CHAPTER II

THE "CHAMBRE INTROUVABLE"

The nature of the Charter. The elections of 1815 and the triumph of the *Ultras*. The White Terror. The trial of Marshal Ney, and its consequences. The extraordinary escape of Comte Lavallette. The debate on the amnesty and the "categories" of La Bourdonnaie. The theorists of the Monarchy and its early Romanticism. Didier's conspiracy. The conflict between the Chamber and the Government. Louis XVIII decides to dissolve the *Chambre Introuvable*.

THE constitutional Charter granted to his subjects by Louis XVIII by virtue of the "free exercise of his royal authority" had been hastily drawn up by a Commission mainly composed of old officials of the Empire. The Allies would brook no delay; the Commission started their work in the morning and in the evening submitted the draft to the King, who in consenting to each clause, constantly repeated, "It is hateful, but I am bound." According to Secretary Beugnot, this document, which was the foundation of the restored monarchy, was flung together like the text of a comic opera.

The Charter.

And indeed it was a hotch-potch—the civil equality of Frenchmen in the eyes of the law and in all matters relating to taxation and the administration of justice; the liberty of the subject; the liberty of the Press and of religious denominations; the inviolability of property including national property, that is to say, property acquired since the Revolution; the permanency of the Bench of Judges; the maintenance of military rank, pensions and the Legion of Honour—all these items followed upon each other in disconcerting confusion. As for the Government, the Charter confided it to the King, assisted by responsible Ministers; it was the King who sanctioned and promulgated laws, and in whom was vested the sole right of proposing them to the Chambers.

The latter consisted of the Chamber of Peers, nominated by the King either for life or as hereditary holders of the title, and of the Chamber of Deputies, elected for five years by the electoral bodies and eligible for re-election quinquennially. This was all that was said regarding the relations between the executive and the legislature.

The Elections.

In July 1815, as the law regarding the method of election had not yet been passed, the electoral bodies as they had existed under the Empire were convoked, but the voting age was lowered to twenty-one and for the right of candidature to twenty-five. The Government feared the return of *ultra*-Royalists as much as that of Jacobins, and regarded with most favour deputies who were constitutionalists supporting the Charter and as far removed from the violent revolutionaries as they were from the *émigré* spirit. But the times were not favourable to moderation. In the north and the east the elections took place under the supervision of the Allied troops; in the west and the south there were civil disorders; the Press had no liberty and the electors were terrorised by the presence of the foreigner. The landowners who had rallied to the cause of the Empire during the Hundred Days were anxious to wipe out their dangerous past, and displayed an exaggerated enthusiasm for the new régime; whilst the timid moderates either did not dare to vote or were prevented from doing so. In short, the Royalist spirit prevailed, and the new Chamber, consisting almost entirely of *Ultras*, was acclaimed

Triumph of the *Ultras*.

by the Comte d'Artois and his followers, who had not expected such favourable results. Louis XVIII, who was more broad-minded, thought they were almost too favourable, and less from conviction than from a wish to be witty—a temptation which he found it difficult to resist—dubbed it the *Chambre introuvable*.[1] Was it representative of the will of the people? In this connection suffice it to say that the 402 deputies were returned by 48,500 electors.

Most of the new-comers were small landowners, honest, upright and disinterested country gentlemen with sincere convictions, who brought with them an indescribably crude

[1] The "Prodigy Chamber," because it surpassed the most sanguine expectations of the Royalists themselves.

provincial royalism which soon exasperated Paris. Their success was made the occasion of loud demonstrations on the part of the Life-Guards, who let themselves go against anything that had the smallest taint of Napoleonic tyranny, and at the theatre hooted Mademoiselle Mars, whose Bonapartist proclivities were well known. The Liberals retorted that Mars had nothing in common with the Life-Guards, whereupon the latter gave an ovation to Mademoiselle Bourgoing, another actress, who professed the right opinions. Any reminder of "the crime of the Hundred Days" was met with execration; there were loud cries for vengeance and reprisals, and for an example to be made of all the generals and officials who, on the 20th of March, 1815, had abandoned or betrayed the Crown. Peace had been made with Europe, but France herself was by no means pacified.

If at Orleans the people confined their expression of loyalty to burning the Emperor's portrait in the Place du Martroi and breaking up his bust with bayonets; if at Carcassonne they sacrificed a live eagle caught in the mountains, which had succeeded in surviving the first Restoration, the disturbances in other places assumed graver proportions.

In le Gard, the bands of Trestaillon, Truphémy, Servent and Jean Graffaud organised a methodical massacre of Bonapartists.

The White Terror.

Religious passions mingled with the political feeling; 130 victims lost their lives, and the murderers were not brought to justice. At Marseilles, the garrison had to evacuate the town owing to the commotions, and 100 of their men were killed, whilst citizens of the town who were known to hold Republican views or to be attached to the Imperial cause were massacred. All who had the reputation of holding seditious ideas were plundered and despoiled, and the authorities did not dare to interfere. Throughout the south companies of Royalist volunteers, known as "*verdets*"—they wore a green uniform the colour of the Comte d'Artois' livery—had been enrolled, and terrorised the countryside. At Toulouse, General Ramel, in spite of the fact that he had not returned to duty during the Hundred Days and was in command of the town in the King's name, tried to disband these new Prætorians; but on the 15th of August, 1815, he was assassinated without anyone having the courage to go to his help. At Avignon, Marshal Brune was murdered as he was crossing the town under the protection of a safe-conduct, and such was the terror inspired by his murderers that the verdict returned was one of suicide. But his death was not sufficient—his coffin was broken up and his body, which was cast into the Rhone, was afterwards recovered more than fifty miles below Avignon.

"The people of the south have been made to stand up to their knees in blood," said a contemporary, "and neither the citizens nor the authorities dared to take steps against the culprits, even when they were disarmed, so terrified were they of finding some powerful protector behind them."

And indeed the Government let them be, or feigned ignorance. The old *émigrés* and "fugitives from Ghent" urged it to take a high hand; they were filled with that thirst for revenge which follows upon humiliating panic, and on this point were almost in accord with the Allies. As had been the case in 1793, names were demanded, and denunciations poured into the King's cabinet. From the Prefect to the humblest official, the administration, according to these zealous informers, was entirely made up of suspects. The slightest word was twisted round, and trial and imprisonment followed. Daunou, the head of the Archives, furnished, at the request of the Court, a list of the members of the Convention who had voted for the execution of Louis XVI; and this was significant.

Urged on by public opinion and without waiting for the meeting of the Chambers, to whom he had relegated the task of naming the culprits, the King had eighteen generals court-martialled. The first victim was General Labédoyère, who, together with his regiment, had gone over to the service of the Emperor at Grenoble. Although he was connected with a Royalist family, he was shot on the 19th of August; he was only twenty-nine at the time. The Faucher brothers—"the La Réole twins" who had commanded the Pyrenees army during the Hundred Days—were in their turn executed on the 27th of September. But the man upon whom the hatred of all was concentrated, and for whose chastisement the *Ultras* were clamouring, was Marshal Ney.

Having rallied to the Bourbon cause in 1814, Ney, as soon as he heard of Napoleon's landing at the Gulf of Juan, boasted that he would bring his old leader to the Tuileries in an iron cage. Louis XVIII, who was present, murmured, "We do not expect as much as that from him." And he was right. The Emperor arrived, crowned by the prestige of his victories, amid the acclamations of town and country, and borne aloft on the enthusiasm of the people. "The eagle flew from belfry to belfry towards the towers of Notre Dame." Ney found it impossible to resist such a spectacle; the cause of the Bourbons appeared to him to be hopelessly lost, and hypnotised by the Master, he fell into step with the rest and led his troops over to him. His defection was a thunderbolt for the Tuileries, who had no one else upon whom they could count. With the vanishing of this last hope the road to Paris lay open, and there was nothing to bar the advance of the Usurper. At Waterloo, Ney fought with the courage of despair, knowing full well that on the issue of this battle his fate depended. In the thick of the fight he called out to d'Erlon, "As for us two, if the English bullets don't do for us we shall only be killed like dogs by the *émigrés*." They were prophetic words. When he saw that defeat was inevitable he went in search of death; four horses were killed under him, but he was spared.

Marshal Ney.

On the list of generals to be court-martialled his name was the first to appear. Warned by his wife, he sought refuge in a castle in Cantal belonging to one of his relatives, Madame de Bessonis. A Royalist denounced him to the Prefect, and the castle was surrounded. From one of the windows the fugitive could see an officer of the gendarmerie. "Who are you looking for?"—"Marshal Ney."—"Come up here, sir, and I will point him out to you." And he gave himself up.

When Louis XVIII heard the news he cursed the zeal of the Prefect. "That is a piece of stupidity which will cost us dear!" he exclaimed. Then, referring to Ney himself, he added, "The wretch! By giving himself up he will do us more harm than he did on the 13th of March when he went over to Bonaparte!" In his heart of hearts he almost tried to find excuses for the Marshal's treachery; the latter had left his cabinet a loyal subject with every intention of remaining so to the end, but events were too strong for him. The *Ultras* did not see the matter in the same light; they were thirsting for a regular execution, and grew impatient at the length of the trial.

Marshal Moncey, indeed, refused to preside over the court-martial or to express any opinion as to the guilt of Marshal Ney; such an ordeal was more than he could bear. Whereupon he was cashiered and given three months imprisonment. But other Marshals, endowed with less nobility of temperament, consented to take their seats. Through the instrumentality of one of his counsel, Ney denied their competency and, pleading his right as a peer of the realm, demanded to be judged by the Court of Peers. The members of the court-martial, which consisted partly of comrades of the Marshal who had also served during the Hundred Days, though they had displayed more skill than he had done, eagerly seized upon this means of escaping a painful duty, and by a majority of five to two declared themselves incompetent. Ney was pleased, and remarked to his lawyer, " What a service you have done me! Those blackguards would have killed me like a rabbit! " Possibly he was wrong.

Trial of Ney.

When the prudent decision of the court-martial became known, there was an outburst of hatred and indignation on the part of the *Ultras* which seems astonishing to us now, and the like of which is perhaps to be found only in certain episodes which took place at the time of the Convention. Women who as a rule were sweet and gentle became changed to furies at the thought that Ney might possibly escape punishment. " Don't let them keep either him or us waiting! " Some of them went into appalling paroxysms of rage or grief. " What ferocity! " wrote Benjamin Constant at the time. " The words they found it possible to utter we find it impossible to write! " And indeed the embroidresses of 1815 had nothing to learn from the knitters of 1793. Among the foreigners the same passions were roused and the same language was used. The Russian Ambassador declared to Monsieur de Vitrolles, the Secretary of State, that if the French were incapable of punishing the traitor, the Allies would undertake the task themselves—they would kidnap him and his like and deport them to Siberia.

Among the King's Ministers, Richelieu, wise and noble-minded though he was, allowed himself to be influenced by this bloodthirsty impatience, and when an order of the 11th of November, 1815, referred Ney to the Court of Peers, he read the following statement: " It is not only in the name of the King, my Lords, but in the name of France, long since shocked and indignant and now filled with amazement, and even in the name of Europe that we have come to conjure you and at the same time request you to sit in judgment on Marshal Ney. We would even dare to say that the House of Peers owes the world handsome reparation . . ." These words proved only too conclusively that the policy of France was no longer in the hands of her own people, but that Europe was bearing down the destinies of the country with all its weight.

Before the trial opened, Bellart, the Attorney-General, " a sort of judicial wolf," who had served the Empire and the Restoration with the same verbose devotion, who had displayed delirious enthusiasm on the birth of the King of Rome and passionate hostility to Napoleon in 1814, submitted that the culprit had gone unpunished long enough and that the matter should be ended forthwith without an opportunity for defence being allowed. The Peers, however, did not dare to go as far as that, and on the 4th of December the proceedings opened. It was obviously impossible for the counsel to attempt any apology for the Empire—they were Royalists—but they brought forward certain legal arguments.

Article 12 of the capitulation of Paris granted formal amnesty to all persons, " whatever their functions, opinion and conduct "; again, the Treaty of the 20th of November stipulated that nobody born in the districts that had been ceded could be molested by reason of his conduct or his political opinions. Now Ney was a native of Sarrelouis, one of the said districts. But when he learnt that, in order to save his head, his counsel wanted to make him out a foreigner, he became indignant, " I am French, and as a Frenchman I shall die ! " From that moment his fate was sealed. After the evidence of General Bourmont, proving that Ney had acted with premeditation, his condemnation was certain. A verdict of " Guilty " was returned by 159 votes to one, one member abstaining from voting. It was the young Duc de Broglie who voted against the verdict and declared, "There are certain events which in their nature and bearing are beyond the domain of human justice, albeit they are odious in the eyes of God and man." The vote on the sentence was then taken; 139 pronounced in favour of death, seventeen in favour of deportation, whilst five peers abstained and recommended the prisoner to the clemency of the King. But the popular fury overcame Louis XVIII's better judgment; although he quite clearly foresaw the remote consequences of condemning the Marshal to death, he did not dare to exercise mercy.

Execution of Ney.

On the morning of the 7th of December, 1815, Marshal Michel Ney was shot on the Avenue de l'Observatoire. When he was facing the bullets he proved the fine soldier he had been on the field of battle, refusing to be blindfolded and to kneel down. "A man like me does not kneel down!" He was dressed in a blue frock-coat, black breeches, black silk stockings and a round hat. After saying his last words to the *curé* of Saint Sulpice, he turned to face the firing-party and exclaimed, "I protest before God and my country against the sentence passed upon me. I call upon men, posterity and God to bear witness. *Vive la France!*" Then, taking off his hat, he cried, "Soldiers, fire straight at my heart!" and pierced by twelve bullets he fell dead.

It is said that an Englishman made his horse jump over the body, but another foreigner drew a different conclusion from the drama. "The French," he said, "are behaving as if there were no such thing as history or the future." Some of the Royalists were much of the same opinion; they regarded the condemnation of the Marshal as no doubt inevitable, but when once sentence had been passed he ought either to have been pardoned or else solemnly executed in the presence of the army and the people. "To shoot this man clandestinely was not only weak, but actually cowardly." And indeed the death of Ney, a fine death, full of nobility and courage, wiped out at one blow all the mistakes of his life, and his idealised figure joined that of the Emperor in the hearts of the soldiers. The Restoration "had washed him clean in his own blood." As for the

Government, which thought it had given proof of energy, and handed over hostages to the fury of the Royalists and the Allies, the only result it had obtained was to arouse the hatred of the army against the new régime.

The very day on which Ney fell beneath the bullets of the firing-party, an old *émigré*, who was trying to curry favour with the Duc de Berry, the King's nephew, observed to him, with an ingratiating gesture, " Only two or three more little executions, Monseigneur, and France will be at your feet." One of the victims for whom he was waiting was Comte Lavallette, who had been Postmaster under the Empire and had been condemned to death for having been guilty on the 20th of March of a usurpation of office and of conspiring against the monarchy. Quite a number of people were trying to save him, for all he had done was to take possession of the General Post Office a few hours before the arrival of Napoleon in Paris. Moreover, he inspired sympathy, and had conferred many favours in the past without distinction of party, whilst his wife belonged to an *émigré* family. In order to commute his sentence, all the King required was a word from the Duchesse d'Angoulême, whose decisions the *Ultras* respected. But when the Duchess was approached by Richelieu, who also wanted him to be pardoned, she refused to speak on behalf of the prisoner. When Madame Lavallette threw herself on her knees before her in the Guard Room in the Tuileries, holding out a petition to her, she tore herself away violently, casting a furious glance at the suppliant. " I knew it," sighed Louis XVIII, and thinking of his brother and those about him, he added, " *They* are implacable, but if I braved their displeasure I should not have a moment's peace." After which he answered all further solicitations on the part of the prisoner's wife with vague phrases : " Madam, I pity you, but I am bound to do my duty."

Escape of Lavallette.

But the *Ultras* were in a fine fix when they learnt that Lavallette had escaped from the Conciergerie, where he had been imprisoned. On the 21st of December, 1815, the eve of the day on which the prisoner was to have been executed on the Place de Grève, his wife had come to see him, as was her daily custom, about five o'clock in the evening. At seven o'clock she was seen to leave, leading her daughter by the hand. A few minutes afterwards, when the gaoler went to make sure that the condemned man was still in his cell, he found not Lavallette, but his wife. She had given her clothes to her husband, and thus disguised he had passed out, respectfully saluted by the warders. When the news was heard in Paris, the people rejoiced wholeheartedly. It would not have required much to make them illuminate the city, and enthusiastic songs were sung in the streets, in praise of Lavallette and his heroic wife. The rage of the *Ultras* did not abate, and the King was in a quandary: "You will see, *they* will say that we have done it!" Decazes, who had succeeded Fouché as head of the police, sent out his agents in all directions, had the gates of Paris closed, and the houses of Lavallette's friends searched. He mobilised the royal forces, from the generals to the *gardes champêtres*, and gave orders for the frontiers and the ports to be watched. Every post chaise and private travelling coach was subjected to the most rigorous scrutiny, whilst the passports were examined at every stage. All in vain! "Lavallette must be found, cost what it may," wrote Richelieu, "otherwise the result will be terrible."

And he was right. The passions which had been aroused over the trial of Ney broke out afresh with renewed vigour. A young woman was seen asking Barbé-Marbois, the old Keeper of the Seals, the man whom Talleyrand used to call a reed painted to look like iron, "When will they give us back our good old executions?" The *Ultras* maintained that Lavallette, who was fat and portly, could not have escaped unrecognised, as his wife was tall and slim, and that his flight was the result of a vast revolutionary plot in which the Ministers themselves were involved. Whereupon Decazes redoubled his efforts and sent criers through the streets with a proclamation calling upon every householder and tenant to reveal the presence of any lodger beneath their roof under pain of two years imprisonment. It was all labour in vain. The whole of France was engaged in the search for Lavallette; but he could not be found. As a matter of fact he was hiding in the very buildings of the Ministry for Foreign Affairs where Richelieu lived, and on the 9th of January, 1816, the day on which he was executed in effigy on the Place de Grève, he reached the Belgian frontier in the disguise of an English officer.

Meanwhile the Chambers had met. At first concord seemed to reign supreme. The deputies inspired the King with confidence, and when Decazes one day presented himself before the Bar of the House in order to read the will of Marie-Antoinette, which had just been found, there was a moment of unanimous emotion. Surely the King could not complain at having to govern with a majority so wholeheartedly Royalist?

As a certain parliamentary poet of the day put it:

> " Excès d'amour, excès de zèle,
> C'est le vrai portrait d'un ultra.
> Trop amoureux et trop fidèle,
> Les jolis défauts que voilà ! " [1]

The Amnesty Bill.

But when the Amnesty Bill came up for discussion the disagreement between the Government and the majority came to a head. Richelieu was in favour of leniency; the majority, on the other hand, wanted to make further examples. At the sitting of the 10th of November, 1815, La Bourdonnaie, one of the ultra-Royalists, brought forward a motion for the exclusion from the amnesty of all holders of high military and administrative posts under the Empire, the generals and corps commanders, and all who had been Prefects under Napoleon, and finally members of the Convention who had voted for the execution of Louis XVI. Death was to be the punishment for the former, and deportation for the latter; whilst in both cases the property of the condemned was to be confiscated. If it had been passed, the measure would have meant the death of 1200 persons. " It is only by dragging down the leaders from the heights to which their crimes have raised them," cried La Bourdonnaie, " that you will teach a salutary lesson of moderation and virtue! . . . In order to put an end to their criminal machinations, you must have recourse to chains, executioners and punishment. Death, and death alone, will frighten their accomplices and put an end to their plots! "

Richelieu had only consented to act as head of the Government with the greatest reluctance. " I shall not rule the country

[1] " Over-much love, and over-much zeal, that is the true picture of an *Ultra*. Too loving and too faithful, what splendid defects are these! "

as you expect me to rule it," he informed the *Ultras*, "and you will be sorry for insisting." He felt that it would be less difficult to save the King from his enemies than from his friends, and he was justified by events. The mad enthusiasm of La Bourdonnaie, which seemed ready to carry away the whole Chamber with it, filled him with anxiety, and comparing his own lot with that of the landowners and *émigrés* who had been despoiled by the Revolution, he tried to make them listen to reason. "I really do not understand your hatred and indignation and your feelings of resentment, which can only lead to fresh disasters. Every day I pass by the mansion which used to belong to my ancestors; I have seen my great family estates in the hands of new owners; in the museums my eye falls upon pictures that once were mine. All this is very sad, but it does not exasperate me or make me implacable. Indeed, I sometimes think that you, who have remained in France, are mad." And thus a compromise was reached. No further steps were taken with regard to La Bourdonnaie's "categories" and the confiscation of property was not carried out. But in spite of the opposition of the Government, the regicides were excluded from the amnesty and were obliged to go into exile, among them being the painter David. This measure, though it violated the terms of the Charter, which had forbidden any inquiry into opinions held before the Restoration, was passed, to the accompaniment of cries of "After all long live the King!" which showed the attitude of the majority.

But the latter, not content with meting out punishment for the crime of the Hundred Days, were determined to destroy the Revolution. With this object they passed a law against all seditious cries, speeches or writings, whereby threats against the King, even if they led to nothing, and the mere exclamation of "*Vive l'Empereur!*" were to be punished by deportation. The liberty of the subject was at an end, and the preventive arrest of people without trial was declared legal. At the same time the Chamber re-established the *Cours prévôtales*, the object of which in the old days had been the repression of vagabondage. They were now competent to deal with crimes of rebellion and of military sedition; there was no appeal from their verdicts, which were carried out within twenty-four hours, and they constituted a sort of engine of war for securing the loyalty of the army to the Crown. One deputy, anxious to perfect and extend their deterrent power, even went so far as to suggest that the guillotine should be replaced by the gallows.

In 1816 the machinery for thus policing the country and administering justice was in full swing. "The enemies of the State" were arrested *en masse*, and in this category was included anybody who was pleased to see the Government and the administration in difficulties; this provided wide scope for the activities of the disciplinary courts. Chateaubriand remarked, "If there are no Royalists in France they must be created," pointing out that with the help of a Bishop, a commanding officer, a Prefect, a Public Prosecutor, a President of the *Cour prévôtale*, an officer of the gendarmerie and a commandant of the National Guard, nothing could be easier. "If these seven men belong to God and the King, I will answer for the rest!" Indeed people were terrorised into Royalism, and until July 1816 capital sentences were carried out to this end, the last of these being the execution of General Mouton-Duvernet, who, imagining that passions had had time to cool, had given himself up. He was condemned to death, and shot on the 29th of July. Once again Louis XVIII did not dare to exercise mercy.

At this the hunted Bonapartists made up their minds to go into exile, and two generals, the Lallemand brothers, founded a colony in Texas, the *Champ d'Asile*, where 400 soldiers sought refuge. Here for some time they dragged out a miserable existence, giving to the streets lined by their hovels names commemorating the glories of the Empire. But Spain, to whom Texas at that time belonged, growing alarmed at this invasion, called upon the exiles to take their departure. In vain did *la Minerve*, a Liberal journal, open a subscription on their behalf; driven out by the Spaniards, the colonists of the *Champ d'Asile* had no alternative but to scatter over America.

The *Ultra* Party were triumphant all along the line; they had the majority in Parliament and could rely upon the loyalty of the recently appointed Government officials. Thus France seemed ready to "disgorge" the Revolution. The task of purgation extended even to the Academy and the Institute, from which

The Theorists of the Monarchy.

all scientists, writers or artists whose names recalled unpleasant memories of the Republic or the Empire were excluded; and when everything had been thoroughly cleansed, the theorists of the Restoration were free to lay the foundations of a new society. This was the work of Joseph de Maistre, Bonald and Ballanche.

Reduced to its simplest elements, their doctrine may be formulated as follows:—all power comes from God, society has been created by Him, and though all the Charters in the world were to proclaim the civil equality of citizens, inequality would nevertheless remain the law of nature. The individual has no rights; society alone rejoices in privilege, and the Prince, as God's representative on earth, "administers his territory as a landowner does his estates." Carried into practice, these principles had the result of founding not a monarchy modified by a constitution, but a monarchy by divine right. The agents of the latter were the clergy charged with the task of education and the maintenance of the civil State, and the large landowners, the landed aristocracy, who ruled the masses in the name of the King. Centralisation, "the creation of the spirit of innovation and revolution," was to be exchanged for decentralisation, or local Government under a monarchy as it was known in France before 1789.

Romanticism.

At the same time as they propagated this mystic doctrine of the Restoration and this political philosophy, the *Ultras* endeavoured to turn the literary current towards Christianity and the great traditions of Kingship. Chateaubriand had set the tone some time previously; and they developed the themes which were his creation. And indeed in the new monarchical society, classical antiquity, precedents from Plutarch, Republican heroism and the Roman virtues struck a discordant note. Fresh standards had to be created and new life breathed into the national traditions, and the sacred legends illustrative of the rise of the royal house of France. Brutus was taboo, and Clovis and Charlemagne held the stage; there was an efflorescence of old tales, epic ballads and poetry "of the troubadour species." The writers set to work, historians and scholars coming to the support of the poets; Creuzé de Lesser, Marchangy and Raynouard provided the material for "the friends of the Muses," and the long-forgotten Knights of the Round Table, and the heroes of the Celtic, Italian and Spanish epics, and all the characters in the great "emprises" of the Middle Ages were again revived. Walter Scott, who was translated at this time, was received with enthusiasm; he was the chronicler, the story-teller and the poet for whom the Royalists were longing; in him their aspirations were made articulate, and from that time they were able at their leisure to admire the *châtelaine* in her high hennin, the damosels, and the minstrels playing the lute and the viol in the lofty halls of crenellated keeps. The beau ideal of the knight was Jehan de Paris, as he was depicted in the charming vignettes adorning the romantic little booklets bound *à la cathédrale*, with his sword and harp clasped to his breast, on his head a bonnet or helmet with a long curling plume, a turned-down collar, a slashed tunic trimmed with velvet, a scarf tied in a large knot, white trunk hose and yellow boots. He was a knight devoted to the service of God, a squire of dames; but his greatest passion was for the King. He it was who sang:

> "Que le Roi vive et la France prospère,
> Sur ses autels que Dieu soit respecté,
> Ce sont les vœux et l'unique prière
> Des Chevaliers de la Fidélité." [1]

This early romanticism, picturesque, artificial and lacking in vitality, was destined to be a passing vogue, but it served the purpose of directing men's minds to a class of study hitherto undeservedly neglected; and to it was due the interest aroused in the treasures of mediæval France. The Gothic style, which even the best-informed and most cultured minds of the eighteenth century, like President de Brosses, regarded as barbaric, returned to favour, and the treasure house of French literature was enriched by popular legends and national folklore. In this connection the influence of the *émigré* element in France was very great. Writers who had lived in exile returned to France with a new conception of history and a way of looking at men and events hitherto unknown in their own country, enriched by experience gained in German universities. It was at this

[1] "Long life to the King and prosperity to France, and may God be worshipped at her altars; such are the wishes and the one prayer of the Knights of Loyalty."

time that Madame de Staël's book on Germany and Sismondi's book on the literature of Central Europe, both of which had been published under the Empire, came to be fully appreciated, and through their instrumentality the spiritual horizon of France was widened.

In the domain of literature Royalist enthusiasm was not only inoffensive, it was actually beneficial; but in the political sphere, on the contrary, it presented grave dangers. For Bonapartism in alliance with Liberalism refused to allow itself to be cut down without a struggle, and consisting as it did chiefly of men who had been on active service, it looked to a *coup de force* to overthrow the new régime.

It was at Grenoble that the first conspiracy against the Bourbons broke out in 1816. The man who organised it was Paul Didier, once head of the *École de Droit*, who had been a Royalist in 1814, but had turned Orleanist after Waterloo. As it was necessary for him to have a flag, he chose the most popular, that of Napoleon II, the King of Rome, and succeeded in organising troops of men in various cantons who were to be relied upon at a given signal—the lighting of two fires on the mountain top—to take Grenoble by surprise with the connivance of the officers of the garrison. The most prominent members of this conspiracy were soldiers on half-pay, chemists, postmasters, not to mention country lawyers, showing that the discontent with the policy followed by the *Ultras* was not confined to any one walk of life. The rising was arranged for the 4th of May. On the previous evening, the Prefect, who had been warned through some mysterious channel, had already made several arrests, and when Didier, at the head of 400 men, presented himself before the gates of the town, he fell in with the troops under the command of General Donnadieu, an ardent Royalist, who held the military command in the Isère district. The insurgents, met by a fusillade which killed six of their men, took to flight and sought refuge on the mountain, whilst Didier fled to Savoy; whereupon Donnadieu wrote to the Government: "Long live the King! The bodies of his enemies are strewn all along the roads for three miles around Grenoble. . . . His Majesty's troops have covered themselves with glory." As,

Didier's Conspiracy

according to Donnadieu, the rebels numbered at least 4000, the Government imagined it was faced by a general rebellion, and invested the authorities with discretionary powers. A state of siege was proclaimed, and a price set on Didier's head; whilst anybody who gave him shelter was "to be handed over to a military commission to be shot," and his house razed to the ground.

Terror reigned in the Isère district. Twenty-four culprits, among whom was a boy of sixteen, were summarily condemned and executed, whilst Didier, who had taken refuge at Saint-Sorlin d'Arves in Savoy, was betrayed by an inn-keeper and arrested in a solitary barn in the mountains. He was extradited and executed a month later, on the 8th of June, 1816.

At the time of his trial Didier declared himself to be a Bonapartist, but he was more probably a partisan of the Duc d'Orléans, who was at that time in England. Louis XVIII, with his characteristic sensitiveness, was doubtless aware of this preference for the junior branch when, in describing the Duke, he said, "He does not stir, nevertheless I can see that he makes headway. This motionless activity makes me anxious. What can one do to prevent a man from walking when he does not move a step? This is a problem which it still remains for me to solve. I hope I shall not be obliged to leave its solution for my successor."

And the King had good reason to feel concerned about the future of his dynasty. The police had just discovered a fresh plot in Paris, organised this time by working men, which gave food for reflection. Three men were condemned to death and seventeen deported, but still peace was not restored. There was a strange feeling of unrest in the country. It is true that the Press, which was carefully censored, did not publish any news, but it was conveyed from mouth to mouth, and there were rumours of the return of Napoleon and of the massacre of nobles and priests.

Louis XVIII very wisely endeavoured to pacify men's minds, but he had his work cut out with his own immediate circle. The Duc de Berry in particular let himself go to lengths of brutality both in word and deed that threatened to become dangerous. One day he exclaimed, "The marshals are going to be hunted down. Eight must be killed ! " This was reported to the King, who took his nephew severely to task. " You will bring about the overthrow of my dynasty," he told him. On another occasion the Duke flew into a passion with a colonel of the Guard, and tore his epaulettes off his shoulders. The colonel put his hand to his sword, but the King, who was present, made a sign to him, and exclaimed, " Colonel, my nephew has just torn off your epaulettes because he knew that I was going to give you those of a general." And thus the King, who had learnt from experience, made up for the violence of his supporters; but it was difficult to act in the same way with regard to the violence of the Chamber.

Conflict between the Chamber, the Government.

The conflict between the Government and the majority had reached a head. The Budget of 1816, presented by Corvetto, the Finance Minister, arranged for the deficit in the previous Budgets to be made good and the debts contracted during the Hundred Days to be paid off; the sums required were to be raised in part from the sale of woods that had belonged to the clergy. The *Ultras* immediately declared that the Budget was entirely imbued with the revolutionary spirit and that the property of the Church should not be made security for expenses incurred by Bonaparte. Whereupon the Government, giving up the idea of selling the woods, was obliged to have recourse to Treasury expedients. Every measure that was proposed, whether it concerned electoral reform or the University system, which they wanted to put in the hands of the clergy, only served to emphasise the antagonism. And it was an extraordinary thing that the *Ultras*, who in regard to general politics professed the most rigidly absolutist doctrines, showed themselves resolutely Liberal in Parliamentary matters, aiming at increasing the powers of the Chamber at the expense of the royal prerogative, which was defended by the Liberal minority. It was a curious spectacle to see the champions of divine right insisting upon the integrity of Parliament and the power of the majority over the Government.

And indeed the Charter had not solved the problem of the relations between the executive and the legislature, that is to say the question whether the Government depended upon the

King or upon the Chamber. In the former case, the Chamber was practically nothing more than a consultative assembly; if, on the other hand, the Government could only exist in agreement with the Chamber, the latter became the sovereign power. The *Ultras*, being in the majority, interpreted the Charter to their own advantage against the Government, which they considered too lukewarm, and against the King, who supported it. But the minority at this time would not agree. "The day on which the Government shall be dependent upon the majority in the Chamber," said Royer-Collard, "on that day there will be an end, not only of the Charter, but also of our monarchy." And Monsieur de Serre declared, "It is said that the Chamber of Deputies is the organ of public opinion, and that it represents the interests of the nation. If these expressions are not exaggerated, it follows that the Chamber of Deputies represents the whole of France; in which case who would be able to resist this preponderating influence? Who would refuse to bow down before it?"

Louis XVIII was of the same opinion—the *Ultras* entered into the spirit of the Charter, but "as the Greeks entered into the Trojan horse"; if the Charter became null and void, they would have a free hand under the benevolent eye of the Comte d'Artois, whose accession they desired. And the opposition to the Government did, as a matter of fact, emanate from the Pavillon de Marsan, the residence of the King's brother, and the mansions in the Faubourg Saint Germain, where the old aristocracy lived. Artois—"Monsieur" as he was called—had learnt nothing since the sojourn at Ghent. Surrounded by a band of enthusiasts, he maintained a private body of police openly opposed to the official police under Richelieu and Decazes. In this "little office," which was also a government on a small scale, suspects were denounced, jobs provided, and even the person of the King was not spared. "Union and oblivion," had been the words of Louis XVIII. To the friends of Monsieur this meant union with the Bonapartists, and oblivion of the Vendée, which had always supported "the legitimate King." Was it not a scandal to see the King reserving his favours for those who had been his implacable enemies, humouring erstwhile members of the Convention, like Abbé

Grégoire, buying pictures by David the regicide and helping the sister of Robespierre? A crowned Jacobin, a King-Voltaire, a dressed-up comedian, fit subject for doggerel and penny a liners, who had just thrown an English Charter to France—such was the picture drawn of Louis XVIII in the conventicles of the *Ultras*. "I should like to send him to Pondichery," exclaimed Baron de Frénilly, one of their number.

The King was at the Tuileries, and was doing his best to hold out against Frénilly, whom he used to call Monsieur de Frénésie, and his friends in the Chamber. He was even making preparations to get rid of them.

Foreigners had long been warning him of the dangerous consequences likely to arise from the policy followed by the majority. Were they not heading for a popular revolution? Public opinion passed from anxiety to exasperation. By its insane tactics and its attacks upon the Chamber of Peers, which had remained moderate, "the coterie of the Comte d'Artois" was leading the monarchy straight to ruin. But the Powers did not feel disposed to "countenance his follies," and the English newspapers even went so far as openly to discuss the possibility of the candidature of the Duc d'Orléans. This touched Louis XVIII on a sensitive spot. At the time of Lavallette's escape he had already declared that he reserved to himself the right of "consulting the nation" for the purpose of discovering whether the Government had really forfeited its confidence, but the *Ultras*, fearing a dissolution, had taken it for granted. The effect of this, however, was short-lived, and it was necessary to have recourse to fresh efforts.

Richelieu was indignant at this foreign intervention against the *Ultras*, and the idea that his Government might have the appearance of being supported by the Allies was odious in the extreme. When the question of a dissolution was broached, therefore, he at first refused. "It would be a disaster for a monarchy to dissolve a Chamber because it was too enthusiastically Royalist." But when Decazes pointed out to him that the *Ultras*, if they were allowed a free hand, would condemn France to a partition of her territory or to a revolution, the probable result of which would be the proscription of the Bourbons, he allowed himself to be convinced. Decazes had less difficulty in persuading the King. "I have no intention of being the King of Diamonds," [1] Louis declared; and dissolution was decided upon.

Dissolution of the Chamber.

It took place on the 5th of September, 1816, to the accompaniment of the well-rounded flowery phrases of which Louis XVIII possessed the secret—an appeal to the friends of peace, the inviolability of the Charter, the danger of innovation, etc. The *Ultras* were filled with indignation. Monsieur, in high dudgeon, asked to see his brother, hoping to secure the repeal of the order; but the King shut the door in his face, and Monsieur, having been worsted, went off to hunt, which was his method of sulking. Chateaubriand, who had just finished his pamphlet on *La Monarchie selon la Charte*, added a postscript implying that the order did not represent the personal feeling of Louis XVIII, but was merely a proof of the disastrous influence of Decazes. Whereupon the latter fell into disfavour among the Royalists. As he still had the disposal of offices in his hands, however, they continued to solicit his favour, but as they passed under the lamp outside his house, they would have liked to see him hanging from it. The King, for his part, congratulated himself on the dissolution, which released him from tutelage, siding wholeheartedly with Decazes and crossing the name of Chateaubriand, who had expressed doubts concerning his personal good will in the matter, from the list of Ministers of State.

In judging of the work of the *Chambre introuvable*, it is not only the violent attitude it assumed that should be considered. The majority in it, among whom there were no business men, proved themselves stern economists, and the financial regulations it passed remained for a long time the basis of the French economic system. These country squires and landowners possessed a fund of wisdom and good sense which came into play as soon as the material interests of the country were at stake.

Such was France's first experience of parliamentary government. The *Ultras* had been on the point of proving that a determined majority could put a check on the royal authority

[1] In popular language the Ace and Knave of Diamonds signify despicable people and Louis' remark is evidently a play on this association of ideas.

and seize the real power itself. Later on the Liberals were to profit by this example. Although he was friendly to the *Ultras*, Baron d'Haussez was of opinion that the dissolution, while it was a calamity, was absolutely necessary, for the Chamber was proclaiming revolutionary doctrines in the name of Royalist principles. And indeed France as a whole approved of the order of the 5th of September; for between the Liberals, who, though they did not openly say so, did not want the Bourbons, and the *Ultras*, who wanted them, though under the conditions of the *ancien régime*, there existed a vast body of people who welcomed this dynasty under certain conditions—the mass of peasants, tradesmen and bourgeois anxious to carry on their business and grow rich in peace.

BIBLIOGRAPHY.—R. André, *L'occupation de la France par les Alliés en* 1815 (1925). F. Baldensperger, *Études d'histoire litteraire* (1907). *Le mouvement des ideés dans l'émigration française* (2 vols., 1924). Beugnot, *Mémoires* (2 vols., 1866). Louis Blanc, *Histoire de Dix Ans* (5 vols., 1842) (introduction to Vol. I). L. de Carné, *Souvenirs de ma Jeunesse au temps de la Restauration* (2nd ed., 1873). Maréchal de Castellane, *Journal* (5 vols., 1896–7). Chateaubriand, *Mémoires d'outre-tombe* (Ed. Biré) (6 vols., 1898–1900). E. Daudet, *La Terreur Blanche* (1876). Ducoin, *Histoire de la conspiration de* 1816, *Paul Didier* (1844). de Frénilly, *Souvenirs* (1908). Guillon, *Les conspirations militaires sous la Restauration* (1895). d'Haussez, *Mémoires* (2 vols., 1896–7). H. Houssaye, 1815. *La seconde abdication. La Terreur Blanche* (27th ed., 1905). Lanzac de Laborie, *Les passions politiques sous la Restauration* (*Correspondant*, 1900). Lucas-Dubreton, *L'évasion de Lavallette* (1926). MacDonald, *Souvenirs* (1892). Madelin, *Fouché* (2 vols., 1900). Michon, *Le gouvernement parlementaire sous la Restauration* (1905). Molé, *Sa vie. Ses mémoires* (Published by the Marquis de Noailles) (4 vols., 1922–5). Montgaillard, *Souvenirs* (1895). Murst, *l'Histoire par le Théâtre* (3 vols., 1864–5). Nettement, *Souvenirs de la Restauration* (1858). Poumiès de la Siboutie, *Souvenirs d'un médecin de Paris* (1910). *Procès du Maréchal Ney*, 1815. de Reiset, *Souvenirs de* 1814 *à* 1836 (3 vols., 1900–2). Rousset, *Le Marquis de Clermont-Tonnerre* (1885). Sers, *Souvenirs d'un préfet de la monarchie* (1906). Talleyrand, *Mémoires* (5 vols., 1891–2). Thureau-Dangin, *Le parti libéral sous la Restauration* (2nd ed., 1888), *Royalistes et républicains* (2nd ed., 1888). Vitrolles, *Mémoires et relations politiques* (3 vols., 1883). E.-M. de Vogüé, *Le procès du Maréchal Ney* (*Revue des Deux Mondes*, 1893). Welschinger, *Le Maréchal Ney* (1893).

CHAPTER III

GOVERNMENT BY CHARTER

The composition of the new Chamber. Louis XVIII and the false Dauphins. The system of moderation. The parties. The Liberals : La Fayette, Benjamin Constant, Manuel, General Foy. The pamphlet and the song. Paul-Louis Courier and Béranger. The Doctrinaires. Royer-Collard and his group. The *Ultras* : the Comte d'Artois and his followers. Decazes in favour. The *Ultras*' hatred of him: the Riverside Plot. Victory of Decazes. The policy of the Liberals : the electoral Bill. The army law of Gouvion Saint-Cyr. The liberation of the occupied territory, the work of Richelieu. The Press law, the work of M. de Serre. The secret note.

THE drama of the Restoration was enacted on a very different plane from that of the Empire. Foreign affairs, on the whole, played only a minor part in it, whilst the stage was no longer a field of battle but the lists formed by a parliamentary chamber, the precincts of a party and the palace of a King. During the years that followed the dissolution of the *Chambre introuvable*, the French people, in the midst of economic difficulties and conspiracies, served a hard apprenticeship to representative government. Unlike what had happened at the beginning of the century, the nation relied on its own resources without regard to the foreigner, though it acted under the supervision of the latter. It tried to recover its equilibrium and moral health, and, gradually rising from its defeat, it shook off the yoke that was weighing it down, till little by little the France of to-day emerged. The spectacle was not lacking in grandeur.

The New Chamber.

Chateaubriand had prophesied that the new Chamber would be the child of the Convention. As a matter of fact, out of 262 deputies elected—the King had wisely reduced the number of representatives to this figure—three alone had been members of the Convention. The majority consisted of moderate Royalists, constitutionalists and a few Liberals—in short, of Government candidates. And this majority was destined to remain in power for four years.

Louis XVIII was satisfied. In the Speech from the Throne with which the session opened (4th of November, 1816) he assured his people "of his firm determination to repress all malevolent attempts and to hold in check any manifestation of exaggerated zeal." And he proceeded to outline the policy he intended to follow: if it was necessity that had driven him to grant the Charter, he now regarded it as a bill of exchange bearing the signature of Bourbon, and foresaw that the day on which that letter was protested his dynasty would disappear. He had within him "the steadfast desire to die upon the throne, and sufficient wit and wisdom for this desire not to be vain." As the elections seemed to show that France was gradually moving towards stability, reasons of state directed him to avoid anything that might rouse public opinion again.

But at this very moment there were disturbances in some of the provinces, the cause of which was directly connected with the King. In January 1815 Louis XVIII had given instructions for the bodies of Louis XVI and of Marie-Antoinette to be exhumed from the cemetery of la Madeleine and had given honourable burial to "these august remains," paying reverent homage to the memory of the martyrs. But where was the body of the Dauphin Louis XVII, the *orphelin du Temple*, whose death had been announced in June 1795? Had he really succumbed to the villainies of the infamous Simon?

The false Dauphins.

As early as 1798 a boy of thirteen, named Hervagault, who was said to be the lost Dauphin, had appeared in the department of Marne. Fouché had thought of making use of this Pretender against the Bourbons, but Bonaparte had refused his consent to such methods. Hervagault had died a miserable death at Bicêtre in 1812, and the name of Louis XVII was buried in silence. At the time of the celebrations held in honour of the King's return his name was not pronounced, and no ceremonies were held in his honour. This indifference created considerable surprise; for a large number of Royalists really believed that Louis XVII had undoubtedly escaped from the Temple, and were awaiting the return of "Joash escaped from the massacre," suspecting that the King had no right to be on the throne. Thus when, in the month of December 1815, a new Dauphin appeared, their enthusiasm knew no bounds; hailed by thousands of the old Royalists, Mathurin Bruneau, surnamed Charles of Navarre, was soon surrounded by an adoring court at Rouen, whither he had been relegated. The Tuileries were alarmed; the Pretender was put in solitary confinement and condemned to seven years imprisonment.

Nevertheless the popular agitation was not calmed. The clergy and the old Royalist families still persisted in believing that the Dauphin was alive, and Chateaubriand demanded from the rostrum, "Where is the brother of the *Orpheline du Temple* (the Duchesse d'Angoulême)? Where is he to be found, that I may ask him the terrible but all too familiar question: Capet, art thou sleeping?" Whereupon the Government made a pretence of directing the search. Months passed by, and the agitation seemed to abate. But for posterity "the mystery of Louis XVII" still remained unsolved.

Was Louis XVIII certain of his title? His attitude at the time of Bruneau's arrest, and his refusal to shed light on the subject, seem to point to the fact that he, too, believed in the escape of the Dauphin. Nevertheless, it is difficult to believe that a prince, permeated as he was by Royalist traditions, would knowingly usurp the throne of the legitimate heir, and one would prefer to think that in his heart of hearts he had no doubt as to his death.

Moderation of Louis XVIII.

At all events, this much at least is certain—he did not wish to dig up the past. Rich in the virtue of patience which he had acquired in the days of exile, "he did not meet events half-way, but let them come to him." He awaited them in his armchair, and endeavoured to counteract them if they were a menace to peace and order—negative, opportunist qualities, if you will, for which the politicians upbraided him, but at the time when he put them into practice they had their uses, and even possessed a certain nobility.

Those who had worked with Napoleon were astonished to find Louis XVIII so easy-going; long reports bored him to death. Somebody once observed to Talleyrand, "The King sat in Council for three hours. What passed?" "Three hours," replied the diplomat. Another remarked, "The King wishes to give the appearance of activity, and prefers the men who make the task of government easy." But this was due to wisdom, and not to laziness on his part; for he mistrusted innovations and counted, as Machiavelli did, upon the healing touch of time. After Ghent he adopted a perfectly clear policy—in order to create the elements of the representative system he was obliged to turn to two sources, those who had been loyal to the old system and those who upheld the new venture, "and to bring them together," as Tocqueville afterwards observed, "joining the principle of modern liberty to that of the old hereditary system." This policy of moderation was, in his opinion, the only one which would prevent France from wrenching herself from his grasp. Placed outside and above parties, filling the rôle of mediator, he hoped to become the King not of two hostile peoples, but of a single nation, of which he would be the worthy personification in the eyes of victorious Europe, "by the pride of his bearing doing honour to his country's grief."

The mechanism of Parliament was different in those days from what it is at the present time. The Chamber of Deputies, which was elected for five years, had a fifth of its number re-elected every year. When the session was opened, the King went in state to the Palais Bourbon, where he read the Speech from the Throne in the presence of the assembled peers and deputies. But the two were not treated in the same manner. The King himself bade the peers to be seated, whilst the Chancellor afterwards informed the deputies that His Majesty gave them leave to sit down—a proceeding savouring of red tape and reminiscent of the *ancien régime*, which made a distinction between the King's supporters and the representatives of the electoral body. The Chambers answered the Speech from the Throne by an address in which they made known their sentiments as a rule in a purely formal manner.

The deputies did not nominate their President, who was chosen by the King from a list of candidates drawn up by the Chamber, whereby he was able to exercise a certain control over the proceedings which were only open to the public in the Chamber of Deputies. As for the Ministers, they supported proposed legislation, not as representing the majority, but as representing the King, and the latter had to give his consent to amendments before they were proposed in the House.

What was the appearance of the Palais Bourbon when the House was sitting? Against the end wall, behind the President, were statues of Greek and Roman legislators—Romanticism had not yet conquered Parliament; facing the President were the benches of the deputies, arranged in a semi-circle; above were the seats reserved for the public. On the left sat the Liberals or Independents—Bonapartists and Jacobins who had played an active part during the Hundred Days, deputies who had at first rallied to the Monarchy, but had afterwards been forced into opposition by the excesses of the *Chambre introuvable*. These members, though sprung from such diverse sources, were united by hatred of the *ancien régime* and attachment to the principles of 1789, but they did not dare openly to avow their anti-dynastic sympathies, and made a pretence of loyalty. To safeguard the liberties that had been won and to secure further rights, above all the freedom of the Press, which had been promised but never conceded; to carry the Charter to its logical conclusions, and so to modify it that it should no longer be in the nature of a benevolent concession on the part of the royal authority, but a regular contract; and to seize parliamentary power by means of a judiciously arranged electoral system—in short, " to bind the Crown without destroying it "—such was their programme. They did not dream of establishing a democracy; very far from it! To grant political rights to the mass of the people seemed to them a dangerous delusion; voting was only possible on a basis of enlightenment, and if civil equality was a protection against the aristocracy, political inequality alone seemed compatible with the aspirations of the bourgeoisie and the essential prerequisite of good government.

The Liberals.

These Liberals—lawyers, doctors, holders of national property, ex-soldiers, industrialists or business men—owed allegiance to a member of the aristocracy, La Fayette. The latter, indeed, was less an orator and a politician than a flag. A sensitive man, and a humanitarian after the fashion of the eighteenth century, La Fayette enjoyed

La Fayette.

a great reputation, owing to his conduct at the time of the American War of Independence. He was "the hero of two worlds," and in the end he so sincerely shared the admiration in which he was held that he came to believe himself "the Buddha incarnate of Liberty." But had he really got the qualifications of a party leader? It is extremely doubtful. Mirabeau, who knew him very well during the Revolution, called him "the Vacillator," or "Gilles-le-Grand." An unrepentant conspirator, La Fayette confessed to his followers that the greatest moment of his life would be the day on which he should mount the scaffold and make confession of his political faith. Meanwhile, however, he possessed no gift for organisation or capacity as a leader; he was merely a name round which the Liberal bourgeoisie rallied in case of alarm.

Benjamin Constant.

The strategist of the party, the man who did more than any other to make the parliamentary system take root in France, who formulated, explained and applied the dogma of constitutionalism, was a man of far greater worth than La Fayette. Behold this aged youth, with the refined and faded features, framed in long, lustreless fair hair, to whom the President has just given the floor. He spreads little scraps of paper in front of him, which he is continually arranging and re-arranging; his voice has an effeminate ring, his delivery is jerky, laboured and monotonous. But hearken to his words; the subject is summed up in a few brief, poignant sentences, whereupon follows an outburst of irony, biting and scathing. In vain do the Royalists protest against the onslaught; the orator, in no wise disconcerted, continues in the same vein, calmly envenoming the debate and entangling his adversaries in a political syllogism. Occasionally a flash of wit or an aphorism may enliven his speech, but on the whole it is entirely lacking in rhetorical flourish. Such is the picture of Benjamin Constant on the rostrum, the man who had just written that extraordinary psychological novel *Adolphe*, that sentimental tale, which is yet so crude and full of bitterness and hate. The novelist and the politician were welded into one. The *Ultras* held him in detestation. "A venomous reptile, a hideous and ghastly figure filled with cruelty, impudence, envy and malice." The younger members were astounded by his reasoned violence and his lack of enthusiasm; his enemies, calling to mind his dubious reputation and his various changes of opinion, accused him of corruption; whilst Sismondi's mother declared that "he had much wit, but no soul." These qualities were perhaps an asset in a party man. At all events, the fact remains that as long as he sat in Parliament, Benjamin Constant was one of the main pillars of Liberal doctrine, its theorist and tactician.

Manuel.

Beside him stands a lawyer from the south, tall and thin, with melancholy features not altogether devoid of beauty, and very simply dressed—it is Manuel. His speciality, if one may use the expression, was in season and out of season to oppose France of the *ancien régime* and the Emigration by France of the Revolution. As frigid in appearance as Benjamin Constant, he unloosed the fury of the Right by his constant apology for periods of upheaval. Trained in the school of Fouché, he was well versed in the art of inflicting deep wounds by means of arguments which seemed almost innocuous. Always master of himself, he went his way implacable, smiling at abuse and dominating the Assembly with his lofty disdain. "A tiger in the guise of a cat, with ingratiating manners and the soul of a hyæna," observed one of the *Ultras*.

Benjamin Constant and Manuel made but little appeal to sentiment. They doubtless enjoyed a certain measure of popularity, but they failed to rouse the enthusiasm of the mob, and reason played a greater part than affection in the admiration bestowed upon them. For two years the sentimental tribune, the moving orator, was not to be found in the ranks of the Liberal Party; but after 1817 this gap was filled.

General Foy.

One day there appeared in the Palais Bourbon a man who held himself proudly erect; his forehead was lofty and as it were illumined by enthusiasm, his mouth was strong, with boldly outlined curves, and there was "something chivalrous about his head." Whereupon the debate, which until that moment had been dry and arid, was suddenly transformed. The words which fell from the lips of the speaker were endowed with a strange warmth of conviction, an odour of virtue, which won the hearts of his listeners. He recalled the triumphs of the Empire, referring to the life of the soldier heroes who had returned to their homes, with a noble sincerity and a profound and unaffected love which prevented the *Ultras* from protesting. "There is an echo throughout France," he exclaimed, "when in this place the words 'my honour and my country' are pronounced!" Along all the benches, from the Right to the Left, ran a tremor. After such manifold divisions, and an endless chain of calamities, a phrase such as this resounded with peculiar force and for a moment welded the souls of all in one. Such was the first appearance in the House of General Foy. An old soldier of the Revolution, a General under the Empire, and at one time a favourite of Napoleon, who during the war in Spain knew how to appreciate his clarity of vision and his cool courage, a man with a magnificent record of service behind him, of unimpeachable probity and disinterestedness, fifteen times wounded—the last time at Waterloo—this plebeian from the North hated the *ancien régime* and the old aristocracy. Nevertheless he gave his allegiance to the Bourbons, refusing to join in any conspiracy against them, and became in Parliament the defender of the Imperial army and of the heritage of glory won by France which the Restoration, in spite of all political considerations, was bound to respect. As a military orator was a novelty, the Opposition welcomed him with open arms; General Foy had a martial bearing, he ascended the rostrum as though he were rushing to victory, and his almost blatant magnanimity convulsed his hearers. Moreover he had a gift for discovering striking phrases and tags which pleased the passions of his party. When in the course of a debate he referred to the possibility of France one day returning to the tricoloured flag, and added, "It will not be the shades of Philip Augustus and of Henry IV that will wax indignant at seeing the *fleur de lys* of Bouvines and Ivry on the flag of Austerlitz!" and when, irritated by the tedious matter-of-fact arguments of a certain Minister of Finance, he exclaimed, "I know nothing about gambling on the Stock Exchange; it is on a rise in the national honour that I stake my all," he was greeted with loud applause, and even the young Royalists felt inspired with respectful affection for this soldier. "His fine profile," said one of them, "stands out like an antique cameo. Speeches which are always laboured, and which from the lips of anyone else would stink of oil, are redolent of gunpowder when they come from him."

The Liberals used to foregather at the house of La Fayette or of Benjamin Constant, in the Rue d'Anjou Saint Honoré, where they discussed the tactics of their party. For purposes of propaganda they had their own periodicals—*le Mercure*, founded by Benjamin Constant, which on its suppression was replaced by *la Minerve ; le Constitutionnel*, which survived for a long time; *la Bibliothèque Historique* and other minor papers such as *le Miroir*, "the hussar of the Press, a charming swashbuckler," which, under the editorship of Jouy, Arnault and Jal, "every day sent out some broken gleams from the sun of the Empire." But until 1819 the newspapers, which could not be published without permission and were subjected to censorship, did not dare to discuss general politics, but confined themselves to anecdotes, and like *le Constitutionnel*, for instance, kept watch "by the soldiers who died in their beds," and advanced no further. Thus it was impossible through the Press for the detested Liberalism of the Bonapartists to exercise any real influence upon public opinion; hence the recourse to pamphlets and songs, and the success of Paul-Louis Courier and of Béranger.

The Liberal Journals.

The former, who had been an officer of no distinction under the Empire, and had been for ever disgusted with war by the massacre of Lebau, at which he was present, was at heart "an aristocrat of the intellect," a Hellenist who had accidentally tumbled into politics. Posing as a peasant of Touraine, he repeated *ad nauseam* that he was a man of the people, with no knowledge of the upper classes, and with the disgruntled son of toil as his theme, told the rulers what he thought of them. If he pretended to admire "the autocratic behaviour" of Napoleon, it was only in order to hold it up in contrast to the hypocrisy of the Bourbons, and of Louis XVIII, who bought the votes of the deputies and smiled approvingly on "representative Government, as the source of all prosperity." If, as an artist and a writer of some refinement, he declared himself in favour of the black bands who were destroying castles, it was because Blois and Amboise only called to mind "shameful debauchery and

Louis Courier.

infamous treachery," and because all traces of the *ancien régime* should be for ever obliterated.

This sham democrat, who had no respect for history, and had acquired, through books, an admiration for Greece alone, made a pretence of ingenuousness and roundly declared the Government of his dreams was like " a coachman who is paid to drive us not where he pleases, but where we wish to go." Every event, even the most trifling—an ill-advised decision on the part of some mayor, or an arbitrary arrest—furnished him with a pretext, and he set to work to put an edge on his pamphlets and to hew out phrases at once artful and perfidious : " Every day charity grows weaker, as the nation turns to labour, and will soon be as dead as a door nail if the Holy Alliance does not restore order." And—a fact which gives one no very high opinion of the taste of the period—this far-fetched and laboured style of writing was a popular success. After the lapse of time the excellence of the manner alone survives, the rest fades into oblivion, and the political work of Courier joins hands across the centuries with the *Satire Ménippée* against the League.

Béranger.

Béranger's case is not so complicated. A Parisian born in Paris, who had hardly ever left the Rue Montorgueil, except to pay a visit to Péronne or Dieppe, he knew the masses well, and was imbued with the genius of the metropolis. He was " an ignorant knave, after the fashion of Montaigne," in this respect resembling Courier ; but his frankness possessed greater vitality, his writing was more lively, and smelt less of printer's ink. According to Benjamin Constant, the first time he put a song into verse it took the form of an ode, and thereby, at one stroke, appealed to men's hearts and found " the spot where he could best be heard." He had in him some of the qualities of a second-rate Beaumarchais, whose work, with a youthful smile and concealed malice, reflects the spirit of the Age, the atmosphere of the day; and in this respect his poems are admirable documents. Whether he sings the glory of the Emperor, ridicules the *émigrés*, or attacks the parlementarians or the Jesuits, his verse is nearly always happy and its magic lucidity haunts the mind.

Louis XVIII, who was by nature a man of letters, and had inherited the wit of the previous century, said, " One cannot help forgiving the author of *Le Roi d'Yvetot* a good deal." But this revolutionary song, saturated with Liberal and Bonapartist ideas, sank deep into the minds of the people; it was imitated, sometimes intelligently, by other "Cellar Alcæuses," who founded societies whose names sufficiently indicate their nature —The Society of the Jolly Franks, of the Rabbits, of the Imperial Veterans, of the Friends of Glory. One song-writer, Brazier, has preserved the picture of one of these heroi-comic gatherings, convened in the name of the Emperor, and of Liberty, whose leaders were all old soldiers. The invention and development of this quasi-lyric poetry were entirely the work of Béranger. His sentiments may have been of a low order, there may have been in his poetry a tinge of vulgarity, and Proudhon may have been right in saying, "Béranger rendered good service to the Revolution, but he debased the moral sense and destroyed the political sense"; nevertheless, from the standpoint of history, it must be remembered that his songs accomplished more for the Liberal cause than many a speech or newspaper article, and that under the Restoration, Béranger was really the *vox populi.*

The Doctrinaires.

In the centre of the Chamber sat the deputies of the Third Party, who supported the Bourbons and the Charter, and wished to put an end to the Revolution, whilst maintaining the liberty that had been won. Having in the past sought a practical compromise between the France of 1789 and that of 1815, they thought they had discovered it in the legitimate monarchy in alliance with the representative system. Distinct from the Liberals, inasmuch as they maintained that the King's authority was superior to that of the majority, and also from the *Ultras,* since they would have nothing to do with a return to the *ancien régime,* they laid down the principle that "the monarchy was to be nationalised and France was to be royalised." They were enamoured of abstract ideas and theoretical speculations, convinced that everything should bow to reason, and, "reason was naturally that which seemed reasonable to themselves." They were called the Doctrinaires.

Royer-Collard.

These great and haughty bourgeois, who were absolutely sincere and were not really on a level with their colleagues, but above them, owed allegiance to a famous orator whose name has been handed down to history and who crystallised the programme of his party into maxims —Royer-Collard. His grave features, his tall stature and his majestic bearing, together with his noble and dignified gaze which occasionally condescended to come down from the heights to the level of his interlocutor, made Royer-Collard a fairly typical representative of the Jansenist bourgeois. He affected a sort of plebeian simplicity, scandalising the courtiers by brandishing a large red handkerchief in the presence of the King and blowing his nose in it loudly; but this in no way detracted from his dignity. On the rostrum he read out in a loud, drawling voice cleverly constructed speeches with boldly rounded periods, denouncing the faction born of the Revolution which was always aiming at usurpation, as well as the opposite party of privilege who were outraged by equality and wished to destroy it. His speeches were effective, for he touched on the philosophic aspects of every problem, and there was no danger with him of grovelling in the base contingencies of reality. His Royalist sympathies won him the confidence of the Right, whilst his leanings in the opposite direction made him *persona grata* with the Left. Thus constituted, he dominated the Assembly, hurling his opinions and prophecies at their heads; strengthened by his study of politics, he gladly played the part of augur, and prophesied the slow but certain rise of the middle classes.

In addition to him there were theorists who developed his doctrine. In his historical works Guizot described the gradual rise of the bourgeoisie to power and its forthcoming supremacy; Cousin, the spiritualistic philosopher, proved that the "natural rights" of the eighteenth century had found their confirmation in the Charter; and finally in Parliament, a few superior minds—Camille Jordan, de Serre and the Duc de Broglie—ranged themselves about Royer-Collard and supported him with the full weight of their authority.

This reasoned outlook, this attitude of disdain, this determined stand on high altitudes gave rise to a certain amount of ridicule. "They are four," said a certain Liberal paper, "who at one moment declare that they are only three, because they think it impossible for there to be four such great minds in the world, and the next make out that they are five, in order to frighten their enemies by their number." But in reality,

Royer-Collard, in spite of the position he occupied, was outstripped by the march of events. He used frequently to declare, "There is nothing that I despise so much as a fact," and when he was confronted with a fact which brought a train of disaster in its wake, he confined himself to cursing it and withdrew into his own world of thought. His bigotry and love of pedantry, and the way in which he observed, "I have always been an unpleasant customer," made it hard to get on with him. When, later on, de Serre, who had left the Doctrinaires, reproached his old chief with not having followed him, and brought forward many excellent reasons why he should have done so, Royer-Collard replied, "I do not follow, I remain where I am." And, here again, he gave proof of his powers of divination; he did indeed remain where he was, submerged by the facts he despised, at the very moment when the bourgeois monarchy of 1830, which he had dogmatically predicted, had come into being.

The Ultras.

In contrast to the Liberals, the Constitutionalists and the Doctrinaires, the *Ultra* minority was impressive by reason of its numbers as well as owing to the fact that it was supported by the National Guard, who took their orders from the Comte d'Artois. At that time they had as their leader Chateaubriand, who, as a counterblast to *la Minerve*, had just founded *le Conservateur*. The contributors to this journal, the perusal of which even at the present day is extremely absorbing and stirring, bore the most distinguished names in France, though the zeal of humbler aspirants was not discouraged. Thus by the side of names like Levis and Fitzjames, whom Chateaubriand had made into writers, there appeared that of a certain young priest named Lamennais, whose vehement articles created a sensation by a certain savage and far from aristocratic energy. In addition to *le Conservateur*, *la Quotidienne* and *le Drapeau Blanc*, which was edited by Martainville, "erstwhile buffoon of the *Grivoisiana* and the *Pied-de-Mouton*," and hetman of the *émigré* forces, carried on the fight. The design on the latter paper represented an officer of the Royal Guard brandishing an unfurled banner with the device: "*Vive le roi quand-même!*" This constituted the whole of the Royalist programme against Louis XVIII.

Since the dissolution of the *Chambre introuvable* the *Ultras* had made no attempt to conceal their hatred of the Charter, "the source of all our ills." It was at bottom, they maintained, merely a confirmation, not, it is true, of the crimes of the Revolution, but of the ideas that served to produce it, and consecrated the work of '89. To restore the administration to hands that were clean, to return to the *émigrés* any of their property that had not been sold, or, if the sale had already taken place, to give them compensation, to subject the Press to censorship and only allow the publication of papers of right ideas, to entrust the work of education to the clergy, and, if the King refused, to ride rough-shod over him—such in brief outline was the political system of the party, that was ousted in 1816. They used to meet at the house of one of their members, the lawyer Piet, in the Rue Thérèse. "We used to sit round in a circle," Chateaubriand afterwards said, "in a room lighted by a lamp that smoked. In this legislative fog we would discuss the law that had been proposed, the motion to be carried, and which of our members were to be raised to office. And we would retail the most depressing news." This pessimism continued during the meal, to which each member brought his contribution—a haunch of venison or a turkey. La Bourdonnaie was conspicuous among them for his violence, waxing indignant at the very thought of any dealings with the majority and accusing the Minister Decazes of every crime under the sun.

Decazes.

Decazes was at this time at the height of his power. Once secretary to Madame Laetitia, the mother of Napoleon—whom the *Ultras* called *Mère-la-Joie*—he had rallied to the support of the Bourbons. A native of Gascony, free and easy, obliging and never insolent, and on the whole extremely clever, he possessed all the qualities calculated to please Louis XVIII; his gaze could be kindly and his voice persuasive; moreover he was animated by a warmth of devotion which won the King's heart. In 1815 he had asked leave to cross out the name of his friend Montalivet from the list of suspects in such moving tones that the King had held out his arms to him, exclaiming, "You are a good fellow! Kiss me!"

For Louis XVIII, the presence of a favourite, of a "Narcissus" as Royer-Collard remarked, was an innate desire which he could not suppress. And thus Decazes became his friend, his son; he worked with him every morning, and told him the scandal of the day, for he had kept in his pay the excellent police of the Empire, an act which the extreme Royalists never forgave him. Gradually Louis XVIII dropped into the habit of using the familiar " thou " to him, and at a Cabinet meeting, since he could not converse alone with him, he used to hand him affectionate notes. Every day they were at each other's beck and call, exchanging flattering attentions which enlivened the existence of the old King and to which the favourite added the finishing touch by demonstrations of romantic attachment. " I shall raise him so high," said Louis XVIII of his favourite, " that the highest in the land will be jealous of him ! " And this was literally true. For close on four years Decazes guided the destinies of the nation, which sufficiently explains the hatred he aroused in the breasts of the *Ultras*.

Le Drapeau Blanc openly accused him of conspiring to restore the Empire under Napoleon II, but the King refused to lend credence to such a tale. Although such elections as had taken place had added to the ranks of the Independent or Liberal deputies, he remained faithful to his Minister, who represented his system of moderation. In 1817 there was great scarcity of food in France, due in part to the occupation by the Allies, who reduced the stocks of cattle and terrorised the peasants. Disturbances broke out owing to the high price of corn, the roads were full of beggars leaving the impoverished provinces, and bands of starving men, particularly in the Cher district, held up the carriages on the Paris road and demanded money from the occupants, so that it became necessary to send out troops against them. The Right immediately held Decazes responsible for these calamities; but Richelieu bought corn abroad to meet the shortage. Thus peace was restored and the favourite remained in office.

Whereupon, in order to frighten the King and prove to him the power of the revolutionary party, the *Ultras* engineered in all its ramifications a plot which broke out in Lyons in June 1817. The insurgents demanded bread at a penny a pound—it was worth fivepence ha'penny—whilst others shouted, " *Vive Napoleon II !* " The army was immediately mobilised, and the *Cour prévôtale* convened; 155 men were charged, twenty-eight were condemned to death, of whom sixteen were sentenced by default. But some of the depositions were so peculiar that the Government charged Marshal Marmont to hold an inquiry, the result of which was that the plot was proved to have been the work of the police and of General Canuel, who were whole-hearted adherents of the *Ultras*.

This abortive demonstration, which cost the lives of many innocent people, in no wise discouraged the Right, and the Comte d'Artois made up his mind openly to demand from his brother the dismissal of Decazes, "Otherwise," he added, "I, together with my children, will leave Court." "There are such things as fortresses for rebels," replied Louis XVIII. "The Charter does not allow of State prisons," was the reply. This unexpected appeal on the part of the leader of the *Ultras* to the "hated Charter" entirely stopped the King's digestion; his gout flew to his stomach and he almost choked. But this was merely a trifling encounter. In the end, the hardened Royalists, exasperated by the Liberal régime, which reduced them to impotence, decided upon a grand attempt—nothing less than the placing upon the throne of the Comte d'Artois, with the title of Charles X, "without waiting for heaven to dispose of Louis XVIII." This conspiracy, called the Riverside Plot, since it was hatched on the terrace of the Tuileries alongside the Seine, was easily discovered by Decazes's police; but it would have been unwise to seize the ringleaders, and only the rank and file were arrested, to be set free as soon as they had confessed. The King was informed of the affair; he had already deprived his brother of the command of the National Guard, and this fresh attempt on the part of the vanquished *Ultras* bound him all the more closely to Decazes.

The Riverside Plot.

Certain of the support of "his father" and of the co-operation of the majority, Decazes, whether he were President of the Chamber or not, deliberately directed the Government policy against the rival Court in the Pavillon de Marsen, and thus it came about that the Chambers passed one after the other the Electoral Bill, the Army Bill and the Finance Bill, required for the evacuation of the occupied territory.

The Electoral Bill, which was the work of Lainé, the Minister of the Interior, whom the *Ultras* accused of wishing to restore the Republic, established the simplest possible method of voting—the direct nomination of the deputies by the departmental colleges by means of the *scrutin de liste* (multiple vote system). Every Frenchman who had reached the age of thirty and paid 300 francs in taxation had a vote; the candidates had to be forty or over, and to pay 1000 francs in taxation. In short, out of 29,000,000 Frenchmen, 90,000 had the vote, whilst 16,000 were eligible for election. This system, little democratic though it was—in 1791 in France 429,000 had the vote though the population was smaller—roused the anger of the Right. The meeting of the voters in the capital of the department gave an advantage to the Liberals of the towns and destroyed the influence of the landed gentry in the country districts; on the other hand, the Government, who appointed the Presidents of the Colleges, brought all its weight to bear on the choice of the electors, and legislatively established the official candidature.

The Electoral Bill.

As in 1815, the Right thereupon took up the defence of the doctrines of liberty, and Monsieur de Villèle, one of its most remarkable members, moved that any deputy who was promoted to office or to a permanent position should stand for re-election, but the Minister de Serre replied that "the Government had need of every possible means of increasing its power." The law was passed (February 1817) and secured the progress of the Liberal Party, and the urban bourgeoisie, as opposed to the rural Royalists, until 1820.

For the future of the country, the Army Bill, drawn up and supported by Marshal Gouvion Saint-Cyr, was of far greater importance. Since 1815 the army had been reduced to 150,000 men, under the command of lieutenant-generals with the title of divisional governors, almost all of whom were drawn from the ranks of the aristocracy. General Clarke and General Latour-Maubourg had carefully sifted it. The officers whose names were on the roll on the 20th of March (the date of the Emperor's return) were divided into twenty-one categories, according to the degree of their complicity with the Usurper, and relegated on principle to the inferior ranks and placed under the supervision of a secret police in the pay of the Duc d'Angoulême, the eldest son of Monsieur.

The Army Bill.

Of this army, which was regarded with suspicion, Gouvion Saint-Cyr wished to make a national army, whereby France would be able to prove to Europe that she had recovered her strength and was now able to maintain order on her own account and to dispense with the presence of the foreign troops. According to the new law, recruiting was to be carried on by means of voluntary enlistment, and also by ballot. The word conscription, which had been abolished by the Charter, was not pronounced, but the reality was there. Nobody could obtain a commission without having been a non-commissioned officer for two years or a pupil in a military school; promotion was given by seniority to two-thirds of the officers up to the rank of lieutenant-colonel; and lastly the veterans' legion—from which the reservists of to-day developed—was created.

This law, which arranged the military organisation of France for many years to come, was violently attacked by the Right, which regarded the army as its traditional domain. According to Bonald, recruiting by ballot was nothing less than "white slavery"; the institution of the veterans' corps amounted, according to Chateaubriand, to the creation of a second army, trained by the Empire, over and above the royal army; the new rules of promotion deprived the Crown of the right of choosing the officers, made the non-commissioned officers the real masters of the soldier and undermined the privileges of the aristocracy—it meant an invasion on the part of the men on half-pay, a revolutionary invasion. Nevertheless the Bill was passed (1818) and one of the *Ultras*, Frénilly, exclaimed, "To think that a King could be found to accept such a law! Is it possible to love one's country without despising such a man?"

But in fact the system of seniority was not applied, and promotion continued to depend upon the King's pleasure and that of his nephew, the Duc d'Angoulême, though the Army was increased from 150,000 to 240,000 men; thus providing an argument in the negotiations with the Allies.

Liberation of occupied Territory.

By the Treaty of 1815 the occupation by the Allies was to be reduced to three years, provided it could be proved to be no longer necessary and France had paid off her arrears of debt. Richelieu, to his eternal credit, devoted himself wholeheartedly to the task of liberating the occupied territory, but he was confronted by enormous difficulties. The foreign sovereigns were demanding the payment of indemnities dating from the Seven Years War, whilst one German Prince was claiming the return of the sum paid to 4000 reiters who had been raised on behalf of Henry IV! It was necessary to compromise and come to terms. Thanks to Richelieu's efforts, a convention signed at Paris on the 25th of April, 1818, limited the obligations of France to 265 millions (francs), and financial arrangements were made whereby the loans to meet the sum could be raised. At the Congress of Aix-la-Chapelle the withdrawal of the Army of Occupation was agreed upon, whereupon France once more resumed her place among the Great Powers; she was released from tutelage and recovered her liberty of action. But this wiping out of the "disgrace of 1815" did not satisfy the Allies; they were determined not only to cling to the right of surveillance over France, but also to intervene if necessary in her internal affairs.

Thus the adventure of the Hundred Days was in part liquidated. According to Monsieur Charléty's calculations it had cost France about two milliards.

Richelieu had just delivered the country from the yoke of the foreigner, and his personality rightly overshadowed that of Decazes; but it was impossible for the two men to work together for long. Frightened at the policy pursued by his colleague, and finding it extremely distasteful to carry on the Government in opposition to men who for five-and-twenty years had defended the monarchy, and many of whom were his personal friends, Richelieu demanded the resignation of Decazes from the King. But Louis XVIII could not bring himself to take the step, and it was Richelieu who sent in his resignation. After an acrid debate, the Chamber voted this loyal servant who retired from office a poor man—he had had to sell his jewels—a grant of 50,000 francs, which he at once handed over to the hospitals of Bordeaux. In his place the King gave the Presidency of the Chamber to General Dessolles, whose name had been unearthed from the pages of the *Almanach Royal*; but the acknowledged head of the Government was Decazes, who leant more than ever upon the Left, and in order to ingratiate himself with them, introduced fresh schemes of legislation with regard to the Press.

Until that time newspapers had been treated more or less in the same way as they had been under Napoleon, who said, "The Press is an arsenal reserved for those who enjoy the confidence of the Government." The new laws which were passed in May and June 1819 abolished the rule that no paper could be published without permission, a mere notification now being all that was required. Infringements of the law were no longer to be dealt with by the *tribunaux correctionels*, but were to be tried by jury. Nevertheless, as the Liberals were anxious that the Press should not be used as an instrument by means of which the masses could easily be moved, security was demanded, and the existing stamp duties prevented the papers from being circulated too cheaply. They remained an article of luxury, a subscription costing about 80 francs a year. The sale of single copies was non-existent.

The Press Law.

These laws were supported, not by Decazes, who was content to set the ball rolling, but by one of the Doctrinaires, who in this instance proved how powerful political faith allied with the highest integrity can be. Monsieur de Serre, although he was an old soldier of the Emigration, had broken off connection with the *Ultras*, who, to use his own words, were "Pharisees, who, with the letter of the Charter on their lips, only sought opportunities for violating the spirit of it." He was convinced that if liberty was to be established it was necessary to secure the Bourbons on the throne, and with wonderful loyalty he supported the work of Decazes for three years. The *Ultras* did not forgive him for this. One day de Serre declared that the majorities in the revolutionary assemblies had almost always been sound in their judgments. "What! Even the Convention?" exclaimed La Bourdonnaie. "Yes, sir, even the Convention; and if the Convention had not voted with a pistol at their heads, France would never have had to bewail the most horrible of crimes." This was greeted with loud applause from the Left. On the other hand, when the question of allowing the return of the regicides was mooted, de Serre answered with a "Never!" which expressed a rigid determination, and it was the turn of the Right to applaud. Such was the nature of this man, who was wholeheartedly devoted to the interests of the monarchy, superior to party and disdainful of intrigue. Lamartine, who was quick to recognise greatness and energy when he met them, felt that the eloquence of Monsieur de Serre was illumined by a rare spark of genius, "a spark in which there is no human alloy."

And thus the policy of the Liberals was triumphant, though the minority did not lay down their arms. Whilst Richelieu was negotiating for the liberation of the occupied territory, it had no scruples about sending to the Chancelleries of Europe a note which made France appear in the light of a volcano ready to set the whole continent alight. This note, drawn up by Frénilly but recast by Monsieur de Vitrolles, the confidant of the Comte d'Artois, suggested that the panacea was the dismissal of Decazes, and, in order to stop the advance of the Revolution, begged for the Allied occupation to be continued. It was seized by the police and published, thus placing the *Ultras* in an extremely unenviable position. Nevertheless they refused to acknowledge themselves beaten.

The Concordats.

At this juncture negotiations were being carried on with the Pope for the signature of a fresh Concordat. If by its instrumentality the clergy recovered the power they had enjoyed under the *ancien régime*, the minority would receive a fresh access of force. In 1815 the parishes were in a terrible condition. Out of 12,000 livings, which were recognised to be necessary, 5000 only were filled, and Lamennais was right in saying, "There is not sufficient alarm felt at the depopulation of the Church; every year the number of priests grows less and religion becomes weaker." In 1817, Monsieur de Blacas, the French Ambassador in Rome, signed a new Concordat, which annulled the one in force under Napoleon and restored the Concordat of 1516 passed under Francis I. But its acceptance by the Chambers seemed indispensable, and yet no one had the courage to present them with the treaty. The negotiations dragged on interminably, and in spite of the efforts of Portalis, the jurist, a fresh scheme failed, owing to opposition from the Court of Rome. In the end the Concordat of 1801 was renewed without modification or change; the only stipulation being that the number of dioceses should be increased. This was another rebuff for the *Ultras*.

In 1819 the hatred of his enemies for Decazes knew no bounds, and the Duc de Berry, with his usual impulsiveness, observed out loud in front of some hundred people, "The wretch! He is destroying everything—the King, France and the monarchy! In the old days we were at least fortunate enough to see the people meting out justice to these favourites!"

BIBLIOGRAPHY.—De Barante, *La vie politique de Royer-Collard* (2 vols., 1878). Béranger, *Ma biographie* (1857). Brazier, *Histoire des petits théâtres de Paris* (1838). Charléty, *Une conspiration à Lyon en 1817* (*Revue de Paris*, 1904). De Cisternes, *Le Duc de Richelieu* (1898). Combes de Patris, *Le Comte de Serre* (*Revue Universelle*, 1924). Timon Cormenin, *Le Livre des Orateurs* (2 vols., 1836). Baron de Damas, *Mémoires* (2 vols., 1922–23). E. Daudet, *Louis XVIII et le Duc Decazes* (1899). Comte Ferrand, *Mémoires* (1897). De Guichen, *La France morale et religieuse au début de la Restauration* (1911). General d' Hautpoul, *Mémoires* (1906). Hyde de Neuville, *Mémoires et Souvenirs* (3 vols., 1892). S. Lapointe, *Mémoires sur Béranger* (1858). G. Lenotre, *Louis XVII et l'énigme du Temple* (1921). Ch. de Mazade, *Le Comte de Serre* (2 vols., 1881).

CHAPTER IV

THE ASSASSINATION OF THE DUC DE BERRY AND THE FALL OF DECAZES

Results of the policy of Decazes. Public opinion in 1820. The growth of Liberalism in Europe. Decazes decides to make concessions to the Right. The assassination of the Duc de Berry. Decazes accused of complicity. His overthrow by the *Ultras*. Consequences of Louvel's Crime—now only two parties in the Chamber. Exasperation of the public. The electoral struggles. The disturbances of June 1820. The conspiracy of the French Bazar. Defeat of Liberalism. Madame du Cayla becomes favourite. Resignation of Richelieu. Satisfaction of Louis XVIII after the birth of the Duc de Bordeaux.

FOR three years the King, the Government and the Chamber had been in agreement with regard to a policy of moderation, and it was only on the part of the Peers that any signs of independence were shown. Louis XVIII used artfully to invite some of them to drive in his carriage with him in order to make them see reason or miss a division, but Decazes chose a more radical means and created seventy-three new peers at one fell swoop. The Right protested that it was the ordinance of the 5th of September over again, another *coup d'état!* In the Palais Royal, in the smoke-laden atmosphere of the Café Valois—the café of the orthodox as opposed to the Café Lemblin, where the Bonapartists used to meet—Martainville, the editor of the *Drapeau Blanc*, circulated abusive lampoons against the favourite. Since Louis XVIII seemed to have been irrevocably corrupted by "the new Sejanus," the hopes of the minority were now entirely centred in the Duc d'Artois; and as a bad rhymster put it:

> "Pour raffermir le trône ébranlé sur sa base,
> Il faut changer le sol, et de serre et de case." [1]

[1] "To consolidate the throne, shaken to its foundations, the ground must be changed, and the edifice rebuilt from attic to cellar." The play on the names de Serre and Decazes cannot be translated.

Meanwhile parliamentary institutions were becoming more settled and Liberalism was gradually taking root in the country. The Left brandished the Charter in all directions; their propaganda was untiring, and it was even printed on tobacco pouches and scarves; it was the palladium of their party. In 1819, when he was on a mission of inspection in Metz, the Duc d'Angoulême was acclaimed with cries of "*Vive la Charte!*" and the Prefect had great difficulty in prevailing upon the National Guard to shout "*Vive le Roi!*"

At the same time there was a revival of the literature of the eighteenth century, of the Encyclopædists and of "works of philosophical import." They formed the principal element of libraries, of which the most famous was *La Tente*, given by the bookseller Ladvocat to Captain Gauthier, who had been badly wounded in the Napoleonic wars. Another officer of the late Imperial Guard, named Dulac, a wine merchant of the Rue des Jeûneurs, shed lustre upon his trade by selling book-bottles bearing such labels as *Esprit de Voltaire*, *Esprit de Rousseau*, *de Molière*, *en l'honneur de Tartuffe*, etc., whilst close by *La Bibliothèque du XIX Siècle* undertook in a hundred volumes to transvalue morality, science and history for the instruction of the rising generation. One Catholic journal estimated the number of books hostile to religion published between 1817 and 1824 at 2,741,000.

The person of the King and his dynasty remained to all appearance above such controversy. In 1818, when the twenty yoke of oxen, which were transferring the bronze statue of Henry IV to the Pont Neuf, got stuck in the mud, the crowd unharnessed them and conveyed "the Béarnais" themselves through the Champs Élysées, the Place Louis XV and the Tuileries to the appointed site. But could this proof of loyalty on the part of the people of Paris be interpreted as a sign of general devotion to the Bourbons? It is not easy to answer this question, for the Press, although it was free, had not yet shaken off its shackles, whilst the electoral system, under which the number of potential candidates had been drastically reduced and no salary was paid to the deputies, yielded results which gave no criterion of the real state of public opinion. We find a confirmed Liberal, like Manuel, for instance, being returned by Vendée, which was an ultra-Royalist department.

The chart of public opinion in France about 1820, however, has been drawn up as follows by Monsieur Charléty, who was the first to study the question. The North was almost entirely absorbed in business and gave no trouble to the Prefects; in the East, on the contrary, hatred of the foreigner and coolness towards the Bourbons predominated; Lorraine was suspicious of the aristocracy and, trodden underfoot by the Allies, remained on the *qui vive;* whilst the Alsatian for his part was "as good a Frenchman as he was a bad Royalist." Burgundy was conspicuous for a spirit of contradiction and backbiting and for a profound indifference with regard to religious matters. On the Côte-d'Or, eighty out of 400 communes remained without incumbents, and the *Ultras* played no part either there or in the Franche-Comté. In Lyons, although the majority was Liberal, the Royalists, as the police conspiracy of 1817 proved, were strongly organised. In the south they had the upper hand in Provence, whilst Languedoc was riddled by religious dissension and struggles between Catholics and Protestants, embittered by the White Terror of 1815. In the Gironde, Liberalism and Bonapartism were hand and glove together, though there was a nucleus of *Ultras*, who had recovered all their power in Vendée. To sum up, but for two isolated districts in the south and the west which were wholly Royalist, France could be divided into two political regions—the east on the whole hostile to the Restoration, and the west where interest in politics was feeble and the *de facto* Government accepted. Did this provide a sufficiently stable foundation to ensure the survival of the Bourbon dynasty? It is extremely doubtful.

Public opinion in 1820.

The partial elections of 1819—we have already observed that a fifth of the Chamber was re-elected every year—returned a fresh contingent of advanced Liberals who had no desire to unite the Bourbons to the Charter in their affections. The election of one of their number gave rise to considerable scandal. Abbé Grégoire was not exactly a regicide, but in the course of a debate under the Convention he had declared that "Kings are a pestilential class who are always a cancer in the body of the Government and the scum of the human race." Yet this revolutionary Bishop was elected at Grenoble instead of Decazes's candidate, owing to the support of the *Ultras*, whose dictum was that it was better to return Jacobins than supporters of the Government—any means being justifiable for the overthrow of the favourite. The latter took fright. The Duc de Berry's words had already been reported to him, and since the Duke had married Marie-Caroline, the eldest daughter of the King of the Two Sicilies, in 1816, he had become a personage of the first importance. Certainly he had no love for the King. Impulsive, inclined to "bully the army," whom he rightly suspected of Bonapartist tendencies, and but little fitted to play any part requiring tact and diplomacy, he had no sympathy for the policy of moderation so dear to the heart of Louis XVIII. But as his elder brother, the Duc d'Angoulême, had no children, he represented "the hope of the Legitimists," and it was impossible for Decazes to ignore the hostility of this prince of the blood.

Liberalism in Europe.

At this time there was an outbreak of Liberalism in Europe; German students solemnly burnt the writings of the absolutists, and shouting "*Vivat Teutonia!*" the young band murdered the writer Kotzebue, who was guilty of having defended the policy of Russia. In England workmen's riots broke out in Manchester. The Allies took fright, and the Tsar addressed a Note to France, pointing out the dangers to which her policy exposed the nations united by the Holy Alliance. Whereupon Decazes, aware of "the vague but very real anxiety of men's minds," resolved, with the King's consent, to make certain concessions to the Right, and announced that he would bring forward a scheme of electoral legislation to put a stop to the progress of Liberalism. The Left immediately protested that "the counter-Revolution was raising its head," and Decazes at once lost his popularity. Nevertheless he refused to give way, and with the co-operation of Monsieur de Serre, the scheme of legislation was drawn up and was to have been presented to the Chamber on the 14th of February, 1820.

On the 13th of February the Duc de Berry was present together with his wife at a performance at the Opera, at that time situated in the Rue de Richelieu opposite the Bibliothèque—to-day the Square Louvois. *Le Carnaval de Venise* and *Les Noces de Gamache* were being played, and the house, owing to the appearance of new dancers, was very full. About eleven o'clock the Duchesse de Berry felt tired, and left. Her husband accompanied her to the exit on the Rue Rameau, but as he was about to enter the theatre again, a man who had been hidden behind the sentinel, who was presenting arms, rushed at him, seized him by the shoulders, and planted a dagger in his heart. "What a ruffian!" cried the Duke, who thought he had been jostled by a passer-by who was in a great hurry. But on putting his hand to his breast he found it was covered with blood. "I have been murdered," he cried. "That man has killed me! I am holding the handle of the dagger." The Duchess, whose carriage had not yet driven away, and the gentlemen who were present, clustered round the Prince, who was carried to the little room into which his box opened. Meanwhile the assassin, who had fled by way of the Rue de Richelieu, had been stopped by a refreshment vendor just as he was about to cross the Arcade Colbert.

Assassination of the Duc de Berry.

The doctors, who were hastily summoned to the Duke, found that the dagger had penetrated up to the hilt, and Dupuytren, who was the leading physician among them, did not conceal the fact that in his opinion the wound was mortal. The Comte d'Artois, the father of the Prince, and the Duc d'Angoulême, his brother, were prostrate with grief by the couch of the dying man, who whispered that he would like to see the King. The Latin prayers recited by a Bishop provided a strange accompaniment to the lamentations of the Duchesse de Berry and the jumble of sounds that came from the gala house, for the performance was still going on and snatches of lively music could be heard. Ministers, Marshals of France, personal friends of the Prince, ladies of the Court in evening dress and decked with jewels, hurried up, and the last to arrive stood on tip-toe in the corridor to see. In the little room the atmosphere had become stifling, and the doctors ordered the Duke to be carried into a large room belonging to the management of the Opera, where they laid him on a folding bed and bled him. Dupuytren probed the wound, making the dying man scream with pain. The Duchesse de Berry, with the passion of her race, was unable to control herself, and her cries and lamentations made her husband's death agony even more terrible. Once he opened his eyes and said aloud, "My dearest, control yourself for the sake of our child." And thus those who were present learnt that the Duchess was pregnant, and that there was still hope for the legitimate dynasty. In a neighbouring room the murderer was undergoing a preliminary examination before the Prefect of Police and Decazes.

The Duke again and again asked to see the King. The latter had been told the news at two o'clock in the morning, but on the advice of the Comte d'Artois, who was afraid that the presence of his brother might introduce "the constraint of etiquette" into the tragedy, Decazes had calmed Louis XVIII by promising that he would be kept well informed. In his heart of hearts, the Minister was terrified by the murder, and in his mind's eye already saw Paris in revolt and a conspiracy on foot against the monarchy. About four o'clock all hope had been abandoned, and he decided to return to the Tuileries. "Is it all over?" exclaimed Louis XVIII, as soon as he saw him. "No, sire, but he is asking for Your Majesty. I beg you to summon up all your courage." The King embraced him and said, "Tell them to get me up!" In his state of health this was a long business. He was hoisted into a carriage and drove all the way without saying a word.

On the stairs leading to the Royal Box in the Opera House the porters groaned beneath the weight of the King's chair. The ascent was extremely difficult, and Louis XVIII, jostled about between the banisters and the wall, had a great struggle to reach the landing. As soon as he entered the room in which his nephew was lying, the latter raised himself up and in supplicating tones implored him, "Forgive me, my uncle, I beg you to forgive me!" Louis XVIII sat down, took breath and answered slowly, "There is no hurry. We will talk about that later on, my nephew." "Alas, the King does not consent," continued the Prince, "and yet his forgiveness would have softened my last moments." Whereupon he fell back. Louis XVIII, who, in spite of all, had a heart, turned to Dupuytren and said, "*Superestne spes aliqua salutis?*" Dupuytren, however, knew no Latin, but Dubois, one of the other doctors, replied in perfectly correct

Latin that the situation was desperate. "Then God's will be done," said the King. A few moments later Dupuytren asked for a mirror, and Louis XVIII handed him his snuff-box, the glass of which was held to the nostrils and the lips of the Prince; it was not clouded. "Is it all over?" Dupuytren made a sign in the affirmative. "Help me, I have one last service to render *my son.*" Crippled with gout as he was, the King leant on the surgeon's arm, and while he closed the eyes of the man who had been the dashing Duc de Berry, all present fell on their knees.

That same night, the murderer, who was a sadler in the royal stables, named Louvel, was imprisoned in the Conciergerie. He made no difficulty about confessing the motive of his crime, which had been inspired by hatred of the Bourbons. Owing their return to the foreigners, they were, in his opinion, a disgrace to the nation, and he had taken the law into his own hands and made up his mind to wipe out the ill-omened dynasty, choosing the Duc de Berry, because he was "the trunk," the man who personified the hopes of the monarchy. "And if you had escaped, what would you have done?" "I should have killed the Duc d'Angoulême." "And after that?" Louvel hesitated. He did not dare to name the King.

The inquiry held by the Chamber of Peers, which had been transformed into a Court of Law, revealed the fact that the murderer was a fanatic, who had no accomplices, the spiritual descendant of Ravaillac and Damiens. Brought up in the revolutionary schools, and a convert to Theophilanthropy—a sort of philosophic religion which had a period of vogue during the last days of the Convention and under the Directoire—having emigrated to the Isle of Elba in 1814 out of fidelity to the Emperor, he afterwards fought at Waterloo. This monomaniac insisted on seeing in the Bourbons the cause of all the misfortunes of France, the enemies of his country. It seemed perfectly clear that he was not the instrument of any party or conspiracy; his was a diseased brain, possessed of an *idée fixe* which turned his head. But this conclusion was not one that could be accepted by the Royalists.

On the 14th of February, the day after the crime, Clausel de Coussergues, an *Ultra* deputy from Aveyron, demanded from the rostrum that Decazes should be accused of complicity in the murder which had put France into mourning. It was, of course, absurd. "You are a fool!" said Monsieur de Villèle to the orator behind the scenes. "Your motion is badly worded. You should have accused the Minister quite vaguely of high treason." Nevertheless the motion was put as it stood, and the Press joined in the chorus. "Yes, Monsieur Decazes, it is you who killed the Duc de Berry," wrote the *Gazette*. "Weep tears of blood and beg Heaven to pardon you, for your country will never do so!" The Royalists were agreed in regarding the knife that had struck the Duke as "a Liberal idea"; Charles Nodier, though he could not be regarded as one of the fanatics, advised Decazes "to pick up Louvel's dagger and plunge it into his own heart"; whilst Chateaubriand wrote, "The hand that struck the blow is not the most guilty." A few days later, in speaking of the King's favourite, he uttered the famous words which he afterwards tried to recall, or at least to interpret differently, "Our tears and groans astonished a foolish Minister. His foot slipped in the blood, and he fell."

Decazes accused of Complicity.

In vain did philosophers like Ballanche endeavour to rise above the passions that had been aroused, and denounced in Louvel "the new principle which was convulsing the world, and becoming incarnate in certain individuals, elated them and automatically drove them to crime." When the Chamber moved that the Crown should be called upon to reply to the murder by vigorous measures, it was in vain that General Foy exhorted them to make mention only of the tears shed for a prince who was mourned by every Frenchman, "mourned above all by the friends of liberty, because they well know that this terrible crime will be made an excuse for endeavouring to destroy the liberties and rights which the wisdom of the King has recognised and consecrated." These words of moderation found no echo, even the Liberal Press remaining silent. It was necessary to take reprisals.

The *Drapeau Blanc* openly extolled the fine *coups d'état* of the past, and cited the example of Louis XIII when he dismissed Marshal d'Ancre. But Louis XVIII refused to follow the example of his ancestor; and when he heard of the proposal made by Clausel de Coussergues, he exclaimed, " It is an accusation the extravagance of which is only equalled by its atrocity ! " Nevertheless he was too well advised not to perceive the direction in which the manœuvre tended. " They are trying to exploit my grief, and to separate us, my dear son," he said to Decazes, " but they will not succeed." But shut up in the Tuileries, sick and suffering, it was impossible for him to follow the subterranean machinations of the *Ultras*. In Paris, at the Halle, report had it that the hand of Louvel had been armed by the King's Minister. How could it be otherwise? This erstwhile agent of Fouché, this police officer of Bonaparte, had been nurtured in the antechambers of the despot, and his sham royalism was only a bait to win confidence.

When Decazes presented himself before the Comte d'Artois, he was met by rumours. Warnings from official sources urged him to flee if he valued his life, and his house was guarded by the police. The Life-Guards threatened to make the suburbs rise up against him by marching through them with the bloodstained shirt of the Duc de Berry, " his victim "; and even his friends and those who were under an obligation to him implored him to retire. On the 16th of February he sent in his resignation to the King. The latter collapsed. " Your letter has killed me ! " he wrote to his beloved son.

For the *Ultras* the death of the Duc de Berry " had something providential about it, and was more useful to them than his living presence." But the King insisted upon refusing to accept the resignation of his Minister, repeating, " They shall not separate us." But were they to be stopped by this? Thereupon a regular siege began about the chair of this old man of sixty-five. Meals were eaten amid gloomy depression; the Comte d'Artois appeared with bloated features and extremely pale; the Duchesse d'Angoulême wept in silence; her husband bowed his head, dumb with fear, for until that moment he had been a loyal supporter of the King's policy of moderation. But sometimes the attack was direct; Artois would remark that as the father of the murdered man it was impossible for him to receive Decazes; the Duchess hinted that unless he took his departure there might be a fresh victim. One evening after dinner Decazes found Louis XVIII purple in the face and with bloodshot eyes; in a quivering voice the old man pointed to a place near his chair. "There, but a moment ago my brother and my niece declared to me on their knees that they would not get up until I had promised to sacrifice you. They must have heard my answer in the Carousel, I was so wild and indignant!" But Decazes, who had vainly intimated that he was going to restore the censorship and suspend the liberty of the subject, felt that public opinion had been roused against him. Accused by Chateaubriand of having dyed his Dictator's purple in the blood of the Duc de Berry, he begged "his father" to let him go. "The wolves are only asking the shepherd to sacrifice his dogs," the King said sadly. "Only one of his dogs, sire; the six others can be kept." replied Decazes, alluding to his colleagues in the Government. "You know very well that without you the shepherd will have no dog to protect him," retorted Louis.

Fall of Decazes.

For yet a short while longer Louis XVIII hoped that it would not be necessary for him to sacrifice his beloved son. When the Duc de Richelieu was approached he did, in fact, refuse the Presidency of the Council; but the Comte d'Artois threw himself on his knees and begged him to save the Royal Family, and protect its surviving members from the knife of the assassin. "Your policy shall be mine," he declared. "On my honour as a gentleman, I will be your first soldier!" In spite of his reluctance once more to assume the reins of power, for he knew the troubles and trials of office all too well, and was above any appeal to vanity, Richelieu in the end accepted, and the resignation of Decazes was decided upon. Whereupon the grief of Louis XVIII became lyric: "Come and see the ungrateful prince who has been unable to defend you; come and mingle your tears with those of your sorrowing father!" Everybody had betrayed him, even Angoulême, whom he had trusted; he compared himself to Cæsar, to King Lear, and other tragic heroes of history and drama. He certainly felt the death of his nephew far less.

The few short hours before the departure of Decazes were one long-drawn-out agony. With his own hand the King drafted the warrant for the dukedom to be conferred upon his friend, appointed him an Ambassador with a salary of 300,000 francs, and, not wishing to be deprived of his wisdom, allowed him to retain the title of Minister. He overwhelmed him with flowers and presents and sent note after note to him, heartrending, tearful notes. "My spirit is destroyed. God grant that you are suffering less than your father!" On the day of his departure, be made Elie, the Christian name of Decazes, the password, and the countersign Chartres, the town in which his friend would sleep. In his cabinet he had the portrait of the new Ambassador hung in the place of that of Francis I. Just as he was about to get into his carriage, a valet handed Decazes a piece of paper folded in four, "To my cousin the Duc Decazes. Adieu, my beloved son; it is from the depths of a broken heart that I bless you." And thus the carriage drove off, avoiding the Versailles route, for the police had been warned that some of the Life-Guards were lying in wait for the new Duke in order to harass him.

Within the space of four days, thanks to the crime of a fanatic, the *Ultras* had succeeded in casting down the King's favourite.

But the assassination of the Duc de Berry was destined to have further consequences than the fall of a Minister; it brought about a change such as had not occurred since 1815, and entirely upset the arrangement of parties and the internal affairs of the nation.

Results of Louvel's Crime.

Until that moment the Centre, the Doctrinaires, had hoped to reconcile Liberalism and the monarchy, but Louvel's crime had made this impossible. The scission was complete; instead of three parties, there were now only two in the Chamber, the Right and the Left, the *Ultras* and the Liberals. The men of wisdom and moderation, who clung to the belief that a union between the Charter and the Bourbons was a possibility, had had their day, force of circumstances drove them to the extreme parties, and the system of moderation so dear to the heart of Louis XVIII had once and for all to be abandoned.

Nevertheless Richelieu relied upon the support the Comte d'Artois had promised to give him, and wished "to govern reasonably with the moderate Centre and the help of the Right," but the demands of the latter were not long in rousing public opinion to the highest pitch of excitement. Ever since the 26th of March, 1820, the liberty of the subject had been suspended; a Press law subjected all political writings to censorship whatever their channel of publication. *La Bibliothèque Historique* and *la Minerve* disappeared, and Benjamin Constant was able to assert that " the Government had henceforward condemned itself to knowing nothing except through its salaried officials." An unexpected counterblow was provided by *le Conservateur*, the organ of the *Ultras*, ceasing to appear, for Chateaubriand, with the haughty independence of the writer, would not consent to submit to the tutelage of the censorship. The Press was enveloped in silence, and the papers that were still published beat about the bush without coming to the point and hid their real sentiments beneath a veneer of rhetoric. Soon there was no further need for the censorship. But passions remained none the less violent, and if they found no outlet in print they were expressed by word of mouth and the interpretation of facts. A stranger visiting Paris at this time was astonished by the widespread interest of the public in political events; from the bourgeois to the cab-driver and the porter, everybody was discussing the new scheme of legislation that had been laid before the Chambers, and the last royal ordinance—the street had become the annex of Parliament.

At the same time the atmosphere of the Palais Bourbon underwent a change. Up to this time free and spontaneous discussion had hardly existed in the Chamber, "When," says one eyewitness, "I see the Opposition speakers and the Government speakers mount the rostrum from right and left, I feel as if I were watching two armies dragging their artillery along the opposite banks of a river without ever being able to come to grips." In May 1820 the two armies were to meet in open conflict, and the battle was fought over the debate on the new Electoral Bill.

New Electoral Bill.

The object of this Bill was to substitute for the power of the small property-holders that of the landed aristocracy, by the creation of two electoral colleges, one in the *arrondissement*, the other in the department; but a quarter of the most heavily taxed electors were allowed to meet in the capital and nominate another set of deputies, which enabled them to vote twice over. This law, known as the law of "the double vote," was the work of Monsieur de Serre, who staked his whole political career upon it. After Louvel's crime he had parted from his Doctrinaire friends who were inclining towards the Left, and, convinced that the existence of the monarchy could only be safeguarded by a return to the policy of the Right, he resolutely sacrificed his popularity and ties of friendship to this conviction. He secured the exclusion from the Council of Royer-Collard, Guizot and Barante, to whom he was deeply attached, acquiesced in the rupture of his political career, and on the rostrum defended inch by inch the law which was to give the uncompromising Royalists the majority in the country. Ill as he was at the time—he died shortly afterwards of chest trouble in Naples—he gave proof of extraordinary energy. The spectacle of a man trembling with fever holding his own against the world, capping argument with argument, sarcasm with sarcasm, and recognising among his enemies those who had long been his own comrades in arms, was indeed harrowing. Nevertheless so great was the sympathy he inspired that at the very height of the parliamentary struggle Royer-Collard, the stern Royer-Collard, said to him with a touch of tenderness, "You and I are bound by inexpungeable memories!"

But the Liberal Opposition had no reason to show him any consideration. Manuel coldly declared that the new law, by sacrificing liberty, aimed at subjecting the country to the majority of 1815, whilst on the 27th of May La Fayette made an eloquent appeal for revolt. "Beware," he cried, "of jeopardising the fruits of the revolution, lest you force the people themselves to seize the sacred fasces of the principles of eternal truth and sovereign justice!" De Serre immediately sprang on to the rostrum, and with quite unaccustomed sarcasm reminded La Fayette of certain episodes in his life. "The honourable member put himself at the head of those who attacked and overthrew the old monarchy. . . . On more than one occasion he must have had it brought home to him that when once the masses have been roused, not only is it well-nigh impossible to control them when they rush to crime, but one also is frequently forced to follow—nay, sometimes even to lead them." The majority applauded and the excitement increased, whilst due regard for courtesy and politeness, which in the old days had been characteristic of parliamentary debates, seemed on the point of being cast to the winds. The deputies voted ostensibly by ballot, and the general public took part in the discussion with acclamations or murmurs of dissent.

At the beginning of June 1820 disturbances broke out in the neighbourhood of the Palais Bourbon. Groups of young men shouted, "*Vive la Charte!*" whilst life-guardsmen, in civilian clothes, retaliated with "*Vive le Roi!*" and when they recognised deputies of the Left as they passed by, they brandished their canes at them and shouted, "You will have to pay for it!" One day, Benjamin Constant and one of his colleagues were threatened, whereupon the Opposition immediately seized the opportunity, and Camille Jordan, a Doctrinaire who had gone over to Liberalism, moved that the debates should be suspended until the safety of the Assembly had been secured. The Chamber thereupon adjourned.

Disturbances of June 1820.

On the 4th of June the troops were called out. Although the order had been given not to fire, a young soldier killed a student called Lallemand; whereupon public indignation suddenly burst out, and once again Paris was forced to learn what revolution meant. Officers who had been pensioned or put on half-pay placed themselves at the head of bands of insurgents from the suburbs and marched on the Palais Bourbon. Charged by the cavalry, they retired and reformed near the Bastille, whilst from the terrace of the Tuileries civilians watched the spectacle, which rekindled in the breasts of some among them passions of days long since gone by. Towards evening it began to rain, and the insurgents dispersed. But on the 6th of June, the day of Lallemand's funeral, fresh disturbances occurred, and it was necessary to call out the troops again. On the same day, the Court of Peers condemned Louvel to death, and although very little notice was taken of his execution, the crisis provoked by his crime obsessed the minds of all.

In the Chamber the debates were continued in the same feverish and rebellious atmosphere. De Serre protested against the machinations of the revolutionary faction, whereupon Casimir Périer, one of the Liberal leaders, replied that it was impossible to hold deliberations under a system of oppression. Another deputy, Emile de Girardin, occupied the rostrum for more than four hours without being able to finish the most harmless sentence. At last, however, thanks to the support of some of the deputies of the Left, who, terrified by the disturbances, rallied to the support of the Government, the electoral law was passed. Nevertheless the Liberal Party did not cease to repeat, as though it were an established fact, that the law of the double vote had received a " baptism of blood."

In this state of instability Richelieu contrived to carry on the Government. He gave guarantees to the Right, provided Monsieur de Villèle with a seat in the Cabinet as Minister without portfolio, appointed Chateaubriand Ambassador to Berlin, and, in order to please the clergy, placed secondary education in their hands. But this was not enough for the *Ultras*, who demanded the immediate carrying out of their programme and a return to the traditions of the *ancien régime*.

Meanwhile, the Left was preparing its revenge. Summing up the situation, Guizot said, " In 1820 the great change was introduced, the only fundamental change that had taken place for six years. One Government fell beneath the blows of the counter-revolution, under the ægis of which a new Government was formed which was entirely in its favour. Power suddenly sought and found a fresh camp and fresh friends." Guizot, who was a Doctrinaire, however, was by no means in favour of violent measures; though certain Liberals, on the other hand, favoured a *coup de force*. The existence of a secret Government, which took its orders from the Comte d'Artois and his faithful Minister Vitrolles, had already been denounced in the Chamber on the motion of a certain magistrate named Madier de Montjau. His allegations were true, but in spite of the efforts of Manuel and Benjamin Constant, the vote on the motion did not lead to any split in the new majority.

The Bazar Conspiracy.

Whereupon the Left again had recourse to the Army. A shop known as *Le Bazar Français* in the Rue Cadet, the proprietor and employees of which were old soldiers, was used as a meeting-place by certain Liberals and Bonapartists—the time-honoured alliance born of the treaties of 1815. Encouraged by La Fayette, the leaders of the conspiracy, Captain Nantil of the Meurthe legion, Major Bérard and Lieutenant Maillet, decided to provoke an insurrectionary movement in Paris. Simultaneously with a rising in the provinces, the Château de Vincennes was to be captured, the date fixed being the 19th of August, 1820. A certain number of regiments seemed already to have been won over, when a gunpowder explosion occurred in Vincennes (Alfred de Vigny has given a memorable description of it); the conspirators hesitated, and the Government, who were kept informed by their spies, arrested the ringleaders. This abortive conspiracy gave the *Ultras* the opportunity of maintaining that the dangers threatening the monarchy were by no means at an end.

At the time of the elections of 1820, the Government had very shrewdly reduced the number of voters by granting exemptions from taxation—for, as we know, it was the payment of taxes that determined the civic rights of the citizens—and in the new Chamber, which consisted of 450 members, there were only eighty representatives of the Left. At this juncture the cause of Liberalism suffered a series of defeats throughout Europe; there were risings in Naples and the Piedmont, which were suppressed by Austria; the Greeks, who, profiting by the war declared by the Sultan Mahmoud against Ali Pasha of Janina, had made an attempt to shake off the yoke of Turkey, were defeated by the latter, and Ypsilanti, the patriot leader, took refuge in Austria (June 1821). Everywhere, except in Spain, where King Ferdinand VII had been obliged to accept a constitution, the policy of Metternich was triumphant and the Holy Alliance kept watch and ward over the safety of the legitimate dynasties.

These events had an immediate repercussion in France, and lent encouragement to the *Ultras*. In the Chamber one tumultuous sitting followed another, General Foy exalting the tricoloured cockade and including the Jacobins of the guillotine and the gibbet indiscriminately in his denunciations, whilst Manuel called to mind that the Massacre of St. Bartholomew had been carried out " under the white cockade." In these once academic surroundings the atmosphere became almost abusive; de Serre was called an insolent fellow, which in the old days would have given rise to a scandal, and the Left posed as a victim. " Tell your lictors to drag me to your dungeons!" exclaimed the irascible Casimir Périer. As the Press was gagged and the conspiracies had proved abortive, the call to revolt was transferred to the rostrum and preached from the platform. But the Right pursued their way. Finding Richelieu too lukewarm, and anxious to have at the head of the Government a man entirely devoted to their cause, they attacked his foreign policy. In an address to the Crown, voted in November 1821, the following words occurred: "We congratulate you, Sire, on the continued friendliness of your relations with foreign Powers, fully confident that a peace so precious has not been bought at the price of sacrifices incompatible with the honour of the country and the dignity of your Crown." Louis XVIII refused to accept this insulting address, which contained absolutely gratuitous insinuations. "The very thought that I could ever be guilty of sacrificing the honour of the country and the dignity of my Crown fills me with indignation!" he exclaimed. At one moment it seemed as though in his rage he was going to dissolve the Chamber, as he had done in 1816; but times had changed, and Louis XVIII was obliged to bow to new influences.

Madame du Cayla.

The fall of Decazes had left a gap in his life. A Minister might possibly have taken his place, but Richelieu was too lofty a spirit to curry favour, his colleagues doubtless had not the necessary qualifications, and it was a woman who succeeded the "Sejanus of Libourne."

One day, at a reception at the Tuileries, a young woman who was to be presented to the King accidentally knocked over a little table on which there were some papers. With abject apologies she proceeded to pick up the scattered sheets, and tried to classify them by reading their contents aloud. Then, suddenly realising her clumsiness, she became more clumsy than ever. Louis XVIII was watching her with a smile. At last the papers were sorted, and she held them out to him. "Pray go on, Madam," he said, "so that I may have the pleasure of hearing as well as seeing you." She almost collapsed, but pulling herself together read in calmer tones a report of which she obviously understood not a word. The sight of the charming creature wrestling with a solemn official document delighted the King. He watched her for some time in great glee, then, feeling that she had been sufficiently tried, he said, "Thank you, Madam! I wish I could often have such a charming and intelligent reader. You must come to see me again." Such was the first audience of Madame du Cayla.

Zoé Talon, the daughter of a lawyer at the Châtelet, was separated from her husband, the Comte du Cayla. Sprightly and witty, she adopted an austere pose, affected to despise the fashions of the day and in the Faubourg St. Germain was accredited with being extremely religious; yet at the time she was only thirty-five. She went to see Louis XVIII again, as he had asked her to do; gradually he made a habit of receiving her, and she soon became indispensable to him. One day, when Dambray, the Chancellor, knocked at the door of the King's cabinet in the Tuileries, he replied, "Come in, Zoé!" and from that day forward, Dambray was always called Chancellor Crusoe.[1]

In due course Madame du Cayla became Louis' Egeria. He declared that she acted as an inspiration to him, and used to consult her when he was in any doubt or difficulty and ask her advice on the problems raised by politics or Court intrigues. He had a sincere regard for her mental abilities, and when he was talking to her something of the spirit of his ancestor Louis XIV would pervade his being. "A King," he observed, "whose life is spent in a round of painful duties and tiresome pomp, should he chance upon a lady friend, the like of whom history has never seen before or is likely to see again, clings to her both from inclination and from gratitude; she becomes his life, the very breath of his nostrils; in her presence he is the happiest of men."

Devoted heart and soul to the Comte d'Artois, Madame du Cayla was not altogether unconnected with the fall of Decazes, and as she grew in favour every day, the *Ultras* surrounded her and inculcated their doctrines upon her; she became "the Esther and the Madame de Maintenon of the religious party," and its mouthpiece at Court. Nevertheless Louis XVIII was still bitter against the Right, on account of the address they had had the impudence to vote, and it was by no means easy

[1] The pun is untranslatable, as it depends on the French pronunciation of Crusoe, which is *Cruso-é* and sounds like "Believed to be Zoé."

for the favourite to persuade her protector to lend an ear to them. But she succeeded with charming skill, putting in a word here and a word there at the audiences he gave her, assuring him that the enemies of the Duc de Richelieu were the most devoted servants of the Crown and that a sincerely Royalist Government would give peace to France and incidentally to him who presided over her destinies. She declared that all she had at heart was the happiness of her sovereign lord, who, after so much fatigue and misfortune, deserved the right to rest in peace. Louis XVIII allowed himself to be lulled by her voice.

Richelieu had only accepted office at the urgent entreaty of the Comte d'Artois, and ever since he had been President of the Council he had felt himself the object of the secret or open hostility of the Pavillon de Marsan. Worn out and probably looking back with regret to the years when he had been Governor of Odessa, he remarked to a friend, " What a tiresome task it is to rule these devilish civilised nations ! " When the Right, as we have already described, criticised his foreign policy, he made up his mind to demand a frank explanation from the King's brother. Were Monsieur and his followers for him or against him ? Yes or no. Overcome with confusion, the Comte d'Artois advised him to abandon all connection with the Centre and to come to an agreement with Monsieur de Villèle, and concluded by saying that he did not wish to interfere in any way. Whereupon Richelieu reminded him of the promise he had made directly after Louvel's crime. " Ah, my dear Duke ! " exclaimed Monsieur, adopting the tone of a man of the world, " you took what I said far too literally ! And also things were so very difficult at that time ! " Bursting with indignation, Richelieu at once repeated to the King the conversation he had just had. " What do you expect ? " replied Louis, who knew his brother well. " He conspired against Louis XVI, he has conspired against me, and he will conspire against himself."

Resignation of Richelieu.

But Madame du Cayla again intervened. She was perfectly well aware that the King felt no real attachment to Richelieu, and slowly but surely she continued the process of bewitching him. In the end Louis XVIII was convinced—so firmly convinced, in fact, that he commanded Richelieu to send in his resignation three times in one evening.

The latter was cut to the heart by a dismissal brought about by such odious means. "It is not the King," he exclaimed, "it is not Monsieur, it is not the Chambers that are driving me out! It is an intrigue—yes, a mere intrigue, of which I am the victim—that is showing me the door!" Within six months, on the 17th of May, 1822, Richelieu died of brain fever, handing down his name to history as one of the great servants of his country; the liberation of French territory is one of his titles to glory which will never die out.

It is said that after the fall of Richelieu, Louis XVIII, perceiving his brother's satisfaction, remarked, "At least I have secured peace in my household!" In reality he had all unconsciously signed his own abdication, and handed over the power to the *Ultras*. But his good sense and alertness of mind had been blunted by age, and ever since the birth of the Duc de Bordeaux he had been relieved of all anxiety regarding the future of his dynasty.

The Duc de Bordeaux.

During the night of the 29th of September, 1820, in the presence of a Marshal of France, Court dignitaries and national guards—who had been convened in order to give the lie to the insinuations of the Orleanist Party—the widow of the Duc de Berry had brought a son into the world. From the balcony of the Tuileries, Louis XVIII had shown the people the heir of the Bourbons, saying, "We are all one family, and you are all my children. This infant will one day be your father." It was a memorable scene; the sun was shining, the bells were ringing and the crowd applauded.

> "Il est né l'enfant du miracle,
> Heritier du sang d'un martyr.
> Il est né d'un tardif oracle,
> Il est né d'un dernier soupir."[1]

Never had Louis XVIII enjoyed such popularity. After so many years of uncertainty he at last felt that his subjects were at one with him. Whatever political crises might intervene, how could he have any fears now regarding the overthrow of the

[1] "He is born, the child of miracle, the heir of a martyr's blood. He is born of a belated oracle, he is born of a dying man's breath."

dynasty? The child was the gift of Providence. . . . Richelieu was sacrificed!

BIBLIOGRAPHY.—Duchesse d'Abrantès, *Mémoires sur la Restauration* (6 vols., 1838). S. Charléty, *La Restauration* (Book II, Chap. 1). Chateaubriand, *Mémoires touchant la vie et la Mort du Duc De Berry* (1820). Court of Peers, *Affaire du* 19 *Août*, 1820 (*Conspiration du Bazar Français*) (1820). de Cussy, *Souvenirs* (2 vols., 1909). E. Daudet, *L'Ambassade du Duc Decazes en Angleterre* (1910); *La Police Politique* (1912). Dayot, *Louis XVIII, Charles X d'après l'image du temps* (1902). Deneux, *La Naissance du Duc de Bordeaux* (1881). Germond de Lavigne, *Les Pamphlets de la Restauration* (1879). Duchesse de Gontaut, *Mémoires* (1891). Hapdé, *Historique des Événements Funèbres de la Nuit du* 13 *Février*, 1820 (1820). Lesur, *Annuaire Historique*, (1820). Lucas-Dubreton, *Louvel le Régicide*, (1923). de Marcellus, *Chateaubriand et son temps* (1859). Chancellier Pasquier, *Mémoires* (6 vols., 1893–94). de Puymaigre, *Souvenirs* (1884). de Reiset, *Les Enfants du duc de Berry* (1905). Rochechouart, *Souvenirs* (1889). Roullet, *Récit des Événements qui se sont passés dans l'Administration de l'Opéra la Nuit du* 13 *Février*, 1820 (1862). de Serre, *Correspondance* (6 vols., 1877–78).

Details regarding public opinion in 1820 will be found in the *Archives Nationales;* CC. 503–14 (trial of Louvel). BB^{18} 1060–62–64–74–75–1315 and F^{7} 6745–6746–6906.

CHAPTER V

VILLÈLE. THE CONSPIRACIES. THE SPANISH WAR

Villèle. The Conspiracies. The Spanish War. Villèle in power. Government by the Right. The constitution of the *Congrégation*. The French missions. The Liberal Opposition. *Carbonarism* and the military conspiracies: Belfort, Saumur, Thouars. General Berton. The four sergeants of La Rochelle. Disintegration of *Carbonarism*. The Right carries out its programme and wants war in order to consolidate the monarchy. Situation in Spain. An expedition decided upon. Uproar in the Chamber and expulsion of Manuel. Rapid success of the campaign. Dissolution of the Chamber and rout of the Opposition. Death of Louis XVIII.

FOR the first time since the Restoration, the Right came into power, and forced upon Louis XVIII a Government entirely composed of Royalists, at the head of which, although he was not actually given the office of President of the Council, was a statesman of the highest standing, who was destined to rule the country for six years (1822–28)—Villèle.

Villèle.

This Gascon aristocrat, a short slight man, with sharp features, a nasal voice, and a timid, retiring and almost humble manner, was not to be judged by his looks. But he had served his apprenticeship since 1815, working hard while his friends were wasting time in backstair intrigues, and was the best qualified man in the party to tackle the practical details of administration as well as questions of finance. Moreover, his intellectual activities were not confined to petty problems; he had broad views, a tenacious will and consummate parliamentary skill; his speeches were unpretentious, but of admirable brevity. His enemies made fun of his fragile appearance, calling him, "a phantom in a dress coat embroidered with fleur-de-lys"; but Villèle showed himself supremely indifferent to attacks of this kind. Calm and courteous, he used to mingle freely with the Opposition groups after a session.

> "Et Villèle prisait, en homme tolerant,
> Dans les boîtes de Foy, de Benjamin Constant." [1]

[1] "And Villèle, like a tolerant man, took snuff from the boxes of Foy and Benjamin Constant."

As soon as the *Ultras* came into power the personnel of the Court was constantly changing; they rendered homage to the King as though he were an idol to whom they were accustomed but did not pay much attention. Every morning Madame du Cayla, through the medium of her friend Sosthène de la Rochefoucauld, had the orders for the day conveyed to Villèle; it was she who led the dance, making Louis XVIII want whatever she wanted; and the strange spectacle was presented of a constitutional monarch gradually relapsing all unawares into a sort of absolutism. The experience so dearly bought during exile and the Hundred Days faded away, and the instinct for power once more gained the upper hand.

In order to test the strength of her influence, Madame du Cayla undertook to reconcile the King with his brother—an ungrateful task, for the two men had always adopted diametrically opposite lines of conduct, and their antipathy was but thinly veiled. Nevertheless she succeeded, and Louis XVIII seemed to be definitely converted to the ideas of the Right. "I am using the last years of my life," he wrote at this time, "in a daily struggle against all my family affections; I have denied the men whose hereditary devotion has followed all the fortunes of the monarchy. . . . Liberals, I placed my trust in you; you repaid me only with hatred. Entirely at the mercy of revolutionary passions, you are perfidious rebels—withdraw, I say!" With their enemies thus dismissed, the Right took matters in hand, and found in the *Congrégation* a strong pillar of support.

The Congrégation.

The *Congrégation*, which had been founded in the days of the Republic, was a religious society consisting of laymen and clergy, which, under the leadership of the Abbé Legris-Duval and a Jesuit named Father Ronsin, had for its object "the development of the sphere of good works and the defence of the Faith against bad examples." It held its meetings in the house belonging to the *Missions Étrangères*, in the Rue du Bac. It was here that deputies from the provinces who felt lonely in Paris used to meet, and with the growth of the power of the Right, the members of the *Congrégation* increased in number. Soon branches were opened in the chief towns in France and offshoots were created which widened its sphere of action—the *Société des*

Bonnes Études in the Rue de l'Estrapade, to which young men destined for the Bar, politics or literature belonged; the *Société des Bons Livres*, the object of which was to combat the spread of Voltairean ideas; the *Société des Bonnes Œuvres*, which concerned itself with charity and visited hospitals and prisons; and lastly the *Société de Notre Dame des Victoires*, which aimed at bringing influence to bear on the Army, but was disbanded on account of the hostility of the Duc d'Angoulême.

In 1816 the passing of the law abolishing divorce was supposed to have been due to the influence of the *Congrégation*. From that day forward the number of its supporters steadily increased —clerics, politicians and high officials as well as the Liberals inclining to identify the extreme Royalists with the *Congrégation* and regarding its influence as paramount. And it must be confessed that this belief was to some extent justified, inasmuch as the Government was at the mercy of this secret power. As a matter of fact, in addition to the " perfectly innocent " society of the Rue du Bac, there was in existence another real secret society which conformed to certain rites of initiation—a member would entwine his fingers with those of a stranger in a particular way when he met him—" making the chain," as it was called— and thus recognise a fellow member. This society was purely political, it was controlled by the *Ultras*, and brought pressure to bear alike on the Chamber, the Court, the Press and the Administration; but it remained in the shade.

The members of the *Congrégation* were recruited chiefly from the ranks of the nobility and the upper classes; but in addition there was an organisation entrusted with the task of conducting propaganda among the masses.

The French Missions.

The French missions were the offspring of the old foreign missions which aimed at the conversion of the infidel in Asia and America. The Abbé de Rauzan, an ex-chaplain of Napoleon, supported by the Abbé Forbin-Janson and the Abbé Liautard, conceived the idea of turning their activities towards the evangelisation of France; after the revolutionary upheavals and the spiritual anæmia, so to speak, which had been characteristic of the Empire, this was a work that required to be done. Thus the towns and the country districts beheld the arrival of missionaries, who, after preaching to the people, proceeded to

" ceremonies of reparation "—a cross, sometimes weighing more than a ton, was borne by troops of the faithful; the procession, consisting of the authorities of the place, the Bishop, the Prefect, the General, proceeded to the spot where the cross was to be set up; through the mouths of the missionaries the people made amends, in the first place to the crucifix for the outrages to which it had been subjected, and then to the royal personages who had been massacred during the Revolution. Occasionally, in a transport of repentance, the inhabitants would make a holocaust of the works of Jean-Jacques or Voltaire, giving expression to a sort of general confession of guilt and repentance in which the only disturbing element was provided by the Liberals, who protested against all such demonstrations. The missions exercised a far wider influence than did the *Congrégation*, for their action was direct and objective, and Metternich, who chanced at this time to be travelling through France, wrote, " The only effective force here is provided by missions similar to those which aim at the conversion of savage people."

Impotence of the Liberals.

Thus the old world in its rebirth was continually coming into conflict with the new, and all the cleverness of the politicians was incapable of preventing it. As far as the Liberals were concerned, the *Congrégation* had overthrown Richelieu only in order to set up Villèle; the bourgeoisie, excluded from the highest offices, joined the Opposition; it had access to administrative duties only through the ministerial posts for which it had paid, and was infuriated by the taunts hurled at it by the *Ultras:*

> " Quoi ! je te vois, ami, loin du bagne fatal !
> Es-tu donc libéré ?—Non, je suis libéral." [1]

At the same time the teaching given by the *Frères de l'école chrétienne* gradually superseded the co-operative lay teaching modelled on an English system, the principle of which was " reciprocity of education among students, the more advanced acting as teachers to the backward." The Press no longer counted; in the Chamber the Opposition was impotent, and it afforded but little consolation to greet Cléante's tirade against

[1] " What ! Do I see thee, friend, far from the dread gaol ? Art thou then liberated ?—No, I am a Liberal."

the religious hypocrites of *Tartufe* with frenzied applause in the theatre, or to know by heart Courier's pamphlet making fun of the public subscription being raised for the purpose of presenting the Château de Chambord to the Duc de Bordeaux. " The 12,000 acres of enclosed land constituting the park of Chambord—what a fine present for anyone who knew how to cultivate it! . . . But as for him, what do you expect him to do with it? His task is one day to reign, if God so pleases, and one castle more or less will not help him in any way."

Carbonarism.

Whereupon, finding it impossible to make its voice heard in the country, reduced to complete impotence in parliament, the revolt from the rostrum having apparently fizzled out without giving rise to an echo, the Left reverted to the idea of a *coup de force*. But it now possessed a weapon which it had not had before in the shape of Carbonarism.

" There are certain moments," said an extremely wise man, the Chancellor Pasquier, " when the mania for conspiracy becomes a sort of disease, which, in spite of catastrophes, is almost always contagious." Carbonarism was an organisation for fomenting conspiracies. In 1821, when Benjamin Constant went to Saumur to deliver a lecture, his presence raised an uproar; the Royalists of the cavalry school wanted to give him a rude reception, and in one of his pamphlets Paul Louis Courier portrays an aristocratic lieutenant saying to his sergeant-major, " Pick up your sword, Francisque, and let us make an end of this Benjamin Constant." But Francisque had his own reasons for not obeying. The only tangible result of this incident was the creation by the local Liberals of a society called "*Les Chevaliers de la Liberté*." But the provinces had already been forestalled by Paris.

The Neapolitains—" pure canaille," as their King Ferdinand called them—had founded a society called *La Carbonaria*, the object of which was " to clear the country of the wolves," meaning to free Italy of the foreigner. Although it was broken up through the intervention of Austria after the Conference of Laybach, this society had won a certain notoriety. Two members of the Paris society known as *Les Amis de la Verité* went to Naples, and after being initiated, returned to France with the statutes of the *Carbonaria*. Flottard, Buchez and

Bazard set to work to adapt the latter to the requirements of French politics and the "tendency to conspiracy" characteristic of the moment; and thus it came about that Carbonarism took root in French soil. Each *vente* consisted of twenty Carbonari, and took its orders from the central *vente:* at the head was the Chief *Vente*; every new member swore to render implicit obedience, to put nothing into writing, to have a firearm and fifty cartridges in readiness; whilst, in order to make an appeal to the imagination, mysterious symbols were used—passwords, signals of recognition, "handshakes and clasping of wrists."

Such as it was, Carbonarism enjoyed a dramatic success among the Opposition, attracting not only ex-soldiers, half-pay officers, rich bourgeois, doctors and certain deputies and members of the aristocracy, but also students and intellectuals—historians like Augustin Thierry, artists like the Scheffer brothers, and philosophers like Jouffroy and Cousin. The latter was particularly conspicuous for his neophytic zeal, and in the gardens of the Luxembourg he used to unloose the avalanche of words of which he possessed the secret, and explain his plans for insurrection and the infallible formulæ at his disposal for winning over garrisons and inducing them to revolt. The wolf, in his case, was not Austria, as it had been with the Neapolitains and Silvio Pellico, but the House of Bourbon. No one could tell what the results of a revolution might be, but the revolution itself was possible—nay, even probable.

Carbonarism tried its strength at the funeral of Lallemand, the student who had been killed during the disturbances of the elections of 1820. But this was too narrow a sphere. Intoxicated by its successes in France, it resolved to attempt a movement on a grand scale—two insurrections were to take place almost simultaneously, one on the 18th of December, 1821, in the west, with Saumur as its centre, the other immediately afterwards, on the 29th of December, in the east, at Belfort. It was hoped that these insurrections would kindle an inextinguishable flame and would spread first to Marseilles, and then to Lyons, which was a hotbed of influential Carbonari.

The Military Conspiracy.

But the Saumur conspiracy, of which the Government received due warning, fizzled out on the arrest of one or two non-commissioned officers; at Belfort, part of the garrison followed the leaders of the plot; but there was a lack of unity, and some fifty of the conspirators were arrested. La Fayette, who arrived at this juncture in order to take command of the movement, quickly retired, and to prevent his being compromised, his carriage was burnt on the other side of the frontier. Some of the conspirators had succeeded in making good their escape, and with the object of catching them, together with any suspects in the district, the police, in conjunction with the military authorities, organised a fresh conspiracy complete in every detail; *agents provocateurs* succeeded in convincing a lieutenant-colonel on half pay, named Caron, that it was possible for him to rescue the prisoners in Belfort; and, as a matter of fact, he succeeded in winning over two squadrons, but he was arrested by his own soldiers, condemned to death and executed. The insurrection in Alsace had been stamped out.

Nevertheless the Carbonari in Saumur did not consider themselves beaten. "Give us a General and we shall march out," they informed the Head *Vente*. General Pajol was approached, but refused; another officer, however, offered to make the attempt. General Berton had been imprisoned as a suspect in 1815; he had been set free at the end of a year, but had been shut up again, since when he had been periodically imprisoned every six months. Having forfeited his pay, and seeing his career ruined, he represented the old army which was hated and persecuted by the Bourbons. The plan he proposed was to win over the people of Thouars and the garrison of Saumur by announcing that the revolution had just broken out in Paris; the insurrectionary movement would gradually spread.

General Berton.

Berton alarmed some of the Carbonari by his weakness and vacillation; nevertheless he was entrusted with the command. At Thouars the plot was successful (24th of February, 1822), and the insurgents marched on Saumur; but the further they advanced the smaller grew their numbers, and Berton had only 125 men behind him when he reached the gates of the town. The sub-Prefect had warned the garrison, and about midnight the rebels found themselves faced by regular troops. They hesitated and parleyed, and their general, unable to come to a decision, had scruples about attacking; in the end he beat a retreat, and soon afterwards took refuge at La Rochelle in disguise. He was advised to cross the frontier into Spain, but, taunted with cowardice, he refused, and tried to win success at the very place where he had just been defeated.

The police had an easy task with conspirators of this calibre; betrayed by a sergeant-major named Wölfeld, who had been one of his most staunch supporters, Berton was arrested, and the conspiracies which, as we look back upon them, seem like ridiculous child's play, ended in bloodshed. Sirejean, one of the non-commissioned officers who was most deeply compromised during the first rising at Saumur, was condemned to death by court-martial at Tours. In vain did Madame Récamier beg for his reprieve. Berton died courageously on the scaffold; Dr. Café, one of his accomplices, opened his veins in his prison cell like a Stoic, and another conspirator of humbler rank, named Saugé, just as he was about to be executed, uttered a cry which was unknown to the new generation: "*Vive la République!*"

But the epidemic of conspiracy was not ended. The 45th line regiment, composed of the remnants of the Loire army, and at that time quartered in Paris, was in barracks in the Quartier des Écoles, which facilitated intercourse between students and non-commissioned officers. One of the latter, named Bories, was full of dreams of revenge, and chafed at the inaction to which he was condemned. He joined the Carbonari, founded a *vente* in his regiment, and at a meeting in an inn called the King Clovis, in the Rue Descartes, was given some peculiar shaped daggers by delegates from the Central *Vente*. On the 22nd of January, 1822, the 45th left Paris for La Rochelle. At Niort there was a banquet at which toasts to the triumph of liberty were drunk. Shortly afterwards, Bories, carried away by his youthful enthusiasm, confided his secret to an ex-officer who had retired to Poitiers. The inevitable happened; Bories was betrayed and taken prisoner at La Rochelle, together with three of his companions—Pommier, Raoulx and Goubin, who were regarded as the leaders of the conspiracy. One of the conspirators called Goubillon revealed the names of the members of the Central *Vente* to which the 45th was affiliated, and gave a

The Four Sergeants of La Rochelle.

circumlocution to tell everything which for the last thirty-three years we have had bottled up against each other!" But these were merely oratorical threats calculated to impress the Tuileries, and the latter had no wish to inaugurate a political trial. In vain did the Liberals in the Chamber demand "open discussion" before the people; they no longer counted seriously.

Programme of the Right.

Meanwhile the Right, under the guidance of Villèle, was taking the first steps towards the realisation of its programme. A new law was passed by which misdemeanours on the part of the Press were once again to be tried by the magistrates of the royal courts, instead of by jury; it also made the mere "tendency" or intention of "bringing about a breach of the public peace" a punishable offence on the same footing as open incitement thereto; and the Liberal papers did not even dare to refer to the matter. The ashes of Voltaire and Rousseau were removed from the Panthéon, the École de Droit was closed, the École Normale suppressed, and Guizot and Royer-Collard were forbidden to lecture, whilst Bishop de Frayssinous, whose discourses in the church of St. Sulpice had enjoyed considerable and well-deserved success, was given the title of Grand-Master of the University. These measures were not passed without debate in the Chamber, the Liberal minority making up in vehemence what it lacked in numbers. Girardin dubbed the missionaries "the smugglers of religion," and reminded a certain deputy of the Right that he had once grovelled at the feet of Napoleon; whilst on another occasion he read with great gusto, as though it were his own, a speech once made by Villèle in favour of the liberty of the Press —a polemical device which had become common in parliamentary procedure. Benjamin Constant was greeted with cries of "Conspirator!" and "Rebel!" In short, anything was made an excuse for uproar, whether the matter in debate were the pensions paid to the King's Privy Council, "a well-paid sinecure" (Bonald was given 20,000 francs), the appointment of candidates for office, the instructions given to officials to vote for the Right or to send in their resignations, or the supplies to be voted for elementary education. But the efforts of the Left invariably met with failure.

The more far-sighted among the Royalists, and chief among

them Chateaubriand, did not under-estimate their enemies, knowing full well that the latter had a firm hold on public opinion through the recollection of the victories won under the Republic and the Empire, an advantage which the Right, which could boast of no such past, did not enjoy. In order to destroy the prestige of the Liberal Party, it was necessary for the Restoration also to have a war, a test which would establish it once and for all.

The revolt of Greece against the Turks might have provided France with an excuse for intervention. The Tsar approached the Comte d'Artois, who was now virtually King of France, with a view to concerted action (January 1822). Monsieur had already given his consent, when suddenly the news arrived that Greece, at the Assembly of Epidaurus, had decided to declare herself an independent State. The insurrection had veered round to Liberalism and proclaimed the sovereignty of the people. This no longer served the purpose of the *Ultras*, and all thought of intervention was abruptly dropped. But how was the martial ardour which the Royalist Press had carefully tended day by day to be exploited? The Liberal movement, as everybody knew, had been stamped out in Germany and in Naples. Spain alone remained.

Situation in Spain.

King Ferdinand VII had been forced on the 9th of March, 1821, after the insurrection of Riego, to swear adherence to the Constitution and leave the power in the hands of the moderate Liberals, although he was all the while conspiring against them. The personality of this monarch roused but little sympathy in France, even among the most ardent Royalists, who regarded him as a "Louis XI without genius, and so repellent to look upon that he was like an old bull with a hawk's head," whilst Chateaubriand, without further ado, dubbed him a King of base alloy. Nevertheless, Ferdinand VII, "a prisoner like Louis XVI," was symbolical of monarchy enchained by the Revolution; and his deliverance was a work of piety demanded by the principles as well as by the interests of the party in power in France.

As an epidemic of yellow fever had broken out in Spain, so virulent that "even the birds died of it," the French Government had stationed bodies of troops all along the frontier, who, after the scourge had disappeared, were kept there as an army of observation. And thus France would have found herself ready prepared in case intervention was decided upon.

But there was a lack of unity in the Cabinet. Villèle was first and foremost a financier, who disliked adventures. Moreover, he was terrified by the attitude of England, who at the time was in the throes of a grave economic crisis and was turning the revolt of the Spanish colonies in America to account in order to dump her goods there. She was consequently opposed to the re-establishment of absolutism in Spain. " If the roar of cannon is heard on the Bidassoa," said Lord Brougham, " we shall not remain neutral." Monsieur de Montmorency, the French Minister for Foreign Affairs, on the other hand, who was secretly sending subsidies to the Spanish absolutists, presented himself at the Congress of Verona, which had just met, as the mouthpiece of the most bellicose *Ultras*. Villèle tried to oppose the policy of his colleague, whereupon Montmorency sent in his resignation. But Chateaubriand, who succeeded him at the Foreign Office, was an even more convinced " interventionist." Strengthened by the support of the Tsar, he emphasised the need for a counter-revolutionary war. In order to remain in power, Villèle gave way, and France was charged by the Congress with the task of restoring Ferdinand VII his rights and, as Louis XVIII observed in his speech to the Chambers, " of securing the throne of Spain to a grandson of Henry IV." A hundred thousand men were to be sent across the Pyrenees.

The Spanish Expedition.

Public opinion was not unanimously in favour of the war; business men were afraid that trade would suffer, whilst the Liberals for their part were loud in their denunciations of " this monkish crusade against liberty." Courier published a proclamation addressed to the army; " When you have restored the *ancien régime* in Spain, you will be marched back to do the same thing here," whilst Béranger openly incited them to rebel in a song of which the refrain was " *Demi-tour !* " This state of mind was naturally reflected on the rostrum.

Chateaubriand, the instigator of this war, which he declared was bound to be short and almost free of risk, made a carefully elaborated speech, which was at once " the manifesto of his genius and the manifesto of the Royalist idea before the tribunal of Europe." He was listened to like an oracle by the Right, but the Left protested violently. General Foy, who had fought in the Peninsular War, pointed out the danger of an armed conquest when once Madrid had been passed; whilst Manuel, in characteristic fashion, reminded the House that foreign intervention had in the past been responsible for the death of Louis XVI. "The Royal Family," he declared, "were exposed to greater dangers when the foreigner invaded our territory, and France, revolutionary France, feeling it incumbent upon her to defend herself by means of the new forces and the fresh energy. . . ." He was interrupted by shouts from the Royalist benches, "Order! Order! Treason! He is justifying regicide!" President Ravez called the speaker to order and tried to calm the assembly. But it was no good. "A call to order is not enough! Turn him out!" cried the *Ultras*. "Drive out the scoundrel!" Manuel calm as ever, waited for the storm to blow over.

On the following day the Chamber discussed the motion for expulsion. Manuel conducted his defence in his usual disdainful and irritating manner, reminding the House that Chateaubriand himself had written that Louis XVI had fallen in the midst of an upheaval. But it availed him nothing. In spite of the efforts of Royer-Collard, who condemned "the species of *coup d'état* attempted by the majority," sentence of expulsion was passed against him.

Expulsion of Manuel.

When the House met again Manuel took his seat, followed by all the members of the Opposition, wearing their official uniforms. The President called upon him to withdraw. "I shall yield only to violence," he replied. The National Guard was called in, but the sergeant in command of the detachment, a lace-maker named Mercier, refused to lay hands on the deputy. The Left and some of the spectators shouted, "*Vive la garde nationale!*" Whereupon thirty gendarmes burst into the hall, and their leader, Colonel Vicomte de Foucault, said to his men, "Seize Monsieur Manuel!" Laying hold of him by the collar, they dragged him out of the Chamber, followed, as he had been on his entry, by all his colleagues of the Left, who declared that in future they would take no part in the deliberations of Parliament. Later on Victor Hugo, when he had become a Liberal, celebrated this episode in *Les Châtiments :*

> " Vicomte de Foucault, lorsque vous empoignêtes
> L'eloquent Manuel de vos mains auvergnates . . ." [1]

Nevertheless, the Liberals, who by their retirement from the Chamber lent its discussions " an appearance of illegality, or at all events of tyrannical violence," did not renounce their efforts to prevent the war. They attempted to organise on the Spanish frontier a kind of *pronunciamento*, and spread the rumour that the King of Rome had joined the ranks of the Spaniards. Just as the advanced guard of the French army was preparing to cross the Bidassoa, it was confronted by a body of 150 men surrounding a tricoloured standard, who shouted out, " What are you going to do? It is to set a despot on the throne again that the French tyrant has sent you out to fight liberty ! " General Walin, one of the old officers of the Empire, who was in command of the advanced guard, replied, " like an honourable man," by four rounds of grape shot, which laid low forty of the insurgents.

The Spanish expedition turned out to be little more than a somewhat straggling military march. At the beginning it met with certain material difficulties, for victuals and supplies, carriages, horses and wagons were lacking. But eventually everything was arranged through the instrumentality of a shrewd man of business named Ouvrard.

The French in Spain.

This " brazen and corrupt rogue " presented a curious and hitherto almost unknown figure in the society of the Restoration. According to Monsieur de Clermont-Tonnerre, he was endowed with a certain loftiness of vision and depth of ingenuity; handsome and witty and with ingratiating manners, he possessed no property in his own name, and was thus able to live a life of opulence, although he was a bankrupt. According to his own tale, he had never in his life given money to anybody. " It is most unfortunate," he used to declare, " but I am terribly absent-minded. Sometimes without thinking I put my pocket-book

[1] " Vicomte de Foucault, when you seized the eloquent Manuel in your coarse Auvergnian hands. . . ."

on the mantelpiece while I am talking; and then I forget all about it. But the strange thing is that never has a single one of those wretched pocket-books been returned to me." Thus gifted, Ouvrard became the chief contractor for the army in Spain, and thanks to his ingenuity he found the post extremely profitable. His method was as follows: his agents used to follow the troops, inform the *alcades* (the mayors) of the villages that requisitions would not be paid for, and offer them a sum amounting to a quarter of their worth, whereupon they recovered from the commissariat department the full value of the goods.

The Liberal armies in Spain offered no serious resistance, whilst the French were now supported by those who in 1808 had been their irreconcilable enemies—the peasants, the monks and the majority of the people who were in favour of the restoration of an absolute monarchy. The only feat of arms worthy of the name was the capture of the Trocadero. This success, which under the Empire would have had as much importance as "the capture of a defended post," was won with the loss of thirty-five men, and brought the war to an end (September 1823).

But as the French army advanced, the Spanish counter-revolutionaries made reprisals on the Liberals, "the *negros*," as they called them, and in order to prevent massacres from taking place, the Duc d'Angoulême, who was Commander-in-Chief, was obliged by the ordinance of Andujar to take the government of the country, which he had at first placed in the hands of a regency established at Madrid, back under his own control. The Absolutists immediately lodged a protest. Had France come in order to fight the revolution or had she not? The ordinance was repealed, and the massacres broke out afresh. Ferdinand VII, who was now a free agent, subjected his people to a sort of White Terror, under the very eyes of the French army of occupation, which did not dare to interfere. Meanwhile England's influence with the Spanish Liberals increased, as did also her commercial supremacy; but thanks to Ouvrard, the cost of the war to France rose to 200 millions instead of the estimated 100 millions, and she found the part she was playing in the Peninsula reduced to that of passive supervision.

But, as Monsieur de Martignac, a deputy who was beginning to attract attention, remarked, "The question of the Spanish war is in no way connected with strategy; it is entirely a social and political concern." The Liberal movement across the Pyrenees obviously in no way threatened the Restoration; nevertheless the intervention of France produced the result the *Ultras* had expected. The abortive attempt on the Bidassoa turned the attention of the army away from conspiracies and broke up the secret societies upon which the revolutionary party relied; the officers became reconciled to the white flag, and Chateaubriand was able to say, "Eight years of peace did not do so much towards establishing the legitimate throne on a firm basis as a war lasting twenty days."

The Royalists did all in their power to exaggerate the importance of the victory, and organised a triumphal reception for the army on its return from Spain—there were rejoicings, illuminations, *Te Deums* and processions of troops. The Duc d'Angoulême, who had a fairly accurate notion of the value of his accomplishment, dubbed this bombastic return of the forces sheer Quixotry, whilst Marshal Oudinot remarked, "What annoys and disturbs me most about the whole affair is that these people really believe they have made war." But the *Ultras* did not look at the matter in this light. That the note of victory sounded by the trumpets of the Spanish army sounded somewhat cracked, as Hugo declared, concerned them not at all; all they wanted was to derive as much profit as possible from this inglorious expedition—to foment popular enthusiasm, demolish the Left and secure themselves in power for some considerable period. And, indeed, the Chamber was dissolved on the 24th of December, 1823, and after the elections the Liberals found their numbers reduced to fifteen out of a total of 430 deputies, which meant the utter rout of the Opposition. Whereupon, reassured by this almost unlooked-for success, Villèle arranged for the passing of the law which was to secure for the Chamber, which was no longer the *Chambre introuvable* but the *Chambre retrouvée*, the certainty of being able to legislate in peace for seven years without having to fear changes in public opinion (the Septennial Law, May 1824). "The work of the Royalists," wrote *la Quotidienne*, "is not finished; it has only just begun."

Dissolution of the Chamber.

Louis XVIII, when he granted an audience to General Walin,

who had dispersed the French insurgents on the banks of the Bidassoa, said to him, "General, your shots have saved Europe." Flattery, no doubt; but the fact remains that the King regarded the Spanish War as the most important event of his reign; and in this connection, the testimony of Monsieur de Puymaigre, one of the old *émigrés*, is instructive. Louis XVIII received him sitting at a table, his legs covered by a rug which reached to the floor. He talked with some effort, and seemed both preoccupied and worn out. The conversation was flagging when Puymaigre ventured to remind him of the recent victories of his army in Spain. Whereupon the King's eyes lighted up; he pulled himself together, sat up in his chair, and as though he had suddenly been told the verdict of posterity, exclaimed in a firm voice, "Yes, that will be a fine page in my history!" Then his head fell back on to his shoulder, and in low almost inaudible tones, he added, "The last page."

And indeed he was already breaking up. He only took sufficient part in affairs to avoid the accusation of having abandoned all interest in them. "A King who abdicates," he added, "always repents of having done so." But in his heart of hearts he was only too anxious to be spared the necessity of making important decisions; when he was called upon to choose a Minister, he referred the matter to his brother. "I am old and I don't want to make a choice without knowing what would best suit him. Take the list to him." Madame du Cayla remained his Egeria, the one charming inspirer of his reign. When Chateaubriand, who was suddenly suspected of Liberalism, no longer gave satisfaction to the Comte d'Artois and Villèle, she swore she would "throw the cat down." Louis XVIII, duly convinced, immediately said, "I never wish to see that man again. The vagabond has betrayed us." And Chateaubriand was sacked like a lackey.

On the 25th of August, 1824, which was his saint's day, Louis XVIII appeared once again in public. He was doubled up on his throne, his head, which had shrunk to the size of a child's head, almost touched his knees, and he could only watch "his people pass before him" out of the corners of his eyes. But although the gangrene in his legs grew continually worse and gave him terrible pain, he did not allow a word of complaint to escape his lips, or make any serious reference to his condition. "*Non pedes sed caput faciunt regem,*" he said. "It is not the feet which make a king but the head." Even those who had no love for him could not help admiring the prodigy of steadfastness and moderation he presented. Never had he been so much a King, so resolute in the performance of the duties and offices of his rank, and the strength of will that sustained a body that was beginning to decompose was indeed worthy of admiration. For he was literally falling to pieces while still alive; and his valet almost fainted when, on taking off his master's stockings one night, he found fragments of the toes of his right foot in one of them.

Death of Louis XVIII.

Until that moment he had refused to take to his bed, quoting, with the scholarly erudition that characterised him, the following maxim of Vespasian: "An Emperor should die standing up." It was only on the 12th of September, 1824, that he yielded to the entreaties of his physicians, bade a gracious farewell to Madame du Cayla and gave his blessing to his relatives. His death agony lasted over three days and presented one of those terrible royal deathbed scenes that take place in the midst of a crowd of courtiers, in stifling heat, amid silence broken only by the groans of the dying man, to whom the frequent dressings caused untold suffering.

At last, on the 16th of September, towards four o'clock in the morning, the gentleman who was holding the bed curtain let it fall, and turning to the Comte d'Artois, said, "Sire, the King is dead." A few moments later, both wings of the door leading from the bedchamber to the salon were flung open and an usher shouted in a loud voice, "Gentlemen, the King!" And Charles X stepped forward.

If we turn to his contemporaries for a verdict on Louis XVIII, we are astonished by their severity; Liberals and *Ultras* alike expressed their antipathy for him. The former denounced his duplicity and hypocrisy; the latter, unable to forgive his moderation, accused him of "doing his best to destroy the monarchy," whilst the constitutional Royalists themselves, those who had been his servants, censured his pettiness of mind, and his valetudinarian egoism, not to mention his inhumanity.

It is true that his haughty manner and his habit of dissimulation, which he regarded as indispensable to royalty, won him few hearts, and among the crowd that followed his coffin to the cathedral of St. Denis, few indeed were his friends. A certain man who had once been a Royalist spy remarked rather wittily, "The King had in him something of the old woman, something of the native of France and something of the scholar." Admitted that he was all this, he nevertheless accomplished great things, and the politicians who took an active part in public life after his death knew how to appreciate him. "He came too late and he left too soon," said the lawyer Berryer, whilst Thiers declared that he was the best of the constitutional Kings. If he failed to become attached to the men about him, it was because he was testing them. Were they working for France? If so, he kept them. Had they ceased to be useful? He dismissed them at once with magnificent cynicism. His attitude towards the Charter was similar; he refused to destroy it because in practice it seemed to him to suit his people, and secure order and tranquillity.

The outstanding merit of this monarch, who passed more than twenty years in exile, consisted in the fact that he placed his hand on the bleeding heart of his country and, in spite of his upbringing and prejudices, understood that a policy of prudence and moderation was the only means of salvation. Let us consider him in his own day and hour—the successor of Napoleon, and that, too, when the country was in the throes of an invasion. What a trial for an impotent old man! Nevertheless this old man succeeded in gradually rallying together the men of the Empire, as Napoleon had rallied the men of the Republic, "With his sceptre he warded off the calamities that threatened his country," and left behind him a France prosperous and tranquil and at peace with her neighbours.

What was to become of this feat of sagacity in the hands of Charles X?

Bibliography.—Chateaubriand, *Congrès de Vérone* (2 vols., 1838). G. de Grandmaison, *La Congrégation* (2nd ed., 1890). *L'Expédition Française en Espagne en* 1823 (*Revue de Paris*, 1925). Guillon, *Les Conspirations Militaires Sous la Restauration* (1895). P. de La Gorce, *Louis*

XVIII (1926). Lucas-Dubreton, *Louis XVIII* (1926). Marchangy, *Plaidoyer Prononcé dans la Conspiration de la Rochelle* (1822). de Neuilly, *Souvenirs* (1865). *Paris Révolutionnaire* (2 vols., 1834) (Vol. II. art. de Trelat). Pontois, *La Conspiration du Général Berton* (1877). *Procès des Conspirateurs de Thouars et de Saumur* (1822). Vaulabelle, *Histoire des Deux Restaurations* (1857) (Vol. V).

CHAPTER VI

CHARLES X. THE FIRST YEARS

The coronation at Rheims. Villèle the prisoner of the *Ultras*. The indemnity granted to the *émigrés*. Popularity of the Left: funeral of General Foy. The law concerning sacrilege. The pamphlets of Monsieur de Montlosier. Justice the issue. The Right against Villèle. The proposed "law of justice and love." Review of the National Guard; its consequences. Dissolution of the National Guard and subsequently of the Chamber. Coalition between "*la pointe*" and the Left. Independence of Greece and the victory of Navarino. Villèle misunderstood; his fall.

ENDOWED with a certain natural grace, with something undefinably pleasing and chivalrous in his bearing, generous and even in a sense good-natured—such was the figure presented by Charles X when he succeeded his brother on the throne. But, unlike Louis XVIII, experience had not matured him; he regarded it as the highest good never to change, and preserved a marked predilection for the *ancien régime*. He had turned pious in his old age—he was sixty-seven—but certain features of the elegant and frivolous young noble of Versailles, about whom the ladies exclaimed, "Artois is our only hope!" might still be traced in him. Exile, the adventure of the Hundred Days, and all the political vicissitudes that had taken place under his eyes during well-nigh ten years, had not wrought any change in him. The Charter remained in his eyes a criminal concession. "The people want it," he observed in 1814, "and so it must be given a trial; but if at the end of a year or two it is not found to be an unmitigated success, we shall return to the natural order of things." The natural order consisted of absolute monarchy, for any constitution was, in his eyes, an attack on the prerogatives of royalty. "I would rather chop wood," he declared, "than reign after the fashion of the King of England." During the lifetime of Louis XVIII he was always either secretly or openly in opposition, and when his friends came into power he exhorted them to be patient.

"Make the best of the present," he exclaimed, "I will answer for the future."

At the time of his accession, however, he was wise enough not to give expression to his deepest feelings. Never had the situation been more favourable for the Royalist Party; there was peace at home and abroad, the army had rallied to the cause of the Bourbons, the country was in the enjoyment of a financial prosperity unknown since 1815 (the 5 per cent. loan stood at 102), and a parliamentary majority was assured for seven years. Well-known writers, and not merely Royalist theorists like Bonald and de Maistre, but such men as Lamartine and Hugo, lauded the blessings of monarchy, and Charles X had some justification for believing that he had the support of public opinion. In order to reconcile the Liberals and to secure unanimous support, he abolished the censorship set up by his brother, and pardoned political offenders who had been sentenced.

And thus his reign opened in an atmosphere of confidence, though signs of anxiety soon made their appearance. The King had already revived old titles, bestowing the designation of Dauphin on the Duc d'Angoulême and that of minions on the gentlemen of his suite. This decision caused considerable surprise, which was only increased when it was learnt that Charles X was going to be crowned at Rheims.

Louis XVIII had had a similar intention, but the state of his health had prevented him from carrying it out; for the ceremony of coronation was extremely exhausting. But Charles X survived it with ease, and on the 29th of May, 1825, from seven o'clock in the morning until midday, the ceremony was carried out in all its magnificent pomp and glory.

The Coronation at Rheims.

Inside the cathedral a sort of theatre had been constructed, so that the spectators were almost inclined to ask, "Where is my box?" Under a canopy, clad in a tunic of crimson satin, Charles X was anointed at the hands of the Archbishop of Rheims with oil from the Sacred Ampulla. The latter had been broken in 1793 on the pedestal of a statue of Louis XVI by Ruhl, one of the members of the Convention, but a few drops of the sacred oil had been miraculously preserved, and it was possible to say that the substance that had been poured on the brow of Clovis was in no way different from that which was used for the coronation of his successor. Charles lay stretched out on cushions; seven apertures had been made in his clothes, through each one of which the Archbishop pricked him with a golden needle; after which Marshals Moncey, Soult, Mortier and Jourdan in turn presented him with the sword, the sceptre, the hand of justice and the crown. Whereupon a tremendous ovation followed; the great curtain that cut off the end of the cathedral was drawn aside, and the crowd rushed in, the bells peeled and the organ played a triumphal march. Outside the cannon replied to the musketry fire, and from the vaulted roof of the cathedral bird-catchers let loose a flock of doves, which fluttered about terrified in a cloud of incense.

Charles X showed himself to the people surrounded by the Marshals of France; he had given his consent for the oath in the old ritual for the extermination of heretics to be replaced in the present ceremony by one swearing fidelity to the Charter; but, in spite of these precautions, the people were astonished by this revival of mediæval splendours and obsolete forms and ceremonies. The coronation of Napoleon, impressive and religious though it was, had avoided such things as "prostrations on pillows." Surprise turned to mockery; in vain did Lamartine and Hugo chant in dithyrambic strain the majesty of the festival of Rheims; it was Béranger's rhymed satire "*Le Sacre de Charles le Simple*" which caught the people's ear, although it cost its author nine months imprisonment.

The King's coronation, however, had a more profound significance; it signalised the return to the pomp and ceremony of the *ancien régime*, to the pageantry of the ancient House of France. At all events the Royalists regarded it in this light, and when once the outward form was restored they wanted to secure the inner substance as well.

Villèle and the *Ultras*.

When Charles X succeeded to the throne, Villèle remained in office. With obvious single-mindedness and no parade of words—"a great light burning at small cost," as the English statesman Canning said of him—he did his best to maintain the prosperity of the country, and with this object in view to avoid any action likely to excite public opinion. Above all, a cautious man, he was of the opinion of Baron Louis, one of his predecessors, who said, "if you want sound finance you must have a sound policy"; and indeed the measures he inaugurated in this department remained for a long time the basis of the French financial system.

But, willy-nilly, he was the representative of the *Ultras*, and was forced to carry out their programme or resign. But Villèle had the weakness of wishing to remain in power, and it was under his ægis that laws were passed of which he frequently disapproved, but upon which the Right insisted.

The latter had for a long time been protesting against the irrevocability of the sales of national property guaranteed by the Charter, and maintained that the *émigrés* who had been despoiled by the Revolution had the right, either to have their lands restored to them or to be paid an *ad valorem* indemnity. Since restitution was impossible without violating the Charter, Villèle proposed raising a loan of a thousand millions at 3 per cent., which should be assigned to the payment of this indemnity, the basis of valuation being twenty times the revenue of the properties in the year 1790. It was a good and perfectly sound idea; "it would free the national possessions from the moral mortgage which weighed them down," and put an end to a cause of friction which had been in existence since 1814. But the problem of the Emigration was closely connected with that of the indemnity; once again the Restoration found itself confronted with recollections of the Revolution, and the debates on the Bill gave rise to storms.

Indemnity for the *émigrés*.

The indemnity, declared the *Ultras*, was only just restitution, the repayment for robberies committed in evil times. "Not at all," replied the few Liberals who had resumed their seats in the Chamber. "The indemnity has no foundation in law; it is mere generosity for which there is no justification, a fine imposed on the nation." And finally, certain Royalists, who were in favour of summary resolutions, declared themselves opposed to the law, which, in their opinion, sanctioned the acts of the revolutionaries. The tone of the debate grew more and more acrid. "Let the sons of those who bought the public lands remember that in these precincts their fathers have been called robbers and scoundrels ! " exclaimed General Foy. And as the Right interrupted him, he added, " And if anybody tries to tear from them by force the property of which they are legally possessed, let them remember that they have on their side the King and the Charter and that they are twenty to one." In spite of this appeal to the people, the law was passed (April 1825); but in the eyes of the *Ultras* it was merely the preliminary to a reform upon which they had particularly set their hearts—the restoration of the old estates of the nobility through the revival of the right of primogeniture.

The proposed law, which would have repealed certain clauses in the civil code, and aimed—as its authors took no trouble to conceal—at setting up a barrier against the progress of democracy by putting a stop to the partition of property, was first presented in the Chamber of Peers in March 1826. But this Chamber, which was chiefly composed of ex-officials and Ministers—the peerage being a sort of consolation prize bestowed on Ministers who had been turned out of office—had retained a vague Liberal tradition, and this reform, which in spirit, though not so much in its practical application, amounted to " a manifesto against the established order of society," frightened it. In vain did Comte Marc-René de Montalembert maintain that the civil code merely secured equality in poverty, and tended " to turn France into a vast warren in which each individual had his hole "; the majority threw out all the principal clauses of the Bill. Paris applauded, and the Chamber of Peers forthwith enjoyed an unaccustomed popularity, whilst in the restaurants the heads of families gave banquets to their juniors.

This check was enough to enlighten Villèle. He heard all round him discussions about administrative reforms, of " *généralités* " to take the place of Departments, of a remodelling of the magistracy, of the sale of offices, and of provincial assemblies. What barrier could be erected against this political flood, which seemed likely to restore the France of the old days, as though the Revolution were merely a nightmare that had vanished without leaving a trace? His position was extremely difficult, for although he had the support of the

King, he felt himself threatened not only by the Left, but also by the Right. Chateaubriand, who had not forgiven him for the way he had been driven from office, had gone over to the Opposition of his own accord, and was conducting the conflict in the *Journal des Débats* with unflagging animosity. His genius and his gift of intuition made everything he said carry great weight. He posed as a prophet, and indeed, in the realm of politics, he could be extraordinarily far-sighted " when he did not stand in his own light." Villèle had once remarked, " We refuse to become embroiled with brawlers ! " He was now in a position to measure the inconvenience of having abandoned this attitude. One day he tried to reason with Bertin, the director of the *Débats*. " You overthrew Decazes and Richelieu by preaching Royalism; if you want to overthrow me you will have to preach revolution." The *Débats* did not bring about a revolution, but it announced its advent, and Chateaubriand, when he met his friend, Hyde de Neuville, on his return from his mission to Portugal, welcomed him with these words: " Have you come to see how a throne falls ? " Whilst the catastrophe was pending, it was a matter of open war on the part of the counter-Opposition, of " *la pointe*—the defection " as it was called—against the Government, which La Bourdonnaie, one of the most important members of the group that met in the Rue Thérèse, but a second-rate fighter, led with all his usual violence.

Chateaubriand's defection.

The opposition from the Left was less dangerous for Villèle, at all events in Parliament. But since the death of Louis XVIII the Liberals had changed their tactics—they no longer attacked the Bourbons, and their rallying cry had become " *Vive la Charte !* " This device included their whole programme and seemed to leave the very existence of the dynasty out of the discussion. Moreover they enjoyed the advantage of fighting for their ideas without troubling about office, for whilst Villèle was exposed to the machinations of the deputies belonging to his Party, who gave him their support only on certain conditions, the orthodox Liberals presented a united front, and were supervised by truculent overseers like Dupont de l'Eure, " a block of granite whom not even a revolution could move," and defended on the rostrum by orators who had the makings of statesmen.

Casimir Périer.

It was at this juncture that Casimir Périer began to make a name for himself. A thin, bald-headed banker, with spectacles on his forehead "which only came down to their proper position to help him to read," he "was the constant provoker of President Ravez' bell." He sat on the left out of hatred for the aristocracy, but the vehemence of his feelings did not disturb his political acumen; he loved order and gave the impression of being endowed with more than common energy. Moreover he was *persona grata* with the advanced Royalists. "Périer?" said Frénilly, "Périer is a good fellow, the crater of a volcano which is always smoking and sending out sparks. He is a madcap, but sincere and endowed with wit. If he were Minister he would work whole-heartedly for the monarchy, possibly better than certain others of our acquaintance."

Funeral of General Foy.

While they were reduced to a mere handful in Parliament, the Liberals had a great part of France behind them. Villèle was given proof of this in November 1825 at the funeral of General Foy, when a crowd of more than 100,000 followed the hearse of the demagogue whose name recalled the victories of the Revolution and the Empire. It was a vast procession that made its way from the Rue d'Antin to the Père-Lachaise; "above the sea of heads, the coffin, borne on the shoulders of young men, might be seen rising and falling on the waves of this human flood." A subscription was opened on behalf of the General's children, who were left penniless, and at the end of a few weeks it had reached a million francs. Monsieur de Barante, one of the Liberals, astonished by this expression of public opinion, wrote, "We are much stronger than we thought."

Two years later the Opposition could boast that it had not lost any ground. Manuel, who since his expulsion from the Chamber had sunk into complete oblivion, had just died, and with his death recovered all his old popularity. He was given a funeral befitting a martyr of liberty, and Béranger bought the horse-hair mattress upon which his friend had died; "and reverently slept upon the sacred relic."

What were the reasons for this progress of Liberalism throughout the country?

"Our age," wrote one of the Liberal papers, "will be very difficult to explain to our grandchildren. Theological controversy is the order of the day; and we hear of nothing but monks, Jesuits and mandates." And indeed from the rostrum excommunication was discussed, and the Chamber assumed the aspect of a Council charged with the task of defining sin. At the Palais, the lawyer Dupin invoked the liberties of the Gallican Church, whilst the judges passing sentence endorsed the Declaration of 1682 drawn up by Bossuet. It was an entirely new state of mind; there had been nothing of all this under the Empire. Thanks to the combined efforts of the clergy, the *Congrégation* and the missions, the religious question had assumed pride of place.

Law concerning sacrilege.

On the 15th of April, 1825, a law was passed punishing sacrilege—that is to say, the theft of sacred objects from the churches—with death, whilst the profanation of the Host was put on a par with parricide. Villèle was at first opposed to this measure, which he regarded as unwise. "We ought not," he observed, with extraordinary good sense, "*to place ceremonies above ideas.*" But the Right insisted on making an outstanding example of piety; according to its calculations, 538 thefts from churches had taken place between 1821 and 1825; and it was imperative that the sin of sacrilege, when added to that of felony, should fall within the arm of the law.

It was at this juncture that theology made its appearance in the Chamber and that dogma was "raised to the level of legal truth." This attitude of mind, hitherto unknown in parliamentary annals, gave rise to protests on the part of the jurists. "Sacrilege," declared Royer-Collard, "is an attack made upon Jesus Christ. But as soon as any one of the dogmas of the Catholic religion passes into the realm of law, that religion in its entirety should be regarded as true and all others as false." Chateaubriand added that the law harmed mankind without protecting religion; Molé, that martyrs of unbelief would be created who would be endowed with the odour of sanctity; whilst others conjured up the spectre of mediæval intolerance, and pointed out the danger of passing "a law which was an anomaly in the conditions of the present day." But the majority had made up their minds, and Monsieur de Bonald, after citing the authority of the Decalogue, ended his speech with the following words: "As for him who is guilty of sacrilege, what do you do by passing sentence of death except to send him before his natural judge?"

As a matter of fact, the law concerning sacrilege, owing to its definition of what constituted the crime, was impracticable and was never enforced. Nevertheless it attained its object —it was a great demonstration of piety, a proof of the new state of mind existing in France.

Various religious manifestations thereupon followed one another. At the time of the Jubilee celebrations of 1826 three solemn processions took place at which the King and all the Royal Family were present; this was followed by a ceremony in expiation of the death of Louis XVI. The missions redoubled their activities, and the question was mooted of making religious marriage obligatory and of placing the ceremonies connected with birth and death also in the hands of the clergy, as they had been under the *ancien régime*. Officials vied with each other in zeal; when a certain doctor left his Book of Hours at the Tuileries, the sceptics remarked, "When certain people lose their hours they do not lose their time." Marshal Soult, who in the past had enjoyed the reputation of being far from religious, now went to Communion in full uniform at the church of St. Thomas Aquinas, escorted by his children and all his servants in livery. The old days of 1815 seemed to have returned.

The Liberals immediately rose up in arms against this legislation, "the brilliance and audacity of which could not be denied." They brandished the bogey of theocracy, prating about Church tithes and the reprisals made by the old order against the new. "The present administration," said the Duc de Broglie, "finds no support in the customs of the people confided to its care." After the vote on the law of sacrilege, the domination of the "priest-party" became the subject of daily polemics, and, contrary to all expectation, it was a member of the Right, Monsieur de Mont-

Montlosier.

losier, a peer of France, who was loudest in his denunciations of the dangers to which the influence of the clergy exposed the monarchy.

Montlosier, although he was a staunch Royalist, hated government by priests and Jesuits. This hatred had become a mania. "He might have had a Jesuit on his nose, just as Pascal believed he had a fly on his." A Gallican of the old school of Louis XIV, and convinced of the necessity of protecting the Church of France against the encroachments of the religious bodies, he pointed out, in two *Mémoires*, which enjoyed considerable success (eight editions in a week) the four great scourges which, in his opinion, threatened the Throne—the *Congrégation*, the Jesuits, the Ultramontanes and the usurpations of the priests. As a matter of fact he confessed himself unable to give any precise definition of the real nature of the *Congrégation*. "The body is so constituted that it can, whenever convenient, vanish like a shadow," but its power was very real; this illicit society had members drawn from the highest officials of the State—it possessed accurate information regarding all postal and police arrangements in Paris—whilst its intelligence service and spy system included even the army. As for the Jesuits, their society, forbidden by the old monarchy, had been illegally revived, and ought to be dissolved.

Montlosier immediately became the darling of the Liberal Party. The *Débats* dubbed him "the torch of France"; *le Constitutionnel* and *le Courrier* expounded his arguments, whilst Béranger, faithful to his usual method of attacking religion "in a narrow-minded, commonplace and clumsy way," covered the disciples of Loyola with ridicule. The most absurd tales were circulated in order to impress the people, and it was repeated everywhere that soon nobody would be able to secure office unless he were a Jesuit. "The rule of fanaticism," wrote a certain Liberal pamphlet, "will be far more fatal to your fields, your workshops and your factories than the anarchy of the most rabid revolutionaries." Another pamphlet, entitled *Les Jésuits Modernes*, made a particular attack on the novitiate of Montrouge, whose Superior, it declared, "can raise a thousand hands well armed with daggers for the assassination of princes"; the author declaring that "once a week at nightfall, in a darkened chamber, all the novices swore to cast the crowns of the world at the feet of St. Ignatius." And these ridiculous statements were believed; the Jesuit was the ever-present invisible foe; his hand was seen everywhere and he became the butt of the cartoonists. As for Charles X, their acknowledged head, he was depicted wearing the mitre of St. Basil or even officiating, for a rumour was current to the effect that he had taken holy orders and been consecrated Bishop—had he not been seen following the Jubliee procession dressed in purple robes?

It is true that the Court of Paris, to which Montlosier had addressed his denunciations, while announcing that the establishment of the Jesuits was illegal, nevertheless declared itself incompetent to dissolve the societies mentioned; but on the rostrum Monseigneur de Frayssinous, the Minister for Ecclesiastical Affairs, "who was less exclusively a priest than many a layman," had the simplicity imprudently to acknowledge the existence of the *Congrégation*; and the Left was triumphant. "There, it has been officially recognised!" exclaimed Casimir Périer, "that mysterious *Congrégation!* It is not a chimera, but they have forgotten to tell us its family name." The Liberal propagandists found in this avowal a new force, which they proceeded to exploit. The *Congrégation* and the Jesuits, it is true, were not alarmed, but the following of the Opposition increased every day. The journals of the Left and Right, which were against the Government, had a circulation in Paris at this time of 44,000, whilst that of the Government papers amounted only to 12,580.

In vain did Villèle endeavour among his friends to make loyalty to the Government outweigh loyalty to their party.

Villèle's difficulties.

Entirely at the mercy of the *Ultras*, he submitted most unwillingly to their programme, and with the clarity of despair saw his Ministry becoming ever more and more compromised. "The absence of revolutionaries," he had observed a few months previously, "is going to break the Royalist Party. Instead of uniting in the fight, we are going to fire on each other and destroy our own cause." And he was perfectly right. As Michaud, the Director of *la Quotidienne*, observed, the counter-Opposition "were shooting from the windows of the sacristy"; the bench of magistrates was independent, almost revolutionary, and to the applause of the spectators, who shouted, "*Vive la Charte!*" acquitted the papers which had been prosecuted for attacks on the Government or for "a tendency to throw contempt upon persons or things connected with religion." Even the Army seemed to be losing its loyalty, for in December 1824, on the anniversary of Austerlitz, fifty-six lieutenant-generals who had fought under the Empire were put on half pay, whilst "sorry invalids who had never seen a shot fired" were kept on the active list.

In order to recapture public opinion, Villèle made a secret attempt to buy the Opposition papers, but Michaud divulged the plan, and Chateaubriand gave himself the pleasure of describing the homes of the Ministers as "a kind of bazaar where consciences were put up to auction." Whereupon Villèle raised the price for the transport of newspapers, but this indirect measure was only the prelude to stricter methods of repression. Through the instrumentality of the Minister, de Peyronnet, a Bill was presented by which the most insignificant printed publication would have to pay a preliminary deposit and stamp duty, and any infringement of the law would be punishable by heavy fines. It amounted to the suppression of printing. "A vandalistic law," exclaimed Chateaubriand. "They are trying to raise humanity to the happy innocence of the brute beast!" added Royer-Collard. "In the realm of religion, civil society and the Government, the law is becoming reactionary." The *Académie Française*, strongly Legitimist though it was, dared to protest, which roused the indignation of Charles X; Michaud and Lacretelle were deprived of their posts as reader to the King and dramatic censor, whilst Villemain lost his position of *Maître des Requêtes*. The whole affair had been extremely clumsy, and it was turned to ridicule when a certain wag dubbed the measure "the law of justice and love." Nevertheless the Government scheme secured a majority in the Chamber of Deputies. The Peers, however, having appointed a Commission which was against the Bill, it was thrown out amid the acclamations of the Parisian people and above all of the printers, who had been threatened with the loss of their means of livelihood (April 1827).

The "Law of Justice and Love."

Villèle was furious. "I will create so many peers," he exclaimed, "that it will be a disgrace either to be one or not to be one!" But he was fully aware of the force of public opinion, and the smallest incident was sufficient to increase his unpopularity. At the funeral of the Duc de la Rochefoucauld-Liancourt, for instance, some students belonging to the Châlons *École des Arts et Métiers*, of which the Duke had been patron, wanted to carry his body on their shoulders, but as they were coming out of church, the police told them to place the coffin on the hearse; whereupon a disturbance took place, in the course of which the bier fell half broken on to the pavement, amid general indignation.

A flood of complaints reached the ears of the King, who, feeling himself being gradually engulfed in the hostility directed against his Minister, answered impatiently, "Villèle! Always Villèle!" In one caricature the latter was depicted seated before a table, his head turned towards a half-open door through which the profile of Charles X appeared, and Villèle was saying, "For Heaven's sake leave me in peace! Haven't I given you a permit to hunt?" And thus the King was represented as a puppet in the hands of the President of the Council; he was regarded as being incapable of exercising any will of his own and of being entirely engrossed in attending Mass and the hunt, and whenever he showed himself in Paris he was given a cold reception.

Whereupon, anxious to restore the confidence he was losing, Charles X decided to hold a review of the National Guard, for the first time since his accession. Villèle perceived the disadvantages of the idea, and on this point found himself in agreement with Chateaubriand, who, stifling his rancour, wrote to the King pointing out the danger to which he would lay himself open. At one moment there were thoughts of cancelling the review, but the remedy would have been worse than the disease.

Review of the National Guard.

On the 29th of April, 1827, a huge crowd assembled in the *Champs de Mars*; when the King passed in front of his troops there were some shouts of "Down with the Ministers!"—"Clermont-Tonnerre," observed Charles X with a smile, to the Minister for War, who was with him, " they are saluting you ! " But suddenly one of the guards left the ranks and, planting himself in front of the King's horse, exclaimed with wild gesticulations, " Down with the Jesuits ! "—" I came here to receive homage and not instructions," replied Charles X. But the spark had caught. The Duchesse d'Angoulême and the Duchesse de Berry were greeted with insolent shouts, and when the former, with tears in her eyes, turned her head aside, the guards sneered, " She does not even deign to look at us ! " When the review was over, and the troops were marching past the offices of the President of the Council, the drums were suddenly silenced and a tremendous shout arose : " Down with Villèle ! " Behind the windows of the Ministry, Villèle was moving from room to room, following " the march of the maniacs," and that same evening he said to the King, " The National Guard is a revolutionary institution. It has insulted Your Majesty, and you must reply by breaking it up altogether." Clermont-Tonnerre objected, " But that is not strength, it is violence. It will be sufficient if the guilty units are disbanded." But Villèle insisted, and on the 30th of April the order for dissolution was given.

The National Guard disbanded.

The news gave great satisfaction to the Royal Guards, who despised the citizen militia. " Monsieur Pigeon " (this was the nickname given to the National Guard), they said " took its flight early this morning." But wiser spirits thought differently. The National Guard had been one of the instruments of the Restoration in 1814, and had shown equal zeal and devotion during the Hundred Days. Moreover, it was not the King but his Ministers who had been attacked, so why thus light-heartedly bring about a divorce between the monarchy and the citizens of Paris ?

Nevertheless the order for disbanding gave rise to no disturbances. Villèle was astonished. " Paris has not raised a finger," he wrote ; whilst the Duc de Rivière, who was constantly at Court, emboldened by the spectacle of this resignation, summed up the situation by saying, " The King can do anything."

But, as a matter of fact, the bourgeoisie and trades-people, although they found service in the guards a nuisance, resented the disbanding as an insult levelled at themselves, and joined the ranks of the Opposition. And thus, one by one, the largest classes in the community abandoned the Government.

Thereupon Villèle had recourse to extreme measures. An ordinance of the 5th of November, 1827, dissolved the Chamber; another created seventy-six new peers, the majority of whom, it was said, belonged to the *Congrégation;* whilst a third, calculated to palliate the effects of the two first, abolished the censorship that had been set up. This was tantamount to making the country the supreme arbiter of the conflict. But Villèle remained apparently unperturbed. When fears were expressed regarding the result of the elections, he replied, "If we were not certain we should deserve to be sent to the madhouse!" And in fact he had taken every precaution. A circular was sent to all the Prefects instructing them to insist upon their officials voting and doing all in their power to ensure success. But the coalition between "*la pointe*" and the Left presented a formidable obstacle. "What support has the Government among the people of Paris?" asked Benjamin Constant. "It has incensed them. What about public opinion? It has outraged it! And the peerage? It can control it only by flooding it with fresh creations. And the magistracy? The Bench opposes it in the name of justice!" The Ministers were accused of conspiring against the necessary union between the King and his country, and the polemics of the last few years bore fruit. The idea of a possible catastrophe—though what sort of a catastrophe, it was impossible to say—gradually crept into men's minds. "There is a general feeling of nervousness," wrote Lamennais; "people are frightened and they don't quite know why. It is like a nightmare."

Coalition between "la pointe" and the Left.

The elections took place in an atmosphere of feverish unrest. The order for the day was, "Down with the Government!" Committees were formed to draw up lists for a coalition, and in spite of a police conspiracy organised in Paris to strike terror in the Departments, the Opposition won the day, securing a majority of sixty in the new Chamber.

The domestic policy of Villèle had been condemned; and his foreign policy met with no better success. Faithful to the principle he had done his best to get adopted at the time of the Spanish expedition, he was convinced that war could only be prejudicial to France, and consequently adopted an attitude of wise neutrality. But this drew down upon his head the gibes not only of the Left, but also of the Right, who accused him of being the pawn of England and of failing to defend the honour and interests of his country. And, as a matter of fact, he had not opposed the recognition by England of the independence of the Spanish colonies, and this constituted an attack on the rights of Ferdinand VII. He had also freed the French colony of St. Domingo of its allegiance (it was already slipping away) on the payment of an indemnity of 150 millions, to be divided among the dispossessed colonists (April 1825), and Chateaubriand inveighed against "that great business promoter, that prudent mariner who would never have discovered the New World," but wanted to confine France to her own territory "and tie her down."

The Greek War.

But the Greek War of Independence was to force Villèle to come to a decision. The war had lasted for seven years, during which the Turks had been guilty of horrible atrocities and the Greeks had shown heroic resistance. The massacres of Scio (April 1822); the exploits of Kanaris, who with his fireships destroyed the Turkish vessels; the success of Miaoulis, who at Samos defeated the fleet of Ibrahim, the son of the Pasha of Egypt, whom the Sultan had summoned to his assistance; the siege of Missolonghi, where Byron had met his death; the capture of that town, which the primate blew up before it was taken, whilst the inhabitants on their knees called upon God to save them; the siege of Athens, which was defended by a Frenchman, Colonel Fabvier—this succession of tragedies one after the other excited public opinion and united the leaders of the various parties by a common feeling of admiration, Chateaubriand rubbing shoulders with La Fayette at the "Philanthropic Society for helping the Greeks." The war was popularised by artists and writers; in the Salon of 1824 Delacroix' picture *Scène des Massacres de Chio* was hotly discussed, not only because the composition and technique were new to the French School, but also on account of the subject itself. Subscriptions were opened and gradually a league was formed inspired by love and enthusiasm for an illustrious nation which was struggling to be free and "cast off its chains."

Villèle endeavoured to stem the current, but he was carried along. Even Charles X himself was converted to the idea of intervention; disturbed by the fact that he was unable to govern in conjunction with the Chamber, he relied upon success abroad to consolidate his position. In October 1827 the Russian, English and French fleets, charged with the task of forcing the mediation of the three Powers on Turkey, appeared in the roadstead of Navarino. They hoped to convince Ibrahim, the representative of the Sultan, without having recourse to any act of hostility, but the frigate *la Sirène*, which was the flagship of Admiral de Rigny, was received by a cannon shot from a Turkish vessel. Whereupon the battle was opened, and two hours later the Turkish fleet was destroyed and Greece was saved (20th of October).

Battle of Navarino.

From the political point of view, the victory of Navarino was profitable only to Russia, who immediately invaded Turkey. For France it was nothing more than a great moral success, and the fleet, whose glorious victory helped to wipe out "the shame of the treaties of 1815," was lauded to the skies. Public feeling was triumphant, crowing over Villèle, who had been against the war.

The President of the Council, having lost the confidence of the electoral body, tried in vain to find support in the landed aristocracy, who would be well satisfied with a state of financial prosperity. Prudence prompted him to retire, but he still believed in his influence on the Assemblies and the efficacy of his limpid speeches, which calmed the bitterest discussions, "like a bucket of water thrown on to fighting bull-dogs." When they opposed him by Chateaubriand, he replied with infinite wisdom, "I am not jealous of him, he is endowed with far greater wit than I am; but I have better judgment, and it is not wit that makes use of judgment, but judgment that makes use of wit." He believed he had been born for the supreme guidance of affairs, and since he had become accustomed to the exercise of power, he clung to it,

Villèle misunderstood.

and refused to capitulate gracefully. When Charles X asked him the plain question, "Have you a majority?" he replied, "No, Sire; if it is a matter of preventing the Chamber from demanding the dismissal of the Cabinet. But for everything else, yes, if this demand is refused by the King and only measures of general interest are brought forward." This was sheer optimism. He tried to approach the Left, but the financial situation at the end of 1827 had become worse, and the taxes were coming in badly, with the result that his reputation as an administrator, which might have helped him once again to overcome the crisis, was undermined. In the end he made up his mind to send in his resignation on the 3rd of January, 1828.

His Resignation.

If Villèle retired "under a cloud of general disapproval," it was because he had governed for too long, and was saddled with the weight of blunders for which he was not altogether responsible. But even those who had been against him—with the exception of Chateaubriand, who refused to lay down his arms—did justice to him. Bertin, the Director of the *Débats*, declared that he was the most remarkable of all the Ministers of the Restoration, and added, "Under Louis XVIII he would not have fallen." Frénilly, while denying him "the qualities of the statesman," confessed that he was the greatest financier that France had seen since Colbert. And Villèle, it is true, put wonderful order into the administration; under his guidance Government stock rose to 120 francs and the rate of interest was reduced to 3 per cent., and yet capital did not cease to flow into the French market from every source.

Doubtless the mistake he made was to misunderstand the state of mind of his contemporaries, who were less concerned with securing a good administration, and with tangible and profitable realities, than with ideas and thoughts of liberty and glory. The wound of 1815 had not healed, and the Bonapartist fever, though it calmed down from time to time, broke out again more virulently than ever. But Villèle had neither the temperament nor the qualities to satisfy the mentality of the French nation.

Nevertheless his retirement was not unattended with danger to the monarchy. When he went to take his leave of the Duc d'Angoulême the latter could find nothing better to say to him than, "You had become too unpopular!"—"Monseigneur," replied Villèle, "God grant that it was I!"

Bibliography.—Apponyi, *Journal* (1901) (Vol. I). D'Audiffret, *Souvenirs de l'Administration Financière du Comte de Villèle* (1855). Auriant, *Charles X et Mehemet-Ali* (*Rev. Bleue*, March 1923). de Barante, *Souvenirs* (5 vols., 1890). Bardoux, *Le Comte de Montlosier et le Gallicanisme* (1901). de Bonald, *De la Famille Agricole, de la Famille Industrielle et du Droit d'Aînesse* (1826). Bourgeois, *Manuel de Politique Étrangère* (2 vols., 1905). Bourgain, *l'Église de France et l'État au XIXe Siècle* (2 vols., 1901). F. Dreyfus, *Larochefoucauld-Liancourt* (1903). de Guichen, *La France Morale et Religieuse à la Fin de la Restauration* (1912). Lanson, *La Défection de Chateaubriand* (*Revue de Paris*, 1901). de Montbel, *Souvenirs* (1913). de Peyronnet, *Discours sur le Sacrilège* (1825). de Villèle, *Mémoires* (5 vols., no date). Saint-Edme, *Législation du Sacrilège Chez Tous Les Peuples* (1825).

CHAPTER VII

SOCIETY AND IDEAS UNDER THE RESTORATION

The old aristocracy, its *salons* and way of life. The new generation—Jouffroy. Foundation of the *Globe*. Romanticism in search of a definition—Stendhal, Duvergier de Hauranne. The founders of Romanticism. Poetry—Lamartine, Hugo. History—Augustin Thierry. The theatre—Hugo, Alexandre Dumas. "The *ancien régime* of language is destroyed." Reactionary attempt of the classicists. Romanticism in art—Delacroix. Music—Berlioz. Charles Nodier and the Salon de l'Arsenal. Neo-Catholicism—Lamennais, theocracy. The reformers—Saint-Simon. The economic condition of France. It differs but little from that under the *ancien régime*. Poverty of the people. Inertia of the public bodies.

AFTER the military drama of the Empire, the Restoration provided a breathing-space. The society that had been overthrown was trying to find stability once more; everywhere there was lassitude, enervation and disorder. Everybody wanted to restore his own position and introduce order into his own affairs; but the needs were no longer the same, society had been revolutionised and the aspect of the country changed. Yesterday was no longer sufficient for to-morrow, and people asked themselves what would be the new star to guide the destinies of France in the hour of her defeat. Hence for fifteen years the atmosphere was, as it were, leaden and disturbed, and passions and desires were in continual strife; tradition meeting the spirit of innovation in a confused and troublous conflict. The Restoration was a prolonged effort towards reconstructing the nation and setting it once more on its feet.

The Salons.

It was only the *salons* of the *ancien régime* that quickly recovered their stability and returned to their old ways; a familiar institution, they stood in no need of alteration. The palace of Princess de La Trémoïlle was a court at which politics were discussed; at the house of the

Marquise de Montcalm, the sister of the Duc de Richelieu, constitutional liberalism took pride of place. As for the Faubourg St. Germain, it regarded itself as the heart, the very life-blood of France; the routine of life there was conducted with the utmost regularity—six months in Paris, the rest of the year at the country seats; balls during the Carnival, concerts and sermons in Lent, marriages after Easter; the theatre very seldom and travelling not at all. Madame de Sévigné's dictum that "A woman should never move her bones unless she is the wife of an Ambassador," was carried out to the letter. The time was whiled away at card-playing and discussing the members of the royal family: "a thousand and one grievances were nursed, together with a profound disapproval of the Charter," and a bottomless contempt for the system of moderation.

The Old Aristocracy.

Life in this stronghold of aristocracy was conducted "with magnificence tempered by an appearance of old-established custom that saved it from any tinge of ostentation"; the meals were lengthy and substantial, the head of the house carved himself, the old serving-man put in his word, "there was neither awkwardness nor display." Old ladies possessed a gift of speech which was soon to die out, they used words and expressions dating from Louis XIV; their conversation was sprightly and they were not shocked by anecdotes that were inclined to be salacious; but on occasion the arrogance of "the good old days," which lay dormant, would suddenly flash forth.

Those who had managed to save their fortunes almost intact entertained on a grander scale and engaged the celebrities of the day for the diversion of their guests—la Pasta, and la Malibran, of whom Talma observed, "What a pity it is that woman insists on singing!" or Mademoiselle Sontag, who, though somewhat stilted, played the part of Rosine in the *Barbier de Séville* adorably.

The New Generation.

This class, who founded their lives upon the past and upon well-defined hopes, was confronted by a generation of young men born after 1789, who had played no part in the wars of the Empire but who had experienced the counter-blast. This did not mean that they were Bonapartists. They were far from being Bonapartists!

They were suspicious of the bellicose sentimentalism which seemed to have lost all recollection of the rule of the despot, and of the intellectual suffocation from which France had suffered under Napoleon. In their eyes Béranger was merely a vulgar rhapsodist. They were equally suspicious of the old Voltairean Liberalism of the bourgeois, which took refuge in the repetition of threadbare themes and battles of words between encyclopædists or revolutionaries, and they spurned any alliance with the theorists of political or religious absolutism like Bonald or Lamennais. They wanted to be themselves, to see with their own eyes, judge with their own reason, free from all prejudice, as far removed from philosophic intolerance as they were from Jesuitism. Free from all constraint, attached to no school, they read the works of Joseph de Maistre or of Benjamin Constant, and placed them in the same category, distributing praise and blame indiscriminately right and left with youthful intrepidity.

Modesty was not their most conspicuous quality, but they were endowed with sincerity and conviction and a very real desire to break down the barriers surrounding thought, and to give it free scope. Their manifesto was drawn up in 1825 by a first-class writer, of whom the best was never seen, for he died young, but who still, even now, awakens sympathy—Jouffroy.

Jouffroy.

This native of Franche-Comté, a man of almost feminine delicacy, whose pale blue eyes "seemed as if they were turned inward upon his own soul," was an ardent intellectualist. He joined the Carbonari at the same time as his friend Cousin, and in 1822 opened free classes in the Rue des Fossés-Saint-Honoré at which historians, philosophers and critics like Vitet, Burnouf, Damiron and Sainte-Beuve used to lecture. United by an ardent love of the things of the spirit and of intellectual freedom, the members of this coterie were concerned with the discovery of new standards which would help to guide their generation. In a manifesto entitled "*How Dogmas Die,*" Jouffroy defined the position of the youth of his time as follows: "Superior to all that surrounds them, they refuse to be ruled either by the reviving spirit of fanaticism or by the selfish unbelief that pervades society. They sit in judgment on the past. They understand what their fathers failed to understand, what their corrupt tyrants never perceived; they know what a revolution is and they know it because they arrived in the nick of time."

Ever since 1824 this band of *élite* had had their own organ, the *Globe*, founded by a young typographical printer named Pierre Leroux. To give all the news, foreign, industrial and social, and, unlike the other papers, which were full of Paris affairs, to present a picture of life in the provinces, and in regard to literary doctrine to observe "the principles of liberty and respect for the national taste"—such were the aims of this new journal. By way of apology for their boldness, the editors added: "If our forms are somewhat dogmatic, it is because we are accustomed to certainty." They wished to avoid being taken for young Doctrinaires.

The *Globe*.

Thus constituted, the *Globe* developed into a powerful organ. In it ideas were aired, theories discussed, and reforms indefatigably and eagerly suggested, often with nobility and candour and occasionally with extraordinary depth of wisdom. As the free lectures had been stopped by the *Ultras*, it was in the *Globe* that thought found refuge. Cousin, who no longer had a chair from which he could let off the superfluous "electricity" with which he was endowed, contributed articles characterised by that facile vehemence and mimicry which led Lamartine to observe, "There is something clownish about that fellow!" But in spite of his ridiculousness and his lust for power, he had a remarkable capacity for rousing enthusiasm. Jouffroy, for his part, "who beneath a colder exterior hid a fiercer fire," was the conscience of the group.

Goethe, who was a regular reader of the articles in the *Globe* and confessed that they provided him with much food for reflection, thought that the editors were "men of mature years." What greater tribute could have been paid to these old heads on young shoulders? As a matter of fact, none of Jouffroy's friends had reached the age of forty, and were therefore ineligible as deputies. Parliament was closed to them; but their intellectual outlook naturally inclined them towards Liberalism in politics and in literature towards Romanticism.

Since 1816 a change had taken place in the latter. The

troubadour fashion was beginning to lose its charm; it was old almost before it was born. What was wanted now was not only fresh subjects, but the discovery of a less conventional, a more lively and spontaneous form of art, which would appeal direct to the heart; inspiration and lyric beauty were to take the place of mechanical structure; the canons of beauty and ugliness, of the "lofty" and the trivial, immutably fixed by the old masters, were to be discarded, and the writer, spreading his wings freely, was to express himself without troubling about established rules. The poets of the *Cénacle*, which had taken the place of the *Muse française*, expressed their horror at the exalted style that called coffee "the bean of the moka," the butterfly "an insect that to its own bewilderment came into being," pins, "darts for the aid of beauty," and linen "salutary hemp." Such foolish phrases, dubbed graceful conceits, had had their day; it was time they were for ever banished.

Romanticism.

The Liberals of the old school, who had disapproved of the early Romanticism as being reactionary in tendency, were offended by this new attitude. In their eyes La Harpe had once and for all "drawn the map of good taste"; they remained faithful to the classical tradition, to the pompous, oratorical style which had come into vogue since the Revolution and still reigned supreme on the rostrum. The *Ultras*, for their part, were terrified by this spirit of innovation which threatened law and order and held up independence to admiration. Thus, in their fear of Romanticism, the extreme Right and the Left joined hands.

Nevertheless the new school had as yet no doctrine; it possessed aspirations rather than certainties. It stood in need of definition, and it was towards this object that the *Globe* turned its activities. Stendhal, in *Racine et Shakespeare* (1825), after declaring war on classicism, "the chief characteristic of which is boredom," wrote: "Romanticism is the art of presenting to the world literary works which in the actual conditions of life and state of belief are best calculated to give the greatest possible pleasure." The doctrine was vague enough, but the author made it clearer by means of personal examples. "What would the public, sectarian or otherwise, say if it were called upon to choose from the point of view of wit and talent between Monsieur Droz and Monsieur de Lamartine, Monsieur Campenon and Monsieur de Béranger, Monsieur Daguesseau and Monsieur de Lamennais ? " The *Globe* sought for a more general definition, and Duvergier de Hauranne, one of its chief editors, made the following suggestion : " Obedience to the laws of the language; independence in everything else." Vitet capped this with " Taste in France is awaiting its 14th of July " ; another writer placed like a device above his article the following inscription : " The old man : Let us carry on.—The young man : Let us examine.—There is the nineteenth century in a nutshell ! "

And indeed the literary tendencies of these young reformers still escaped definition, and in order to find a way out, one writer in the *Globe* confessed : " Romanticism is neither a party nor a doctrine ; it is the law of necessity, the law of all that happens, of all that changes, the law of everything in the world." Jean-Jacques Ampère was already advocating a measure of prudence, a golden mean which was hardly in keeping with the attitude of his friends : " Do not let us sacrifice Shakespeare to Racine, or Racine to Shakespeare. They are two powerful gods ! Why make them hostile deities ? Their worship stands in no need of sacrifices."

But Romanticism, in spite of all that its friends could do or say, was no ready-made article that sprang into existence one fine day under the Restoration. It could not deny its distant ancestor, Rousseau, or its acknowledged father, Chateaubriand. The latter had been the first " to turn against the eighteenth century, and had unexpectedly shown it a shield blazing with light, some parts of which were pure diamond." He it was who had taught the new generation that restlessness of soul, that feeling of exaltation which at first had no goal but which was destined to find satisfaction in lyricism. " There are few among us," said Lamartine, " who do not owe him our past, our present and our future." And Augustin Thierry, who felt he was a historian when he read in *les Martyrs* the description of the Frankish army marching out to battle, added, " We have all met him at the beginning of our studies, as the first source of inspiration." It was Chateaubriand, in short, who had sounded the religious note which we find again in the first poetic attempts of Hugo and Lamartine, not to mention Sainte-Beuve, and which constitutes their keynote.

This purely national influence was supplemented by foreign influences, some of which had already played a part in Royalist romanticism—Byron with his satanic irony, Walter Scott with his popularisation of history, Young, whose *Nights* flooded the libraries, the nebulous reveries collected under the name of Ossian and Grey. The "Lake Poets," Wordsworth, Southey and Coleridge, whom Sainte-Beuve made his particular study, fed French poetry on deep melancholy hovering over wide landscapes. Germany, in addition to Werther, contributed her legends and her philosophy of history, which was to guide Michelet and Quinet in their youth; and Spain her collections of romances, "that rich pearl necklace" that has not its like in Europe.

From this repertory "of pictures, sounds and colours," the Romanticists borrowed freely, transforming their material according to their temperament, talent and genius; and little by little the new art came into being.

Lamartine.

With the publication of the *Méditations*, Lamartine sprang into the front rank poets. With its vague and misty lyricism, its exaltation towards God, Love and Beauty, "which has neither dwelling-place, symbol nor name," and with its dissection of the soul, its utterances sounded strange to the ear; but surprise turned to admiration and then to enthusiasm. He was followed by others, and gradually the parts were allotted; Lamartine remained the poet of the morning, of awakening, of the dawn; the poetry of Hugo, on the other hand, belonged "to midday, to the fierce sunlight, to the deep fantastic shadows"; whilst Vigny "awoke only after the secret hour of midnight." Pain and love-sickness found an incomparable interpreter in Marcelline Desbordes-Valmore, who, as a child, had learnt spelling from the tombstones in a graveyard, and, during the vicissitudes of a tragic life, learnt to speak in accents of unprecedented intensity. It was a wonderful efflorescence of elegiac poets, a burgeoning of youth above the barriers of the old classicism.

Hugo.

A similar freedom of spirit made its appearance in fiction (for which the *Obermann* of Senancourt set the tone), in the historical novel which was destined to have a dangerous success, as well as in history proper. Here a certain tact was necessary; Walter Scott could not be accepted as an acknowledged model. But a revival of historical studies occurred similar to that which had taken place in other departments of literature. In 1820, Augustin Thierry published in *le Courrier Français* his *Lettres sur l'Histoire de France*, in which he declared war on "those writers without learning who have been unable to see and those writers without imagination who have been unable to depict." According to him there was no history of France in existence describing the ideas, the sentiments and the customs of those who had handed down the name of Frenchman through the ages. He despised—though with but little justification—such men as Mézeray, the elder Daniel, and Velly, and proved, this time with some show of reason, that it was absurd to ascribe to Clovis the royalty of Louis XIV. At the cost of immense pains, he succeeded in establishing four principles which in his opinion should in future guide all research into French history—the necessity of distinguishing between races, the recognition of the influence of the southern peoples in the establishment of the Frankish Empire, a due regard for the leading part played by the enfranchisement of the communes, and lastly an appreciation of the importance of the popular songs, of legend and of folklore. Time has destroyed much that Thierry wrote, but the noble passion and fervour of this author, who went blind through work, will always stand out conspicuous, and it is impossible to show sufficient admiration for the manifesto which serves as a preface to his *Dix Ans d'Études Historiques*: "If I had to begin my journey over again, I should take the same road as has led me where I am. Blind and ill beyond hope of recovery and almost always in pain, I can yet bear this testimony to myself which will not be suspect from my lips—there is something in the world which is higher than material pleasures, higher than wealth, higher even than health, and that is devotion to science."

Augustin Thierry.

One field still remained for Romanticism to conquer, and it was indispensable if her victory was to be complete—the theatre.

Here Casimir Delavigne, who had been destined by his father for the crockery trade and had become the official dramatist of the Restoration, and Scribe, the protégé of the Duchesse de Berry reigned supreme. Scribe delighted the *Gymnase* audiences by his comedies of middle-class life, the protagonists of which were either a soldier of the Empire, proud and melancholy, a generous banker, a solicitor or an attorney. Actual events and allusions to contemporary history frequently formed the subject of plays, and the theatre became the arena in which the parties met. In 1819, when Arnault's *Germanicus*, the performance of which was forbidden at the time in Belgium, was produced, a regular "battle of walking-sticks," as a certain wag described it, took place; this was followed by the "calico war" declared against the shop assistants who wanted to give themselves martial airs and only made themselves look ridiculous. Delavigne's *Les Vêpres Siciliennes*, showing how a nation wins back its liberty, was regarded as a leading article in perfect verse, and the *Ultras* accused the Opera, which presented *Masaniello* and *La Muette de Portici*, of teaching the people the best way to rebel.

The Theatre.

Thus the ground seemed ready prepared for the invasion of Romanticism. The melodramas of Pixérécourt had already completely broken away from the traditional rules and, drawing their inspiration from the maudlin style, wrought upon the masses by means of terror or pity. But this only made the task of Hugo and his friends all the more difficult; it was necessary to "outdo" melodrama, to rise above it, and make use of symbolism and synthesis—in short, "to embrace the infinite." A hard task indeed! Romanticism was obliged to force its note and adopt a frankly provocative attitude towards classicism, and aim bluntly at "terrifying the bourgeois." The "ancient usages of the language" were to be cast out, right of asylum was to be granted to every word, the lowest as well as the noblest; lines were to be broken by cutting up the Alexandrine and the use of enjambment; whilst, master of this more pliable instrument, the poet was to speak to the people and predict the future by his images.

Whilst Duvergier de Hauranne in the *Globe* was solemnly discussing the question of the "unities" and defending the happy blending of the comic and the tragic, the dramatists were setting to work, turning history to their own purposes in order to make it produce a different effect from the chronicle-dramas, which it was quite impossible to act, published by Vitet. In 1827 an English company presented a series of Shakespearean plays in Paris; it was a revelation. " Imagine a man born blind whose sight was suddenly restored ! " wrote Alexandre Dumas, who, with his superabundance of life and strength, had espoused the cause of Romanticism with all the zeal of youth. France stood in need of a Shakespeare; that was perfectly clear; and Hugo, putting himself at the head of the movement, wrote in the same year the preface to *Cromwell*, and threw down the gauntlet of the new school to " the reactionaries of thought."

Dumas' *Henri III et sa Cour* and Hugo's *Hernani* put a match to the powder; the classicists and the romanticists confronted each other; the latter might be seen dancing round the bust of the author of *Phèdre* singing, " Down with Racine ! " Later on, Emile Deschamps, who happened to be passing the Théâtre Français just as the audience were leaving after a reading of *Marion Delorme*, said, " And they are going to act *Britannicus !* " At the first performance of *Hernani*, when the hero, learning that Ruy Gomez has entrusted his daughter to Charles V, exclaims, " *Veillard stupide ! il l'aime !* "[1] one of the audience, Monsieur Parseval de Grandmaison, who was a little bit hard of hearing, understood him to say " *Vieil as de pique !* "[1] and could not help protesting : " Ah, now, that's going a bit too far ! " Whereupon Lassailly, a confirmed romantic, immediately retorted, " Sir, he is quite right; cards had been invented." Excitement reached such a pitch that at the same performance, which has remained famous in the annals of the theatre thanks to Théophile Gautier, a romantic from the gallery shouted out to the classicists in the stalls, poking fun at the old bald-heads, " To the guillotine with those bare knees ! "

This reminder of the Terror was not inopportune. According to Jouffroy, Madame de Staël and Chateaubriand represented the Constituent Assembly in the romantic revolution, Charles

[1] Phonetically *Veillard stupide!* and *Vieil as de pique* may be confused. Literally translated they mean " Foolish old man ! " and " Old ace of spades ! "

Nodier and Lamartine the Gironde, Hugo and his friends the Convention. And the conventional period, it is true, opened under the joint dictatorship of Hugo and Dumas. Whereupon the *Globe* gave vent to shouts of victory: "Nothing that is against us is young; youth, power, work and faith are on our side!" The classicists replied with a cry of alarm; in truth this literature oozed scandal and took a delight in despising any moral: *Henri III et sa Cour?*—a tortured woman. *Hernani?*—a gentleman pirate; and the whole filled with incoherent incidents and degraded by base expressions. Did not Hugo boast of calling a spade a spade? It was even worse than "the plays of Mademoiselle Clara Gazul," and of Merimée, about whom one of the classicists wrote: "Romanticism is not ridiculous; it is a disease like somnambulism and epilepsy." The disease was now developing into madness; and the terrified bourgeois, whether Liberal or *Ultra,* held the new school responsible for the increasing number of suicides.

Resistance of the Classicists.

Certain members of the Academy thereupon sent an address to Charles X begging him to use his authority to prevent the influx of Romanticism into the theatre; but in this case the King proved himself the gentleman of Versailles that he had been in the past. "In a matter of this sort," he replied, "I, like everybody else, have only a seat in the pit." The romantics—those steam engines, as their enemies, in their consternation, called them—celebrated this success in their own way; and when Dupaty, a well-known classicist, was made an Academician, everybody repeated Hugo's remark: "I thought one reached the Academy by the Pont des Arts; I was wrong, apparently one reaches it by the Pont Neuf."

Chateaubriand had not the courage to lend his name to these audacities. One day when he was trying to persuade Brifaut, another Academician, to vote for Hugo, the latter remarked, "You are like Louis XIV, you are trying to make us legitimise your bastards." But Chateaubriand had no such object in view at the moment, and in his heart of hearts he even denied so compromising a paternity: "If I had not already written *René,* I would not write it now."

Nevertheless "the magnificent covey of 1815," mentioned by

Renan, had found its wings. Asked to choose between authority and liberty, it had pronounced in favour of the latter, and courageously set up its banner, not only in the domain of literature, but also in that of politics. The step had been taken, Royalist Romanticism had had its day and Jouffroy wrote: "The hour of persecution is at hand, the stakes of the Jesuits must not lack for victims!"

Art.

The battle over *Hernani* had been won by the art students—that is to say, the evolution of Romanticism progressed side by side in literature and in art. Dumas, who had a gift for simple and striking classifications, saw in Paul Delaroche a Casimir Delavigne, and in Delacroix a Hugo. The *Globe* had provided the painters with the programme they required—what was wanted was truth, not convention, the picturesque, fine dresses, local colour, no moralising, and above all richness. The subjects? There were plenty. Greece and Rome and the field of mythology had been exhausted, crystallised by the classicists, but what splendid material was afforded by Dante, Shakespeare and Chateaubriand, by the chronicles and the memoirs that scholars were continually publishing, not to mention the tragedies of contemporary history!

Delacroix.

This appeal was heard. Scheffer, the former conspirator, Géricault and Delacroix "illumined," as the romanticists called it, the Salon of 1824, and once again the classicists gave vent to cries of horror. Delacroix above all, with his violence, his disregard for subjects and poses and time-hallowed technique, seemed to them "an act of war and a cause of war"—the man painted "with a drunkard's broom." And indeed what must the bourgeois of the Restoration, accustomed to an ordered and noble art, tragic and dignified, have felt when they looked at the *Barque de Dante*, black with the horrors of hell, or the *Massacres de Chio*, with the green flesh-tints of its dying figure? Their great artist was Gérard, the painter of the *Entrée d'Henri IV à Paris*, a picture which was the gem of the Salon of 1817, whose talent was so versatile that Molé, who was a good judge, declared, "He is the painter of this century because he is endowed with more spirit than verve, greater powers of observation than warmth of feeling, and because he addresses himself to reason, taste and judgment rather than to imagination, enthusiasm and the senses." Baron Gros, the painter of the Napoleonic era, was also typical of the school.

The actual and the ordinary, and even more the picturesque, shocked the unrelenting admirers of David; accustomed to the classic nude, the harmonious folds of the chlamys, a riding-boot in a historical picture seemed to them a monstrosity. To make a statue of Napoleon otherwise than as a Roman Emperor could only be done for a wager! "It is impossible to produce a fine work with the subject in trousers," was their dictum. They regarded the work of Delacroix as nothing short of an insult to good sense and morality; to dare to indulge in such orgies of colour and savage contempt for the classic canon was, as the *Figaro* expressed it, a degradation of the noblest institution; and Ingres, the artist whose drawing was above reproach, was of much the same opinion. In front of a picture by Rubens, he used to say to his pupils, "Salute it as you pass, but do not look at it"; for the romantics he showed less consideration, calling them wicked, and Delacroix a dishonest creature. Romanticism in art did not succeed in ousting the old school, although it was helped and popularised by that constellation of draughtsmen, illustrators and lithographers known as Boulanger, Célestin Nanteuil, the Johannot brothers, Charlet, Daumier, Gigoux, Achille Devéria, and Eugène Lami; nevertheless, thanks to these admirable artists, "the romantic life" unflaggingly developed its modes of expression; and Goethe found his own visions surpassed by the illustrations of his *Faust* by Delacroix.

Music did not escape the contagion. Hitherto under the distinguished patronage of the Duchesse de Berry, who was a Neapolitan, the Italian school had held the field. But in 1824 Weber's *Freyschütz* showed the public how much emotion could lie concealed in a romantic subject treated romantically. Whereupon Berlioz arose. More impassioned than any other member of the new school, possessed by the desire to astonish and terrify the bourgeois musicians of the Conservatoire, who lulled themselves sanctimoniously with the sober harmonies of Méhul, Spontini or Cherubini, he composed in 1825 a Mass full of "sinister vibrations," followed by the *Francs-Juges*, in which

Music.

Berlioz.

the brass instruments were unloosed in an orgy of fierce fanaticism—it was his way of showing his hatred for the Philistines, the classicists, and society itself. His dishevelled hair, his aquiline profile and the sacred transport by which he seemed to be shaken, gave him an aspect of satanic genius. In 1828 he conceived the idea of giving the finishing stroke to the bleating school of music by a descriptive symphony of which *Faust* was to be the subject.

The disciples of Romanticism, the writers, poets, painters and illustrators, met together and confirmed each other in the faith at the house of a scholar of almost universal talent, whose curiosity was inexhaustible and who was equally interested in philology, the occult sciences and coleoptera.

Nodier.

Imagine a salon in the Arsenal and, standing in front of the mantelpiece, a man with a long, lanky body, long arms, long, pale hands, angular features and lively, tired eyes. With an animation tempered by a strong Franche-Comté accent, he relates a Scotch or German legend, and then explains how, as he was walking along the quays, he picked up an extremely rare volume at Crozet's or Techener's. He was Charles Nodier, the typical man of letters, "the rich, amiable and illusive polygrapher" and author of *Jean Sbogar*, the *Dictionnaire des onomatopées* and many other books, whom even Sainte-Beuve admired. In his house were to be found "all the fine banners, the fine colours, and the daring claims of the vanguard of the Romantic movement, as well as every form of adventure." Here were gathered together the Johannot brothers and Louis Boulanger with their drawings, Barye the sculptor, who seemed to be in search of some marvellous animal, and Francisque Michel, the record grubber. Here too was Musset, still almost a child, dreaming about his *Contes d'Espagne et d'Italie*, Vigny, who seemed as if he could hardly deign to mix with men; here too were Lamartine and Hugo. The master of the house turns towards the latter. "Now that's enough of prose!" he says. "Give us poetry, poetry!" And the young Hugo, his fine head with its broad forehead peering above a black cravat, gracefully does as he is bid. It was here, in this library rich in memories of the past, that the romantic revolution was developed under the eye of a scholar who was ready to welcome any daring innovation, and who possessed the gift of eternal youth, the man to whom Musset said :

> " Si jamais ta tête qui penche
> Devient blanche,
> Ce sera comme l'amandier,
> Cher Nodier." [1]

In its desire to recast existing standards, and to replace the old framework, Neo-Catholicism was the brother of Romanticism, though its aims were infinitely higher.

Neo-Catholicism.

In 1817 a book appeared signed by an almost unknown name, *L'Essai sur l'indifférence en matière de religion*, by the Abbé de Lamennais. As de Maistre declared, it was a clap of thunder in a leaden sky. The author,

Lamennais.

a native of St. Malo and a member of the petty nobility, after a youth full of activity and greedy of adventure—his teachers in order to keep him in his place used to fasten a turnspit to his belt—had attempted on the return of Napoleon to make a livelihood in England as a teacher, but the noble families to whom he presented himself thought he " looked too stupid." He was small, fragile, pale, prematurely lined and so shy that he stammered, and he sat with his head bent forward, his hands folded and his feet pulled back under his chair. In 1816 he had taken holy orders; and France then learnt what concentrated passion supported by a burning faith can achieve.

After the heroic but irreligious days of the Empire, Lamennais was a spiritual revivalist pure and simple. He shook " that deep lassitude, that debility of all kinds " which had spread through the society of his time; and regarding religion from a higher and nobler point of view than the *Congrégation* had done, he not only declared war on the philosophic spirit, but also maintained that the future lay in theocracy. It was necessary, he declared, that the Church should be independent of the State and of parties, and that she should be delivered from political bonds—that is to say, from atheism. For the State was atheistic; it recognised all forms of worship and professed a

[1] " If ever thy bowed head becomes white, it will be like the almond tree, dear Nodier."

monstrous neutrality : " A child is born, and it is registered just like an animal has to pay toll at the gates of our towns." And death, what was death for the State, except " a matter of sanitary precautions "? Owing to these disgraceful practices, society was sinking to the lowest depths ; a sort of ready-made Catholicism made up of miserable concessions, owing allegiance to salaried officials (the Bishops) who claimed membership of a national, Gallican Church, had been manufactured for its use. " Poor foolish society," exclaimed Lamennais, " which goes to the Salpêtrière through the portals of the Morgue ! "

For his own part, he gave his allegiance neither to the House of Bourbon, nor to the Charter, nor to parliamentarism. " I cannot help thinking," he said, " that God allowed representative Government to be invented in an age of pride in order to humiliate men by showing them to what lengths human stupidity could go." If any one party found grace in his eyes, it was that of extreme Liberalism, because it repudiated ancient institutions and " placed the Catholics of modern days in a position of struggle."

Near Dol, in the mists of Chesnaie, " where the sun is only a glorified fog," Lamennais laid the foundations of the society of the future, preaching the reconciliation of the modern world to Catholicism, through the instrumentality of the lower clergy, who had remained pure and under the supreme authority of the Pope. His aim was the realisation of perfect ultramontanism, of an international Catholicism, of a universal Church to take the place of the national Churches each held in subjection by its own State, a Catholicism which was to dissipate the miasma of atheism that was corrupting the nations, and bring about the alliance between religion and liberty.

This philosopher, who was at once Christian and revolutionary, was acceptable neither to the ecclesiastical nor the lay authorities. Regarding the law on sacrilege as atheistic, censured by the Bishops, condemned by the tribunals, predicting the fall of the Bourbons, he accepted the yoke of none, but freely and openly confessed his faith ; and this attitude, this sublime passion on the part of a priest, against whose morals no indictment could be brought, for he was guided by the spirit alone, seemed a terrible anomaly—he was " the Savonarola of the nineteenth century."

And indeed Lamennais had the gift of rousing the people; disciples flocked to him, priests, men of letters, aristocrats and commoners—among them the Abbé Gerbet, Montalembert and that strange creature Eckstein, a Danish Jew who had been brought up as a Protestant but became converted to Rome and founded *Le Catholique.* The master taught them and explained to each his mission. "Behold this clock!" he would say. "Were anyone to say to it: 'If you strike in ten minutes time you will have your head cut off,' nevertheless in ten minutes time it would strike the hour it was destined to strike. Be like this clock; whatever happens, strike your hour!" Gradually he became the great agitator and flooded the world with ideas which even to this day have preserved their strength and vitality.

Whilst Lamennais was discovering in theocracy the law of the future, there were others who were animated by more terrestrial aims. "Make haste," said Senancour to those who were enamoured of sylvan landscapes, "make haste, for the day is at hand when this rude nature will exist no more, when all the ground will be cultivated and every man will be enervated by human toil."

Saint-Simon.

The very forms this industrialisation was to take were predicted by a man of genius, but according to him, instead of enervating society, it was destined to restore it. Saint-Simon, a man of noble family—he was descended from the author of the Memoirs—an ex-revolutionary who had once been a manufacturer of playing-cards, and, by speculating in public property, had made a fortune which he had subsequently lost, was essentially the type of man whose creative imagination turns to the realm of reality. The world about him, with its isolated individuals and its social order, seemed to him an absurdity, and the methods of government a played-out farce. All this, he maintained, was out of date; but if this decrepit society was to recover, it must continue its onward march and, instead of inventing a new constitution, which would be merely chasing a will o' the wisp, it should proceed to a fundamental reorganisation of its forces. And, guided by the results of scientific investigation and the teaching of history, together with the observations he had made himself during his journeys,

Saint-Simon proclaimed that the future lay with the industrial State, the association of men in labour and the orderly exploitation of the world's resources. The transformation of the soil on which we live was to be the work not of the legislators but of scientific progress. The real revolution " would be the railway."

Such were the principles which Saint-Simon outlined in a series of pamphlets, in his *Catéchisme des industriels* and *Le Nouveau Christianisme.* He died in 1825, in poverty, after having tried to commit suicide. But his message was such that it could not fail to influence those youthful minds who were eager for social reform and grandiose schemes. It found ears to hear, and was developed by a band of admirers whose enthusiasm verged on the mystical and who were destined to found a new religion upon the teachings of their master.

" The crisis," wrote Saint-Simon with reference to the France of his day, " consists essentially in the change from a feudal and religious system to an industrial and scientific system. . . . France has become a huge factory and the nation a colossal workshop. The real temporal power of to-day is to be found in the industries and the spiritual power in the men of science." This was a vision from the heights which was far in advance of his time.

Fresnel, it is true, laid the foundation of the science of optics in his *Mémoire sur la diffraction* (1818), Ampère and Arago that of electrodynamics; whilst Sadi Carnot, developing the theories of the mathematician Fourier, anticipated the discovery that " heat is nothing else than motive power or rather motion in a different shape "; and thus gradually the law of the conservation of energy was enunciated. Other great problems, which were more accessible to the general public, were raised by natural science, more particularly that of the immutability of species. In this domain Cuvier was opposed to Geoffroy Saint-Hilaire, the former upholding the traditional belief in their immutability and citing the authority of the Bible, the latter expressing his doubts and outlining the theory of transmutation, which was to prove so fruitful.

The Royal House was not indifferent to the progress of science, and contemporary historians of the Restoration point out that Louis XVIII founded a Chair of Sanscrit at the *Collège de France,* as well as a Chair of Chinese to be filled by the sinologist Rémusat, whilst the Duc d'Angoulême consented to become the patron of the *École Polytechnique.* But the spirit prevalent in the latter institution was far from good; there was much more discussion about Bonaparte and Carnot than about the reigning King, and the efforts of the authorities to introduce a Royalist tone into the studies met with no success.

Thus the men of science had not yet become "the priests" of the new religion heralded by Saint-Simon; but meanwhile, before the results of the zeal for innovation, which animated the writers, the artists and the politicians, had had time to make themselves felt, what was the aspect presented by the France of the Restoration? Was she throwing off the economic bonds of the *ancien régime,* was there any progressive change in the classes of society, and were there any visible signs pointing to a modification of the social organism?

Economic Condition of France.

With regard to foreign trade, protection remained the rule—to prevent competition from abroad as well as the lowering of prices, and to secure the monopoly of the national market to the landed proprietors and industrialists, were the aims that had been followed since 1814, and which found their full development in 1826. On this point the industrialists, who were generally Liberal, and the *Ultras,* who were drawn from the great landed proprietors, were in agreement, and thanks to their combined efforts, prohibitive tariffs ousted English iron goods and textile fabrics from the French market. The importation of cereals was actually forbidden between 1821 and 1830, and gradually almost all agricultural produce, including cattle, was treated in the same way. The wine-growers insisted upon an increased duty on tea because that herb "was injurious to the national character, endowing it with the seriousness of the North, whilst wine bestowed a gentle gaiety." At the same time the French colonies remained subject to the colonial treaty made under the *ancien régime*—the Government flag kept the monopoly of transports and trade with Guadeloupe, Martinique and Senegal, which had been returned to France by England, and with Guiana, which had been handed back by Portugal.

Such a strict system of prohibition and such exclusive

commercial regulations inevitably led to retaliation from abroad and were conducive to fraud; it was the golden age of smuggling. In 1826 an economic crisis which occurred in England had an immediate reaction on the French market, and proved that protection was possibly not devoid of danger; and gradually a Free Trade party came into being which tried to point out that it was absurd to expect never to buy and always to sell, " and to support exports by means of prohibitions." But the industrialists and the landed proprietors imagined they would be lost if the established system were attacked, and although public faith in protection had been shaken, it still remained in force.

At home, economic progress was slow; except in the art of printing, which made wonderful strides, and in the manufacture of articles of luxury, there was no real development. The mail-coach, a Government service, and the national stage-coach were the only means of transport; they took four days to go from Paris to Lyons, and the *diligence* double that time. In 1817 the steam engine was introduced in the spinning-mills in Rouen, but although at Saint Etienne " rail-roads " were constructed to carry coal (1828), the idea of conveying passengers by rail was never entertained. The post remained in an embryonic condition; as late as 1829 35,500 communes out of 37,300 had no post office. The Stock Exchange was monopolised by a few great bankers, and in 1830 only thirty-eight securities were registered there. If to all this it is added that from the point of view of agricultural perfection France was " at the bottom of the scale of northern European nations," it is clear that the industrialisation predicted by Saint-Simon had not yet entered the realm of reality.

Poverty of the People.

In 1826 the population of France rose to 32 million inhabitants, of whom more than 22 millions were agriculturists, and according to certain statistics, the large estates still accounted for half the territory, proving how little the aspect of the country had changed since the Revolution. The agriculturist lived on his land, frugally. It has been estimated that in the south the annual income of a peasant household averaged 451 francs (£18), in the north 508 francs (£20 5*s*. 0*d*.).

The industrial worker too was in a miserable position, for

wages fell, whilst, owing to protection, the prices of articles of prime necessity increased. Consequently in the north half the workers were on the books of charitable institutions. The majority were illiterate, and the number of foundlings reached alarming figures—over 118,000 in 1830.

Inertia of the Public Bodies.

What were the remedies applied for the alleviation of this distress? The political parties, who cared for nothing except interests represented in Parliament—that is to say, the interests of the "*élite*"—remained indifferent, and the public bodies followed their example. A few charitable societies alone began to organise help by means of work, to found homes of refuge and savings banks, which very often did well; but the part they played was chiefly to guide and direct the workers' mutual benefit societies. The latter, intolerant of this supervision, gradually severed the connection, and aimed at managing their own affairs and securing reasonable wages by means of secret united efforts. This mysterious, corporative character was revealed for the first time in 1827 in the statutes of the *Société des Mutuellistes de Lyon*, founded by a silk worker named Charnier, and future Governments were soon to learn the power of these fighting organisations.

To sum up, in spite of changes of thought, the Restoration from the economic and social points of view still remained virtually bound to the traditions and customs of the *ancien régime*. "All social institutions," said Saint-Simon, "should have as their aim the physical and moral improvement of the most numerous and poorest class." Under Charles X this goal was still remote.

BIBLIOGRAPHY.—de Bassanville, *Les Salons d'Autrefois* (4 vols., 1862). A. Boschot, *La Jeunesse d'un Romantique, Hector Berlioz* (1906). G. Bourgin, *Legislation et Organisation Administrative du Travail Sous la Restauration* (*Rev. politique et parlementaire*, 1910). G. Brunet, *Le Mysticisme Social de Saint-Simon* (1925). S. Charléty, *La Restauration* (Book III); *Histoire du Saint-Simonisme* (1896). Alexandre Dumas, *Mémoires* (10 vols., no date). Duine, *La Mennais* (1922). E. Dupuy, *La Jeunesse des Romantiques* (1907). Gaffarel, *La Politique Coloniale en France de 1789 à 1830* (1908). H. Girard, *Un Bourgeois Dilettante à l'Époque Romantique : Emile Deschamps* (Vols. II and III of *La Bibliothèque de la Revue de littérature comparée*). Hourticq, *France* (Coll. Ars Una) (1910). Jouffroy, *Le Cahier Vert* (pub. by P. Poux) (1924). Lanson,

Histoire de la Littérature Française (1898). J. Larat, *Études sur les Origines du Romantisme Français : Charles Nodier* (2 vols., 1923). M. Leroy, *Vie du Comte de Saint-Simon* (1925). Levasseur, *Histoire de la Classe Ouvrière et de l'Industrie en France de 1789 à 1870* (2 vols., 1903). Marsan, *Notes sur la Bataille Romantique* (1913). Renan, *Essais de Critique et de Moral* (1859). Rosenthal, *La Peinture Romantique* (1900). Sainte-Beuve, *Portraits Littéraires* (3 vols., 1845); *Portraits Contemporains* (3 vols., 1846). Ch. Sainte-Foi, *Souvenirs de Jeunesse* (1911). M. Salomon, *Charles Nodier et le Groupe Romantique* (1908). Souvestre, *Causeries Littéraires sur le XIXe Siècle* (1907). Stendhal, *Racine et Shakespeare* (edition published by P. Martino) (1925). D. Stern, *Mes Souvenirs* (1877). Trahard, *Le Romantisme Defini par " Le Globe "* (1925).

CHAPTER VIII

THE JULY REVOLUTION

Charles X resigns himself to accepting a Liberal Ministry. Martignac. The ordinances of 1828; instability of the Government. Confidence of Charles X and fall of Martignac. Effect produced by the Government of the Prince de Polignac. His inertia. Thiers becomes the leader of the Opposition. The Address of the 221. Dissolution of the Chamber and defeat of the Right. The Algiers expedition. Resolute attitude of Polignac. The capture of Algiers encourages the King. The ordinances. Their effect upon the people. The insurrection breaks out on the 28th of July. Retreat of Marmont's troops to the Tuileries. 29th of July; capture of the Tuileries. Charles X leaves Saint-Cloud for Versailles. Candidature of the Duc d'Orléans. He is appointed Lieutenant-General of the Kingdom and acclaimed at the Hôtel de Ville. The mob marches on Rambouillet. Exodus of Charles X. The Charter revised; Louis-Philippe King of the French. The nature and work of the Restoration.

IF he had followed his own inclinations, Charles X, on the fall of Villèle, would have called upon his friend, Prince Jules de Polignac, the French Ambassador in London and a prominent *Ultra*, to take up the reins of power. But the attitude of a certain section of the Right—that "*pointe*" which had given its support to the overthrow of the Ministry—was doubtful; the Left had just won the day at the elections, and the King was obliged to resign himself to a policy of moderation, similar to that followed by Decazes and Richelieu.

Martignac.

The Vicomte de Martignac, although he was not given the title of President of the Council, became the head of the Government. This Bordeaux lawyer, with his elegant figure and his love of letters and the theatre—he had once founded a comic-opera company—was the sort of man to please an assembly; he had a gift of eloquence which, though superficial on occasion, was always prepared for grand rhetorical effects, and his hearers allowed themselves to be bewitched by "his voice, which was tired and gentle as though he were a man on whom women had bestowed something of their own weakness and charm." Courageously and in all good faith, Martignac made up his mind to make representative monarchy take root in France, "by silencing the presumptions of the Royalists and the prejudices of the Liberals."

But as soon as he came into office he saw that it was impossible for him to rely on the King. "It is only fair to tell you," the latter informed him, "that I am parting with Monsieur de Villèle with the deepest regret. Public opinion has been misled with regard to him; his system was mine, and I hope you will do your best to conform to it." And in truth Charles X had but little sympathy with these Ministers who were not of his own choosing. He said of Martignac, "He is just a beautiful organ of speech." Or, after he had made a speech in the Chamber, "Have you heard la Pasta?" La Ferronnays, the Minister for Foreign Affairs, had once had a grave dispute with the Duc de Berry; Hyde de Neuville, the Naval Minister, was a friend of Chateaubriand—both very good reasons for their not enjoying the confidence of the sovereign. He tolerated them for the time being; whilst Villèle still remained active behind the scenes, carrying on a correspondence with the King and taking no care to avoid creating difficulties for his successors.

Nevertheless the new Government was favourably received; there was a feeling of relief and "things looked brighter." The Liberals seemed to have come to the conclusion that the Restoration was an established fact, and Marshal Soult observed to the King, "Sire, you must not be misled. France is Left Centre." But Charles X refused to be convinced. When in an address the Chamber poured abuse upon "the deplorable system of Villèle," he became angry: "I will not allow my Crown to be thrown in the mud. I shall give this address the reception my brother gave to the address which brought about the fall of Richelieu!"—"Your Majesty," replied Martignac, "has doubtless considered the measures for suppressing the upheaval." The King drew himself up indignantly: "Do you really imagine it would come to that?"—"Yes, Sire; and all my colleagues are as convinced as I am." On the following day Charles X's rage had cooled; no doubt Villèle had advised him to temporise, and no incident occurred.

In order to satisfy the Left, whose numbers had just been increased by the partial elections, Martignac had a law passed for the revision of the electoral lists, the aim of which was to reduce the despotic power of the administration. He also made new regulations for the Press—the classic method of unfurling a Government standard. The censorship and the offences of tendency were abolished, but the preliminary deposit and the jurisdiction of the ordinary courts remained unchanged. A certain section of the Left, regarding these reforms as insufficient, declared against the Bill. Martignac now perceived the difficulties of carrying on Government with such a hotch-potch majority. Hardly had his Cabinet been formed when it seemed on the point of falling. As Fontenelle said on his death-bed, he found "it difficult to keep alive," and Villèle's old friends now always spoke of the Government as Monsieur de Martignac's "sufferance Ministry."

New Laws.

The latter now determined to deal rigorously with the Jesuits. He had already dismissed two high police officials, who were avowed Congregationists, but as the Left still continued to inveigh against the encroachments of the priest-party, he wanted to disarm their criticism once and for all and thus regain their confidence. On the 16th of June, 1828, two ordinances were published, the first subjecting the Jesuit secondary schools to the jurisdiction of the University and forbidding members of illegally established communities to teach; the second setting a limit to the number of pupils in ecclesiastical schools and, in order to palliate the severity of this regulation, giving them certain grants. This was the most revolutionary measure that had been passed since 1814. Nevertheless Charles X gave his consent to it, for in spite of his deeply religious nature, his kingly conscience spoke more loudly than the voice of piety. Moreover he had taken counsel with Bishop Feutrier, the Minister for Ecclesiastical Affairs, and with Father Ronsin, the head of the Jesuits. "Let the storm blow over," had been the advice of the latter.

Ordinances of 1828.

The June ordinances aroused considerable excitement in the ranks of the clergy and of the *Ultras*. Through the mouth of Clermont-Tonnerre, Archbishop of Toulouse, the Bishops gave voice to their official protest; after carefully considering their obligations to Caesar and their obligations to God, "they contented themselves with a respectful *non possumus.*" But the Pope refused to lend his support to such an act of rebellion; he preached obedience in order to avoid creating trouble for the King, whose piety he admired, and even went so far as to agree that the pretensions of the clergy to act as guides to young men who were not destined for the priesthood were exaggerated. The Bishops regarded this as final, and Archbishop Clermont-Tonnerre alone, faithful to his family motto: *Etiamsi omnes, ego non,* refused to submit.

After this victory it would have seemed only natural for the Left to rally whole-heartedly about Martignac. But this was very far from being the case. In spite of his oratorical success and his charm of voice, which forced one of his opponents to cry out, "Silence, you siren!" he felt that he was not trusted. The Right regarded him as too advanced, the Left as too cautious; above all he was unpopular because he had not changed Villèle's officials; in the hands of men who were determined not to enforce them, Liberal laws remained a dead letter. But on this point Charles X was obdurate. "Do you want me to dismiss all my friends?" he asked. "No, Sire, only those who are opposed to Your Majesty's Government."—"I will do nothing *en masse;*" replied the King, "I wish to see each name. The staff must not be disorganised, otherwise my Crown will fall in the dust." A man entirely animated by party, almost by clan spirit, the King disliked changes of personnel more than anything else; in his eyes such tactics amounted to surrendering his sword. Nevertheless he resigned himself to making certain concessions, and his antipathy for Martignac increased accordingly. He had him attacked in the Royalist papers, and when the editors of the latter asked him whether they were not much too hostile to the Minister, he replied, "No, no; go on!"

Unpopularity of Martignac.

A visit he paid about this time to Alsace confirmed him in his belief that he had regained his popularity. He was greeted with one long ovation, for, in this home of Carbonarism, the people thought that the King had been won over to Liberalism and had become sincerely constitutional. Charles X was touched. "Do you hear?"

Confidence of Charles X.

he observed to Martignac. "Are these people shouting '*Vive la Charte?*' No! They are shouting '*Vive le Roi!*'" At about the same time the Duchesse de Berry was making a triumphal journey through Vendée, acclaimed by the old Royalist insurgents, those "veterans of civil war" who were whole-heartedly devoted to the throne and the mitre. Abroad, General Maison's expedition, which had been sent to force the Turco-Egyptian troops to evacuate the Morea, had met with complete success, and had thus confirmed the belief that the monarchy was Liberal. The King, in his innocent pleasure, confided to Casimir Périer, "If I had known that I was so much loved, I should have kept Villèle."

The coldness of the Chamber and the persistent hostility of Charles X deprived Martignac of all hope, and he confined his efforts "to leading the monarchy to the foot of the stairs again," whilst, but for him, it would have been thrown out of the window. He saw only too clearly that the King, though he pretended to listen to the advice of the Parliament, was resolved to make his own will prevail; the very existence of the Charter was menaced. At all events, in order to set his conscience at rest and make one last attempt to secure the union of the Right and Left about the monarchy, he introduced two Bills with reference to the organisation of the communes and the departments which substituted election for nomination as the method for the appointment of municipal and general councillors.

It seemed reasonable to think that these Bills would please both the Liberals, since they inaugurated local Government, and the Right, since they favoured the idea of decentralisation. But quite a contrary effect was produced. The Right accused the Government of trying to create 30,000 republics, whilst the Left persisted in making the perfectly illogical demand that the departmental law should be passed first. The conflict raged round this trivial point, and thanks to a coalition between the extreme Right and the Left, the Government was put in the minority. This collusion between the two wings of the Chamber produced a feeling of stifled alarm, "a dull murmur, like a sinking ship." Martignac was seen to beat a hurried retreat, and it was thought that he was going to send in his resignation to the King. But a few minutes later he returned with the announcement that the Bills had been withdrawn.

Charles X accepted this defeat with a smile. Everything was developing according to plan and as he had hoped. "Didn't I tell you," he observed to Martignac, "that it was impossible to come to terms with these people? They would take us further than I am prepared to go." But as Polignac happened to be ill in London at the time, he was obliged to keep the moribund Ministry yet a while longer. In vain did Martignac endeavour to ward off the storm. The King disapproved of his appearances on the rostrum. When a deputy of the Right scoffed at the constitution and the legal system, and the Minister in reply made an eloquent defence of his work and especially of the June ordinances, Charles X said to him on the following day, "Why the deuce did you want to speak? It was a mistake on your part; *they* will not forgive you."

But Martignac would not give in. In an almost prophetic memorandum he showed the necessity for modifying the personnel of higher administrative posts, and the danger of even a temporary suspension of the Charter, which would bring about the ruin of the monarchy. But the King regarded the whole thing as nonsense. When Hyde de Neuville talked to him in the same strain as Martignac, he replied by pointing to the Place Louis XV beyond the Tuileries. "One would think you could see the guns over there!" he said. The *Ultras* were openly discussing a Royalist revolution and citing article 14 of the Charter, by which the King was given dictatorial powers, and extolling Louis XIV's action when he arrived booted and spurred and whip in hand to reprimand the Parliament. It is high time, wrote *Le Drapeau Blanc*, to revive the constituent power which is vested in the King alone, and to cut at the roots "of the poison tree which insensate or perfidious planters have raised."

On the 28th of July, 1829, the Prince de Polignac was in Paris, and on the following 6th of August Charles X dismissed Martignac. The fall of the latter was due to his efforts to reconcile opposites; he talked to the Liberals about the King and to the *Ultras* about the Charter, and succumbed beneath the onslaught of "this

Fall of Martignac.

immoral and unnatural coalition," the members of which were to meet with condign punishment later, the former under a Government set up by a *coup d'état*, the latter by a revolution.

The King had made up his mind; in future he would allow the affairs of the monarchy to be conducted only by those who were in complete accord with his own political faith, and the Prince de Polignac, or Jules, as he called him in private, seemed to him just the man to decide once and for all the question at issue between the legislative and the executive power "by placing the Crown above control."

Polignac.

Extremely elegant, thin and supple, with a long face and noble features, which gave him a certain resemblance to Charles X, whose son he was said to be, affecting English manners, and at once affable and commonplace, Polignac, in Liberal eyes, was the Counter-revolution incarnate; and indeed there was some justification for this opinion. A descendant of the favourite of Marie-Antoinette, the charming Duchesse de Polignac, one of the original *émigrés* at the time of the Revolution, the accomplice of Cadoudal, a prisoner under the Empire, and a peer of the realm who had refused to swear obedience to the Charter after 1815, he seemed to have drawn down upon his head every possible reason for unpopularity. But he did not trouble about it. In his childish infatuation he believed himself to be in possession of the truth, and relied on God no less than on the King, "for he regarded himself as the predestined instrument of the former and the personal friend of the latter." He had in him something of the mystic and the visionary; "a Jean d'Arc chosen for the salvation of the monarchy," as Monsieur de Semonville observed.

Unpopularity of the Government.

When, on the 8th of August, 1829, the *Moniteur* appeared with the list of the members of the new Cabinet, and beside the name of Polignac appeared those of La Bourdonnaie and General Bourmont, the public were moved by feelings of anxiety as well as of anger; it was, as it were, "a red rag to a bull." La Bourdonnaie, that termagant and firebrand detested by Chateaubriand, recalled the excesses of the *Chambre introuvable* against the Bonapartists, "the categories" to be sent to the scaffold. Bourmont was even worse; he had betrayed Napoleon in 1815 on the eve of Ligny, and in making this man, who, to use Odilon Barrot's expression, was regarded as "denationalised," Minister for War, an insult was levelled at the Army. This appointment, "which reeked of a *coup d'état*," seemed like a declaration of war in the heyday of peace, and had the immediate effect of alienating public opinion from the King, "as the hatchet strips the bark from the tree so that it can never be put back in its place."

But for a handful of uncompromising Royalists, discontent and even hatred were everywhere prevalent. "Coblentz, Waterloo, 1815," exclaimed the *Journal des Débats*, "those are the three principles of this Government. Press it and squeeze it, and it will only exude humiliations, misfortunes and dangers." Royer-Collard, the Doctrinaire, who had been made President of the Chamber, sighed, "So Charles X has remained the Comte d'Artois!" whilst in well-informed circles it was whispered, "Can't these people see that they are paving the way to the throne for the House of Orleans?" And, putting the matter in a nutshell, the carter in the street whipping up his horse called the animal Polignac.

And indeed it seemed as though Charles X took a delight in inflaming the passions about him. Yet he had received warnings enough. "This is an adventure," the Duchesse d'Angoulême had told him, "and I have no love of adventures; they have never brought us any luck." And Admiral de Rigny, the victor of Navarino, not wishing to be the colleague of Bourmont, refused the portfolio of Naval Minister; when he gave his reasons, the King replied testily, "Bourmont! he has never done anything except under secret orders from me and at my express command"; whereupon the Duc d'Angoulême, who was a whole-hearted supporter of his father's ideas, went even further, and declared, "Bourmont would get up on horseback behind me if it were necessary." With this unwieldy Cabinet, which was destined to make the monarchy leave the path on which Martignac had placed it, Charles X saw his dream realised; although in public, in order to calm the fears that were being expressed, he made a show of doubting the capacities of his friend. "Poor Jules," he would say, "he is so incompetent!"

In spite of his blind infatuation, Polignac felt that it would be as well to say a few soothing words. He therefore made professions of loyal attachment to the Charter. But nobody was taken in, and Chateaubriand summed up the general feeling when he said, "He loves the Charter in his own way, he loves it at too close quarters." He regarded Polignac as a dumb man eminently gifted for the strangling of an Empire.

Polignac's Incompetence.

Everybody was waiting to see what the Government would do; but they did nothing. It was as if the curtain had been raised for a great play and the actors had failed to appear. And for a very good reason: the Ministers had no bond in common; with the exception of Polignac, La Bourdonnaie and Bourmont, the names of the majority had been picked out from the *Almanach Royale* almost haphazard. Could they draw up a programme of legislation? It was doubtful, and Lamartine wrote to a friend: "Polignac turns up with Liberalism in one pocket and something else in the other. I am very much afraid that there is nothing at all in either of them." In the privacy of the Cabinet, whilst Polignac relied on the influence of the clergy, La Bourdonnaie believed in the gendarme, and, furious at not being President of the Council, complained of being surrounded "by fools who did not know how to take sides." Charles X had chosen him only in order to test the kind of man who is always grumbling, and when La Bourdonnaie declared that he was going to resign because "when he was risking his head he liked to hold the cards," he was allowed to go, on being granted, at his own request, a peerage and a substantial pension.

Meanwhile Polignac persisted in reiterating that he was not going to attempt a *coup d'état*. "I am extremely sorry to hear it," replied Michaud, the director of *la Quotidienne*. "Why?"—"Because, as you have on your side only men who want a *coup d'état*, if you refuse to attempt it, you will have nobody." But, in spite of his public declarations, the President of the Council went his way. The fact that he had not a majority troubled him but little; he would not have known what to do with it. As for his colleagues, if some among them were obstructive, "he would fling half of them into the sea."

In the eyes of the Liberals the acknowledgments of the *Ultra* journals allowed of no ambiguity—the conflict between the sovereignty of the Crown and the sovereignty of the people, between the *ancien régime* and the Revolution, between the white flag and the tricolour, was now engaged. The Charter had failed to settle the question as to who should have the last word, the King or the Chamber, and this uncertainty had been a millstone about the neck of politics ever since 1815. The time had come to put an end to the deadlock, but was it possible to do so otherwise than by force?

At this juncture a new man made his appearance at the head of the Opposition—Thiers. He was a young lawyer from Aix, who, together with Mignet, a friend from Provence, destined to make a name for himself in literature, had left the provinces in order to conquer Paris. One of the editors of the *Constitutionnel*, and the author of a *History of the Revolution*, which, on account of its lucidity, made a sensation at the time, he was often to be seen at the house of Laffitte, a Liberal banker who, after having risen from nothing, was at this time a sort of king of the salons. A man of short stature, jerky in his gait and swaying his shoulders as he walked, "which proved that he had more originality than distinction," Thiers hardly seemed to have the presence of a statesman; but his wonderful intellect, "the ideas with which Nature had endowed him ready-made," his almost cynical realism and his dislike of abstractions made him unique.

Thiers.

He immediately discovered the angle from which the monarchy should be attacked. The Charter, as the Duc de Broglie had remarked, was the stronghold in which Louis XVIII had placed his dynasty. "Let us shut the Bourbons up in the Charter," added Thiers, "and close the doors tightly; they will inevitably jump out of the window." But who was to take their place? Here the English Revolution of 1688 by which the House of Orange had replaced the Stuarts, offered a remarkable precedent. This Revolution had been accomplished without shedding a drop of blood—by the mere change of one person. Why should not France do the same? The *Globe* and the new Liberal journal *le National*, of which the moving spirit was a writer of first-class ability, Armand Carrel, himself the author of a history of the Revolution in England, enlarged upon this theme; if he violated the Charter, Charles X would meet the fate of James Stuart, and "the people would crowd round curiously to witness the departure of a King whom they would have liked to love."

But Polignac paid no heed to these warnings. "The fall of the monarchy had become merely a question of time," and he complacently continued his policy of tame inactivity, turning a deaf ear to the advice which poured in upon him from every side, and praying by the side of the King in the chapel of the Tuileries.

On the 2nd of March, 1830, the Chambers met. As he was mounting the steps of the throne Charles X tripped, his cap fell to the ground, and the Duc d'Orléans hastened to pick it up; the incident assumed a symbolic significance. The Speech from the Throne, in spite of the colourless tone characteristic of this type of rhetoric, contained a thinly disguised menace; when everybody was hoping for a programme, the following words alone were forthcoming: "If culpable machinations were to raise obstacles in the path of my Government, which *I refuse to anticipate*"—the King emphasised these words—"I shall find the strength to overcome them in my determination to preserve the public peace, in the just confidence of the French people and in the love they have always shown for their King."

The Address of the 221.

The Chamber did not allow itself to be impressed, and Royer-Collard himself pronounced in favour of an energetic reply. "We must strike hard and swiftly," he declared; "and not allow time for the folly and ineptitude of a few men to destroy liberty." By 221 votes the Chamber passed an Address in reply to the Speech from the Throne which contained the following passage: "The Charter makes the participation of the country in deliberations concerning the public weal a sacred right. . . . This participation renders it necessary for the political views of the Government always to be in keeping with the will of your people to secure the smooth working of public affairs. Sire, our loyalty and our devotion force us to tell you that this agreement does not exist."

Never had a sovereign crown, not even that of Louis XVI, declared a certain Liberal, received such a challenge; and this lesson in constitutional procedure ended in a perfectly clear conclusion—"Dismiss your Ministers!"

But Charles X would not hear of it. When the deputation

from the Chamber solemnly presented him with the Address, he received it sitting down, and, "with a far from royal gesture, drew from beneath him a paper, which he unfolded." It was a dismissal in due shape and form: "I have announced my decisions. . . . They are unalterable. . . . My Ministers will inform you of my intentions." The *Ultras* applauded: "Behold the royal word at last! Those people did not know what a King was; they know it now; a breath has dispersed them like chaff."

On the 19th of March the Chamber was prorogued by ordinance to shouts of "*Vive le Roi!*" from the Right. The public retorted with "*Vive la Charte!*" and the Right angrily demanded the clearance of the galleries. "The Chamber no longer exists," said Royer-Collard, who was presiding, as he gloomily descended from his seat. On the following 16th of May the Chamber was dissolved and the elections were fixed for the end of June and the beginning of July.

Defeat of the Right.

Charles X was counting upon the Army. At the end of the previous year he had held a grand review on the Plain of Grenelle, and although the acclamations with which he was greeted were far from enthusiastic, his confidence had been increased. When he was told, "The Army will never fail the King for the defence of the throne and the Charter, but if it is a question of restoring the *ancien régime* . . ." he broke in, "The Charter, who wants to violate the Charter? What has the Army in common with the Charter?" If the electors proved seditious he was firmly resolved "not to get into the tumbril," as his brother Louis XVI had done, but to get up on horseback; if the need arose he would dissolve the Chamber again and carry on the Government by means of ordinances.

Nevertheless there were occasions when he contemplated the future with less serenity, and knowing that Metternich was of opinion that a *coup d'état* would prove fatal to the Bourbons, he observed to the representatives of the diplomatic corps, "I know that I am undertaking a difficult struggle. I have the country against me. But tell your masters that my determination is unshakable. I have duties to Heaven."

Meanwhile the Left was preparing for the conflict, combining with the extremist parties and the Republican group, under the leadership of Godefroy Cavaignac, whilst the prophets continued to give utterance to dark forebodings. " We are quietly sinking under sail," said Beugnot; Lamennais, on the contrary, believed there would be disturbances. " The sick man was quietly passing away, and he will perish in convulsions, that is all ! " Foreigners were astonished at the apathy of Polignac, who was endowed with " the fatal obstinacy of the martyr, a species of courage more dangerous than any other," and the Ministry for Foreign Affairs reminded them of the fool's paradise of Milton. " The spirit pervading it is that of the madhouse," remarked the Duc d'Alberg. Villèle looked on helplessly at this collapse of the monarchy, " which is mined and undermined in every direction, so that the smallest spark will blow it all up," and Royer-Collard summed up the general feeling in the words: " An end? Certainly. A loophole of escape? I see none."

Whereupon Charles X made another mistake; he intervened in the electoral campaign by means of a proclamation, and brought his royal person into play instead of remaining above party. But his optimism had become unbounded since he had discovered in his foreign policy a means of counteracting the difficulties he met with at home.

The Right had remained faithful to its bellicose programme, which was to surround the monarchy with a halo of glory to wipe out 1815. Chateaubriand had in mind a grand recasting of Europe, which would give to France the Rhine frontier from Strassburg to Cologne, and Polignac dreamed of the annexation of Belgium; but these hopes proved abortive, and a fresh conquest of territory had to suffice.

Algeria.

Ever since the sixteenth century France had been in possession of settlements on the coast of Algeria called " African concessions," for which rent was paid to the Bey of Algiers. The payment of these dues, as well as the acts of piracy committed by the Barbary natives, provided perpetual causes for conflict, which from 1827 onwards assumed an acrimonious character. The Bey Hussein complained of not having been paid, and demanded the recall of the French Consul Deval, heaping insults upon his head. " Do you take me for a clown, a man of straw, a raggamuffin? It is you who have told the Minister not to write to me. You are a wretch, an infidel, a traitor!" And so saying he struck him with his fly-whisk.

As a result of this action Algiers was blockaded by a French fleet, and the blockade, which was far from being effective, lasted two years. In July 1829 an attempt at reconciliation was made, but Admiral La Bretonnière's ship was bombarded by the guns in Algiers.

Blockade of Algiers.

This amounted to direct provocation, the classic *casus belli*—the violation of the right of nations, piracy, insult to diplomatic agents. Whereupon Polignac considered the possibility of inciting the Pasha of Egypt against Algiers; but he was forced to admit that the enterprise was impracticable, and a French expedition was decided upon.

It failed to arouse popular enthusiasm, for the presence of Bourmont at the head discredited it. The *Ultras*, however, acclaimed it with joy. "We are going to skirmish against the Bey, but the real and glorious war will be when the army comes back."

Nevertheless there was an obstacle in the path in the shape of the opposition of England, who threatened to send a squadron to cruise along the Algerian coast. On this occasion Polignac proved himself a diplomat and a *grand seigneur*; he vouched for the disinterestedness of France and calmly continued the preparations for the expedition. But d'Haussez, the Naval Minister, made matters clearer to the English Ambassador, Lord Stuart de Rothesay. "I have no intention," he told him, "of treating the question diplomatically. You will find the proof of this in what I am going to tell you—France cares not a straw for England."

At the end of May 1830, a fleet of 103 battleships and 350 merchant vessels, under the command of Admiral Duperré, carrying 37,000 soldiers and 27,000 sailors, weighed anchor from Toulon for Algiers. It did not fall in with a single English boat, so convinced were the authorities in London that the expedition was doomed to failure. After the disembarkation at Sidi-Ferruch and the battle of Staouëli, the French artillery proceeded to bombard the Fort l'Empereur, which commands Algiers. Here alone did they meet with serious resistance. The old fortress, dating from the sixteenth century, held out for four days; "through the gaping embrasures and above the ruined merlons, the men serving the guns could be seen falling and others taking their places one after the other." At last, on the 5th of July, 1830, Algiers capitulated; in the Bey's treasury 48 millions were found, the approximate cost of the expedition. The French had lost 415 men all told.

England lodged a protest against the *fait accompli.* But Polignac, although he had the reputation of being an anglophile, replied haughtily, "In the taking of Algiers I had only the dignity of France in mind; in deciding to keep it or return it I shall consult her interests alone."

Capture of Algiers.

Charles X was at the moment uneasy on account of the results of the elections, which had belied all his expectations. Although Polignac had assured him that the mass of the people were concerned only with their own material interests and cared but little about politics, he found the Opposition triumphant with 274 deputies, and almost all the signatories of the Address—the 221 as they were called—again returned. But the capture of Algiers, the news of which was known in Paris on the 9th of July, lent him fresh courage, and he fondly hoped that after this glorious success he was master of the situation, and determined on resistance. He received encouragement from every quarter; when a *Te Deum* in honour of the victory was sung in Notre Dame, the Archbishop of Paris, publicly addressing him, said, "May Your Majesty soon return to give thanks to the Almighty for further wondrous and no less welcome and brilliant achievements!" And the spokesman of a deputation of colliers—a body of men who were Royalist to the backbone—added, "Sire, the collier is master in his own house. See that you are master in yours."

Moreover the financial market showed no signs of alarm, whilst public credit continued to improve. Had not a loan of 80 millions standing at 102 at 4 per cent. been raised at the time of the expedition? There was no need to exaggerate the importance of the elections; the people had confidence in their King and loved him, and the time was ripe for advancing without fear. Rare indeed were the monarchists who thought like Chateaubriand, " This victory delights without reassuring me. Providence can at one stroke enlarge a kingdom and overthrow a dynasty."

And indeed the conquest of Algiers hardly touched the people, who, thanks to Liberal propaganda, were far less concerned about the defeat of the Bey than about the way in which the struggle between the King and the Chamber was going to end. In May Paris had witnessed a sort of renewal of disorder. At an evening party given by the Duc d'Orléans at the Palais Royal the King was a guest; the mob broke into the gardens, set fire to the chairs, shouting, " Down with the aristocrats ! " and applauded the speeches made by extempore orators—all of which gave food for reflection to those who had seen the beginnings of the Revolution of 1789. In the provinces, and particularly in Normandy, repeated acts of incendiarism occurred; there were 178 between the 18th of February and the 7th of July in Calvados and the Manche and Orne districts, burning brands being thrown on thatched roofs and straw ricks by culprits who were never discovered. They were doubtless acts due to " pathological infection," but in the atmosphere of panic that prevailed everybody was inclined to accuse the Ministers.

Renewal of Disorder.

But Polignac remained unperturbed. Guernon-Ranville, one of his colleagues, deplored the fact that the Government had neither plan nor goal; they had certainly recognised the necessity of freeing themselves from the limitations laid down by law, but how? On being questioned about this, Polignac replied, " You are the man who raises difficulties; everything will turn out all right, you'll see. This is a mere surface disturbance which a whiff will disperse. There is nothing to fear; we have taken every precaution." But, it was objected, what about the middle classes who fringe the people? " Bah ! only the obstreperous bourgeois will be touched. The people will not move." And thus the President of the Council marched towards the abyss with the rigidity of a somnambulist—the Holy Virgin, who had just appeared to him, was leading him by the hand and dictating all his plans. " Under such celestial guidance any hesitation would have been criminal."

The Ordinances.

What the plans of Polignac were became known on the 25th of July, 1830. On that date, which fell on a Sunday, at a Cabinet meeting held after Mass, a lengthy report was read aloud proving that by virtue of Article 14 of the Charter, which recognised the right of the Crown "to publish such ordinances as were necessary for the safety of the State," the King had the power, not doubtless to change existing institutions, but to consolidate them. Whereupon five ordinances followed; the first suspended the liberty of the Press; the second announced the dissolution of the Chamber; the third modified the electoral system by reducing the number of representatives and strengthening the powers of the administration; the fourth convoked the electors for the month of September; whilst the fifth contained a list of *Ultras* appointed to hold high office. When the reading was over, the King observed, "The more I think of it the more convinced am I that it is impossible to act otherwise." He seemed agitated, his face was flushed and he breathed quickly. Nevertheless he took the pen and signed the document; the Ministers appending their signatures to his. When they had finished, the King said, "I count upon you, gentlemen, and you may count upon me. Our cause is one. It is a matter of life and death for us."

Polignac again declared that the military forces quartered in Paris were sufficient for the safeguarding of peace, whilst Mangin, the Prefect of Police, wagered his head that he could keep order. Whilst the ordinances were being printed (to the great perturbation of the chief editor of the *Moniteur*, "an old man who had seen the days of the Revolution") the President of the Council set ostensibly to work to prepare the speech which the King would make on the opening of the Chambers.

The secret had been scrupulously guarded. Marmont, to whom in case of trouble the command of the army had been entrusted, and Champagny, the Under-Secretary of State for War, had not been informed, and the Duc d'Angoulême rubbed his hands and said, "Champagny will be very much surprised when he reads the *Moniteur* to-morrow."

This paper appeared on the 26th of July a little later than usual, about ten o'clock. At Saint-Cloud, where the King was in residence, everybody was triumphant; the Duchesse de Berry ran to her father-in-law, and throwing herself at his feet, kissed his hand, exclaiming, "At last you are reigning! My son will owe you his crown!" Charles X kissed her and then mounted his horse; he was going hunting at Rambouillet.

Their Effect upon the People.

In Paris the impression produced was somewhat different. Crowds gathered round the doors of the reading-rooms to learn what the *Moniteur* had to say, for the Prefect of Police had forbidden newspapers to be published without leave. *Le National* retaliated by appearing and advising its readers to refuse payment of taxes; and at the same time Thiers, in the name of forty-four journalists, drew up a protest in which he declared, "The rule of law is at an end, and that of force has begun. . . . Obedience has ceased to be a duty." Nevertheless Paris remained calm; *rentes*, it is true, fell four francs; Talleyrand told his friends "to speculate on a fall, as the opportunity was ripe!" and Chateaubriand, faithful to his rôle of prophet, sighed, "Yet another Government is deliberately throwing itself off the towers of Notre Dame!" But there were no signs of disturbance. Only at about five o'clock, in the neighbourhood of the Palais Royal, did bands of printers and students begin to collect together, shouting "*Vive la Charte!* Down with the Ministers!" Polignac and d'Haussez, who happened to drive past at the moment, were recognised and hooted—the dismissal of the Ministers was all the crowd seemed to demand.

On Tuesday the 27th, the journals of the Left having been published in spite of the Prefect's prohibition, the latter gave orders for their presses to be broken up. But the operation was not performed without difficulty; Baude, one of the editors of the *Temps*, protested, with a copy of the law in his hands, against "this act of burglary," and the only man who consented to carry out the orders of the police was a locksmith whose business it was to rivet the chains of convicts.

Outbreak of Insurrection.

The agitation increased. Bands made up of bourgeois and workers, "the frock-coat cheek by jowl with the blouse," paraded the boulevards; armourers' shops were looted, and the Liberal deputies met at the house of Casimir Périer in order to organise the movement and keep it within legal bounds. Meanwhile Marmont,

Duke of Ragusa, arrived at the Institute, of which he was a member, where he learnt that he had been put in command of the garrison. "This is the most cruel proof I have had of the fatal destiny that dogs my footsteps!" he exclaimed. Like Bourmont, he had once betrayed Napoleon, and did not know how unpopular he was; for the people of Paris "*raguser*" meant to betray, and in appointing Marmont to this post, the King "had dragged the people into the affair."

Nevertheless the Marshal carried out his orders, occupying the boulevards, the Carrousel, the Place Louis XV and the Pont-Neuf with troops. There was no serious resistance; only at about three o'clock a man was killed in the Rue du Lycée, near the Théâtre Français, whilst later on insurgents set fire to the guard-house of the Bourse. Whereupon order was everywhere restored and, with his mind at rest, Marmont sent the troops back to barracks.

Outwardly the night seemed calm, but in the shadows—most of the street lamps had been broken—forms were moving, and there seemed to be a dull rumble of activity in the streets. The printers and the Liberal industrialists had dismissed their staffs, who joined the ranks of the combatants. The members of the National Guard again took up the arms which had not been taken away from them when they were disbanded in 1827; the old Carbonari reappeared and, in conjunction with the Republicans, organised insurrectionary committees; the paving-stones of the streets were torn up and barricades erected. When day dawned the people were ready. Shouts of "Down with the Bourbons!" had taken the place of "Down with the Ministers!" The disturbances, as Marmont wrote to Saint-Cloud, were assuming the appearance of a revolution.

With one rush the mob seized the Hôtel de Ville and Notre Dame, above both of which the tricolour was soon floating, and captured the guard-houses, the powder magazines and the arsenals; the fire-drums beat, the tocsin sounded; on the boulevards, the tradespeople, moved partly by self-interest and partly "by patriotism," occupied themselves with cutting down the trees which unfortunately obstructed "the showing of their wares" and which, when thrown across the road, made excellent barricades. Whereupon Marmont made three of his columns advance, one on the Hôtel de Ville, another in the direction of the Bastille and the Faubourg Saint-Antoine, and the third on to the quays; and the battle was fought "under a sky white with heat in which a fiery sun was floating."

The tactics of the insurgents were as follows—a large group advanced against the regular forces, behind the barricade, and opened fire; the soldiers replied, whereupon one section of the insurgents held their ground, whilst another rushed to the doors of the houses, and running upstairs shot on the troops from the windows, pelted them with stones and threw down pieces of furniture upon them. As soon as the column had passed on, the insurgents came down again, and after again setting up the barricade which the soldiers had destroyed and posting a few men to guard it, went by side streets to rejoin their main body.

The soldiers were tired out; they had been fighting since seven o'clock in the morning in tropical heat, averaging 95 degrees, borne down by the weight of their arms and equipment, with nothing to eat or drink; for in its ineptitude the Government had foreseen nothing, and the military bakeries were in the hands of the insurgents. The enthusiasm of the latter, on the other hand, steadily increased; they seemed to be acting in obedience to some strange secret word of command. It is true that they shouted "*Vive la Charte!*", but he whom they acclaimed was above all the Black Prince, "the mysterious prince of darkness" who appealed to their imagination; and for this prince, who, unknown though he was, satisfied their vague instinct for poetry, they fought without ceasing, melting down lead pipes from the houses for bullets, and with their pockets full of cartridges, returning to the thick of the fight.

They were guilty of no excesses; wine and brandy were forbidden, and the order was scrupulously obeyed; they drank only liquorice water, or "coco" as it is called. Their discipline was perfect; anyone in a black coat or in uniform took precedence of the man in a smock, and a pupil at the *Polytechnique* would find himself addressed as "*Mon petit général!*" There was an ingenuousness, a simple courage and a modesty born of inexperience in all this, which no subsequent revolution was destined to see.

By five o'clock in the evening Marmont had recaptured the Hôtel de Ville, but almost the whole of Paris was in the hands of the insurgents, and the Marshal received orders to concentrate his troops, who were utterly exhausted, between the Tuileries, the Place Vendôme and the Place des Victoires.

Retreat of Marmont.

Polignac continued to live in the clouds, "his elbow resting on his ministerial portfolio as though it were a litter." The Holy Virgin had again appeared to him and encouraged him to persevere. "Pray reassure His Excellency," he said to a messenger from a foreign Ambassador who had asked him for a safe-conduct, "it is nothing. In two hours it will all be over." When it was suggested to him that the military bakeries ought to be recaptured in order that the troops might be fed, he replied, "You are an alarmist; when the time has come for action, four men and a corporal will be enough." At the same time he was sending perfectly calm and reassuring despatches to the King.

The latter, who had remained at Saint-Cloud, gave his own explanation of the situation: "The people of Paris are in the throes of anarchy. And anarchy will bring them back to my feet. If they lay down their arms they can count upon the most generous pardon." The usual routine of life in the castle was not changed; during the course of the day the Royal Family met once more round the whist table, and sat down to play at the usual hour, and when through the open window the roar of the guns could be heard, Charles X merely flicked the tablecloth as though he wanted to remove a speck of dust.

Charles X at Saint-Cloud.

The journalists, the staff of the *Globe*, and the Liberal deputies formed no clearer view of the situation. Thiers, who was not a man to run risks, spent the day in the country, whilst at Casimir Périer's loyalty to the King was still the ruling thought. But the course of events, and the entry of the people and the Republicans into the lists, left the petty prudence of the bourgeois lagging far behind. Périer was the first to see this. "After the start the people have just made," he said, "we shall be disgraced if we do not make common cause with them." It was no longer a question of dismissing the Ministers—La Fayette was demanding the appointment of a provisional Government.

About eleven o'clock at night the tocsin ceased to ring and the firing stopped. There was not a breath of air, "the heat was paralysing," whilst here and there burning buildings cast red reflections in the sky. A solemn silence reigned.

Marmont felt confident of being able to hold out for a fortnight in the Tuileries; and in the courtyard of the palace, Monsieur d'Autichamps, the aged Captain of the Guard, sitting crippled in an arm-chair, urged his men on to the fight. On the morning of the 29th of July, the insurgents opened the attack, this time under the command of the Republicans—Cavaignac, Bastide and Joubert. A child climbed on to the colonnade of the Louvre by means of a box and showed itself to the soldiers, who immediately jumped to the conclusion that the mob had invaded the palace. A general panic ensued. Marmont's army fled in disorder towards the Champs Élysées; the tricolour was planted on the Pavillon de l'Horloge and two line regiments went over to the side of the insurgents.

Capture of the Tuileries.

On the left bank of the Seine the rebellion met with equal success; bands of insurgents marched past waving black or tricoloured flags, "covered with inflammatory inscriptions." They were no longer the combatants of the previous day; the prisons had been forced open and looting began.

The Liberals had met to discuss the situation at the house of deputy Laffitte. Suddenly the sound of firing could be heard. "The royal guards are marching on us!" a voice exclaimed. Whereupon they all took to their heels, leaving Laffitte, who was laid up with gout, all alone. But it was a false alarm. The discussion was resumed. In face of the success of the revolution there was but one alternative open to them—to make common cause with the insurgents. A municipal council of five members to sit at the Hôtel de Ville was appointed, and La Fayette, "*le drapeau La Fayette*," was put in command of the National Guard.

Meanwhile Marmont arrived in hot haste at Saint-Cloud. "Sire," he exclaimed, "the battle is lost. I failed to hold my own in Paris. A bullet aimed at me killed an officer's horse close by. I only wish it had pierced my skull." Everybody crowded round the King, who refused to dismiss Polignac; they fell on their knees before him, pointing out the dangers to which the Duchesse d'Angoulême, who was some distance out of Paris, was exposed. The Council met and decided to rescind the ordinances and make certain changes in the Cabinet; and the Duc de Mortemart, who had the reputation of being a Liberal, took the place of Polignac. Three messengers conveyed the news to Paris. "And here I am in the same position as my unfortunate brother in 1792!" sighed Charles X. But gradually he became calmer, and assured the Duchesse de Berry that in twenty-four hours everything would have been settled.

He still clung to his illusions. But it was too late. The King's envoys were not admitted to the Hôtel de Ville; at the Palais Bourbon the deputies declared that, before coming to any decision regarding their attitude, they would await the arrival of the Duc de Mortemart; but the latter failed to appear. Moreover, what could be the use of these eleventh-hour negotiations? After the three days that had just elapsed any attempt at reconciliation between Paris and the Royal Family was out of the question. Talleyrand, when he saw the troops fleeing through the Tuileries, had already observed to his secretary, "At five minutes past twelve to-day the elder branch of the House of Bourbon ceased to reign."

Charles X flees to Versailles.

At Saint-Cloud confusion reigned. The Duc d'Angoulême, who had been appointed Commander-in-Chief, came to words with Marmont, and in trying to snatch his sword from him wounded himself in the hand. "Monseigneur," cried the Marshal, "you can shoot a man like me, but you may not lay hands on me." This set the tone. The King in the end decided to move the Court to Versailles, and ordered his Ministers to see to their safety. "Our cause," he said, "is the cause of God. The Almighty is putting His servants to the test." Then he added, "Nothing is yet lost to our House. I am going to fight with one hand and carry on the Government with the other."

There were at this moment three different authorities in Paris—the Chamber, which, although it had been dissolved, had worked for the revolution, and considered itself called upon to rule through the medium of the 221; the municipal Commission of the Hôtel de Ville, which had been invested with executive powers; and lastly La Fayette, " who had got astride his eternal gee-gee—a white horse bedecked with the tricolour," and seemed to be the lord of the moment. Between these three Thiers manœuvred skilfully, and brought forward the candidature of a prince about whom the majority seemed not to be troubling their heads.

The Duc d'Orléans.

The Duc d'Orléans had a revolutionary past. His father, one of the regicides, had died on the scaffold; he himself had fought at Jemmapes and had ever since carefully abstained from compromising himself in any way with the *Ultras*; and it is well known that Louis XVIII stood in fear of his underhand machinations. The Palais Royal, where he lived, served as a rendezvous for the opponents of the elder branch—men of letters, courtesans and artists who had incurred the displeasure of the Tuileries. He was popular with the bourgeoisie on account of his affable manners, and had his sons educated at an ordinary school. " They are the first," observed Courier, " to have been educated in this way since schools and princes have been in existence." In short, he enjoyed a certain reputation in a limited circle, affected airs of unimpeachable loyalty, and scouted the idea of becoming Regent. " Never," he declared, " shall I be another Philippe d'Orléans to a second Louis XV."

But on the morning of the 30th of July passers-by stopped in front of placards posted on the walls, bearing the name of the Duc d'Orléans in every line, apparently with the object of impressing his merits on the minds of the people. The latter seemed but little moved, however. " What dangers has this prince run? What was he doing yesterday and the day before? He should be either on the King's side or on ours." But Thiers and his friends were clever enough to circumvent La Fayette. " Will you take upon your own shoulders the responsibility of establishing a republic? " they demanded. Whereupon La Fayette, who two days previously had been anxious with the help of the tricoloured flag " to produce a revolution and not a revolt," was overcome by fear. He hesitated. He knew that in the Hôtel de Ville Cavaignac and others were discussing the convocation of a constituent assembly, he saw a Jacobin Government already looming on the horizon; the accession of a member of the House of Orleans who would give guarantees to the people was perhaps the most satisfactory solution of the crisis, and the best suited to France. He gave way.

Thiers at once hastened to Neuilly, the summer residence of the Duc d'Orléans, where he experienced no difficulty in winning over Madame Adelaide, the latter's sister. But Louis-Philippe himself could not make up his mind. Was it safe to run the risk? At last, on the evening of July 30th, he came to a decision, and dressed in ordinary civilian clothes, and accompanied by two aides-de-camp, he entered Paris by the Barrière de l'Etoile. Gloom and depression reigned in the city; only a few solitary candles flickered in the windows, there were barricades every sixty yards; now and again a funeral procession wound slowly by, or a mounted messenger bearing orders galloped past; it might have been the day after an assault. But near the Palais Royal the people were keeping watch about their bivouacs, and these men, most of whom had fought for the Republic, got out of the way in order to allow the unknown citizen, who had come to raise the fallen monarchy from the dust, to pass by.

Louis-Philippe Lieutenant-General.

On the following day, escorted by the Orleanist deputies who had just nominated him Lieutenant-General of the Kingdom, Louis-Philippe went to receive the popular confirmation of his appointment at the Hôtel de Ville. But the enthusiasm, which at first was half-hearted, gradually turned to hostility, for the proclamation of the Lieutenant-General in which he declared that "the Charter would henceforward be a reality," did not satisfy everybody. The Charter? Something more than the Charter was wanted after the bloodshed that had occurred. Then suddenly at one of the windows of the Hôtel de Ville, Louis-Philippe appeared, holding a tricoloured flag, and he kissed La Fayette. Thereupon a tremendous ovation greeted him; the sight of those colours, scorned for fifteen years, and now once more raised to honour, that reminder of the glories of the Empire which wiped out the humiliations that had been endured, "that republican kiss" bestowed on the hero of two worlds—for thus they persisted in calling La Fayette—cemented the union at one stroke. Thanks to the skill of Thiers and the marvellous piece of staging of which demagogues possess the secret, Louis-Philippe conquered both the Legitimists and the Republicans.

Charles X remained to be dealt with. He had left the Trianon for Rambouillet, and as soon as he heard of the turn of events in Paris, he tried to forestall circumstances by nominating "his cousin" of Orleans Lieutenant-General, and sending in the abdication of both himself and his son, the Duc d'Angoulême, with instructions that the Lieutenant-General was to proclaim the Duc de Bordeaux, the son of the Duchesse de Berry, King of France, with the title of Henry V. Louis-Philippe, who had been duly installed at the Hôtel de Ville, took no notice of all this. He held his authority from the Chamber, and not from the King, and wrote to the latter informing him that his letter of abdication would be deposited with the Chamber of Peers, and advising him in all friendliness to make good his escape; measures would be taken to protect him on his flight.

Charles X at Rambouillet.

But Charles X was apparently determined not to take flight until his grandson had been proclaimed King. Whereupon it was decided to frighten him. On the 3rd of August an undisciplined band, armed with guns, halberds and swords, with vehicles of all kinds dragging along in their train, made for Rambouillet. It was a procession very similar to that which in October 1789 had set out for Versailles; it had a similar object in view and adopted similar methods. Charles X still had 8000 men and forty-two guns. He was in a position to put up a good defence, and those who were nominally in command of the people's militia were not altogether free from anxiety. "At the first round of grape-shot, they will take to their heels," declared Colonel Jacqueminot.

But the commissioners sent by Louis-Philippe succeeded in persuading the King that, if he wanted to hasten on the proclamation of Henry V, his wisest plan would be to quit Rambouillet—for a large and angry mob was advancing against him. Charles X gave orders for departure; he was counting on the intervention of the diplomatic corps, but they did not raise a finger—England was having her revenge for the Algerian expedition.

Flight of Charles X.

By short stages the royal train made its way to Cherbourg.

It was a sorry exodus, in carriages with the coat of arms obliterated and guarded by men appointed by the new Government. The Duchesse d'Angoulême, who had just rejoined her family, sat still and silent, the tragedies she had already survived passing once again before her eyes—the Revolution, exile, the return, the flight during the Hundred Days, and exile again. The Duchesse de Berry, on the other hand, was feverish and excited, talking of resistance and a new Vendée. As for the King, he was still majestic, observing the strictest etiquette, even in the humblest village. The bodyguard surrendered their colours, and in sepulchral silence Charles X embarked with his family on an American vessel belonging to the Bonapartes which was sailing for England.

The Charter Revised.

Meanwhile in Paris all the talk was of guarantees, the drawing up of a new Charter, or the revision of the old one. "The monarchy holds the Chamber, the usurpation the Palais Royal, and the Republic the Hôtel de Ville," observed Chateaubriand. But in order to secure the support of the various parties, the victorious usurpation was obliged to make concessions. By what right was Louis-Philippe to ascend the throne? What were to be his relations with the elected representatives? After prolonged discussions, in which the framers of constitutions gave themselves free rein, the following decision was reached—the people were to call upon the Duc d'Orléans to rule over them, which meant that the legitimate line had been broken, and right divine replaced by right by contract; the new King was to take the name of Louis-Philippe I and not Philippe VII, which would have been a vexatious reminder of the old connection. The Charter was to be kept, but it was to be revised. The preamble to it was done away with; it was no longer to be a benevolent concession of a constitution on the part of the King; it was the people who were once again resuming the sovereignty. Article 14, on which Charles X had based his ordinances, was modified, the censorship abolished once and for all, and the initiative in legislation vested in the Chambers and the King alike. Such was the arrangement which obtained the sanction of the Parliament; "219 deputies, who in ordinary circumstances would have

Louis-Philippe King of the French.

constituted a majority of only two, modified the Constitution, announced the downfall of one dynasty and set up another in its place."

On the 9th of August, 1830, before a joint sitting of the Chambers, the Lieutenant-General swore to observe the new Charter, and surrounded by the same marshals who five years previously had witnessed the coronation of Charles X at Rheims, he was acclaimed King of the French.

The majority of those who had remained faithful to the fallen King held their tongues; the *Ultras* seemed to have vanished into thin air. Meanwhile, in the Chamber of Peers, Chateaubriand rendered one last tribute to the legitimate line: "After all I have done, said and written on behalf of the Bourbons, I should be the most despicable of wretches were I to deny them, at the moment when for the third and last time they are treading the path of exile"; and in terms of magnificent oratory he tore the policy of Polignac to bits, "that palace terror organised by eunuchs, which was expected to take the place of the republican terror and the iron yoke of the Empire," whereupon he lauded the courage of the people, those shopkeepers who sniffed powder with gusto, and ended by tolling the knell of the Restoration: "The idolatory of a name has been abolished; Monarchy is no longer a religion."

Paris had carried out the revolution single-handed, believing that Waterloo was being avenged in the streets of the capital and proud of driving out a dynasty that had been restored by the hand of the foreigner. The provinces did not stir. "We despatched our revolution to the departments by coach," wrote a contemporary; "they only had to acknowledge the receipt." It thus became clear to all how small a place the Bourbons held in the affections of the people, and the triumphant bourgeoisie were able to cast aside the mask. "We have been play-acting for fifteen years," wrote the *Globe* in the month of August 1831; "there have been conspiracies, either active or passive, to overthrow the throne of the Bourbons, and the conspirators time and again swore the oath of fidelity to Louis XVIII and Charles X, some in their capacity as soldiers, others as deputies, lawyers or officials." The ardent band of youth which had been responsible for the circulation of so many new ideas, and which, a few years previously, had felt itself uplifted by "the great hope based on human reason," saw its dreams realised in the accession of the Duc d'Orléans, in the quasi-legitimacy of his dynasty, and in "a throne surrounded by republican institutions." Some among them, however, regarded the solution as paltry; mounted on the height, they had hoped to perceive a grand and consoling spectacle, but all they saw beneath their eyes was a sort of "plain already deep in mud into which the Liberal hordes were rushing."

Thus ended the programme of revolution inaugurated by the rich bourgeoisie, which was realised and surpassed by the people, by the nameless masses. The insurrection had no recognised leader; Dubourg, a retired colonel, had to be decked out in General's uniform in order to represent authority; and who was the man who on the 28th of July had the inspiration to plant the tricolour on the tower of Notre Dame? Indeed, the disturbances of 1820, after Louvel's crime, had been better organised. The Republicans who, on the second day, placed themselves at the head of the movement, derived no advantage from their action; they were caught unprepared, whilst the Orleanists had a programme, and a scheme of Government ready to hand. Cavaignac confessed as much: "We only gave way because we were not strong enough. It was too difficult to make the people who had fought to the cry of *Vive la Charte!* understand that their first act should have been to arm themselves for its destruction. Later on it will be different."

In short, the Republican Party regarded it as a historical fact that the bourgeoisie had "juggled away the revolution" for their own benefit, and they were frankly hostile to the new system. In vain did Louis-Philippe endeavour to win them over by giving their leaders every assurance—their hostility persisted. Soon it was to be transformed into hatred.

The Work of the Restoration.

The Restoration was a period of originality and power; there was a clash of ideas and doctrines; the old world that was striving to return to life was opposed by a new world fighting for breathing-space—it was a time when cause for conflict lay ever latent and sometimes became acute. Ardent spirits met in conflict and allowed themselves free play in a fresh atmosphere; this frankness of outlook, this confidence and youth, not to mention this ingenuousness of mind, were never to be seen again.

From the political point of view the Restoration was the golden age of parliamentarism; people believed in the virtue of systems, in the value of reason, in the power of order, and it was not regarded as a duty to despise the enemy. After a few timid attempts the struggle was loyally entered upon and supported by military tribunes, like Foy, political philosophers like Royer-Collard and Benjamin Constant, and statesmen animated by deep convictions like de Serre and Richelieu. The efficacy of back-stair intrigues and underhand machinations, to which some had already had recourse, had not as yet become a dogma.

Never since the seventeenth century had the administration of France been better; honesty was almost universal, there were no scandalous trials, no corruption or embezzlement. The financial situation on the eve of 1830 was still excellent, for the methods of Villèle and his prudent foresight had borne fruit.

But it was above all in the domain of thought that the Restoration gave evidence of greatness. Under the Empire but little was written; under the Restoration much was written and there was much to be said. The appellation of man of letters, poet, historian, philosopher and even of controversialist was always honourable and the end to be attained a lofty one. There was inexperience, it is true, and occasionally an assurance that raises a smile, but which at least had the merit of originality; the tone was firm and full of energy, the outcome of sincere and lively conviction. This was true even of the newspapers; *le Conservateur* of Chateaubriand, *la Minerve* of Benjamin Constant, and the *Globe*, though differing widely in origin and tendency, were united by a common and disinterested pursuit of truth, and desire for the improvement of morals and the perfecting of the human spirit.

Conquered and exhausted in 1815, humbled in the sphere of diplomacy and suffering for her past greatness, which had brought down upon her head the jealousy and hatred of the foreigner, France found her feet again under the Restoration; she reorganised her forces and recovered her self-confidence. She freed herself from her tutelage to the Holy Alliance; peace reigned, but it was not a servile peace; Algiers was conquered freely and deliberately in spite of and against the wishes of England.

The glory of having nursed and facilitated this French renaissance is due to Louis XVIII. With his subtle intellect and his rigid good sense, he understood that the safest policy, and the one most profitable both to the monarchy and to his subjects, was that very system of moderation which exasperated the *Ultras*.

Charles X, on the other hand, a slave to cliques, narrow-minded and chivalrous, but " utterly lacking in energy, even the energy of fanaticism, with nothing great about him, not even his pride," believed that he owed it to himself to misunderstand the new France, and without a thought for established rights and habits of liberty, to bring her back by devious ways beneath the yoke of some sort of absolutism. The word Restoration meant for him a return to the *ancien régime*. Feeling that public opinion was against him, he became evasive and opposed his own Ministers—a course which Louis XVIII had never adopted—and allowing himself to be dragged into a policy of adventure, he attempted a *coup de force* which was badly conceived and badly carried out, and which resulted in the immediate fall of himself and of his dynasty. And it was Polignac who was the man of destiny.

BIBLIOGRAPHY.—D'Andigné, *Mémoires* (2 vols., 1900–1901) (Vol. II). Th. Anne, *Mémoires sur l'Intérieur du Palais de Charles X* (2 vols., 1831). *Journal de Saint Cloud à Cherbourg* (1830). J. B. Barrès, *Souvenirs d'un Officier de la Grande Armée* (pub. by Maurice Barrès) (1923). Odilon Barrot, *Mémoires* (4 vols., 1875–76) (Vol. I). S. Bérard, *Souvenirs Historiques de la Révolution de* 1830 (1834). Comtesse de Boigne, *Mémoires* (new ed.) (5 vols., 1922–24). E. Daudet, *Le Ministère de M. de Martignac* (1875). Dayot, *Journées Révolutionnaires*, 1830–1848 (no date). Duchesse de Dino, *Chronique* (Vol. I) (1909). Gautherot, *Un Gentilhomme de Grand Chemin. Le Maréchal de Bourmont* (1926). Hugo, *Choses Vues* (1888); *Choses Vues* (New Series) (1900). La Cour-Gayet, *La Duchesse de Dino* (Revue de Paris, Dec. 1922). Marmont, *Mémoires* (8 vols., 1856). Mazad, *Mémoires pour Servir à l'Histoire de la Révolution de* 1830 (1832). Montalivet, *Fragments et Souvenirs* (2 vols., 1899) (Vol. I). de Rumigny, *Souvenirs* (1921). de Saint-Chamans, *Mémoires* (1896). Sainte-Beuve, *Causeries du Lundi* (no date) (Vol. VI., art. on Marmont). de Salaberry, *Souvenirs Politiques sur la Restauration* (2 vols., 1900). Vaulabelle, *Histoire des Deux Restaurations* (ed. cit. Vol. VIII).

THE JULY MONARCHY

CHAPTER I

THE BEGINNINGS OF A DYNASTY

Character of Louis-Philippe. He temporises whilst awaiting an opportunity for the establishment of personal rule. Attitude of the bourgeoisie towards him: the King-citizen and the citizen-King. The fundamental laws regarding elections and the National Guard. The intellectual and political opposition; the riot of ideas. The parties. The Legitimists: Berryer. The Republicans: Armand Carrel. Republican Bonapartism. The party of resistance and the party of progress. La Fayette and Laffitte. Trial of the Ministers of Charles X; the march on Vincennes; the removal of the accused; their condemnation. Resignation of La Fayette. Looting of Saint-Germain-l'Auxerrois and of the Archbishop's Palace. Foreign affairs: the Case of Belgium. The King keeps the peace. The insurrection of Poland. Fall of Laffitte.

Louis-Philippe.

IN 1830 the King of the French was fifty-seven years of age. Matured by exile, as Louis XVIII had been, endowed with extremely sound common sense, he had seen poverty face to face, and in the course of his various peregrinations in Europe and America had learnt to know human nature. In him there came to light again "the pupil of Madame de Genlis (who had guided his boyhood's days on entirely realistic lines), the secretary of the Jacobins' Club, the general of the Republican armies and the prince of the blood of Louis XIV." Life had made him a sovereign of somewhat complex character.

He had kept a very lively recollection of the Revolution of 1789, and knew every detail of its history. Hugo relates how on one occasion "he corrected from memory the whole of the letter A in the alphabetical list of the members of the Constituent Assembly." The Republic terrified him not only on account of its excesses, but also by reason of the lamentable notoriety it had bestowed upon Philippe-Égalité, his father, who had voted for the death of Louis XVI; and he regarded this form of government with the holy horror that certain Asiatic tribes feel for the devil, "as a malevolent being who must be flattered and treated with consideration, but never opposed."

His habits were above reproach and simple in the extreme. Rising early, he used to light his own fire in the winter, and shave himself at the same time as he received his aides-de-camp; whereupon, after a frugal breakfast—the only form of food of which he was really fond was soup—he settled down to work. This had been his routine when as a poor exile at Reichenau he had given drawing lessons in order to earn a livelihood.

Out of doors he did not show himself with all the pomp and ceremony of his predecessors. He wore a grey hat, "which presented a happy contrast to the white plumed hat which Charles X never laid aside, even when he was hunting," and carried the large "sentimental umbrella" which Heinrich Heine the poet and Henry Monnier the caricaturist each immortalised in his own way. He used to walk on foot through the mud, bowing affably to the passers-by, which made him popular with the bourgeoisie, who saw themselves reflected in him—he was their man.

Like them, he looked carefully after his own concerns and the management of his fortune; he took legal advice only as a matter of form, and if a lawsuit were pending he would hand over to Maître Dupin a regular brief which filled the lawyer with astonishment. He lived a family life, surrounded by his daughters and his five sons, "young men whose equals were rarely to be met, and who as princes had not their like on earth." In short, he seemed to possess all the qualities of the victorious class—domestic virtue, thrift and urbanity. The pomp and show of the old monarchy had had its day; bourgeois monarchy had made its entry upon the scene of history.

But although Louis-Philippe had lost or abandoned the habits usually associated with royalty, he remained nevertheless a prince of the blood. Thanks to his upbringing, he believed himself better fitted than anyone else to discover an ingenious unravelment of the threads of European politics, and doubting neither his capacity nor his intelligence, would allow nothing to stand in the way of his decisions. When one of his Ministers expressed astonishment at the fact that he read only foreign newspapers and never a French journal, he replied, " I know what is happening better than the journalists." In his heart of hearts, he felt he possessed the gifts required by a statesman, and would have liked to govern by himself; but his wisdom, his appreciation of the circumstances of the case, and that somewhat machiavellian prudence which he had acquired during his years of obscurity, prevented him from revealing all he thought. When he heard of the publication of the ordinances of Charles X, his sons heard him mutter, " They will get themselves driven into exile ! Oh, well, for my own part I have already been in exile twice. I am tired of it; I shall remain in France." And it was in this conciliatory frame of mind, adopting the attitude of a prince who intended to respect the Charter and defend law and order, that he presented himself at the Hôtel de Ville and accepted the formula : " A throne surrounded by republican institutions." Thus Louis-Philippe had a very definite aim, which was to guide the policy of the country personally. But in 1830 any such pretension was out of the question; it was necessary to temporise, to consent for the time being to be merely the first citizen of France, and above all not to allow that sympathy and that recent popularity which had brought him into power to wane.

His Aim.

Unlike the mob who had fought in the streets, the bourgeois of 1830 did not regard the revolution as just retribution for the treaties of 1815. Historians like Guizot and Augustin Thierry persisted in pointing out to him that French history in the past had really been nothing else than a slow advance of the middle classes towards securing the reins of government, and that the process was now complete. This simplistic philosophy satisfied and flattered him. From that time forward the bourgeois of July made up his mind " to take his place in the new monarchy as though it were his own fief," and presented himself at the Palais Royal not as a subject—this word, once tactlessly uttered by one of his Ministers, was met with horror

—but as a citizen-King paying his respects to the King-citizen. It now became apparent how in every democracy "officialdom takes the place of aristocracy"; there was a general rush, a stampede of applicants for office, a regular scramble, making Paris a sink of iniquity which Auguste Barbier, in a moment of genial scorn, has described for us:

The Citizen-King.

> "Où chacun cherche à déchirer
> Un misérable coin des guenilles sanglantes
> Du pouvoir qui vient d'expirer."[1]

Few and far between were such men as Baron Louis, Minister of Finance, who replied to the crowd that thronged the ante-chambers, "What do you want of me? Your advice? I have no use for it. Denunciations? I do not listen to them. Posts? I have only one at your disposal—and that is my own. Take it if you like." Louis-Philippe was inclined to be more circumspect. He had a naturally amiable disposition, he expressed himself good-naturedly and inspired confidence; and those who approached him found him "plain and outspoken," kingly, no doubt, but not awe-inspiring. In his person the monarchy descended from its lofty and isolated heights.

Queen Marie-Amélie, an Italian princess of consummate dignity who was universally respected, had not desired her husband's accession to the throne. Guided by a sure instinct, she had foreseen the dangers, but she acquiesced in the accomplished fact and did all in her power to support the King, for whom she had a deep affection and whom she regarded as the most honest man in France. In her salon she received the wives of "the officers of the citizen militia" and did her embroidery in their company. Meanwhile Louis-Philippe held a review of the legions of the National Guard, "the husbands of these ladies," and addressing them as "his dear friends," said that he was happy to find himself in their midst.

The Queen.

From Paris, from the suburbs and from the provinces, deputations hastened to pay their respects to him; he had a kindly word for all of them, and his abundant good humour delighted

[1] . . . "where everybody is trying to tear off a miserable shred from the bloodstained rags of the power that has just died."

these worthy people. But his life became extremely arduous —it was one continual parade. In the evening the loafers crowding round the railings of the Palais made themselves hoarse with shouts of "The King! The King!" and Louis-Philippe was obliged to appear on the balcony and sing the *Marseillaise* with the crowd, beating time with hands and feet. What would Charles X have thought of such a spectacle? His opinion might have been expressed in the words of a certain deputy—a commoner, be it said—who observed to a lady, "Really, one cannot dine with the King any longer; he keeps such bad company."

One of the Court officials asserted that Louis-Philippe detested "this revolutionary, democratic and bourgeois coarseness and brutality, which constituted the penance of the first years of his reign." And this is highly probable. But was it possible for him to refuse to flatter the bourgeosie, or make no attempt to win the people over to him? Doubtless he would have preferred to ascend the throne gently raised upon the wings of right divine, but Fate had decreed otherwise; his royal house was founded upon those barricades which he had broken through, while he was yet unknown, during the night of the 30th of July.

Two Fundamental Laws.

In order to secure for the new monarchy a solid support which would never be found lacking, it was necessary to give the possessing classes an interest in its stability and prosperity. It was with this object in view that the two fundamental laws of the reign of Louis-Philippe were promulgated—the electoral law and the law concerning the National Guard (March to April 1831). By the former the assessment for deputies was lowered from 1000 to 500 francs, that of electors from 300 to 200 francs, and in the case of certain citizens, such as members of the *Institut* and officers on half pay, it was only 100 francs. Thus the number of electors was increased to about 190,000 out of a population of 32½ million males, the figure returned by the census of 1831. By this the bourgeoisie proved that they had no intention of allowing their political rights to be infringed by means of imprudent concessions; their class remained, as it had been under the Restoration, the only one represented in Parliament, and Louis Blanc was able truthfully to declare that "the criterion of the country *qua* electorate is money."

The National Guard, which Charles X had disbanded, was reorganised upon a new basis. Charged with the task of defending the sovereignty of the Charter and of safeguarding or restoring public peace and order, it was henceforward to consist of every Frenchman between the age of twenty and sixty. The legions appointed their own officers, with the exception of those of the highest ranks, who were still nominated by the King. But only those citizens who paid direct taxes were forced to serve in its ranks, and the necessity of paying for their own equipment effectually excluded working men, so that in this instance also the bourgeoisie maintained their prerogatives; political power was secured to them by means of the electoral law, and material power through the instrumentality of the National Guard. But even before these laws were passed the party of law and order was put to the test.

The National Guard.

On one occasion, in replying to a deputation from the provinces, Louis-Philippe declared, "As for domestic policy, it will be our endeavour to observe a *golden mean*." These words met with astounding success; they became as it were the motto of the new *régime*, the symbol of the "system." Some regarded them as the most appropriate expression of the best of Governments, others as an act of treachery, an abdication of the great principles for which they had fought. And indeed it was in the interpretation of the July revolution that opinions differed.

The Golden Mean.

The old Liberals, those who had risen up against Charles X and the ordinances, flattered themselves on having secured the triumph of law and order. That was all they wanted. "There has been no revolution," said Casimir Périer, "there has merely been a change in the person of the head of the State." But in the ranks of the advanced Liberals and the Republicans, and among the intellectuals, this prudent and extremely limited interpretation was not accepted. Only the former editors of the *Globe*, and those who had found a place in the new *régime*, "those who were satisfied," whether they were historians like Guizot, or,

The Opposition.

like Cousin, philosophers of a kind, preached a return to order and a mild respect for the liberties that had been won. The majority wanted something more; still irritated by the recent struggles, they indulged in dreams of the future which in loftiness and splendour surpassed all previous conceptions—the physical upheaval was followed by an upheaval in the realm of thought.

Revolutionary Romanticism.

Romanticism, which had been Liberal, now turned revolutionary. It became the fashion to exalt all that was low, ugly and deformed, to denounce the iniquity of the "*fait social*"—which Stendhal was destined to accomplish with forceful irony. In *Notre Dame de Paris* (1831), which met with phenomenal success, the sympathetic part was allotted to the monster and the Bohemian woman; the nobleman and the priest were, in comparison with them, merely objects inspiring contempt and horror. All unconsciously art became impregnated by democratic ideas. The sufferings of the people, the vengeance of the destitute, indignation at the inequality between the classes, at the privileges of rank and fortune, at the inadequacy of the bourgeois philosophy of life, were soon to become the ordinary themes of the novel and the drama.

Lamennais.

Among the Catholics who surrounded Lamennais the ferment was just as great. The author of the *Essai sur l'indifférence* openly went over to the side of democracy and prayed for the advent of a republic based upon religion. In his opinion the union between Christianity and liberty would bring about the transformation of the world. In the month of April 1830, with the help of Montalembert, the son of a peer of the realm, and of Lacordaire, "a young man with refined features, and sparkling black eyes, bearing the stamp of purity and manliness of soul," Lamennais founded *l'Avenir*, the motto of which was "God and Liberty." The paper lived up to its motto, and in the ardour of its democratic aspirations almost went beyond the programme of the Republicans. It was no longer merely a question of bringing about the separation between the Church and the State and the abolition of the grant for public worship; there was to be freedom of association, freedom of the Press and of education, the extension of the right of suffrage, including universal suffrage. From the little smoky house, number 20 Rue Jacob, in which the offices of the paper were situated, Lacordaire, supported by a lively faith and the enthusiasm of youth, launched his appeals to the faithful, to the people. "Catholics!" he exclaimed, "behold what the millions of the State are costing you—freedom of conscience!" He announced the advent of a new state of affairs; Kings were to be swept away, their day was done; it was for the Pope and the clergy to place themselves at the head of the popular movement in order to lead and purify it!

These theories were put into practice. The editors of *l'Avenir* founded local societies, and in order to force the authorities to settle the question regarding freedom of education, they opened a school in the Rue des Beaux Arts. The teacher was Lacordaire, helped by Montalembert. "Though we are few in number," said the former, "let us remember that but few are required for the winning of liberty—the heads of three children will suffice if courage be added unto them." The police closed the school and the Government took proceedings, which were solemnly conducted before the Court of Peers, of which Montalembert had become a member, and the founders were condemned. No matter! The question had been put. And thus the loftiest minds felt themselves drawn by a natural and impetuous desire towards democracy; and the bourgeoisie, who wanted nothing better than the maintenance of the new order of things, found themselves confronted by an opposition at once intellectual and political. How, in these circumstances, were the parties to be classified?

The Legitimists.

Ever since the July Revolution the Legitimists seemed to have disappeared. Chateaubriand, after his final confession of faith, had retired into his tent; nobody had taken his place, and the aristocracy of the Restoration, entrenched in the Faubourg Saint Germain, turned a deaf ear to the advances of the Palais Royal. There was one man, however, who tried to bring this vanquished party back to life.

Berryer was an orator of the first rank; with his handsome head, his broad shoulders, at once "gentle and strong," as soon as he made his appearance, faultlessly attired in a blue coat with gold buttons, he produced an impression of elegance and vigour. With a just appreciation of circumstances, he tried to convince his friends that, whilst preserving as far as possible their loyalty to the legitimate King, it was necessary to introduce changes, and to march with the times, and he declared himself a partisan of universal suffrage and the abolition of the money qualification for the electorate. But this was asking too much of the circle about Charles X, and of those who in the mists of Holyrood in Scotland were charged with the education of the Duc de Bordeaux and took care to impress upon the young exiled prince that the whole population of France were his subjects. Berryer was the voice of one crying in the wilderness, and he subsequently confessed his disillusionment to Lamartine: "If there is any hope left, it is beyond the reach of human ken; it hovers above an unknown horizon."

Berryer.

For the Legitimists Louis-Philippe represented "the King of the barricades," the usurper. The Republicans were of the same opinion, though their reasons were different. They perceived that in 1830 they had played the part of dupes, and worked for the establishment of a dynasty which had nothing democratic about it; and they were filled with the bitterest resentment against Louis-Philippe, who had turned the victory of the people to his own account.

In the Republican Party there were as yet no members of the populace to be found; it consisted entirely of bourgeois, and the sons of flourishing and well-to-do bourgeois or tradesmen carrying on lucrative businesses, together with intellectuals, most of whom had served their apprenticeship with the Carbonari. The leaders of the Party, G. Cavaignac, Guinard, Trélat and Raspail, it must be confessed, had no definite programme, but 1792 had set a precedent that commanded respect. So they returned to the vocabulary of the Convention—Cavaignac was the son of one of its members—they brought it up to date, remodelling it to the taste of the day and made use of the same methods

The Republicans.

as their "glorious ancestors," working through the agency of clubs and newspapers.

The political societies, which were animated by an ever-growing spirit of hostility to the monarchy, played the part of recruiting agents, swelling the ranks of the enemies of the established system and bringing discontent to a head. The earliest of them, the *Amis du Peuple*, exercised a very real influence. The members of this society maintained, with a zeal that was altogether laudable, that the lot of the "proletariat" should be the constant concern of those in power; they recalled the glories of the Revolution, the heroes of the great days of the Republic, heroes who, according to one witness who observed that the meetings of the society "had the smell of an old, much-read, greasy and worn copy of the *Moniteur* of 1793," were somewhat out of date. But this in no wise discomfited the Republicans. With the rage of warriors who had been deceived, they immediately went to extremes, and glorified the Terror, whilst Cavaignac's mother remarked of her son, "He is a Brutus."

The Press seconded the efforts of the Republicans in the work of propaganda, and here the most remarkable journalists of the day were to be found Moreover, since 1830 journalism had acquired an influence hitherto unknown. On *la Tribune* there was Marrast, "the marquis of the Revolution," a native of Provence, with refined features and abundant locks, "a scoffer like Desmoulins, with something of the mocking spirit of Beaumarchais." But it was only later on that Marrast won real popularity; the man of the moment, the most upright as well as the most intelligent of them all, was Armand Carrel.

Armand Carrel.

He was the son of a merchant of Rouen, and had been to Saint Cyr. One day when he had to be reprimanded for some offence, the General in command of the school threatened to send him back to his father to measure bales of cloth. "If I ever pick up my father's yard-measure again," he retorted, "it will not be to measure bales of cloth!" And he kept his word.

Carrel took part in the conspiracy of Belfort under the Restoration, and in Spain tried to win the regiments over to Bonapartism and to bring about the failure of the expedition sent to restore Ferdinand VII to the throne. Arrested and acquitted, he felt that he had been misled; the July Revolution found him sceptical; and he had no faith in the success of the revolt against the ordinances. On the accession of Louis-Philippe his attitude was at once prudent and sarcastic; but seeing Thiers, his old colleague, on the *National*, a convert to the new *régime*, he soon altered his tone. The barter of liberty and the scrimmage for office certainly filled him with disgust; like Hugo and Lamennais, he hoped for better things, and it was with an air of haughty disdain that he eventually made his appearance at the end of 1830.

With his long, thin face, his pale complexion, his features bearing the imprint "of something indescribably sharp and hard as steel," with his thin lips, his extremely black brows meeting above his nose, his eyes sunk deep in their sockets and, according to a terrified contemporary, darting "flames of infernal fire," he had preserved his military, aristocratic bearing; and dressed with elegant simplicity, booted and spurred and whip in hand, he had nothing of the demagogue about him. Indeed, he filled everybody with astonishment. "He is a character!" they exclaimed. He was opposed to violent measures and was a stern judge of the politicians of his Party. "They are madmen, bunglers, jealous and impotent scoundrels. Their qualities are only of use in entirely exceptional circumstances; their drawbacks are ever present." He had profound convictions, but when he turned democrat he could not bring himself to adopt the characteristic vulgarity of bearing. His courage was magnificent, and Chateaubriand rendered him homage in the following words: "He defended with his sword the ideas which the quill-drivers drew from their scabbards."

Carrel's one idea, to which he gave expression in season and out of season with ever-increasing vehemence, was that of vengeance for 1815. "Between our friends the Prussians and the July Monarchy," he said, "peace will only be signed when not a single soldier remains on the left bank of the Rhine." To the Holy Alliance of Kings he wanted to oppose the Holy Alliance of Peoples, and proclaimed that it was the mission of France to come to the succour of the nations that were bowed down beneath the yoke of Absolutism. Lamennais and Edgar

Quinet gave expression to the same ideas, and thus all three touched the profoundest depths of the nation's soul.

The tale is told of how a certain Boulogne fisherman who had been at sea for some days saw the tricoloured flag waving on the jetty when he entered the port on the 30th of July. "I knew that *he* was not dead!" he exclaimed. *He* was Napoleon; and indeed Napoleon still lived in the memory of the people; there had been no achievement conspicuous and glorious enough to oust him from his pinnacle since Waterloo; his shadow was cast upon the throne of Louis-Philippe as it had been on that of Louis XVIII and Charles X. A trophy on which none could lay hands!

Republican Bonapartism.

The Republicans immediately adopted this great name; just as the Liberals under the Restoration had taken to their bosom the erstwhile tyrant and metamorphosed him into a champion of liberty, so the democratic opposition of 1830 sought shelter beneath the imperial flag. When, at the time they were trying to frighten Charles X in order to hasten his flight, Cavaignac observed, "It would be easier to push Paris towards the Rhine than towards Saint-Cloud," he accurately voiced the feelings of the people. What magic resided in these memories of past triumphs! The victors of July only asked to be allowed to fight again in order to win independence for foreign nations and at the same time wipe out the disgrace of their own defeat in 1815.

In 1831 Victor Hugo's *Ode à la Colonne* was published in *Les Chants du Crépuscule*; and Napoleon and Liberty were worshipped as twin gods. The youth of the nation, "who were changing," in their ingenuous enthusiasm confounded Republicanism and Bonapartism, and in their mind's eye pictured a resplendent future crowned with victories, glory and peace, a free fraternity amid the clash of arms. And this passion was duly exploited. In the theatre Napoleon was presented at every stage in his career in all his classic poses; for actors who had his figure and could imitate his gestures this vogue proved a gold-mine. In the space of a few days the worthy Dumas, commissioned by a shrewd director, scribbled off a *Napoleon* in several scenes. The Conservatives were alarmed by this infatuation, and the more clear-sighted among them discerned beneath this cloak of Bonapartism the Phrygian cap of the Republic. "The anarchists," said Thiers, "are using the name of Napoleon because they know it is more glorious than their own."

Between these two extremes, the Legitimists apparently defeated, the Republicans or democrats, eager to set out on fresh conquests, and the bourgeois deputies, the representatives of the system established by law, wavered, some regarding the revolution as having achieved its end and opposed to any fresh concessions, the others carried along by the swift rush of events, convinced that there were still further developments to be expected from the July Revolution. Hence the establishment of two parties which were destined to oppose each other for eighteen years—the party of resistance, and the party of progress.

The Two Parties.

The former had as their spokesmen Casimir Périer and Guizot. Their programme never changed—peace abroad and peace at home, the maintenance of law and order, and no encouragement for democratic passions. This party was supported by the majority of the "legal country," the electors who were recognised as such by the law of 1831.

The party of progress, on the other hand, though they did not accept the Republic—recollections of the horrors of '89 were still too fresh in the minds of the bourgeoisie—kept in touch with the Republicans and considered it politic to accede within bounds to popular demands. The undisputed leader of this party was La Fayette, the Commandant of the National Guard. The man who had installed the new monarchy at the Hôtel de Ville, "basking in the sweet sunshine of the people's smile," the erstwhile conspirator of the Restoration, was made a sort of civil and military High Constable; his power and fame were greater than those of Louis-Philippe. His house was a rendezvous for all France and even for all Europe; republicans, foreign refugees, ambassadors and men of letters came to render him homage; "mud-stained boots and silk stockings trod the parquet of his rooms," and his house became the Pavillon de Marsan of the revolutionary party.

La Fayette.

whose rooms in the Palais Royal looked out on to the Rue de Valois, was awakened by shouts of "Death to the Ministers, or the head of King Louis-Philippe!" Terrified out of her life, she had the King and Queen warned; and reinforcements for the National Guard arrived just at the moment when "the rioters" were beginning to ascend the great staircase. "The popular lion," so carefully caressed, so magnificently lauded by the romantic poets, seemed insensible to all these attentions. After that night in October its roar was to be heard more than once.

Disunited and without a policy, the Government was quite incapable of restoring order, and the bourgeoisie were filled with fear. General looting was expected, and the women hid their jewels or sent them abroad, whilst in the Luxembourg quarter—the trial was to take place before the Court of Peers—the shopkeepers put their shutters up. "Paris was enveloped in gloom and seemed to be weighed down beneath a crushing burden." Whereupon Louis-Philippe decided to try a Government chosen from the party of progress, and sent for Laffitte (2nd of November, 1830). "The most advanced elements," he thought, "cannot complain of such a choice."

The Trial.

The trial of the Ministers opened on the 15th of December, and lasted for six days. The accused behaved with great nobility, and the peers were filled with admiration for the pride and moving words of Peyronnet, and the serene good grace of Polignac. The latter was defended by Martignac, who, already a prey to the malady which was to carry him off shortly afterwards, pleaded eloquently on behalf of the man who had once driven him from power. The proceedings were conducted without incident, though now and again the sound of disturbances outside reached the hall in which the trial was being held. For the mob had turned a deaf ear to the exhortations of Lamartine, who, in the verses he wrote in condemnation of the death penalty, exclaimed:

> "C'est ainsi qu'un grand peuple, au jour de la justice,
> Dans la balance humaine au lieu d'un vil supplice
> Jeta sa magnanimité!" [1]

[1] "And thus a great people, on the day of justice, threw its magnanimity into the human scale instead of a dread sentence of death."

But there was no longer any likelihood of this; each day the disturbances looked more and more like insurrection. Crowds, held in check with difficulty by line troops, surrounded the Luxembourg, and in vain did La Fayette repeat his appeals for peace and try to convince " the misguided citizens that the cause of justice was not served by intimidating the judges." On the evening of the 20th of December, while the lawyer Crémieux was defending Guernon-Ranville, shouts accompanied by the beating of a drum drowned the voice of the speaker; one of the peers hurriedly approached Pasquier, the President of the Court, and said, " You have not a moment to lose to close the sitting." Whereupon panic seized the assembly. Crémieux fainted, and from one bench to the other the alarming news was handed on—the people were blockading the Luxembourg, the call to arms was being sounded in the streets, the regulars had been outnumbered and the National Guard were not to be relied upon. " It is no longer safe to continue the proceedings," said Pasquier. And the meeting was adjourned.

Fearing disturbances, the troops bivouacked round bonfires during the night. Meanwhile, Montalivet, the Minister of the Interior, a confidant of the King, was discussing with Pasquier, La Fayette, Sébastiani, the Minister for Foreign Affairs, and Odilon Barrot, the Prefect of the Seine, the means to be adopted for the conveyance of the accused, who, after each sitting of the Court, were sent back to the Luxembourg prison; it was necessary to avoid any meeting between them and the National Guard, which was becoming more and more hostile. La Fayette was not in favour of such methods of evasion, which might undermine his popularity; but Montalivet was firm. On the 21st of December, in the late afternoon, the four accused got into a carriage, and escorted by a few riders and Montalivet himself, drove in hot haste to Vincennes. At six o'clock in the evening, whilst the Court was still deliberating, a cannon shot rang out—it was the signal announcing the arrival of the prisoners at Vincennes.

That same night the ex-Ministers were condemned to imprisonment for life, whilst Polignac was further sentenced to civil death. This decree sent the people into a paroxysm of rage; civil death was not enough, the least they would be satisfied with was the head of Polignac! The appearance of La Fayette, who held a review of the legions of the Guard, restored order for a moment, but it was evident that the insurrection was still simmering. In vain did the deputies of the democratic party endeavour to bring the insurgents to reason. "We are of the same opinion as yourselves," Arago assured them. "Those whose clothes are not made of the same material as ours cannot be of the same opinion," came the reply. For the monarchy the danger was very great; was the Guard, to whom the maintenance of the public peace had been entrusted, going to support the enemies of the Government? The Chamber, in alarm, thereupon voted the abolition of the post of Commander-in-Chief of the National Guard, and La Fayette, who was thus directly attacked, sent in his resignation, so that Louis-Philippe was relieved of the dictatorship which had hampered all his decisions since July.

Condemnation of the Ministers.

Resignation of La Fayette.

Ever since his advent to power, Laffitte had shown but little capacity for reaching a decision. In trying to please the deputies of the Left, and to reassure the friends of order, he succeeded only in displeasing both sides. On the 14th of February, 1831, an unforeseen incident occurred which put his statesmanlike qualities to a severe test.

On that day, in the church of Saint Germain l'Auxerrois, the Carlists—that is to say the devotees of Charles X—were holding a memorial service for the Duc de Berry, who had been stabbed eleven years previously by Louvel. During the ceremony a young man in the uniform of the military school of Saint Cyr came forward and pinned on the catafalque standing in the middle of the nave a lithograph representing the Duc de Bordeaux, the son of the murdered Duke. A tumult immediately arose, and the crowd that had collected before the porch burst into the church and the presbytery, broke up the altars, the statues, the windows and the crosses, and at the end of a few hours left only bare walls and piles of wreckage.

Looting of Saint Germain l'Auxerrois

On the following day, in a sort of destructive frenzy and as it were impelled by the determination to wreak vengeance for the clerical domination which they had tolerated all too long, the same crowd rushed upon the Archbishop's palace and reduced it to ruins. "Every window on the ground floor," says one witness, "became a means of entry that could not be closed." The books from the library were thrown out of the windows into the river, and all the papers in the palace met with a similar fate or were scattered about the grounds. Meanwhile the floors, the ceilings and the stairs gave way, the main walls were attacked, and soon the roof fell in. A gang of a thousand housebreakers could not have accomplished as much in three days. "Furniture, chasubles and cassocks were to be seen floating downstream; on the banks book-lovers were trying to rescue books in magnificent bindings from the wreck. . . ." If Louis Blanc is to be believed, "the loss to art due to the sacking of the Archbishop's palace was incalculable." In the evening guttersnipes ran about the streets dressed up in magnificent dalmatics and spurting water in the faces of the passers-by, crying out, "There's some holy water for nothing!" The riot had degenerated into a sinister carnival.

And of the Archbishop's Palace.

The Government seemed to hold itself aloof from these events. The National Guard turned out, it is true, but they did not interfere. One of their colonels confessed to Arago that he had received orders to put in an appearance and then to return. Thiers, who was prowling about in the crowd and at that time only occupied a minor post in the Government, did nothing to stop the crowd; and men of experience declared that they had seen nothing like it except in the last days of the Directory, in the months preceding the 18th Brumaire. Moreover, among the most rabid insurgents were to be found not only working men in smocks, but also "black coats and smart hats"; it seemed as if the bourgeoisie were taking a delight in this Saturnalia, and it was even asserted that the Government was diverting the rioters from the shops and the Palais Royal and turning them on to the churches. In short, no attempt was made to stop this explosion of popular fury, this unexpected counterblast to the July Revolution. And meanwhile it was clear that the victorious populace had not said their last word, but that they intended to chastise the upholders of the fallen system still further; their store of hatred had not yet been exhausted.

After these days of upheaval, Louis-Philippe thought it would be wise to delete the fleur-de-lys from his coat of arms, which elicited from Casimir Périer the remark, "The rioters pass beneath his windows, and lo and behold he flings his escutcheon into the river!" Laffitte, who in his heart of hearts was perhaps not altogether displeased that the Carlists should be terrified, let things slip; but at this juncture foreign affairs complicated the situation.

Foreign Affairs.

The accession of Louis-Philippe had met with a bad reception in Europe. This monarchy which was born of revolution inspired only mistrust in absolutist or even constitutional Powers. The English Ministers told the King's representatives that they would recognise them, though they would keep watch over them. Austria, through the mouth of Metternich, spoke out more plainly, and compared the July revolution to the bursting of a dyke, and saw in it an explosion of anarchical passion against authority. Russia, frankly hostile, refused to recognise the illegitimate monarchy that France had given herself, and was within an ace of declaring war, eventually only consenting to enter into relations with her on terms that almost amounted to insult.

Louis-Philippe, though he was personally brave, was timid in matters of politics. According to Guizot, who knew him better than anyone else, he preferred diplomacy to force and always tried to get round obstacles instead of making a frontal attack upon them. Thus constituted, he made no attempt to pose as an outraged sovereign strong in his rights; with consummate wisdom and almost in humility he represented himself as the brake, the moderating influence, upon the spirit of revolt that had raised him to power, as the check upon the anarchy that threatened. At his command—since Laffitte counted for little in matters of foreign policy—his envoys reiterated in the Chancelleries of Europe that France was aiming only at the maintenance of peace, that she was respecting the treaties of 1815 and had not the smallest intention of interfering in the domestic affairs of her neighbours.

Thus the King abandoned all intention of extending the consequences of the Paris insurrection to other countries, and gave a formal denial to those who in the "three glorious days"—the classic name for the July Revolution—saluted the dawn of the liberation of the peoples. These assurances, however, did not succeed in disarming the animosity of the old monarchies; and Metternich, faithful to the Holy Alliance which was his own creation, continued to press the right of intervention, "just as a man insists on going to extinguish the fire in his neighbour's house, to prevent it from spreading to his own."

The political events which were taking place outside France were to force Louis-Philippe to adopt a definite attitude.

The Case of Belgium.

Ever since 1814 the Belgians had been protesting against the treaty which had united them to Holland; the two nations were diametrically opposed both in character and religion. On the 25th of August, 1830, during a performance of *La Muette de Portici* in Brussels, the people, excited by allusions in this play which they thought applied to themselves, rose up in rebellion; the movement spread throughout Belgium, and on the 4th of October she proclaimed her independence. The Treaties of Vienna were once more put in question, and it seemed as though war was likely to break out at any moment.

Talleyrand, the French Ambassador in London, immediately proposed that a conference should be called "to settle the Belgian question." Without enthusiasm and only because they were afraid that something worse might happen, the Powers supported him; but the Belgians were resolved to consult only their own interests. Summoning a National Congress, they refused to consider the candidature to the throne of any member of the House of Orange, which was the dynasty established in Holland, and in spite of Talleyrand, who in conjunction with England was supporting the claims of Prince Leopold of Saxe-Coburg, they elected as King of the Belgians the Duc de Nemours, the second son of Louis-Philippe.

It was impossible for England to accept this solution. The

accession of a French prince to the throne of Belgium or the annexation of that country to France amounted in her eyes to the same thing; and when once the decision of the Congress was ratified, war would have been inevitable. Louis-Philippe was well aware of this, and, in spite of the supplications of the Belgians, refused to accept the Crown for his son; and shortly afterwards the influence of England secured the victory for the candidature of Prince Leopold of Saxe-Coburg (4th of June, 1831). Peace was maintained, though not without inflicting a wound upon the self-esteem of the French nation. It was only later on that people perceived the real wisdom of Louis-Philippe's policy; when the neutrality of Belgium was proclaimed by the Powers, the King regarded it, not as a measure directed against France, but as a guarantee; and indeed, for many a long year, it constituted an extremely effective guarantee.

Louis-Philippe Keeps the Peace.

The Belgian Revolution had been acclaimed in France with the greatest sympathy; and when the news of the Polish insurrection arrived the enthusiasm increased still further.

Poland, which had been made a kingdom in 1815, was at this time ruled by the Grand-Duke Constantine, a relative of the Tsar, "a hirsute and hideous giant, whose fits of temper were terrible." Just as he was gathering together his armies to crush the revolt in Belgium, a rebellion broke out in Warsaw among the Polish regiments, and thus Russian intervention against the movement for the independence of Belgium became impossible, and indescribable scenes of enthusiasm occurred in France. The Poles had fought on the side of France under the Revolution and the Empire; for years they had been the victims of absolutism, dismembered, oppressed and downtrodden, at the mercy of the various treaties. And now they came forward as defenders "of the sacred cause of the people's rights." Everything combined to make them popular heroes; in Paris everybody thought and talked of nothing else, and in the streets Casimir Delavigne's song "*La Varsovienne*" ousted "*La Parisienne*," which he had written in praise of the House of Orleans.

Insurrection of Poland.

"I should be glad," wrote Jouffroy at this juncture, "if for a long time to come France were able only to consider her vocation abroad and forget all about her home vocation. But she is doing precisely the contrary—sacrificing foreign policy to home affairs, and the latter go from bad to worse in consequence." Talleyrand had already given expression to similar sentiments when, after the July Revolution, he observed, "What is lacking in all this is a victory or two." And now the insurrections which followed upon each other in Belgium and in Poland, as well as in Italy, who, in her turn, rose up against the rule of the Pope and of the Dukes of Modena and Parma, encouraged the bellicose inclinations of the French. Even among the bourgeoisie the talk was all of rushing to the help of the Italians and of the heroic Poles, and of spreading the blessings of liberty throughout Europe. There was complete agreement on this point between La Fayette, Carrel and Montalembert, between the party of progress, the Republicans and the Catholics, and the refrain from "*La Varsovienne*":

> "Pour de vieux frères d'armes,
> N'aurez-vous que des larmes?
> Frères, c'était du sang que nous versions pour vous,"[1]

was sung with sincerity and fervour. But if the Government followed public opinion, what would be the result? To help the Poles meant war with Russia; to side with the Italians, war with Austria, who was all-powerful in the peninsula. Could France with her 250,000 soldiers embark on such an enterprise?

Louis-Philippe was too prudent and too realistic to take such a step; but, as usual, he did not meet the difficulty squarely. He allowed Laffitte to make generous and grandiloquent declarations from the rostrum, calculated to satisfy public feeling, but in private he told the foreign ambassadors, "My Minister is talking nonsense." And thus no intervention on behalf of the Italians or the Poles took place. "God is too high above us, and France is too far away," said the latter. The politicians, it is true, endeavoured to explain that it was impossible lightheartedly and out of pure sentimentality to run such enormous risks. "Poland," confessed Thiers, "remains, and could not fail to remain, a source of great grief to us." But this failure

[1] "For old brothers in arms have you nothing but tears? Brethren, it was our blood that we shed for you."

to act, this denial of the "principles of July," aroused discontent among the majority of the nation, and Laffitte was not slow to perceive it.

He had consistently hedged and manœuvred, mistrusted by the Left, who disapproved of the feebleness of his foreign policy, as well as by the Conservatives, who considered him incapable of securing law and order at home. And thus Saint-Marc-Girardin was able to write in the *Débats :* "To have a Government that does not govern, but humbly begs to obey, craving pardon for the great liberty it is taking, means that we live in a state that is neither social nor barbarous, but merely one of anarchy and chaos."

And indeed, eight months after the July Revolution, the situation was deplorable—business was bad, bankruptcies occurred every day, there was increasing lack of employment, disturbances in the streets, and everywhere "a vague sense of unrest, without apparent object." The answer of a man who as he was sacking the Archbishop's Palace was asked "What is it you really want?" is typical. "Nothing is working properly, neither labour nor the Government." And he was not far wrong.

In the midst of this anarchy of mind, this bankruptcy of power, Louis-Philippe felt his slender stock of popularity gradually melting away. It was no longer possible to keep Laffitte. Abandoned by his friends, ruined financially and politically, this man, who had regarded himself as the second founder of the monarchy, fell from office, to the satisfaction of all.

Fall of Laffitte.

Abridged Bibliography of the general histories of the July Monarchy.—The most important work is that by P. Thureau-Dangin, *Histoire de la Monarchie de Juillet* (7 vols., 1897–1904), to which must be added *La Monarchie de Juillet* by S. Charléty (Vol. V of *l'Histoire de France Contemporaine*, published under the editorship of E. Lavisse). We would also refer to : Bourgeois, *Manuel Historique de Politique Étrangère* (Vol. III, 1906). Crétineau-Joly, *Histoire de Louis-Philippe et de l'Orléanisme* (2 vols., 1867). Hamel, *Histoire du Règne de Louis-Philippe* (2 vols., 1889–90). de Nouvion, *Histoire du Règne de Louis-Philippe Premier* (4 vols., 1857–61). G. Weill, *La France sous la Monarchie Constitutionnelle* (1912), and above all the work of Louis Blanc, *Histoire de Dix Ans* (5 vols., 1841–44), which ends at 1840.

Bibliography for Chapter I.—de Barante, *Souvenirs* (9 vols., 1890–1901).

RESTORATION AND JULY MONARCHY

A. Carrel, *Oeuvres* (preface by Littré) (4 vols., 1854–58). E. Charavay, *Le Général La Fayette* (1898). Cournot, *Souvenirs* (ed. Bottinelli) (1913). Cuvillier-Fleury, *Journal et Correspondance Intimes* (2 vols., 1903). E. Daudet, *La Révolution de* 1830 *et le Procès des Ministres de Charles X* (New ed., 1907). Fesch, *Lacordaire Journaliste* (1897). Guizot, *Mémoires pour Servir à l'Histoire de Mon Temps* (2nd ed., 8 vols., 1858–67). Lamennais, *Questions Philosophiques et Politiques* (2 vols., 1840). Liesse, *Portraits de Financiers* (1908). de Marnay, *D'Une Chute à l'Autre :* 1830–1848 (1880). Montalembert and Cornudet, *Lettres à un Ami de Collège* (1884). *Procès du Service Funèbre Célébré le* 14 *Février* 1831 *à Saint-Germain-l'Auxerrois* (1831). Renan, *La Réforme Intellectuelle et Morale* (1875). Riballier, 1830 (*Collection : Les Idées Claires*) (1911). Sainte-Beuve, *Causeries du Lundi* (no date) (Vol. VI : article on Carrel). Trognon, *La Vie de Marie-Amélie* (1872).

CHAPTER II

CASIMIR PÉRIER

Portrait of Casimir Périer. How he gained his power over the King, the Ministers and the Chamber. His programme: peace and order. The question of the hereditary peerage and the Civil List. The Lyons insurrection. Outbreak of disturbances in Paris. Activity of the popular societies. Proceedings against the Press. Alliance between the Legitimists and the Republicans: the plot of the Prouvaires. Périer restores order. His attitude to foreign Powers; the Ancona expedition, Admiral Roussin at Lisbon. Fall of Warsaw. Settlement of the Belgian question. Outbreak of cholera in Paris. Death of Casimir Périer. The Duchesse de Berry's plot in Vendée.

Casimir Périer.

WITH a frank open brow, keen eyes beneath bushy eyebrows, gentle features, which at the slightest contradiction suddenly changed and imparted something indescribably morbid and feverish to his face, tall and slightly bent, easy in his bearing and quick in his movements, such was the personality of Casimir Périer at the time when he entered into office (13th of March, 1831).

As President of the Chamber he had witnessed the spread of the spirit of disorder and had come forward as a determined champion of resistance to it. In his eyes 1830 did not represent the inauguration of a new era, the harbinger of a reshuffling of society. On the contrary, he was of opinion that the duty of the majority was to produce from the crisis through which the country had passed "the determined resolution to respect the Charter in its entirety, to acknowledge nothing beyond it and to keep the peace." Anything further meant entering the unknown, "the unknown which was the principle of anarchy," as Jouffroy said.

Accepts Office.

When he was asked to take office, Périer hesitated. "Remember that if I enter the Ministry I shall leave it feet foremost," he replied. He knew that he was ill and subject to sudden fits of passion, and incapable of governing half-heartedly or impartially. But when once he had given his consent he took no trouble to hide his feelings, and revealed his programme with a complete and almost truculent frankness to which the Chamber was quite unaccustomed.

Périer was a financier, a member of the upper middle class. He had no love for the aristocracy, for, as Carrel maliciously observed, the aristocracy of the counter had but little liking for the aristocracy of birth and of arms. And as far as the masses were concerned, he was suspicious of their enthusiasms and of the gregarious instinct that impelled them to follow their leaders. On the day when Louis-Philippe presented himself at the Hôtel de Ville and somebody exclaimed, " How wonderful to have made all this crowd leave their homes ! " Périer retorted, " It will be much more wonderful to make them go back." His chief object, which he pursued with a sort of savage tenacity, was to make the monarchy secure within the framework of the revised Charter, to instruct the bourgeoisie in the true art of government, and show them the path to follow. Louis-Philippe, his Ministers and the Parliament soon perceived that the day of sonorous and empty declamations, or half-measures and platform optimism, was past—a statesman was at the helm in France.

His Policy.

Périer laid down his conditions to the King. He was to see all the dispatches before the latter and to summon the Council in his absence, whilst the Duc d'Orléans, the King's eldest son, and heir to the throne, was not to be present at their deliberations. These stipulations bordered upon hostility; but the King, regarding Périer as indispensable, very wisely gave way. His family, however, did not display similar moderation, and henceforward the President of the Council had to contend with the ill-will of the Tuileries. He cared but little for this, and one day, when he was given a cold reception at Court, he launched his ultimatum, and order was immediately restored. As it was abundantly clear that the Minister was not one to be complaisant, that " he was stiff-necked " and that his backbone did not bend very easily, he won respect. Did not Périer observe with a certain satisfaction of himself, " How can a man of my figure be expected to give way."

With regard to the Ministers who were his colleagues he adopted a less formal attitude. There was only one among them for whom he had any respect, and that was Baron Louis, who in some ways resembled himself. The others he treated with but scant courtesy. Marshal Soult, who was regarded as extremely influential, although his reputation had suffered somewhat since he had commanded the forces in Spain under the Empire, tried to make a show of independence. "Don't indulge in that sort of thing," said Périer, "or I will break you like glass." And when d'Argout, another of his colleagues, was making an irrelevant speech, he motioned to him like a hunter calling back his dog, and exclaimed, "Here, d'Argout!" And d'Argout, obedient though unwilling, went back to his seat on the Ministerial bench. Members of the Government were not accustomed to such parliamentary absolutism; but as a matter of fact they obeyed, and things went all the better in consequence.

The Chamber gave Casimir Périer more trouble. The disturbances in Paris and the insurrections abroad had apparently changed the mentality of the bourgeoisie; in addition to their smugness and love of peace, they seemed to have acquired a taste for revolt. They wanted to maintain law and order, no doubt, yet they bestowed their smiles upon the Revolution. They almost plumed themselves upon it, for the liberation of the nations figured on their agenda. They sold their support of the King dearly, and in their pride as the class that had triumphed, condescendingly imagined they might grant the good folk who had fought in July a few privileges.

Périer was far from agreeing with this point of view. He regarded a reaction as an absolute necessity, abroad as well as at home, and expressed his opinions openly in the Chamber, as he always did. "We do not recognise the right of insurrections to force us into war," he declared, "any more than we recognise their right to push us along the path of political innovations." He refused to destroy peace for the sake of a principle, and repudiated both insurrection and propaganda abroad. In this he gave proof of great courage, for he placed himself in an unpopular position which was difficult to maintain; but such is the power of a strong conviction that he succeeded in winning over the majority who were wavering.

He was mistrusted, no doubt. When the President of the

Chamber was elected—the Charter had recognised the right of the Parliament to make the choice—Girod de l'Ain, Périer's candidate, was returned by a majority of only one. Périer was furious and offered to resign; whereupon sudden panic seized upon the terrified majority, who had no one to lead them. Thus when the Address to the Throne came up for discussion, all the timorous spirits voted for the Government, although it had rejected all idea of intervention abroad. The Conservatives and the new deputies, whom "the legal country" had just returned to the Chamber, fearing the advent of another Laffitte Ministry, gave their solid support to Périer, and the party of resistance took root in France.

The Hereditary Peerage.

The question which at the moment was absorbing the attention of the public was that of the hereditary character of the peerage. Established in 1815, the principle of heredity was a stumbling-block to the bourgeoisie, who saw in it a remnant of the *ancien régime*. Was it not only natural that after 1830 the upper Chamber should divest itself of an aristocracy which had played its part, and that the King alone should have the right of raising to the peerage those citizens whom he considered worthy of the honour? In his heart of hearts, Périer was opposed to this change, not so much out of sentiment as from prudence. But as the reform seemed to him unlikely to have any serious consequences, he left the majority free to decide.

Others took up the cudgels on his behalf and showed but little inclination to emphasise the rupture with the Restoration by this means. "Royalist democracy," observed Royer-Collard, "whether it condescends to keep the figurehead of kingship or not, is or will soon become pure democracy. If the principle of heredity is sacrificed, the peerage will vanish, and with the peerage hereditary monarchy will probably also cease to exist." This was as it were a sounding lead cast into the future, but it produced no effect. The hereditary peerage was abolished by the deputies; thenceforward the King had the right to nominate an unlimited number of peers, though his choice was restricted to certain categories of men of note. And thus the bourgeoisie cut out for themselves an honourable opening in an assembly which, if the truth were told, played but an insignificant part in the State, but whose very name preserved some trace of the glory of its lofty origin. There now remained the difficulty of obtaining from the Chamber of Peers its consent to its own transformation and, in a sense, to its own suicide. This was overcome by nominating a batch of new peers, an old but ever efficacious expedient.

While the majority expected from Louis-Philippe the aggrandisement of their own social and political status, they nevertheless showed themselves singularly susceptible and punctilious with regard to the Throne, and made a point of repeating, "The King whom we made," in order to put him in his place. Doubtless they did not allow their loyalty to be suspect—"We are not revolutionaries," declared the Conservatives—and they surrounded the new monarchy with every sign of respect. But the mystic belief in kingship by divine right had disappeared and its place had been taken by a more practical and realistic point of view. In short, the monarchy was merely an honourable, useful and even indispensable institution, for which, however, too heavy a price was not to be paid.

The Civil List.

When the Civil List was submitted to the Chamber the mistrust of the latter became apparent. The sum proposed was 18 millions (£720,000); Charles X had received 40 millions (£1,600,000); but the business men and the journalists immediately pointed out that 18 millions was thirty-seven times as great as the Civil List granted to the First Consul; while a certain pamphleteer named Cormenin, a writer not altogether devoid of talent who was destined to improve with age, taking this debate for his text, proceeded, under the pseudonym of Timon, to examine the items one by one. This afforded plenty of opportunity for scoffing, which placed the Royal Family in an exceedingly uncomfortable position. "80,000 francs (£3200) for the medical requirements of a King who was perfectly well is scandalous. Louis XVIII, although he was an invalid, was nursed for much less." When Montalivet, the Minister of the Interior, one day had the tactlessness to reply, "If luxury is banished from the palace of the King, it will soon vanish from the homes of his *subjects*," there was an outburst of indignation, and it seemed as if the Civil List would be thrown out altogether.

Unedifying debates followed, which showed up in strong relief the fundamental drawbacks of this monarchy born of revolution. The representatives of the "legal country," the men of means, industrialists, celebrities, and merchants bargained and "haggled" with the Crown as though they were negotiating with some concern to carry out a contract on the lowest possible terms. In the end a compromise was reached, and the Civil List was fixed at 12 millions (£480,000). But the same problems, couched in the same terms, arose later on when the King asked for allowances for his children; with regard to questions of money the bourgeoisie felt they had the whip hand over Louis-Philippe, and they turned this power to account.

Périer despised these quarrels. His mind was occupied with more immediate difficulties.

The silk industry of Lyons provided work for about 30,000 or 40,000 people, some 10,000 master-weavers possessing four or five machines and depending on manufacturers and agents. It was a prosperous industry, but foreign competition had led to a constant fall in wages—a "canut" who earned 4 to 6 francs a day under the Empire received barely 18 to 25 sous in 1831 for fifteen hours work. Whereupon a certain number of manufacturers and master-weavers met together and drew up a tariff of minimum wages, which was approved by the Prefect. The workmen had already declared themselves satisfied, when suddenly the majority of the manufacturers decided not to apply the tariff, which was not legally binding. Filled with indignation, the weavers met on the Croix-Rousse hill on the 21st of November, 1831, whence they marched down into the town, where they came up against the National Guard. Eight workmen were killed, and the tumult increased. Bands of rioters scoured the streets, waving black flags and carrying placards with the inscription "Live working or die fighting." In the end the National Guard made common cause with the insurgents, and the troops, outnumbered, beat a retreat. On the following day, the 22nd, the whole mob from the Croix-Rousse returned to the fight, and by the evening they were masters of the town.

The Lyons Insurrection.

Stupefaction reigned in Paris. In a few hours the second most important town of France had fallen into the hands of the revolutionaries. With Périer at the head of affairs the taking of prompt and energetic measures of repression could be relied upon. On the 5th of December Marshal Soult entered Lyons at the head of an army, with drums beating and bombardiers with their matches lighted. The National Guard was disbanded, the Prefect recalled, and the tariff annulled. It was further decided that a fort should be constructed on the Croix-Rousse which would dominate the town. The "canuts" did not retaliate. They had no proper organisation and were more frightened than elated by their ephemeral victory. But the country had been given a terrible shock. Were the bourgeoisie capable of understanding what lay hidden beneath this sudden revolt, behind this attempt at a servile war?

The drama of Lyons was really nothing but a rebellion on the part of the poor, devoid of any political significance, an uprising due to economic causes. But in Paris things were different.

Disturbances in Paris.

One afternoon in January, about three o'clock, the great bell of Notre Dame rang out; bodies of police hurried in the direction of the towers; a few shots were fired, and on the staircase there were clouds of smoke. Six men were arrested, one of whom, almost a child, burst into tears and said he would confess all. The conspirators, who were seven in number, were making preparations to set the north tower on fire; the conflagration and the ringing of the bells were to serve as a signal, and the people were to rush in a body on to the streets. The fire that had been started was extinguished, but one of the conspirators was missing. Suddenly on the flat roof of the tower a man appeared with his breast bared, calling out, "I surrender!" Asked what his calling was, he replied, "A revolutionary!" His name was Considère and he was the instigator of this absurd plot.

Meanwhile the leaders of the Republican societies did all in their power to keep the public agitation alive. Through their activities every step taken by the Government and every diplomatic difficulty was made a pretext for gatherings in the street.

Louis-Philippe had decided to create an order in commemoration of the July Revolution, which was to bear the inscription "Presented by the King." Presented by the King! That is impossible! exclaimed the Republicans; how can the heroic combatants of the three glorious days accept such a gift from the man who robbed the revolution of its fruits? A disorderly meeting immediately took place in the Place Vendôme, and soon degenerated into a brawl. To restore order, Marshal Lobau, an old soldier who was gifted with ingenuity, had half a dozen fire hoses turned on to the howling mob. The device met with instantaneous success, but the defeat in no way discouraged the demonstrators. They took their revenge by making an effigy of the Marshal dressed in an apron and armed with a clyster-pipe; whereupon they set to work again upon fresh escapades which they hoped would prove more profitable to their cause.

The Popular Societies.

In order to keep their forces in trim, the popular societies organised large subscription dinners, at which excitement waxed high at the thought of future struggles. One evening two hundred Republicans had gathered together at the restaurant called *Les Vendanges de Bordeaux*, and when the toasts were proposed, one of them, a youth named Evariste Gallois—a mathematical genius who was shortly afterwards killed in a duel—brandishing his glass and a large open knife in one hand, exclaimed with all the fury of the neophyte, "To Louis-Philippe!"

The Press Trials.

The Press trials and the prosecutions for incitement to murder or to a breach of the peace provided the "doctrinaires of the Republic" with a platform from which to present their system to the light of day. When the artillery officers of the National Guard, who had been compromised during the disturbances attending the trial of the Ministers of Charles X, were brought up for judgment, Cavaignac, who was one of the accused, proudly confessed his republican faith. With his long red moustache and his military bearing, he aroused sympathy, whilst the ardour of his convictions endowed his speech with a measure of grandeur. The lawyers distinguished themselves by their violence; one of them, Michel de Bourges—he was a strangely ugly creature, who, although quite young, was already bent and bowed like an old man—reminded the jury how bitterly the Restoration had repented the executions of 1822 and the bloody repression of the military conspiracies, and outside the court warned the Government against the danger of punishing political offences.

The public applauded, and the trembling jury acquitted the prisoners. This was another good day for the Opposition.

Little by little the focus of revolt broadened, attracting to itself all the scattered elements of discontent. And, worse still, the police had just discovered a plot revealing the alliance between the Legitimists and the Republicans against the monarchy. They had arranged to force an entry into the Tuileries, where the King had gone into residence when he left the Palais Royal; old servants of Charles X and members of the royal guard had promised their support. The gate-keepers were to open the gates of the Castle and of the Louvre at a given moment. It was common knowledge that on the 1st of February, 1832, Louis-Philippe was to give a great ball; the Royal Family and the high officials, "the indispensable machinery of the system," would be gathered together. It was a unique opportunity for doing away with them all at one stroke. Bands of conspirators, some two or three thousand strong, were to take up their positions in the back streets surrounding the Louvre; one column was to break into the ballroom; little bombs or "maroons" thrown among the carriages drawn up in front of the doors, racks covered with iron spikes placed beneath the feet of the horses, and finally a carefully arranged outbreak of incendiarism, would serve to increase the confusion.

Alliance between Legitimists and Republicans.

It was regarded as impossible for the plan to fail. The Legitimists had distributed bribes all round, while the Duchesse de Berry, the daughter-in-law of Charles X and niece of Louis-Philippe, who was plotting in England to bring about an uprising in the south and in Vendée against "the usurper, her uncle," awaited the success of the movement with all confidence. But in every conspiracy of such magnitude there is always some chatterbox or some spy. The leaders had established their headquarters in an inn in the Rue des Prouvaires; and the police, who had been informed, caught them there.

Plot of the Prouvaires.

And thus the propaganda of the societies and the eloquence of the lawyers produced their effect. A mad thirst for blood seemed to have laid hold of a section of the populace, and one of the most clear-sighted witnesses of this period, extremely hostile though he was to Casimir Périer, was terrified by this lust for revolution. "It is madness," wrote Heinrich Heine, "to revive the language of 1793, as the *Amis du Peuple* are doing." And, with the recent conspiracy of the Rue des Prouvaires in mind, he added, like the unrepentant poet he was, "He who picks up the rosy blooms of spring in order to replace them on the trees after they have fallen is as foolish as he who replants in the sand the faded sprays of the lily."

The well-equipped forces of the bourgeois Doctrinaires were not sufficiently strong to resist the combined attacks of the Legitimists and the Republicans in conjunction with the Bonapartists. "We want a bolt to bar the door against insurrections," said Sainte-Beuve, "something with the strength of a madman." The madman, but a madman of superior calibre, was Périer.

Périer Restores Order.

For a whole year he worked for the suppression of disorder, but the help of the National Guard and of the Chamber was indispensable. Yet he was met by opposition, panic and pusillanimity on almost every side, and all his courage was barely sufficient to overcome these obstacles and force the bourgeoisie to save themselves.

The Prince de Joinville, one of the King's sons, relates how, in the middle of a diplomatic dinner given by his father, the sound of rioting suddenly broke out and put a stop to the conversation. The guests were all looking into their plates, when a loud clatter of arms and the trampling of horses' hoofs were heard—they knew that the cavalry were charging. . . . After which the sky cleared again, and the conversation was resumed, although it required some effort. Similar incidents were frequent; about the Palais Bourbon as well as round the King's residence the insurgents were, so to speak, perpetually encamped.

Whereupon, when fear had laid its hand upon the Chamber, where the deputies already saw in their imagination a repetition of the scenes of the Convention, Casimir Périer appeared, wearing a long grey frock coat somewhat similar to that worn by Napoleon. He had just been addressing the National Guard and the Army in the street, exhorting them to resist the rebels. As soon as he entered, silence fell on the assembly. He quickly mounted the rostrum in order to reply to his opponents, who were accusing the police of having organised the disturbance. "He was so much overcome by indignation," writes an eye-witness, "that at first he had some difficulty in speaking, and remained silent for some moments, his eyes flashing and his nostrils dilated." Whereupon he threw the blame for the disturbances upon the Opposition themselves, and when a murmur of objection rose from their ranks, he turned to the majority. "There has been some talk of danger to your deliberations," he said. "Do not believe it! We have undertaken the duty of securing your safety. You are under the protection of the Army, and of the National Guard. . . ." And with all his might he shouted, "*Vive le roi! Vive la France!*" A storm of applause broke out, the majority pulled themselves together and recovered their self-confidence. It was a grand spectacle, in the subdued light of the great hall, to see this man standing alone on the rostrum, raising his fist in anger against his enemies, and infusing his own courage into the breasts of his friends, literally risking his life in order to put spirit into the assembly that had been depressed by fear, by the rattle of the drums and the rumours from outside.

Yet Périer was obliged time and again to repeat this effort. When he was absent, fear returned, and he was obliged to take up his rôle of professor of energy once more. "It is fear," he declared, "which serves the ends of parties, increases their numbers, creates them, in fact, for it is fear that makes the world believe in their strength." Ever in the thick of the fray, ever vibrating with passion, he dragged in his train that majority whose poltroonery inspired in him a sort of contemptuous wrath, but whom he tried to regenerate by teaching them the value of courage and decision. And he succeeded, though not through his powers of oratory, for he was not the sole author of his speeches. Pacing up and down his office, he used to dictate them, apostrophising his adversaries as though they were present: "Miserable wretches, they think they have got me! This is what I shall say to them!" And a secretary wrote down what he told him, softening the asperities and giving an oratorical form to his invective. Meanwhile the disturbances outside, feeling the hand of a master who despised half measures, died down and were stilled.

Abroad the new Government met with a friendly reception. The personality of Périer and his pacific declarations satisfied England and the absolute monarchies. France had apparently abandoned all idea of propaganda, and the virus of revolution was no longer to be feared. Had not the President of the Council declared, " We concede to no people the right to force us to fight for their cause, and the blood of the French belongs to France alone "?

Foreign Policy.

But the pacifism of Périer was of a peculiar brand. He had no intention of adopting the attitude of a benevolent spectator in the concert of Europe; he wanted to come to an understanding, no doubt, but it was to be an honourable understanding founded upon a basis of perfect equality, and not derogatory to the dignity of the country. If the foreigner threatened to humiliate France, he was up in arms at once.

This became abundantly clear when Austria, after having stifled the rebellion of Modena in Italy, occupied Bologna, a town which formed part of the Papal States. At the command of Périer, Monsieur de Saint Aulaire, the French Ambassador in Rome, lodged a protest: " France, a Catholic country, has need of the independence of the Holy See; and what will become of this independence if the Pope is guarded by the bayonet of the foreigner? " At the same time Périer asked the Chambers for a grant of 100 millions and the passing of a law enabling him to double the size of the Army, and allowed rumours of a landing at Civita Vecchia to be circulated.

This gave Austria food for reflection—for a pacifist, Périer was certainly somewhat rough and rude—and she evacuated Bologna. But six months later she returned there. The retort was swift; on the 21st of February, 1832, a French fleet without striking a blow occupied Ancona, another town belonging to the Papal States. Gallois, the captain of the ship, went beyond the instructions he had received, and arrested the Papal legate in his bed, whilst the French troops fraternised with the Italian Liberals. Paris was delirious with joy. At last the July Revolution had reached an understanding of its mission as an emancipating force! At the Vatican the events were not regarded in the same light. " Since the days of the Saracens," it was said, " nothing like it

The Ancona Expedition.

had been attempted against the Holy Father." Representations were made to the Government, but Périer turned a deaf ear. The step Gallois had taken and the character given to the expedition were doubtless contrary to his intentions; nevertheless he had attained his object—Austria perceived that she could not allow her solicitude for the Pope to develop into the right of conquest, and in the end the latter recognised the right of the French to remain in Ancona. The occupation lasted for seven years. Austria had been beaten on her own ground.

Admiral Roussin at Lisbon.

Périer evidently gave his own interpretation to the principle of non-intervention. In Lisbon, the usurper Don Miguel had inaugurated a sort of reign of terror. At his command two Frenchmen, a shopkeeper and a student, had been arrested and condemned without trial. The safety of the French nationals was at stake, and Périer, unable to obtain reparation, did not hesitate. A squadron under the command of Admiral Roussin set sail for Portugal, and although the Tagus was said to be impregnable from the side of the sea, the French sailors attempted the task of forcing it. They succeeded in breaking through the channel on the morning of the 14th of July, 1831, and the squadron bombarded the forts of Saint Julians and Bugio. At four o'clock it was cruising in full view of the tower of Belem, the navigators' tower celebrated by Camoëns; and an hour later Admiral Roussin wrote to Viscount Santarem, the King's Minister, whom he had warned of his movements: "You see that I keep my promises; I warned you that I would force an entry into the Tagus. And here I am before Lisbon. All your forts are behind me, and all I have before me is the Government Palace. Let us try to avoid a scandal. France, who is ever generous, offers you the same terms as she did before her victory." All the French demands were granted, the sentences against the French nationals rescinded, indemnities paid, and the guilty officials deprived of their posts, whilst Viscount Santarem was obliged to sign the acknowledgment of his defeat on board the French Admiral's flagship.

This extraordinary expedition, which was carried out with such rapidity and certainty, made but little stir at the time, though it displeased England, the traditional protector of Portugal. But Périer's reputation increased.

In Poland events moved rapidly. The Russians crushed the Polish army at Grochow and marched upon Warsaw. On the 6th of September, 1831, the town was bombarded, on the 8th it was captured and half destroyed by fire, to the accompaniment of terrible scenes of carnage. Five thousand Polish landowners were exiled to Siberia, and shortly afterwards a ukase was published declaring Poland an integral part of the Russian Empire.

Fall of Warsaw.

The news reached Paris on the 15th of September. Intense excitement prevailed; business was suspended, the shops and theatres were closed, and the people filled with consternation. "There was but one thought in the minds of all—Poland! There was but one word on the lips of all—Poland!" And Barthélemy, the pamphleteer of the Revolution, who with the help of Méry used to describe current events in verse, wrote in accents which give a fairly good idea of the political poetry of the day:

> "Noble cœur! Varsovie! elle est morte pour nous,
> Morte un fusil en main, sans fléchir les genoux,
> Morte en nous maudissant à son heure dernière,
> Morte en baignant de pleurs l'aigle de sa bannière. . . ."[1]

Consternation was succeeded by indignation. Crowds scoured the streets shouting, "Vengeance! War on Russia!" and on the Place Louis XV—Place de la Concorde—the mob awaited the rising of the Chamber, who were then discussing the situation in Poland. All that Sébastiani, the Minister for Foreign Affairs, could find to say in order to appease public opinion was, "According to the latest news tranquillity reigns in Warsaw," an unfortunate phrase which was turned into the classic "Order reigns in Warsaw." Meanwhile the crowd was becoming impatient; to shouts of "*Vive la République!*" they made for the Government offices and broke the windows, and tried to force their way into the Palais Royal. The carabineers were obliged to charge, and the sight of these giants in armour, who were known as "the shining ones," restored order. Once again Périer refused to give way to pressure from abroad, and stated the position

[1] "Noble heart! Warsaw! she has died for us, died gun in hand, without bending the knee, died cursing us with her last breath, died bathing with tears the eagle on her standard. . . ."

quite plainly: "Peace or war? Who wants war?" And the majority, revolutionary only in order to be in the fashion or from dilettanteism, but conservative at heart, replied that they did not want war.

Finally it was reserved for Casimir Périer to arrange the settlement of the Belgian question.

Settlement of the Belgian Question.

Although the Congress of London had proclaimed the neutrality of Belgium, the King of Holland refused to accept this decision and was mobilising his forces. The French troops intervened, but the King would not give way, and in spite of the treaty, refused to evacuate Antwerp. A fresh expedition became necessary, and preparations were made for the siege of Antwerp. But at this juncture, England, anxious to put a stop to any companionship in arms between the French and the Belgians, insisted upon the latter being excluded from taking any part in the campaign. This had the inevitable result of making the French unpopular with their neighbours, who did not forgive them this humiliation; and in addition to this inconvenience, which was psychological, the isolation of the French army complicated questions of billeting and commissariat. Marshal Gérard, the Commander-in-Chief, however, overcame these obstacles and succeeded in studying the susceptibilities of the Belgians; and after an honourable defence, Antwerp, defended by General Chassé, capitulated on the 23rd of December, 1832.

Thus part of the treaties of 1815 had become a dead letter without giving rise to a European conflict. But Périer did not live to see this last success of his policy.

On the 26th of March, 1832, during a spell of magnificent weather, it was learnt that cholera morbus had broken out in Paris. Its first victim died on that day in a house in the Rue Mazarine.

Cholera in Paris.

Cholera, which came from India, had already decimated the Russian and Polish armies; in February it was notified in London, and now it invaded France. The epidemic was terrible. "The victim was a corpse before the breath had left his body. His face grew thin with extraordinary rapidity, the muscles could be seen beneath his skin, which became suddenly black or of bluish tinge. His eyes were hollow and dry, reduced to half their size and looked as if they were being pulled by a cord through his head towards the back of his neck. His breath was cold, his mouth white and wet, and his pulse extremely feeble. He could only speak in the lowest whisper."

The scourge, which was at first confined to the more populous quarters, where the streets were narrow and dark, quickly spread into the bourgeois districts. On the 9th of April, 861 deaths were reported. The bodies were carried out during the night in artillery wagons, but the clashing of the chains and the rattling of the biers against each other terrified the people, and the wagons were replaced by large removal vans hung with black, on which the coffins were piled to a height almost on a level with the first floors of the houses. " The most terrifying feature," said an eye-witness, " was not the dead piled up anyhow, it was the absence of relatives and friends behind the hearse, and the passers-by fleeing in terror before the sinister convoy."

Whilst the doctors worked heroically and the Royal Family visited the hospitals, those who had hitherto escaped tried to ward off the disease by means of aromatics, bottles of scent and sachets, as the people of the Middle Ages used to do during an epidemic of plague. In order to disinfect the air, large vessels filled with chlorinated water were placed in all the public places. But still the scourge did not abate. On the 11th of April there were 1200 deaths, a figure which the papers did not publish, and panic seized upon the city. In vain did a certain theatrical manager maintain that his theatre was the only one in which not a single case of cholera had occurred, proving its perfect salubrity—the theatres were deserted. All who were in a position to do so took flight, but the masses who were obliged to remain were seized by a kind of madness.

In the suburbs a rumour was spread that the cholera was " an invention," and that in reality scoundrels were going about the streets " pouring poison over the food, into the wine and the cisterns "—in short, that a plot had been made to destroy the populace. Gisquet, the Prefect of Police, an old employé of Casimir Périer, unfortunately lent some support to these rumours by placards which he had set up, whereupon what had after all been only a suspicion was regarded as an officially recognised fact. This led to lynching. A young man was killed " because

who, thanks to him, "no longer bore in her bosom, as a focus of rebellion, a living Poland." They insisted on seeing in him merely a moneyed man anxious to secure the supremacy of the financiers, who were his peers, and the bankruptcy of liberty. But, in spite of all this, they were unable, in the face of his courageous despotism, to withhold a certain tribute of respect. For them Périer was "the Atlas planted between the peoples and the sun of July," a malevolent power, perhaps, but undoubtedly a great one.

In reality this banker was endowed with a noble ardour, a disinterested enthusiasm and an absolute devotion, body and soul, to what he considered the interests of his country. All this could not fail to inspire astonishment and attachment; there are certain great qualities which none can deny. "Believe me," said one of his opponents to another who was trying to cast ridicule upon Périer, "believe me, he is not a man to be scoffed at." Louis-Philippe, for his part, waxed impatient at the state of semi-dependence in which his Prime Minister kept him, and nicknamed him Casimir-Premier. When he heard of his death, he said to one of his friends, "Périer is dead. Is it a misfortune? Or is it a blessing?"

The answer lay with the future.

The Duchesse de Berry.

The July Monarchy was founded, as Vigny remarked, "neither on the voice of the people nor on the right of legitimacy." It rested on thin air, at the mercy of a *coup de force*. Why, in these circumstances, should a fresh Restoration have been impossible? Thus argued the friends of the fallen dynasty, and a royal personage came forward to act as a rallying point for some such attempt—the Duchesse de Berry.

Since the murder of her husband, and above all since the birth of her son, the Duc de Bordeaux, she had been the most popular member of the old dynasty. Unlike the Duchesse d'Angoulême, whose austerity repelled the most loyal, she was quick and lively and attracted all hearts. Ill at ease in the cold and formal atmosphere of the Tuileries, impatient of the restrictions of etiquette, she might have been seen in the past surrounded by a little Court of her own choosing consisting of the young and the gay. Shopkeepers, dressmakers and actors—she kept them all busy; she set the fashion, and subsidised reviews and plays; always open-handed, friendly and natural, she delighted everybody by the simplicity of her bearing and the easy charm of her manner. Moreover, she was very fond of dangerous exercises, in which she indulged from taste and not from vanity, always choosing fiery horses and difficult paths. All this made her a unique figure—the people knew her name.

But beneath her apparent frivolity the Duchesse de Berry concealed a determined love of intrigue, and her belief in her own destiny and that of her son increased when during 1828 she made a triumphal tour of Vendée and the south of France. "My friends," she told the old Royalist rebels who acclaimed her on this occasion, "if fresh storms blow up to obscure the future of our beloved country, it is among you that I shall seek refuge, among you that I shall try to win back the throne of my son!" And she kept her word.

After 1830, exile and the austere life led in Scotland in the gloomy palace of Holyrood, where Charles X had tried to set up the semblance of a Court, became insupportable to her. And when she learnt from her emissaries in France how precarious was the position of "her uncle Philip," she made up her mind to turn it to account. With the ardour of a simplicist, she believed that everything would be settled perfectly easily. Her father-in-law Charles X would abdicate and make her Regent until the Duc de Bordeaux attained his majority, when he would ascend the throne with the title of Henry V. Painful negotiations followed. The old King, who had charge of the young Duke, a boy of twelve, mistrusted the frivolity of his daughter-in-law; first he accepted, then he refused, and in the end made a pretence of giving way. The Duchesse de Berry was appointed Regent, but under certain conditions and subject to the control of the King's favourite, Monsieur de Blacas. But she did not trouble about such distinctions, and under an assumed name, though without taking the trouble to hide her identity, she set sail for Holland and finally reached Italy.

Appointed Regent.

Her plan was as follows—to cross the French frontier by hook or by crook, to make the south and Vendée take up arms, and then march on Paris. At Massa, where the Duke of Modena, in spite of the protestations of Louis-Philippe, had kindly allowed her to settle, she received a flood of appeals from the Legitimists in France. The time was propitious, the nation was waiting, all the regiments quartered between Marseilles and Montauban would declare in her favour, certain discontented generals, like Clausel, would be won over to her cause, and Vendée would take up arms. " If only Madame will show herself, France will be at her feet ! "

This romantic adventure delighted the Duchess. She pictured herself setting the Bourbons on the throne once more, followed by her loyal supporters—Marshal Bourmont, the conqueror of Algiers, and Kergorlay, de Brissac and Mesnard. The failure of the plot of the Rue des Prouvaires did not discourage her in the least. During the night of the 24th of April, 1832, she left Massa and set sail in a ship specially chartered for the expedition, the *Carlo Alberto*; and on the evening of the 28th, after encountering a thousand difficulties, she landed in the neighbourhood of Marseilles. " And now, Marshal," she observed to Bourmont, " we have burnt our boats," and she awaited news of the insurrection that was to break out. On the 30th she received the following note : " The movement has failed. You must leave France." On the horizon, the French frigate *Le Sphinx* was pursuing the *Carlo Alberto*.

In Vendée.

Leave France ! The idea filled her with horror. Was she to give up her plans because the people of Marseilles had not followed her ? " Gentlemen, to Vendée ! " she exclaimed. Travelling through Nîmes, Béziers, Toulouse and Bergerac, she reached Saintonge without being molested, whence she proceeded to Vendée. There she dressed herself up as a peasant, in a green bodice with tarnished metal buttons, a dirty yellow waistcoat and blue coutil trousers, hid her hair under a chestnut wig and blackened her eyebrows with boot-polish—she was " *le Petit Pierre* " of the legends. She felt herself uplifted with hope, for the old men told her that never had such a wonderful Royalist uprising been prepared.

In June the insurrection broke out. It was a lamentable failure—orders and counter-orders, childish foolhardiness and great loyalty uselessly sacrificed ! Balzac, who was a staunch Legitimist, tried to enshrine in his *Comédie Humaine* the tale of the siege of La Pénissière, of that second Saragossa, when sixty Royalists held 500 soldiers at bay; two trumpets were blowing all through the fight, fire was above their heads and beneath their feet. . . . It is the only episode that remains in the memory. The " Philippist " soldiers, the National Guard of the West, were exasperated by this struggle, which recalled to the veterans among them the terrible days of the Peninsular War under the Empire. " A handful of Royalists keeps 30,000 ruffians at bay," exclaimed Lieutenant Saint-Arnaud, who was afterwards Marshal of France. " I shall have the skins of a few or forfeit my name ! " Gradually the men of Vendée grew weary of the fight. They were no longer the disinterested combatants of 1793, or the platonic loyalists of 1828; they had become landed proprietors, and wanted to cultivate their estates in peace, and devotion to the legitimate King faded away in the face of material interests.

The Duchess watched this collapse broken-hearted. The leaders, conquered by the " red breeches," advised her to take flight. Had not a law been passed banishing the senior branch of the Bourbons for ever? To persist would be absurd; it was a question of history and not of romance. But the Duchess refused to be convinced. " They sent for me, and now they are casting me adrift," she replied in fury. Berryer, the Legitimist lawyer, hurried to the rescue from Paris, and implored her " to seek refuge," and escape with him to La Rochelle. " What will happen if you are taken prisoner and shut up? " he asked. But just at this moment a letter—a forgery, no doubt —arrived with the news that the whole of the South was ablaze. Whereupon the Regent of France retorted triumphantly: " I shall not go."

At the beginning of June 1832, shortly after the death of Casimir Périer, she made her way to Nantes, disguised as a peasant woman, slipped through the gates of the town, a basket under her arm and munching an apple, and sought refuge in a house in the Rue Haute-du-Château, belonging to the Duguiny sisters, who were her whole-hearted devotees.

At Nantes.

The police of Louis-Philippe were at their wits' end. They thought they had caught the Duchesse de Berry herself on the *Carlo Alberto*, but, on looking into the matter, they found it was only her maid. Where was the Regent of France hiding herself? In vain did they prosecute their search; not a trace could they find. All they knew was that a central agency existed in Paris which corresponded with "an accommodation address" at Nantes, and Louis-Philippe was extremely worried. He wanted his niece to leave France of her own free will, for he was well aware that princes in revolt were just as inconvenient to deal with in prison as out of it. But, as popular belief of the day had it, Nantes was the tomb of police investigations, and the hiding-place of the Duchess remained an insoluble mystery.

Public opinion gradually grew excited over the matter. Some scoffed at the Government for not being able to arrest a woman; others accused it of deliberate inactivity, and even of complicity. Just at this juncture the war against Holland for the liberation of Belgium was on the verge of breaking out; would not the first shot on the frontier let loose the rebellion in Vendée once more, and relight the fire that was smouldering?

Thus unexpected obstacles rose up before Louis-Philippe, and Casimir Périer was not there to overcome them.

BIBLIOGRAPHY.—A. Bardoux, *La Bourgeoisie Française* (1893). Charette, *Journal Militaire d'un Chef de l'Ouest* (1842). Timon Cormenin, *Lettres Complètes sur la Charte, la Poésie, la Liste Civile* (1832). Dejean, *La Duchesse de Berry et les Monarchies Européennes* (1913). Dermoncourt, *Madame et la Vendeé* (1834). Giraudeau, *La Presse Périodique de* 1789 *à* 1867 (1867). Hatin, *Histoire Politique et Littéraire de la Presse en France* (8 vols., 1859–61) (Vol. VIII). H. Heine, *Französische Zustände. Lutetia* (1855). Prince de Joinville, *Vieux Souvenirs* (1894). Lacour-Gayet, *Les Dernières Années de Talleyrand* (*Rev. Mondiale*, 1922). Montalivet, *Le Roi Louis-Philippe. Liste Civile* (1851). *La Politique de Casimir Périer* (*Rev. des Deux Mondes*, 1874). Nettement, *Mémoires de la Duchesse de Berry* (3 vols., 1837). Thirria, *La Duchesse de Berry* (1900). Tirel, *La République dans les Carrosses du Roi* (1850).

CHAPTER III

THE HEROIC PERIOD. INSURRECTION AND CRIME

"The Summary of Events." The Press attacks the person of the King. Funeral of General Lamarque; insurrection of June, 1832, *le cloître Saint-Merry*. The Ministry of the Duc de Broglie; death of the Duc de Reichstadt; arrest of the Duchesse de Berry. Temporary lull; the law on elementary education. The Eastern Question. Disagreement between the King and his Ministers. Fresh outbreak of disturbances. The Society of *Les Droits de l'Homme*. Law relating to associations. Insurrections in Lyons and in Paris; massacre of the Rue Transnonain. Debate regarding the King's function in the monarchy. Trial of the April insurgents. The Republican Party apparently beaten. Crime of Fieschi; its consequences; the Laws of September 1835. Fall of de Broglie and the Ministry of Thiers. Attempts at a rapprochement with Austria. Their failure owing to the crime of Alibaud. Thiers tries "to strengthen his position through Spain"; his resignation. Death of Armand Carrel.

The Summary of Events.

THE King, confident in his own long experience, believed himself fully qualified to govern alone, and a Cabinet without a leader was by no means displeasing to him—he did not replace Périer. But the death of the latter had brought about a revival in the progressive and Republican Parties, who with one accord drew up a "Summary of Events" addressed to the electors, in which they declared that the Restoration was winning and that the July Revolution had been delivered over into the hands of its enemies. "The old struggle which we believed to be at an end has broken out afresh!" It was a regular declaration of war, the gauntlet thrown down to the system that Périer had defended to his dying day.

Press Attacks on the King.

At the same time the person of the King, which hitherto had been above party squabbles, was subjected to violent attacks. If ever a sovereign knew the blessings of a free Press, it was Louis-Philippe. Caricatures, not devoid of talent, be it said, making fun of him, were displayed in front of print shops; the *Charivari*, under the editorship of Philippon and subsidised by the Legitimists, *le Corsaire*, *le Bridoison*, and *les Cancans*, vied with each other in this campaign of vilification. The King was "*La Poire*"[1] (the Pear) which Philippon had one day drawn on the prisoners' bench at the Palais de Justice. The Duc d'Orléans, his eldest son, was "*Le Grand Poulot*."[2] The pamphleteers had the time of their lives. "The King never plays for money. He is not so silly! He only plays for honour, and he who loses wins. In the arms of France the lees have taken the place of the lys." The hero of a play which was at that time being acted at the Odéon was described as "a fool from head to foot, big, fat and stupid"; these last words delighted the public, and from that time forward were applied to the King. Even among the bourgeoisie the respect that had once been felt for him gradually grew less and less. "He is like all five-franc pieces," they said, "jolly but devoid of genius"; and when they called Louis-Philippe the Napoleon of Peace, Thiers quickly retorted, "He is the intaglio, Napoleon the cameo." Madame Adelaide was treated even more flippantly; for the Queen alone was there still a remnant of respect.

Louis-Philippe was not unaware of these murmurs and insults, but he refused to take them tragically. One day, relates Hugo, he saw in front of his castle at Neuilly a child trying to draw a pear on one of the gate-posts. "You don't know how to do it," he said, and finishing the drawing, he gave the guttersnipe a louis, adding, "The pear is on that too." Meanwhile the combined attacks of the Opposition and the Press, the recollection of the despotism established under the leadership of Périer and the hope of revenge gradually led to a return of the disturbances. There was an atmosphere of rebellion in Paris—it only wanted a spark for the city to be ablaze.

Funeral of General Lamarque.

General Lamarque had just died. He was an extremely popular deputy—a soldier under Napoleon, a friend of La Fayette, he was in the eyes of the people the personification of glory and liberty. He had always refused to accept the defeat of France at Waterloo and was constantly quoted as having

[1] A slang term of abuse meaning "a fool."
[2] A term of endearment meaning "a little fat chicken."

said, "The peace of 1815 is not a peace, it is a halt in the mud."

The Opposition made this worthy man a rallying-point, and on the 5th of June, 1832, the day of his funeral, there was a general mobilisation of the enemies of the monarchy. Members of the secret societies, political prisoners, students, old soldiers, foreign refugees, Poles, Italians and Spaniards, gunners belonging to the National Guard—the Republican Party in the bourgeois militia—followed the hearse in a compact body. The air was heavy, and great black clouds rolled over Paris; with flags flying, drums muffled, to the accompaniment of revolutionary hymns and from time to time prolonged funereal cries of "Honour to General Lamarque!" the procession advanced, and this gathering about the convoy, which gave an impression of strength and unanimity, exasperated the crowd and roused it to violence. A certain section grew frightened. "Where are they leading us?" they asked. "To the Republic," replied a man who had received an honour at the July Revolution, "and you may take it for certain that we shall sup to-night in the Tuileries." And indeed the Republicans believed the hour had come. On the Pont d'Austerlitz the spark burst into flame; the crowd began to sing the *Marseillaise* and to shout "*Vive la République!*" Violent speeches followed one upon the other, and the sudden appearance of a man on horseback dressed in black and waving a red flag had the effect of raising the excitement to the required pitch. The cavalry charged, and barricades were erected. Three hours later half Paris was in the hands of the insurgents.

The June Insurrection.

Although they had been warned, the King and the Government had erred through over-confidence, and were taken unprepared. La Fayette, who was following the procession, had taken to his heels as soon as he saw the demonstration developing into a riot. "If we were to throw the General into the Seine," he heard murmured about him, "how could the Government defend themselves against the suspicion of having sacrificed him?" In the Tuileries terror reigned; in the dark they discussed in low tones the possibility of flight, and the example of Charles X returned to their minds—was there going to be a repetition of the days of 1830? Everything seemed to point to it; the Address of the 221 had only changed its name—it was now called the "Summary of Events." The staff of the Palace seemed to be melting away; "fear had frozen the most ardent devotion," and there were men high placed in the royal favour who meditated coming to terms with the future conqueror.

Louis-Philippe behaved as he always did in such circumstances, with simple sincerity and courage. At nine o'clock in the evening, while the centre of Paris was in the hands of the insurgents, he held a review by torchlight on the Carrousel. At twelve o'clock the following day he rode through the boulevards as far as the Bastille, the Faubourg Saint-Antoine and the quays. The sound of firing could be heard, and the National Guard, filled with admiration for his calm courage, cheered him. Near the Place de Grève, a woman posted in a window aimed at him, but her weapon was too heavy for her and made her hand tremble. . . . The King passed on.

Meanwhile the Republicans, supported by the Legitimists, who supplied them with arms, were still holding their own. The former remarked to the latter, "We may not have the same Paradise, but we have the same Hell." And they opened fire side by side. But gradually the regulars and the National Guard gained the upper hand, and the insurrection was confined to the classic quarter for popular upheavals, the area between the Rue Montmartre, the Passage du Saumon, the Rue Montorgueil and the Cloître Saint-Merry. At this point sixty men, under the leadership of one named Jeanne, held the army at bay; they made bullets from the lead gutter-pipes, plugged their muskets with advertisements torn from the walls, whilst from a lofty window a woman told them the movements of the troops.

The Cloître Saint-Merry.

On his return to the Tuileries the King received deputy Laffitte and two of his colleagues, Arago and O. Barrot, who came to appeal to his mercy—the victory he was on the point of winning must not be too cruel, there were urgent reforms that . . . Suddenly a dull boom was heard which made Laffitte start. "That is the cannon," said Louis-Philippe perfectly calmly. "It has been brought into play in order to force the Cloître Saint-Merry without the loss of too many lives." And indeed by four o'clock in the afternoon the Cloître was cleared and the insurrection stamped out. It had cost 800 victims in dead and wounded.

This June insurrection and the temporary but very real success of the uprising provided a clear proof that it was impossible to abandon the policy of resistance, and that it was necessary to have a man of energy at the head of the Government. At last, after several unsuccessful attempts, Louis-Philippe called upon the Duc de Broglie.

Ministry of the Duc de Broglie.

The Duc de Broglie, a Liberal under the Restoration, was a Doctrinaire in his opinions, he possessed the haughtiness of this group and its dogmatic and somewhat arrogant manner. An aristocrat, with profound convictions, he was endowed with a sort of proud timidity, and considered himself "unfitted for the handling of men." When Louis-Philippe pressed him to accept office, he insisted on having the support of his friend Guizot, who was, like himself, a Doctrinaire. Marshal Soult was made President of the Council and Thiers Minister of the Interior; but in reality the Duc de Broglie, a resolute partisan of resistance, was the leader—the direction given by Casimir Périer was resumed.

Death of the Duc de Reichstadt.

But before the Ministry had been formed (11th of October, 1832) an event had happened the logical result of which was the stabilisation of the monarchy; on the preceding 22nd of July, the Duc de Reichstadt, the ex-King of Rome, had died at Schoenbrunn. The disappearance of the young Napoleon II, in whom the old army had placed all their hopes and whose name had constantly recurred in the conspiracies under the Restoration, deprived the Bonapartist Party of a leader and delivered Louis-Philippe from a pretender who might have become dangerous. Nobody at that time gave a thought to the new heir to the imperial glories, Prince Louis Bonaparte, son of the late King of Holland and of Hortense de Beauharnais. It was vaguely known that he was engaged in conspiracies and showed sympathy for the Republican idea—a dreamer from whom little was to be feared.

But although the monarchy believed itself safe from any revival of the Napoleonic spirit, it had not yet succeeded in warding off the Legitimist menace. The movement in Vendée had doubtless been stifled, but the Duchesse de Berry was still in France, eluding every effort to find her, and possibly ready to give the signal for revolt once more as soon as she thought the time was ripe. The Government determined to have done with the rebel princess.

Thiers was charged with the task. A young and ardent southerner, he felt elated by the difficulty of the undertaking. He sent as Prefect to Nantes, Maurice Duval, a man who was capable of taking a high hand, and drew up a plan of campaign by which the whole of Brittany and Vendée would be subjected to a house-to-house search. But this proved unnecessary. One evening in October 1832, a man named Deutz, a Legitimist agent, who had just returned from a mission to Portugal and Spain, on which he had been sent by the Duchess, presented himself at the Ministry of the Interior and offered to betray his protectress. Thiers concluded the bargain.

Arrest of the Duchesse de Berry.

On the 6th of November the house of the Duguiny sisters at Nantes was surrounded by troops; the police searched it from attic to cellar, exploring the walls and the cupboards; the Duchess could not be found. At last, most unwillingly, the soldiers left the house, but two gendarmes were left on guard in every room. At dawn on the 7th, one of the latter, who was on duty in an attic, threw a bundle of newspapers into the fireplace to keep himself warm, when all of a sudden the register of the chimney opened and a voice called out, "We surrender, we are your prisoners!" The gendarme raked out the fire and to his astonishment saw the Duchesse de Berry, followed by three of her companions, emerge from the chimney. For sixteen hours these four had been shut up in a tiny pyramid-shaped hiding-place concealed in a hollow wall in the attic.

When Thiers heard the news he could not help feeling proud. He had conducted the whole affair single-handed without any help from his colleagues, and it had the result of consolidating the position of the Government and at the same time that of the monarchy. But Louis-Philippe regarded the matter from a somewhat different angle. The arrest of his niece, the Duchesse de Berry, in addition to being somewhat of a shock, lent a singular prominence to the Legitimist problem in the eyes of Europe. Was he going to keep his relative in prison? Princes in captivity inspire deeper passions in the breasts of their followers than they arouse when at liberty. If he had been a free agent, Louis-Philippe would have had the Duchess taken back to the frontier; but the public, and more especially the bourgeoisie, did not see the matter in this light; it seemed to them out of the question to allow a princess who had tried to rekindle civil war to leave the country without being tried and punished.

The King, however, could not consent to such a solution; if the Duchess were acquitted, he would become a laughing-stock; if she were condemned, he would be regarded as a monster; if he pardoned her, he would be accused of complaisancy. In this dilemma Louis-Philippe compromised very cleverly, and prevailed upon his Ministers to refer to the legislature the task of reaching a decision regarding the fate of the Duchess. She was taken from Nantes and sent to the fortress of Blaye, where General Bugeaud, an old officer of the Empire, was put in command. Devoted heart and soul to the July Monarchy and "somewhat thick-skinned," he did not mind playing the part of gaoler. Meanwhile Thiers, who had just paid Deutz 500,000 francs, which was the price of his treachery, defended his conduct on the rostrum and frightened the Conservatives by the prospect of a trial which would inevitably lead to a recurrence of disorders in the event of the Chamber voting that the Duchess should be brought up for judgment. The Government had won the day.

The ex-Regent of France remained in captivity at Blaye, winning the sympathies of all by her courage and the romantic nature of her adventure. "France," said Chateaubriand, "loves those who resist Fate." And indeed petitions crowded with signatures demanded that the captive princess should be set free. Pilgrimages made their way to Blaye, and the Faubourg Saint Germain went into mourning. But later on, when it was learnt that the Princess had secretly married an Italian nobleman, the Count Lucchesi-Palli, the enthusiasm waned—the misalliance had dethroned the widow of the Duc de Berry and the mother of the Duc de Bordeaux.

When the Government perceived that their prisoner was no longer to be feared, and that she had lost her hold on public opinion, they threw open the gates of the fortress, and a frigate conducted her to Palermo. The Duchesse de Berry had played her part—an object of suspicion to Charles X and his supporters, she found herself gradually deserted by her partisans. The Countess Lucchesi-Palli had killed the Regent of France.

After the rout of the Republicans at the Cloître Saint-Merry, the death of the King of Rome and the arrest of the Duchesse de Berry, it seemed as though the political fever might subside. Nevertheless on the 19th of November, 1832, as Louis-Philippe was riding across the Pont Royal on his way to the Palais Bourbon, a pistol was fired at him. He instinctively leant forward in his saddle, and then saluted to show that he had not been hit. A pistol still smoking was picked up on the pavement, and further on another one was found. A few days later a young man named Bergeron was arrested, but for want of sufficient proof the jury acquitted him.

Bergeron.

This attempt gave rise to widespread indignation, and the Opposition was suddenly eclipsed. The suppression of the June riots had involved the dissolution of the Society known as the *Amis du Peuple*; the whole of the insurgent forces had been brought into play and been defeated, and the leaders could not hope to raise such numbers again, for some time to come. The Revolution had almost succeeded, it is true, but its fall was all the greater—Paris and the whole of France demanded peace and order. Tranquillity was restored.

It is from this period that some of the most important laws of the July monarchy date—the departmental law based upon the electoral system, which supplemented the law of 1831 on municipal organisation; the law of expropriation for considerations of public utility, the object of which was to facilitate the execution of the great national works proposed by Thiers; and last but not least the law on elementary education (28th of June, 1833). Henceforward every commune was bound to maintain, either alone or in conjunction with one or several

Law on Elementary Education.

communes, at least one primary elementary school under the management of a lay or clerical teacher, the State reserving no monopoly. Education was to be free for the people of the place, though the sending of children to school was not to be compulsory. This law, cautious though it was, since it did not raise a clamour about principles that had already been sanctioned—free compulsory education for all and lay teaching—met with prolonged opposition on the part of the local communities. "It is vine-dressers we want, not readers," a Medoc peasant informed a school inspector. But Guizot, who was responsible for the law, insisted; and thus the admirable work begun in France in the seventeenth century by J. B. de la Salle was carried on.

In his foreign policy the Duc de Broglie remained true to the principles of Casimir Périer—peace, albeit honourable peace, if necessary armed peace. Like his predecessor, he jealously safeguarded himself from interference on the part of Louis-Philippe. "If England had not set the wise example," he wrote, "it would have been necessary to invent the rule that the King of a free country should communicate with foreign Ambassadors only through the intermediary of his own Minister." And he saw that this rule was strictly enforced.

During his Ministry the Eastern Question was reopened. Mehemet Ali, the Pasha of Egypt, was extremely popular in France, for he derived his inspiration from the work begun by Napoleon, and was trying to revive agriculture and to lay the foundations of industry in Egypt. That his innovations were mere eye-wash and the Pasha "was decorating the European side of the street," may or may not be true; his popularity increased notwithstanding. After his struggle against the Greeks, which lasted from 1825 to 1828, Mehemet demanded the pashalik of Syria by way of reward from his suzerain, Mahmoud, Sultan of Turkey. The Sultan refused, whereupon Mehemet opened hostilities and beat the Turks at Konieh in Asia Minor (December 1832), and pushed his advanced guard as far as the Sea of Marmora. The Sultan was terrified and appealed to the Tsar for help, and the whole of Europe became interested in the struggle. England, who could not consent to see Russia established at Constanti-

The Eastern Question.

nople, pressed the Sultan to grant him the pashalik of Syria; and Mahmoud gave way (Treaty of Kiutayeh). But shortly afterwards the Powers received notification of the Treaty of Unkiar-Skelessi (8th of July, 1833), by which Russia promised the Sultan all the troops necessary for his protection, whilst in return Mahmoud undertook to shut the Straits to all warships, except those belonging to the Tsar, thus making the Black Sea "a huge Russian military port." England and France protested, but in the latter country Mehemet's success was all that public opinion required; nobody would have understood the reason for intervention against Russia, and peace was preserved.

And thus the monarchy, defended by the members of the party of resistance, seemed to have been firmly established; but the relations between the King and the Cabinet became every day more strained. Louis-Philippe declared that Broglie, Thiers and Guizot were "Casimir Périer in three persons." Their supervision exasperated him, and he now began to communicate his opinions to foreign Ambassadors himself and did not hesitate openly to oppose the policy of his Ministers. Thus the unity which was essential for any efficacious action on the part of the Government was destroyed. The threat of danger at home, however, restored it.

For almost a year the revolutionaries had apparently abandoned all idea of organising disturbances on a large scale in the streets, but after this period of respite, this reign of silence, they suddenly entered the arena once more, and expressed their feelings with extraordinary vehemence. It was a sort of league of oratory, a concert of imprecations, mingled with violent syllogisms against the monarchy and the King. The newspapers, and particularly *la Tribune* under Marrast, let themselves go. They were prosecuted and made to pay fines, which at that time seemed enormous; between 1830 and 1834 *la Tribune* alone was prosecuted 114 times, acquitted 91 times, condemned 23 times, and mulcted to the tune of 150,000 francs (£6000) in fines; but a subscription was quickly raised, frequently with the help of the Legitimists, which enabled them to start again with redoubled offensiveness. The newsboys, who were masters of the streets, yelled out appeals to revolt; the police arrested them, but while loudly protesting against the oppression of which they were the victims, these " heralds of upheaval " allowed themselves to be taken without offering any resistance, knowing full well that the courts would acquit them. It became necessary to pass a law against them.

Unpopularity of the King.

The continual campaign of abuse against the King, the scarcely veiled incitements to murder, the poverty of a large proportion of the people and the hard apprenticeship of democracy soon created a strange state of mind. " The old subsoil of barbarism which remained quiescent in times of peace " rose to the surface again; at the corners of the streets porters might be heard sagely discussing the items of the Civil List, censuring the despotism of the King and even shouting out as he passed, " Miser! Chatterbox!" The more hot-headed among them, it is said, used to climb on to the railings of the Tuileries uttering threats and waving knives—the death of the " traitor " in the end became merely a question of expediency to these successors of the terrorists; and they gradually accustomed themselves to the idea. In Vendée the priests begged their congregations from the pulpit to pray for Louis-Philippe, " who would most certainly be assassinated," while the philosophers, watching the trend of events, regarded him as a lost man.

Meanwhile the King remained calm, and to the frequent warnings he received he merely replied, " I shall get the better of the rebels; the assassin's bullet can never reach my heart; my best shield consists of my children."

Les Droits de l'Homme.

Nevertheless the Republicans, who had been beaten in June 1832, were making preparations for revenge; the Society of *Les Amis du Peuple* was succeeded by that of *Les Droits de l'Homme*, which consisted in 1834 of 163 sections bearing symbolical names, Robespierre, Marat, Louvel, Saint-Just or Ça-ira, and with a roll of about 3260 members—that is to say, twenty to each section. This division had been made to evade the law which forbade associations of more than twenty persons, and the revolutionaries regarded this piecemeal organisation as a reason for its success. They had learnt from experience. A so-called secret society whose leaders are, however, known to the police, is doomed to impotence; on the other hand, if the leader remains anonymous and the members do not know the head that commands them, but, apparently dependent upon nobody, at a given signal respond to the orders of a mysterious authority, and if the parent society is crumbled up into tiny associations which suddenly join together and form a solid block against the established power, then the chances of success are enormous.

At the same time as the Republican Party modified its methods it also changed its programme; the very name of the new Society, *Les Droits de l'Homme*, sufficed to show the alteration that had taken place; vague ideology was replaced by positive demands, a central power to be elected for a limited time, universal suffrage, the freedom of the communes, the general application of the jury system, the emancipation of the working classes—in short, a revolution which should be not only political but social; and, to crown all, a federation of Europe.

This manifesto, published by *la Tribune*, terrified the bourgeoisie, who, as they had done in the time of Casimir Périer, demanded repressive measures; and in April 1834 the Chambers passed a law forbidding associations divided into sections of less than twenty persons, and no longer referring infringement to trial by juries, whose weakness and pusillanimity were to be feared, but to the courts of summary jurisdiction. Thiers frankly confessed that the proposed law was one of defence and hostility, and Carrel, in the name of the Opposition, proposed in the *National* that the suspension of liberty should be met by the suspension of law and order.

Law against Associations.

Lyons had already shown the way in this direction. But on this occasion it was not, as it had been in 1831, a rising of the poor, but a regular social upheaval. Mutualism, which had been founded during the last days of the Restoration, had since developed; it had lost its purely academic character and, encouraged by the newspapers and the predictions of the Saint-Simon school of reformers, began to make common cause with the *Société des Droits de l'Homme.*

Insurrections in Lyons.

In February 1834 a strike due to the lowering of wages broke out. 20,000 businesses closed down, but work was subsequently resumed, and it was thought that peace had been restored, when suddenly the newspapers announced that the Government was bringing forward a scheme of legislation with regard to associations. Everything was once again in the melting-pot; the Mutualists, who were directly attacked, protested; six of them were arrested, and on the 9th of April the troops and the people confronted each other and a battle was fought. But the situation was different from what it had been three years previously—the Government had taken precautions.

Not for one moment were the insurgents masters of the city; but the struggle was terrific. Fighting reached even the roofs of the houses, and cannon and bombs were brought into action, whilst the fire from the forts was turned upon the centres of resistance. On the night of the 10th of April there was a fall of snow; round about the fires the harassed soldiers kept watch over their prisoners, men, women and children; on the Saône, boats filled with hay that had been set alight floated downstream, gigantic fireships which destroyed the piers of the bridges. In the end the insurgents took refuge in the church *des Cordeliers,* where in one of the side aisles workmen manufactured powder, whilst others made bullets, and one of the chapels was turned into a dressing-station. When the guns had broken open the church, the soldiers rushed in, and as the fighting began again a man was seen to mount the altar, where, with hands crossed on his breast and his face shining, he cried, "Now is the time to die for our country!"

At last, on the 12th of April, order was restored. 131 soldiers and 170 insurgents had been killed.

Insurrection in Paris.

The revolt of Lyons had immediate reverberations in Paris. The *Droits de l'Homme* gave the signal, and on the 13th of April barricades were erected in the *quartier du Marais.* But the Government had 40,000 men at their disposal; the attack, begun about seven o'clock in the evening, was continued the next day. The insurgents had already been dispersed, when a rumour was circulated that at number 12 Rue Transnonain they were firing on the troops. The latter, exasperated, forced their way into the house and massacred the inmates in a sort of blind fury, without giving

Massacre of the Rue Transnonain.

quarter. It was a terrible scene, which has been immortalised in a tragic lithograph by Daumier, depicting a man in his shirt and a cotton nightcap stretched out at the foot of his bed, covered with bayonet wounds.

This bloody repression afforded fairly convincing proof that the bourgeoisie intended to stifle revolution for ever, and the Government turned the situation to account by obtaining from the Chamber a law against the possession of arms; a vote of 14 millions was passed to raise the Army to 360,000 men, 2,000 suspects were arrested, and an ordinance referred the April insurgents to the Court of Peers. "It is imperative," said Thiers, "to lay hands on this great conspiracy, which is spread all over France and of which *Les Droits de l'Homme* is the centre of action, *la Tribune* the organ in Paris and *le Précurseur* in Lyons."

The Government had restored order and felt sure of a majority; all inclination for revolt seemed to be at an end. The death of La Fayette, which took place on the 20th of May, 1834, and his obsequies, which were officially celebrated, gave rise to no trouble in the streets; so that the Duc de Broglie hoped to carry on the policy of Périer in the midst of comparative calm. But parliamentary difficulties and the lack of sympathy between the King and his Ministers soon complicated the situation.

Put into the minority in the Chamber, during the debate on an indemnity claimed by the United States, de Broglie sent in his resignation, whereupon combinations and intrigues followed upon each other, which after the lapse of years seem petty indeed—a Ministry would last for three days—but which lent a particular emphasis to the divergence of opinion regarding the function of the King in the new monarchy. Some maintained that the King reigned but did not rule, that it was the business of the Ministers to rule; others, on the contrary, including first and foremost Louis-Philippe himself, thought that the King ought to reign and rule at the same time, that he was in effect the permanent President of the Council, whilst the Ministers were concerned with administration alone.

Debate on the King's Functions.

These theoretic discussions reacted on the politics of the

moment, and the public began to grow impatient and alarmed by the kaleidoscopic Government that was imposed upon them. At last, at the end of eleven months (March 1835), Louis-Philippe resigned himself to the inevitable, and, in accordance with his unfortunate habit, confessed to the foreign Ambassadors that, in order not to fall into the arms of Radicalism—that is to say, of the Opposition—he was forced "to swallow the Duc de Broglie." The latter returned to power. And it was high time—the trial of the April insurgents was about to open.

Trial of the Insurgents.

Anxious to give all possible publicity to this business, which had brought the Republicans and their doctrines to book, the Government, instead of allowing the leaders of the Lyons and Paris insurrections to be tried quietly, had collected all the charges together into one huge indictment. A monster trial was being prepared for which a special room had to be built at the Luxembourg. It was an extraordinary piece of imprudence; nothing could have been better calculated to serve the interests of the Opposition—121 prisoners, 558 witnesses for the prosecution, 261 witnesses for the defence, a huge judicial inquiry (17,000 documents), the mobilisation of all the lawyers and magistrates in the kingdom, was not all this sufficient proof of the power of the enemies of the monarchy?

The latter had drawn up their programme, and speech succeeded speech. The accused, led by the Republican Baune with his stentorian voice, refused to take part in the debates, and insulted the judges; and President Pasquier, an old parliamentarian, although he was accustomed to such sittings, tried in vain to secure peace and silence.

Outside, the mob, not noticing the warlike preparations in the Luxembourg gardens, where bayonets were sandwiched in between the orange-trees, shouted out their admiration for the oppressed. It was a repetition of the scenes at the trial of the Ministers, though the time was spring—it was the month of May 1835—and it looked like a regular political meeting verging on revolution, at which justice appeared in the light of a despised supernumerary, whose only purpose was to marshal the items in the programme. All round the hall discussions were being held; young revolutionaries, with pale faces, threatening looks, long moustaches, beards and hair, and wearing Teutonic or Greek caps—the very ones that Chateaubriand saw—were instructing the onlookers in their doctrines. Never had the Republic had such a wonderful tribunal at its disposal.

But the lawyers spoilt everything. A public letter signed by some of them contained the following sentence: "The infamy of the judge is the glory of the accused." Prosecutions were set on foot by the Court of Peers, but most of the signatories of the letter disavowed it; two only, Michel de Bourges and Trélat, in the end declared themselves the authors. This incident, which showed the courage of the Opposition in anything but a good light, immediately reduced the trial to humbler proportions. Shortly afterwards it was learnt that twenty-eight of the leading prisoners, Cavaignac, Marrast, Guinard and others, had escaped by an underground passage from the prison of Sainte-Pélagie, where they had been shut up. "The Revolution was taking to its heels." The Court of Peers passed sentences of imprisonment and deportation first on the Lyons and then on the Paris insurgents. As far as France was concerned the case had been heard—and the Republican Party found itself reduced to impotence for a long time to come.

The Idea of Regicide.

It then became a commonplace to say that the law of the 10th of April, 1834, against associations had saved the monarchy; and the trial of the insurgents confirmed this opinion. But in reality the idea of regicide was spreading in Paris. Every 21st of January the members of "*la Société de la Tête de Veau*," mentioned by Flaubert in *L'Éducation Sentimentale*, met at a cabaret on the outskirts of Paris and celebrated the great day which had seen the execution of Louis XVI, the Capet locksmith; on the table the calf's head symbolised the head of the tyrant. This was merely a retrospective insult, the occasion for a political agape not provided for in the calendar; but ruder natures dreamed of putting words into action. "To-day," observed X. Doudan, one of the wittiest and most polished writers of the period, "the violence of actions is in inverse ratio to the strength of convictions. To-day a man is shot at for a mere whim. And the King is shot at owing to an impulse which in the old days would merely have prevented a man from taking off his hat as he passed."

And everything combined to foster this state of mind. Extravagant romanticism and the revival of the Middle Ages or the Renaissance with all their ferocity—poison, Florentine perfumed gloves, etc.; the impassioned digging into the past for which Victor Hugo had set the fashion; the extremely gloomy melodramas that were acted on the boulevards and whose only acceptable ending was the heaping up of dead bodies in the last act to the accompaniment of curses, lamentations and anathemas; the glorification of Robert Macaire, the gentleman highwayman, the generous knave whom the great actor Frédérick Lemaître had impersonated on the stage; the whole rhetorical category of hatred and threatening demands, and of the exaltation of the poor at the expense of the bourgeois, had the effect of justifying, in the realm of art at all events, revolt and murder. But for those who were not intellectuals and could not distinguish between art and reality, this state of affairs gave rise to very different feelings—they wanted to act on real flesh and blood.

The Conservative papers were well aware of the danger presented by this efflorescence of tales of horror, and inveighed against the decline of manners and the perversion of morals; Dumas' *Antony* and Victor Hugo's *Le Roi s'amuse* were so many examples of deplorable teaching for the people, and they damned root and branch " that heaping up of crimes and acts of debauchery, each one worse than the last." Occasionally their agitation had some effect—the play was hooted off. When a certain drama dealing with the Terror was presented the public shouted in disgust, " Away with the guillotine ! " There was really a glut of corpses and very often a glut of stupidity. But as soon as a new drama was in preparation, the young school made it their own; and thus a continual battle raged from which romanticism more often than not emerged triumphant. The Republic, it is true, did not share in this triumph—the *National* opposed the movement, which it regarded as unbalanced. Nevertheless the taste for blood persisted; a great crime committed in a fit of rage was certain to arouse tremendous enthusiasm.

Cavaignac used to say to his friends, "The King will live only as long as we wish him to; we have in the *Société des Droits de l'Homme* a hundred assassins whose blind devotion only requires to be kept in check." Words that were almost prophetic; but others also possessed a similar gift of divination. On the 27th of July, 1835, the *Charivari*, printed in red, published an article entitled: "Monarchical catacombs; a small memorial tablet to the subjects of His Majesty who died victims to the mistakes of public order." This was followed by a list of the alleged murders committed by the municipal guard and the National Guard, the line troops and the police in the pay of Gisquet, the Prefect of Police, who were dubbed "the Gisquétaires." In all this the massacre of the Rue Transnonain was not forgotten, but in order to enlighten the people and strike their imagination more forcibly than by a simple obituary notice, this number was illustrated by an engraving depicting the King, the eternal "Poire," in an entirely new aspect. A confused mass of dead men and men in chains formed the head, the arms and the feet, and this unsightly conglomeration bore the following inscription: "The victims of despotism." But this list of old grievances was not enough, and in a general news column of the same number, the *Charivari* wrote, as though by the way: "Yesterday the King-citizen returned to Paris with his superb family without anybody attempting to assassinate them."

In the provinces and abroad the same sinister warnings were published; a letter from Paris inserted in the newspapers announced *urbi et orbi* that Louis-Philippe would perish on the 28th of July, the anniversary of the "glorious days"; whilst in Rome *Young Italy*, a revolutionary society under the leadership of Mazzini, told its members to hold themselves in readiness to turn the death of the King to account.

The prophecy was almost fulfilled. On the 28th of July, 1835, at nine o'clock in the morning, Louis-Philippe, accompanied by his sons and his Ministers and followed by his staff, left the Tuileries on horseback in order to review the troops drawn up in echelons between the Rue Royale and the Bastille. He was greeted with but little enthusiasm, the legions of the National Guard

Crime of Fieschi.

alone cheering the master they had chosen. About midday the procession reached the Boulevard du Temple opposite the Jardin Turc, when suddenly a puff of smoke could be seen issuing from a window in one of the houses. The King just had time to say to his son, the Prince de Joinville, who was on his right, "That is for me!" At the same moment a quick irregular crackling was heard, like the sound of platoon-firing. . . . The royal procession seemed to have been mown down; on the ground the dead and the dying were trampled under the hoofs of the rearing horses, whilst the crowd, seized with panic, howled and screamed in the middle of clouds of smoke and dust and pools of blood.

Louis-Philippe was not wounded, although a bullet had grazed his forehead. Setting spurs to his horse, he galloped to the head of the troops, waving his plumed hat and shouting, "Here I am!" A tremendous ovation, such as he had never before received, met him. As a father he saw that his sons were still beside him; as King he glanced at the field of murder, where forty dead and wounded, many of whom were his servants or friends, were lying; then, drawing himself up, he cried, "Come! We must go on. March!" And all that remained of the procession continued its way towards the Bastille.

The news of the crime of Gérard, whose real name was shortly afterwards found to be Fieschi, led to an outburst of rage and terror. The victims of the infernal machine—twenty-four muskets resting on a slanting frame and all firing together—were not royal personages. Side by side with Marshal Mortier and other officers, members of the National Guard, an old man of seventy, "a working-woman without a hat" and a young girl of fourteen might be seen lying higgledy-piggledy. Could anything more odious and at the same time more stupid be conceived? Even those who had been accustomed to laugh at the sinister jokes of which the King was the subject, the critical spirits who without being convinced Republicans felt drawn towards the idea of a Republic, saw that the game was beginning to grow dangerous. The unfortunate victims of Fieschi's muskets inspired pity, and the crime was followed by a revival of loyalty

Revival of Loyalty.

to the monarchy inspired by the splendid courage of Louis-Philippe, the dastardly nature of the means employed to fight it, as well as by fear of fresh disturbances.

At heart the people were tired of this continual agitation which had been convulsing the country almost uninterruptedly for the last five years. They wanted to put an end to it; and business men, shopkeepers and artisans were united in desiring the restoration of peace, and the certainty of being able to carry on their work without interruption. If the Government required arms to secure order once more, they were ready to supply them.

On the 4th of August, 1835, the Chambers, which had been urgently convoked, were presented by the Duc de Broglie with the draft of three laws calculated to put an end to anarchy in the kingdom. "Anxious for her King and for her institutions," he said, "France raises her voice and demands from the Government the protection she has the right to expect." The two first measures arranged for a change in the procedure before the Assize Courts, which were henceforward to be empowered to pass judgment in the absence of the accused; if the latter placed obstacles in the way of justice they were liable to expulsion; and finally the juries were to give their vote on the sentence by secret ballot, the verdict of the majority to hold good. The third law, which was much more important, was concerned with the Press; it created new offences—affront to the King, Republican leanings; it raised the amount of the deposit money as well as the scale of fines, and made it illegal for any drawing to be published without permission having first been obtained.

These proposals might have borne the signature of Casimir Périer; they complemented the laws already in existence concerning newspaper boys and associations; nevertheless they were not passed without considerable difficulty. The old Doctrinaires, like Royer-Collard, writers, like Lamartine, who had only lately taken to politics, and members of the Opposition, united in recalling memories of the Convention and of the spectre of tyranny. But the impulse of public opinion towards order at all costs was too pronounced. De Broglie confined himself to repeating that the proposed measures were indispensable for the completion of the work of defending the Monarchy, and the laws which have remained famous under the appellation of "the September Laws" came into force. Thus Fieschi's infernal machine had succeeded in killing, not the King, but the liberty of the Press. The Opposition was reduced to silence, the papers were ruined by fines, and propaganda by means of pamphlets and caricatures became impossible. Royalty, henceforward above discussion, was triumphant.

Louis-Philippe thought the moment had now arrived for him to assume personal control of affairs. Ever since his accession, feeling himself suspect at the three Courts of Austria, Prussia and Russia, who could not forgive him his revolutionary origin and regarded his kingship as merely temporary, he had remained faithful to the alliance with England. But now he was cutting a very different figure in Europe; having crushed rebellion and restored order, he represented the principles of stability and of opposition to Liberalism and revolution so dear to the heart of Metternich. Hence his desire to come to an understanding with Austria, and to unite the interests of France with those of an Empire whose sole aim was the maintenance of the *status quo*. If he could succeed in arranging a marriage between his eldest son, the Duc d'Orléans, and an Austrian Princess, the "matrimonial blockade" which had hemmed in his family since 1830 would be raised.

Talleyrand, the French Ambassador in London, asked the King, "What more does Your Majesty expect from England? We have exploited our alliance with her and can derive no further advantage from it." Louis-Philippe shared these sentiments; but de Broglie thought differently. The latter had just replied, in his usual haughty and dignified manner, to a manifesto sent by the three Courts, proclaiming the necessity of upholding the integrity of the treaties of 1815 which were menaced. He remained faithful to the alliance with England, the advantages of which in the East in his opinion outweighed all that Russia had to offer. In this his policy was diametrically opposed to that of the King, and conflict was inevitable.

In February 1836 a vote by the Chamber on the question

of the conversion of the *rente* unexpectedly brought about the downfall of the de Broglie Ministry. A plot hatched in the Tuileries, or a parliamentary surprise? It is impossible to say. But Louis-Philippe at all events had attained his end.

Fall of de Broglie.

He wanted a more complacent and amenable Ministry than the previous one had been, with a policy that lent itself to contingencies and convictions that were not too strong and were capable of adapting themselves to circumstances. He turned to Thiers. The latter had tried his hand at everything since 1830—finance, police, commerce, public works and home affairs, and was extremely anxious to secure the portfolio for Foreign Affairs. A zealous worker under Laffitte and afterwards under Casimir Périer, he oscillated agreeably between the party of progress and the party of resistance, always good-tempered, underrating his own importance—though this was mere pretence on his part—and always knowing how to wriggle out of a tight corner. And when Talleyrand said to him, " Monsieur, Europe awaits you ! " flattery won the day and, abandoning his old colleagues, more particularly Guizot, he accepted the Presidency of the Council on the 22nd of February, 1836.

Thiers in Office.

Endowed with extraordinary ability, priding himself on being well informed on the most diverse questions, and though not an orator capable of holding an audience " by means of the thousand and one little cables such as the Lilliputians used to bind down Gulliver," devoid of dignity in his bearing and almost commonplace to look at—he used to wriggle in his clothes, says a contemporary, as if he were trying to get out of them—Thiers felt himself called upon to lay the foundations of peace in France; " in his opinion everything began and ended in his own person." He had the shrewdness to choose as colleagues men who were incapable of bearing him a grudge and whose names made but little stir in the public mind. Thus he stood out conspicuous in his petty greatness, and, infatuated with himself, let it be known that his advent to the Ministry was going to inaugurate a new era. For almost four years, ever since the death of Périer, all hopes of a strong Government had been abandoned; but with him at the helm, people would soon find out what energy supported by science could accomplish, and the monarchy would resume its upward march.

The reality turned out to be less magnificent. Without a constant majority and without a programme, Thiers played a double game, making advances to all the parties and receiving with equal cordiality one day the Doctrinaires, and the next the deputies of the Left. He shelved irritating questions with jealous care and contented himself with passing laws of general utility. In this he acted as Villèle would have liked to do in the past.

But as regards foreign affairs, Thiers saw matters on a grand scale. He had made the conservative policy of the King his own, expressed his disapproval of the revolutionary agitations in Switzerland in no measured terms, and above all energetically prosecuted the negotiations with Austria with a view to the desired alliance. The Duc d'Orléans had gone to Vienna. Tall and slim, with a charming face, eloquent and brave, the Duke, according to Heinrich Heine, "was a typical Frenchman in the best acceptation of the word." He quickly won the hearts, not only of the young Archduchess Theresa, whose hand he had come to ask, but also of her parents. Nevertheless the opposition of a certain section of the Austrian Court, who invoked the "royal will," delayed the celebration of the marriage. Metternich, in his communications with Monsieur de Sainte-Aulaire, the French Ambassador, raised various objections—the difference between the political systems of France and Austria, the bitter feelings that the Revolution of 1830 had left in Austria, etc.; and finally he reminded him of Marie-Antoinette and Marie-Louise, pointing out that the climate of France did not seem to suit Austrian Princesses. The negotiations were dragging on when suddenly the news of a fresh attempt on the life of Louis-Philippe reached Vienna.

Foreign Policy.

On the 25th of June, 1836, as the King was driving out of the gate of the Tuileries to go to Neuilly, a young man fired at him at close range with a firearm in the form of a walking-stick. Had he aimed a trifle lower the King would have been killed; the wad was

Crime of Alibaud.

found in his hair. The would-be assassin, whose name was Alibaud, was arrested on the spot.

"What a lesson for those who support the marriage!" exclaimed Metternich as soon as he heard the news. "How could a father and his daughter consent to a settlement which exposed her to such risks?" A chorus of warnings was raised about the young Archduchess and she was flooded with well-meant advice. "How would you like to get into a carriage through which the bullets of the regicides were flying?" she was asked. Alibaud's crime was far too good a pretext to be allowed to slip, and the negotiations for the proposed marriage failed.

The Duchesse de Dino, a witty woman, observed at the time, "That shot, I am afraid, has killed our Crown Princess." Nevertheless Thiers tried to reopen the negotiations and to intimidate Metternich. But in vain! "The Duc de Chartres (d'Orléans)," came the reply, "might have been a desirable match; but the Crown Prince of the French is not." Louis-Philippe accepted the result with a good grace. "They are as I have always known them," he said; "it is this spirit that for the last fifty years has lost every cause for those who are always looking backwards." But Thiers displayed less constancy and philosophic calm; wounded in his self-conceit, he changed his policy towards the "retrograde Powers" from one day to the next.

Spain.

Spain, ever since the death of Ferdinand VII, had been in a state of civil war, the Regent Cristina carrying on the Government in the name of the young Queen Isabella and opposed by the Pretender, Don Carlos, the champion of absolutism. Thiers found in this situation a unique excuse for intervention. Since the cause of Isabella, supported by the Liberals, was at the time gravely compromised, he would undertake her defence and raise a body of volunteers to go to her assistance; thus he would revive the July tradition and make France return to her "generous mission"; in short, he would show Austria that she had to reckon with him. Beaten in Vienna, "he would retrieve his fortunes in Spain."

But this sudden change was not at all in keeping with the ideas of Louis-Philippe. He cajoled and flattered his Minister.

"You at least," he said, "know your geography." But he had fully made up his mind to preserve peace and not to take reprisals which would precipitate him into an adventure in Spain. Thiers thought the King was following him, but he was mistaken. "Sire, I am very crafty!" he declared to the King, with childish pride. "I am even craftier," replied the King, "because I don't shout it from the housetops." How true this was became evident on the day when Louis-Philippe insisted on the disbanding of the troops raised at the command of his Minister. Whereupon Thiers sent in his resignation, which was accepted (August 1836).

The year 1836 had a sorry ending. The trial of Fieschi and his accomplices—Morey, a harness-maker, and Pépin, a grocer—all three of whom were condemned to death, proved how strong the spirit of rebellion still remained, whilst Alibaud's crime showed in its turn how useless was the policy of intimidation and the September Laws. Men of experience even saw in it a further significance; Alibaud, who was a commercial traveller, had no political interests and was not a member of any secret society. "Could it be possible, then, that the gangrene was reaching the middle classes?" Thiers had declared that the people had been disarmed and factions reduced to impotence, and the reply had been another deed of violence—the lamp was still burning at the foot of the altar of 1793.

It was a pitiable failure. The struggle against the eternal enemies of the Throne had to be renewed. But how was it to be conducted? What fresh measures were to be demanded of the Chambers? Guizot, who was out of power, took no pains to conceal his discouragement. "I am terrified by the state of affairs at home," he wrote to the Duchesse de Broglie, "and the moral condition of the unknown hordes who probably number thousands who have no faith, no law, no heart, no bread, but are cast adrift in the midst of this invertebrate and aimless community."

Shortly after Alibaud's crime a tragic event occurred, which, in the words of the Duchesse de Dino, "once more shed a gloom" over Paris.

A controversy having arisen between Émile de Girardin, the founder of *la Presse*, and Armand Carrel, the chief editor of *le National*, the two journalists fought a duel in the Bois de Vincennes. Carrel was wounded in the groin and died on the 24th of July, 1836, in a delirium in which the words " France, friends, Republic " could be distinguished. He was respected by all parties, who admired his honesty and courage. " He did not refute his adversaries," said Louis Blanc, " he chastised them," and his death inspired almost universal regret. With him there perished a certain indefinable chivalry and disinterestedness, a courageous virtue and military nobility which won him a distinguished place in the ranks of political writers.

Death of Carrel.

About his body enmities were laid to rest. " His pale face," said an eye-witness, " testified to passion at peace; in him death seemed full of thought, his stiffness was that of the warrior, the proud immobility of a sleeping captain." And among the crowd that followed his coffin, Chateaubriand, " the serf of Legitimacy," Béranger the Liberal, Arago the Radical, and Scheffer the conspirator might have been seen side by side.

Bibliography. Duc de Broglie, *Souvenirs* (4 vols., 1886). M. de Camp, *L'Attentat* (Fieschi, 1877). Chenu, *Les Conspirateurs* (1850). Duchesse de Dino, *Chronique* (1909) (Vol. II). Comtesse de Gasparin, *Correspondance et Souvenirs* (pub. by M. Barbey-Boissier) (2 vols., 1902). Gisquet, Prefect of Police, *Mémoires* (4 vols., 1840). Abbé Grivel, *La Prison du Luxembourg* (1861). D. Halévy, *Le Courrier de M. Thiers* (1921). de la Hodde, *Histoire des Sociétés Secrètes et du Parti Républicain de* 1830 *à* 1848 (1850). Lucas-Dubreton, *La Princesse Captive. La Duchesse de Berry* (1925). Mahul, *Souvenirs* (*Revue Retrospective*, 1893; *Sur les Journées de Juin*, 1832). H. Marcel, *Daumier* (no date). Ménière, *La Captivité de Madame la Duchesse de Berry à Blaye* (2 vols., 1882). Montbel, *Le Mariage Secret de la Duchesse de Berry* (*Revue des Deux Mondes*, April–May 1923). Montalembert and Cornudet, *Correspondance* (1905); *Procès des Accusés d'Avril devant la Cour des Pairs* (4 vols., 1835). Tchernoff, *Le Parti Républicain sous la Monarchie de Juillet* (1901).

CHAPTER IV

PARLIAMENTARY AGITATION. WAR ON THE HORIZON

Parliamentary agitation succeeds rioting in the streets. The Molé Ministry. The parties. Dupin senior. Attempt of Louis-Bonaparte at Strassburg. Death of Charles X. Truce between the parties; marriage of the Duc d'Orléans. The coalition. Fall of Molé. Dissensions in the ranks of the coalition. Insurrection of the *Saisons*; Blanqui and Barbès. Thiers returns to power and refuses to introduce electoral and parliamentary reforms. The Eastern Question. The Treaty of London. Bellicose feeling in France; its repercussion in Germany. Louis-Philippe does not want war; fall of Thiers. Attempt of Louis-Bonaparte at Boulogne. Return of the ashes of Napoleon.

AFTER the fall of Thiers, contrary to general expectation, there were no disturbances in the streets, and Alibaud's crime seemed to mark the end of the heroic period. But in reality agitation had not died down, it was merely transferred from the streets to the Parliament, and the danger to the monarchy, though it may have assumed a more academic form, remained just as real. For four years, from the end of 1836 to 1840, France was to know the meaning of repeated changes of ministry, oratorical battles, and unexpected alliances between conflicting parties; the principle of royal authority and that of parliamentary sovereignty were preparing to clash with renewed violence.

Parliamentary Agitation.

Having rid himself of Thiers and his bellicose ardour, Louis-Philippe gave the Presidency of the Council to a man in whom he had complete confidence, a Minister who would be both accommodating and reliable, " Périer having been reliable but unaccommodating, and Thiers accommodating but not very reliable." Molé, who was a peer of the realm, the descendant of an old parliamentary family, had no very pronounced political convictions; he was an aristocrat but not a fanatical one, endowed with a keen intellect—this is

Molé.

apparent from his recently published memoirs—a dilettante rather than a partisan, he had been a zealous though not an ardent public servant under the Empire and the Restoration, and had never compromised himself. He accepted the new rôle the King called upon him to play with an appearance of philosophic disillusionment. "I have never been able," he said, "to choose my task or to mould my own destiny." This position of semi-isolation had its advantages; being free from the discipline of any particular group, Molé was able, in the formation of his Cabinet, to choose first and foremost men who believed in order, and with whom he stood in friendly relations —Gasparin, Rémusat and Guizot, who, on returning to power, took their revenge on Thiers. And Louis-Philippe had reason to hope that the time had come when he would be able to carry on the Government himself.

At this juncture, however, a change took place in the Parliament which involved a reshuffling of parties. Thiers, irritated by his downfall, moved towards the Left, whilst Guizot headed for the Right. The former's motto was "The King reigns but does not rule"; the latter's "The Throne is not an empty chair." At the same time the old party of progress, whose leader was O. Barrot, became "the dynastic Left," which, in conjunction with the Legitimists, formed the Opposition. Finally, the bourgeois group, which would formerly have been called *le Marais* and which was now known as the third party, swung, as it had done before, from Right to Left, without having any precise political direction.

The Parties.

The mouthpiece of this group, the man who personified it and, in this capacity, became the butt of the journalists and the students of the *quartier Latin*, was Dupin. A lawyer, and nothing but a lawyer, he saw in politics only a cause in which he was either counsel for the prosecution or for the defence. According to Louis Blanc, his was an uncouth and bitter personality endowed with biting eloquence, and possessed of a petty though picturesque way of stating a case together with a capacity for exalting the most trivial ideas by means of a compelling flash of wit. A native of le Morvan, he had preserved a certain rusticity and had inherited the old plebeian magistrate's hatred of the nobility

Dupin.

of the sword and the cassock. The incarnation of bourgeois vulgarity, although he knew he was despised by the Doctrinaires—"to plead *à la Dupin* with street-corner arguments," as the Duc de Broglie used to say—he gathered about him the moderates and the provincials who disliked innovations, whose mentality Thiers so exactly described when he said, "The love of the golden mean has a twofold origin—in the first place fatigue, and in the second horror of extreme opinions. The whole of Europe is in this condition, she has had fifty years of revolution, she has known every extreme of human opinion and she naturally turns to those that are moderate."

Thus Dupin represented a power that had to be taken into account; but his programme was extremely limited, his unfortunate efforts to become a Minister had covered him with ridicule, while his paper, *le Constitutionnel*, was a laughing-stock to the Opposition Press. All this had embittered him. Constantly protesting his loyalty to the established system, he became all the more exacting, and as he thought himself qualified for the highest office, his recriminations never ceased. When Louis-Philippe refused to make him Minister for Foreign Affairs, Dupin, taking his foot in his hand, pointed to the nails in his boots and exclaimed, "Is it because of these that I am unfitted to negotiate with England?" And the story goes that the King, losing patience, pushed him out.

Under the influence of Dupin, the third party gradually adopted a critical attitude and gave itself airs of independence. Its hostility was openly declared when two Bills were presented dealing with allowances for members of the Royal Family. As it was a question of money, the followers of Dupin made common cause with Cormenin, the pamphleteer, and allowed themselves to be convinced of the royal cupidity. Molé perceived the danger.

He had already fallen out with Guizot, who, convinced of his own superiority, refused to recognise him as President of the Council, and treated him with a condescension that could not fail to be wounding. A Ministerial crisis supervened. Once again Dupin almost succeeded in obtaining office, but in the end Guizot was superseded and Molé remained in power (15th of April, 1837).

The question of money had not been the sole cause of the crisis. On the 31st of October, 1836, the Government had received a telegram, with the news that on the previous day Prince Louis-Bonaparte had scoured "the streets of Strassburg with a party of . . ." The telegram, which had been cut short by the bad weather, stopped at this point. The Tuileries were alarmed; the Duc d'Orléans had expected disturbances only in Vendée on the part of the Legitimists, and lo! the Bonapartist menace had reappeared! What had happened?

Attempt of Louis-Bonaparte.

Expelled from France as a conspirator, the only sign of life hitherto given by Louis-Bonaparte had been his *Rêveries Politiques*, in which republican tendencies seemed to consort oddly with Cæsarian aspirations—liberty and a strong Government. This was doubtless calculated to win him the sympathy of the Opposition, the Bonapartist Liberals, but it was of no importance, and the Government took no notice of it. Nevertheless Louis-Bonaparte was meditating a sensational return to France.

On the fall of Thiers he thought the opportunity had arrived, and winning over to his cause Colonel Vaudrey, who was in command of the 4th regiment of artillery at Strassburg, he suddenly made his appearance in the quadrangle of one of the barracks at dawn on the 30th of October. Here he addressed the soldiers, and reminding them of the glories of the Empire, prevailed upon them to follow him, and those inhabitants of Strassburg who happened to be up early that day were astonished by the unusual stir among the troops. Up to that moment everything had gone well for the Pretender, but at the Finkmatt barracks he came up against the infantry, who shouted "*Vive le Roi!*" A tumult ensued and Louis-Bonaparte, Colonel Vaudrey and the other conspirators were arrested. The attempt had failed miserably.

The King would have derived no advantage from exaggerating the importance of this affair; the example of the Duchesse de Berry was still fresh in his memory. Louis-Bonaparte was quietly shipped off to the United States, and his accomplices, both civil and military, were brought up before the Assize Court of the Lower Rhine. The trial took place in a feverish atmosphere, for the Republicans and the Liberals had declared themselves in favour of the accused, and in the court the public shouted out to the jury, "Acquit them!" And the jury, in fact, did acquit them. Strassburg was jubilant; and the adherents of the Pretender and some members of the jury held a banquet in honour of the occasion—it was a warning for the Government.

They did not let it pass unheeded, but immediately introduced a Bill called the "law of separation," by which, in the event of a crime being committed by civilians and soldiers, the former were to be tried by the ordinary courts and the latter by courts martial. But the Bill was thrown out by the Chamber, and it became clear how precarious was the majority upon which Molé had to rely.

Only a few days after the Strassburg episode, the news of the death of Charles X on the 6th of November, 1836, reached Paris. The old King, who was eighty—no Bourbon had ever lived so long—had died at Goritz, still surrounded by factitious pomp and splendour and seeing to it that his grandson should be brought up according to strict Legitimist principles. Chateaubriand, who had paid him a visit three years previously, had been terrified by the museum atmosphere of musty antiquity that pervaded the retreat of the fallen monarch. In France Charles X was forgotten, and his death passed almost unnoticed. But Molé turned the occasion to account in order generously to commute the sentences of the Ministers, whose trial had raised such storms in 1830; three of them were given permission to live in the provinces, whilst in Polignac's case imprisonment for life was reduced to banishment for twenty years.

Death of Charles X.

But this did not suffice for Molé. When a fresh attempt was made on the life of the King by a young fanatic named Meunier, he did not abandon his desire to secure a truce between all the parties, and summed up his programme in the following formula: "We prefer to calm passions rather than to be obliged to conquer them." In order to attain this end he pardoned all political prisoners and ordered the church of Saint-Germain-l'Auxerrois, which had been closed since the disturbances of 1831, to be opened again. Lastly he turned the

Truce between the Parties.

marriage of the Duc d'Orléans into a national festival destined to unite the whole nation about the Throne.

Marriage of the Duc d'Orléans.

After his failure at Vienna, the Duc d'Orléans had become engaged to Princess Helena of Mecklenburg Schwerin. It was not an ideal match, but the Princess, "who belonged to a small though distinguished House," was endowed with a charm that compelled sympathy. Her arrival at Fontainebleau, where the marriage was celebrated, and her entry into Paris were greeted with an enthusiasm which appeared to be unanimous; and Louis-Philippe was able to give himself the pleasure of opening the restored Versailles with great pomp and ceremony.

Cournot, an official who was also a philosopher and one of the great intellects of the period, observed that Louis-Philippe was less a King than a paterfamilias, and that he was anxious that the royal demesne should be a means of enriching his children. "He was endowed in no small measure with the tastes of a landed proprietor and took a delight in planting and building on a grander scale, and in administering the royal heritage as though it were an estate." He reconstructed and refurnished Rambouillet, while at Versailles, which was falling into ruins, more than 23 millions from the Civil List were swallowed up, much to the disgust of Dupin and General Bugeaud, believers in the golden mean, who deplored such prodigality. But when the King was taken to task for "his exaggerated love of the trowel," he replied that he sinned in good company, and refused to reform his ways, citing as his examples Francis I, Henry IV, Louis XIV and Napoleon. "I hate war," he remarked one day to Guizot, "I don't care for either gambling or hunting, and I have no mistress, while you yourself are a witness that I do not heap riches on my favourites! All I want to do is to give employment to workers, to encourage the arts, and leave beautiful monuments behind me for France. Such are my follies! Those of my predecessors were sometimes less innocent."

Thus, when he had the leisure, which happened but rarely, for he worked very hard, Louis-Philippe indulged his passion for decorating and improving. He revised the plans, examined the estimates and controlled the accounts with a thoroughness which surprised his subordinates. Then he would go off quite simply dressed like a bourgeois to superintend the workmen; he would chat to each one of them, and as he was cordial and knew what he was talking about, the artisan on his ladder would answer him quite naturally, without long, obsequious preliminaries. This pleased him; here at least he was treated like a worthy fellow, and was not met by either hatred or mistrust; and when his visit was over, he would return to work covered with plaster which stuck in little lumps to his clothes.

In June 1837, when Versailles was opened, he enjoyed a moment of real satisfaction. The guests were allowed to wander at will through the new rooms of the palace, which had been refitted and regilded, with a taste which was at times somewhat dubious; and in the evening, to the light of torches, the Court went in procession to the great gallery. The Duchesse d'Orléans attracted all eyes, and there was a sigh of relief to find she had nothing German about her. "Her supple figure, her long, arched neck, proudly supporting a small, round head, her delicate features and her movements, which were calm, gentle, gracious, harmonious and measured, like those of a swan on the water, were more reminiscent of Polish blood," and Poland was still dear to the heart of the Frenchman. The Duc d'Orléans looked radiant, and the whole atmosphere was full of joy, unanimity and hope: "the most wonderful honeymoon that could be imagined," observed an eye-witness.

Opening of Versailles.

And indeed the excitement seemed to have calmed down. It is true that a fresh plot had been formed by a man called Huber, who aimed at nothing less than wiping out the whole of the Royal Family by means of an infernal machine more diabolical than the one used by Fieschi—small cannons instead of muskets; but attempts of this kind inspired less terror than they had formerly done—people had grown almost accustomed to them. The women who had once been most hostile to the King-citizen "now honoured him with their jewels," and flocked unhesitatingly to the balls at the Tuileries. Never had Louis-Philippe stood higher in public opinion.

Whereupon Molé seized the opportunity in order to dissolve the Chamber and try to secure a majority which would be more whole-heartedly devoted to him. But the results of the elections were disappointing—the main object of the new deputies was " to secure a revival of trade," without troubling about politics pure and simple. This might possibly have best served the interests of the country, but did not conform with the views of the fallen Ministers, who were doing all in their power to revive the old parliamentary disputes which were thought to be at an end (October–December 1837).

The Coalition.

The first to set the ball rolling was Thiers, the leader of the Left Centre. " The King," he said to the Doctrinaires, " is making fun of us; he knows that if we were united his Cabinet of lackeys could not exist for a moment." Guizot made some show of resistance; but in the end, owing to his grudge against Molé, he gave way; Barrot and Dupin followed suit, and there came into being, between the two Centre parties, the Left and part of the Right, " the immoral and sinister coalition " which was openly to declare war upon " the Court Government."

Thiers held a meeting of the conspirators at his own house. His mother-in-law, Madame Dosne, had made herself conspicuous in society by her bitterness against Molé; but as a matter of fact the object of attack was not so much the Government as the King. Balzac describes how in a moment of temper Thiers went so far as to tell Louis-Philippe, " One day under your own roof, in your own interests and in spite of you, I shall lay down my own terms ! " And this was indeed the aim of the coalition, openly avowed by its theorist, Duvergier de Hauranne, when he talked of replacing personal government by parliamentary government and of securing the triumph of " independence over servility, of uprightness over duplicity, and of honesty over corruption." This was a surprising attitude in a moderate, but the coalition were determined to inflame public opinion.

It was impossible for Molé to leave these diatribes unanswered, and at his instigation a Bordeaux journalist, named Fonfrède, replied that the principle of government was government by the King, and that government by the Chambers would be not only bad but impossible. Whereupon the controversy raged, and lasted throughout the year 1838.

At the same time the foreign policy of Molé, that is to say, of the King—the evacuation of Ancona by the French troops, which had followed upon the evacuation of Bologna by the Austrians, and the attempts at *rapprochement* with the absolutist Powers—was subjected to violent attacks. The Minister was accused of humiliating the country and of abandoning the only policy that had been truly national; whilst on the rostrum the coalitionists took every opportunity of inveighing against the encroachment of personal power with all the oratorical devices at their command. According to them, Molé was merely a screen, a talking machine, behind which the King governed alone. "Listen," wrote Madame de Girardin, a witty woman of the day, "listen to the wonderful speeches in the Chamber telling the Crown in more or less plain terms, 'Go and hide! You can be seen.'"

Hitherto there had been only skirmishes, and exchanges of apparently theoretical ideas; but at the end of 1838 a regular battle was fought over the debate on the Address. The Opposition drafted and presented a text which bore an extraordinary resemblance to the Address of the 221 in 1830; it laid down its conditions to the Parliament and the King sitting in assembly—a sort of ultimatum to the Government and a summons to the Crown to release its grip on the latter. The debate lasted for twelve days, and was so heated that a certain deputy, who was usually calm and contained, shouted out to Molé in the tumult, "Go and hang yourself, you dog!" The Minister held his own against the storm, not with the spirit of a Casimir Périer, but with a good sense and a quiet courage which were surprising in this man who was a thinker, delicate in health, and moreover devoid of any gift of oratory.

However, he met with support from an unexpected quarter. Lamartine, who had been a deputy since 1833, had occupied a seat in the gallery like the old Doctrinaires, not out of contempt, but because he wanted to find "support outside the existing parties, in the conscience of the country." Incapable of intrigue, and a poet who had served his apprenticeship in the art of rhetoric, he was irresistibly attracted by the spiritual side of the events that were taking place. He was accordingly quick to discover that beneath its cloak of grandiloquent eloquence, the

Thiers–Guizot–Dupin coalition hid nothing but platitudes and mean ambitions, and in opposition to these politicians, whom he dubbed "vile jugglers and mountebanks," he set up the working masses, who knew nothing of backstair intrigues, exclaiming, "We who do not wear out the rostrum, who are not perpetually filling the stage with our ever new and ever brilliant parts, who do not spend our time in exercising power or in disputing with our rivals, we, I say, rise at last in order to tell you that we refuse to allow power to be wasted, the rostrum to be degraded, and representative Government to be dragged through the mud. Yes, we refuse to ratify your Address, because it is your Address and not the Address of the country."

Molé won the day, but with such a small majority that once again the Chamber was dissolved. The elections took place in a feverish atmosphere. Without perceiving that they were ruining the system they themselves had founded, and were repeating the tactics which in 1830 had led to the overthrow of the legitimate monarchy, the coalition hurled themselves frantically into the struggle, comparing Molé to Polignac and openly attacking the person of the King. "France," wrote *le Temps*, "has not abdicated in favour of Louis-Philippe." In reality this agitation was quite unjustified; economic prosperity was universal, people were pleased with the state of trade, the budgets showed a surplus and the 5 per cent. *rentes* rose to 119, which they had never done before. But the Opposition cared but little for these things—Thiers and Guizot wanted to return to power. They were victorious—the Government lost thirty seats and Molé sent in his resignation (8th of March, 1839).

Fall of Molé.

What would be the fate of a dynasty thus pulled to pieces and placed in the dock, a dynasty whose origin was too recent for it to have pushed its roots very deeply into the country?

One of the most notorious of the coalition that had led the attack on Molé was Odilon Barrot. In 1830 he had, as a commissioner, superintended the exodus of Charles X and, after having dissuaded La Fayette from establishing a republic, he had become the leader of the moderate Left, the opponents of the dynasty. He was

Odilon Barrot.

popular with crowds, because he had the right gestures and voice; but the gift of foreseeing events and sudden changes of opinion was entirely lacking in him. "In the realm of ideas he was always a day late," and a man who knew him well was able to say of him, "He used to think profoundly about nothing." When he had won the day, Barrot hoped to secure a seat in the Government; but he was far out in his reckoning. Dissension soon broke out in the ranks of the triumphant coalition. Guizot, who had hurled himself resolutely into the conspiracy, wished to reap the reward of success, and in any case could not come to an understanding with members of the Left. But Thiers, for his part, suspected him; for their old animosity was by no means dead, and Louis-Philippe cleverly turned these multifarious misunderstandings to account. When the leaders of the various groups met in his Cabinet, he lent a supercilious ear to their discussions; then, raising his thumb in the air, he said, "I am one, you are four," which Thiers interpreted to himself as meaning, "One who knows what he wants will always get the better of the four." And this was exactly what happened, though it took time.

Dissensions in the Coalition.

New combinations had to be tried, all of which were failures, none of the aspirants consenting to yield an inch to another; but gradually the coalition fell to pieces, which was what Louis-Philippe was aiming at. This unstable state of affairs irritated the people, who felt they were being handed over to the tender mercies of intrigue; there were some disturbances in the streets, and the pessimists raised their voices in lamentation. "Our country is going to the dogs, you may be certain of that," wrote the Duchesse de Dino. In the end a fresh revival of the revolutionary party occurred to bring the politicians back to a sense of reality. Ministerial crises had been succeeding each other for three months when the insurrection of the *Saisons* broke out.

Three years previously, in the month of March 1836, in a lonely house, bearing the number 113 Rue de l'Ourcine, a secret powder factory had been discovered. Here, in disquieting unanimity, law students, a doctor, an ex-manufacturer of cotton goods and a workman, the man who had made the framework of Fieschi's machine, worked side by side, providing sufficient proof of the obliteration of class distinctions through common hatred of the established system. The conspirators belonged to a secret society called *la Société des Familles*, formed from the remains of the *Société des Droits de l'Homme*, which had been broken up after the insurrection of April 1834. They had distinctly republican leanings, tinged with Babouvism—that is to say, Communism—and had organised themselves in such a way as to be unknown to the police. Each family consisted of five members bearing false names, who used to meet twice a month under the presidency of a leader.

It was for these leaders that the police were searching, and shortly after "the affair of the Rue de l'Ourcine" they arrested a thin, sickly, red-haired man, with restless eyes surmounted by bushy eyebrows, who had already served his apprenticeship as a revolutionary in 1831 and 1832. He was a cold and violent sectarian, blindly obeyed by his lieutenants; "clean and badly dressed, wearing black gloves, with small hands and small feet," he looked like an aristocrat turned demagogue, a sort of Saint-Just with less to say—his name was Blanqui.

Blanqui.

At the same time a big fellow with clear frank eyes, endowed with a certain ferocious beauty, who said his name was Barbès, was also arrested. Among his papers was found an appeal to revolt, the tone of which surpassed that of the proclamations under the Terror: "Arise, ye people! Do you not see the victims of Saint-Merry and of the Rue de Transnonain showing you their bleeding wounds? They cry aloud for blood! Strike, and strike again! Bare your arms that they may be thrust into the entrails of your tormentors. . . ." How was it that a young man of twenty-six came to indulge in such giddy rhetoric, in such convulsive writing? He was a student and rich. The police made inquiries, and found that he was the reputed son of a priest who had married in the colonies during the Revolution; his mother had died of shame when she discovered the kind of man she had married; his father had killed himself in despair, and this accounted for Barbès having been won over to revolutionary ideas.

Barbès.

After the discovery of the powder plot, the *Société des Familles*, whose statutes had been seized, was dissolved, but it lost no time in starting again under the name of *Société des Saisons*. The organisation remained much the same as it had been before, with the addition of certain improvements dictated by experience—six members under the command of a seventh called Dimanche made up a week; four weeks commanded by July made up a month; three months rendered obeisance to a Season Chief called Spring, and the four seasons to a revolutionary agent. "The calendar was applied to the conspiracy. Every member and every leader was forbidden to write or keep a single line relating to the society, any breach of the rules being regarded as treachery."

Insurrection of the *Saisons*.

The secret was well kept. Blanqui, the man of ideas, and Barbès, the man of action, having profited by the amnesty voted by the Chamber, took into partnership a sort of revolutionary administrator, named Martin-Bernard, and decided to attempt a *coup de force* on Sunday the 12th of May, 1839. The moment was well chosen; races were being held on the Champ de Mars, which meant that the heads of the administration and of the National Guard would probably be away. Moreover, certain garrison changes among the regiments were coming into operation on that day, which deprived the army of the unity of action which means strength. The three leaders of the conspiracy drew up a proclamation calling the people to arms and appointing a provisional Government, and furthermore, in order to make a more vivid appeal to the imagination, they added the signatures of Lamennais and of Voyer d'Argenson, an advanced Republican, to the other names.

On the afternoon of the 12th of May, the insurgents met in groups in the Saint-Denis and Saint-Martin quarters, where they looted two armourers' shops; whereupon led, some of them by Martin-Bernard, and the rest by Barbès, they seized the Palais de Justice and the Hôtel de Ville, and tried to establish themselves on the bridges in such a way as to secure communications with the centre of the city, where barricades were being erected.

The police, although they were informed through the seizure of certain revolutionary journals, *le Moniteur Républicain* and *l'Homme Libre*, which were clandestinely published, were surprised by the suddenness of the movement. But the insurgents, who hoped to gather thousands of recruits on their way, numbered barely 300. The troops and the National Guard easily got the better of them. By the evening of the 12th the Hôtel de Ville and the Palais de Justice had been recaptured and the barricades raised. On the following day an attempt to revive the rebellion failed completely.

"It was not an insurrection, hardly even an affray," wrote Michelet to Quinet, as they congratulated each other on the fact that Lyons had not followed the example set by Paris. Nevertheless the number of victims reached the figure of a hundred, "of whom about thirty were on the side of law and order." Blanqui had disappeared; Martin-Bernard eluded the police for a few days longer, whilst Barbès was arrested, riddled with wounds, on the evening of the 12th, and condemned to death. His courage almost made him an object of sympathy, but Louis-Philippe hesitated to pardon him. On the very eve of the day on which Barbès was to be executed, however, he allowed himself to be moved, for he had received from Hugo the following lines alluding to the death of the Princess Marie, his daughter, and the birth of the Comte de Paris, son of the Duc d'Orléans:

> "Par votre ange envolé ainsi qu'une colombe,
> Par ce royal enfant, doux et frèle roseau,
> Grâce encore une fois ! Grâce au nom de la tombe,
> Grâce au nom du berceau !"[1]

Barbès was imprisoned at Mont Saint-Michel, and became the hero of the Opposition. "In gaol," wrote *le National*, "Barbès will be none the less Barbès, just as Christ on Calvary was none the less Christ."

The serious aspect about the insurrection of *Les Saisons* consisted in its almost exclusively popular character—members from the ranks of the bourgeoisie, like Cavaignac, became more and more rare in the secret societies—and also in its communistic tendencies. It seemed like a return to the time of the Babeuf

[1] "In the name of your angel, who has flown like a dove, in the name of the royal babe, sweet and delicate reed, Pardon once more! Pardon in the name of the tomb, pardon in the name of the cradle!"

plot, when the conspirators were heard discussing the modification and revision of the principle of private property. But this was only a distant menace; for the time being it seemed as though parliamentary agitation was favourable to disorder—and there was tragic evidence of this.

On the 12th of May Louis-Philippe observed to Soult, "Marshal, the waters are troubled. We must fish for Ministers." And that same evening the Ministry was formed. The King had left out "the great egotists"—that is to say, Thiers and Guizot—and given the Presidency to Soult himself. The latter had no deep political convictions; he did not regard them as necessary, but treated politics as he had treated war, "as a brilliant handle to which blades of all shapes and temper could be fastened at need." Behind him Louis-Philippe carried on a Liberal Government.

But although Guizot, alarmed by the disturbances, definitely left the coalition and accepted the post of Ambassador to England, Thiers did not lay down his arms. When, in February 1840, the Chamber was asked to vote an allowance for the Duc de Nemours, who was marrying a Saxe-Coburg princess, he manœuvred brilliantly and came to an understanding with the friends of Molé to refuse the allowance without entering into debate. "The Ministry," observed Admiral Duperré at the time, "has received a bullet in the belly which has gone and lodged itself in the centre of the Crown." And indeed Soult and the King were defeated; the former had to send in his resignation, whilst the latter had once again to submit to the Presidency of Thiers.

Thiers in Power.

The game of see-saw began again, and at the same time the process of disintegration in the Chamber continued; "in the parliamentary night the parties staggered about." Nevertheless, though Thiers troubled himself but little about a programme and carried on the Government from one day to the next, the Left persisted in demanding reforms—first, the reform of the parliamentary system, which would make the holding of public offices incompatible with the mandate of a deputy—there were at this time 150 deputies in the Chamber who were also officials; and secondly electoral reform—that is to say, the extension of the right of suffrage. But Thiers as Minister was very different from Thiers in opposition, and he tried to cajole the Left by means of favours without giving way to them. "The Ministry is working well, exceedingly well," wrote Ximénès Doudan on the 1st of April, 1840, "it seems to be quite alive. Its head leans slightly to the Left, but it is an imperceptible blemish and many might be disposed to think it becoming."

Nevertheless the heaping up of favours was not sufficient, and in order to occupy men's minds, Thiers proposed to have the ashes of Napoleon brought to France. It was a clever diversion, for the name of the Emperor always acted like magic on the people. The idea was greeted with enthusiasm, and "the sublime agony of Saint Helena, as resigned though more prolonged than that of Christ," was called to mind. Those who, like Lamartine, raised their voices against this encouragement of Bonapartist hopes—"this further support given to a widespread literary conspiracy"—were few and far between. The Prince de Joinville was charged with the task of bringing to France the remains of the hero who had been abandoned on a rock in the Atlantic.

But Thiers did not enjoy the fruits of his idea for very long; he was obliged to come to a definite decision with regard to electoral reform. A petition demanding the vote for members of the National Guard was being circulated in France and was covered with signatures; Arago, a man of science, but also a Radical deputy, pressed it in the name of the sovereignty of the people—was it reasonable, not to say prudent, to give the vote only to 200,000 out of the 8 millions of Frenchmen of the age of twenty-five? Was there not a risk that in depriving the masses of their civic rights, the ranks of the "audacious empiricists" would be swelled? Urged to take sides, Thiers adopted the attitude of a Government official, and replied that sovereignty was vested only in the King and the Chamber; and in spite of a vigorous campaign of propaganda, including banquets and demonstrations, the reform was postponed.

For four months, thanks to his talent and shrewdness, Thiers had remained in power, when suddenly an event occurred in the East which cast all the problems of domestic politics into the shade.

The Eastern Question.

In April 1839, the Sultan Mahmoud, urged on by England,

had renewed the struggle against Mehemet-Ali, Pasha of Egypt, and had invaded Syria; but his troops suffered a severe defeat at Nezib. When the news reached Constantinople, the Sultan had just died, leaving as his heir a child of sixteen, and the commandant of the Turkish fleet handed over his vessels to Mehemet-Ali. It looked as though the latter would shortly be master of Turkey.

His success was hailed with joy in France—the victory of the Pasha meant the defeat of England and the restoration of French prestige in the East. Whereupon the Press immediately adopted a bellicose tone. "It is we who should be the arbiters," they exclaimed, "and see that France plays a part worthy of her!" Dupin, however, who was a staunch supporter of the doctrine "Mind your own business," exhorted the Government to make a stand. Was French policy compatible with absolute and unquestioning sympathy with the Pasha? Was it not to be feared that Russia, profiting by the weakness of the Turks, and exploiting the privilege granted her by the Treaty of Unkiar-Skelessi, would occupy Constantinople? England and Austria hastily proposed to France that they should take concerted action with a view to settling the Turco-Egyptian conflict, and Louis-Philippe, as was only wise, accepted.

But as soon as it came to settling the basis of a compromise between the Pasha and the Turks, difficulties arose—almost the whole of Europe was hostile to the Pasha, England fearing in him the possible founder of an Empire which would bar her road to India and in which French influence would be paramount. What was the Government going to decide? If they abandoned the Pasha it would mean an outcry in France. If they supported him and tried to secure him greater advantages, they would be arousing the animosity of Europe.

Treaty of London.

Whilst Thiers was hesitating at the cross-roads, he learnt that England, Austria, Russia and Prussia had signed the Treaty of London of the 15th of July, 1840, without Guizot, the French Ambassador, being informed, and had decided to settle the Turco-Egyptian question by themselves, undertaking to support the Sultan against the Pasha. This amounted to reviving against France the coalition of 1813, which had brought about the fall of Napoleon. The excitement was intense.

Bellicose Feeling in France.

Not consternation, however, but a desire for war, was the prevalent feeling. All parties were united in maintaining that it was impossible to submit to such a humiliation. "The Treaty," wrote the *Débats*, "is an insult, which France will not endure." The people were all in favour of war, and Quinet only expressed the general sentiment when he wrote: "If we submit to treaties written with the blood of Waterloo, we are still legally in the eyes of the world only the vanquished of Waterloo!" The tradition of 1830 was revived—France would wipe out the disgrace of 1815 on the Rhine frontier.

At Court the same spirit prevailed. The princes saw that war was imminent, and even the King did not hide his indignation. "For ten years," he cried, "I have kept the flood-gates of revolution closed at the expense of my popularity and peace of mind, and even at the risk of my life. *They* (meaning the Allies) owe me the peace of Europe and the safety of their thrones, and behold their gratitude! Do they want me to put on the red cap?" He harangued the foreign Ambassadors with such violence that the doors had to be closed: "You are ungrateful scoundrels; you want war, and you shall have it! And if necessary I shall unmuzzle the tiger."

Thiers, who was more bellicose than anybody—he was one of those petty natures that adore war—began to make preparations for the conflict. He made hurried arrangements for the fortification of Paris; and his Ministry, which had been inaugurated on the 1st of March, was thenceforward known as "the Ministry of Mars I." The sole topic of conversation was bombs, bullets, mass levies, muskets and cannon. Paris was to become a huge stronghold which all the absolutist coalitions in the world would be unable to force. Never, even during the Hundred Days, had there been greater activity in making preparations for invasion. There was panic in financial circles, the *rente* fell—the 3 per cent. dropped from 86·50 to 70·70—and there was unrest among the workers. No matter! They forged ahead; it seemed as though the die had been cast.

The Powers had proposed to give the Pasha Egypt with an hereditary title and Syria with a life title, but when he refused they decided to allow him only Egypt. The whole of French policy rested on the resistance and success of Mehemet. A fragile foundation! After the bombardment of Beyrut by the British fleet, the Pasha gave way, recalled his troops and surrendered his fleet to Turkey.

It was impossible to hide the snub France had received. The English Minister, Palmerston, was insolent in his triumph, whilst Germany was even worse.

Madame de Staël had once made it the fashion in France to feel a sentimental regard for the purity and spirituality of Germany, and Heinrich Heine had been trying in vain ever since 1835 to open the eyes of the French. Where he had failed, however, the Treaty of London succeeded. The national feeling of Germany against France was as brutal as it had been in 1813, and even Heine was able to write, "Thiers with his blustering tub-thumping has waked fair Germany from her lethargic slumbers. . . . Already the clash of the brazen bucklers of the Walkyries can be heard, those divine sorceresses who decide the fate of battles!" While Metternich, in less poetic language, declared, "Monsieur Thiers likes to be compared to Napoleon. Well, as far as Germany is concerned, the resemblance is perfect, and Monsieur Thiers even has the advantage. It has required only a short space of time for him to lead that country whither it had taken ten years of oppression under the Emperor."

Germany.

The new King of Prussia, Frederick William IV, who hated France so much that he refused to buy pictures by French masters, encouraged this explosion of hatred, which found its symbolical expression in *The German Rhine* by Becker, a petty official in Poland, who immediately rose to fame: "They shall not have it, our German Rhine!" Scholars and soldiers followed in the footsteps of the poets after their own fashion, reviving a whole catalogue of ancient grievances—the Treaty of Verdun, made between the sons of Louis le Debonnaire, must be restored, Conradin, who had been beheaded by Charles d'Anjou, must be avenged, as well as Valmy and Jena, whilst "Alsace and Lorraine, brothers that had been separated," were to be given back to their German motherland; and to crown their glory they conjured up the ghost of Hermann destroying the legions of Varus. "France," declared a certain German general at the time, "represents the principle of immorality; she must be annihilated, otherwise there will no longer be a God in heaven." And thus, roused by the bellicose ardour of France, the German States, already economically united by the *Zollverein*, became self-conscious—the day on which they combined against France was really "the day on which Germany was conceived."

Paris was filled with astonishment. Cousin, the philosopher, could not understand this violence against his country; Lamartine, magnificently lost in the clouds, replied to *The German Rhine* by *La Marseillaise de la Paix :*

> "Ils ne crouleront plus sous le canon qui gronde
> Ces ponts qu'un peuple à l'autre étend comme une main."[1]

But this only brought down a further avalanche of abuse on the head of France. Thiers, for his part, was utterly at a loss; for the conflict was no longer limited to England, but was becoming European. Whereupon, in a Note of the 8th of October, 1840, he gave way, though only on one point, abandoning Syria to the fortune of war, but demanding Egypt as an hereditary possession for the Pasha; and, without waiting to see the result, he openly and ostentatiously hurried on the preparations for hostilities. Having adopted a bellicose attitude, and fearing the Left, who regarded the Note of the 8th of October as too moderate, he found it impossible to change his ground from one day to the next, and remained with the sword half drawn from the scabbard. But the King stopped him.

The King opposed to War.

As soon as his first outburst of indignation was over, Louis-Philippe regarded events from a realistic point of view—to oppose Europe and follow the dictates of public opinion involved too great a risk, and his mind was soon made up. "I shall not allow myself to be dragged too far by my little Minister," he declared. "At heart he wants war, and I do not." Shortly

[1] "Never again shall those bridges which one people stretches out to the other like a hand crumble beneath the roar of the cannon."

afterwards, on the 15th of October, 1840, as the royal carriage was driving along the Quai des Tuileries, a shot was heard—a man hidden behind a street lamp had just fired at Louis-Philippe. He was arrested. "Your name?"—"Conspirator."—"Your profession?"—"Exterminator of tyrants." This attempt on the part of Darmès made a considerable impression—it strengthened, as it were, the idea of peace. Moreover, during the course of diplomatic negotiations the popular passion had had time to cool.

Thus when Thiers proposed to the King that a menacing declaration should be made, the latter felt himself strong enough and sufficiently supported by the country to refuse; and Thiers, repeating his action of 1836, sent in his resignation.

Fall of Thiers.

Peace was maintained, but the name of Napoleon and bellicose memories continued to vibrate in the public mind. Louis-Bonaparte had not given up the thought of attempting "a return from the Isle of Elba." On the 6th of August, 1840, he landed from England on the beach at Wimereux near Boulogne, bringing with him, in addition to a few partisans, uniforms and arms, and last but not least "a live eagle, for which doubtless a part had been reserved in the drama which was to be enacted." A repetition of the Strassburg scenes took place; the Pretender, who had accomplices among the officers of the 42nd line regiment at Boulogne, prevailed upon some of the soldiers to follow him, and found himself face to face with troops that had remained loyal. A pistol shot wounded a grenadier, and everybody fled. Louis-Bonaparte threw himself into a boat, which capsized, and was taken prisoner.

Louis-Bonaparte at Boulogne.

Brought up before the Court of Peers, since the Government feared the scandal of an acquittal if he were tried by jury, the Prince was calm and dignified, though he surprised those who were present by his clumsy gestures, the dullness of his eyes, and his foreign accent, which was sometimes German and sometimes English. Sentenced to detention for life, he was taken to the Château de Ham, which had been used as a prison for the Ministers of Charles X, and from which he afterwards escaped.

The leader of the Bonapartist Party had just failed at Boulogne even more miserably than he had done at Strassburg, and yet the cult of Napoleon was in no way undermined.

The Ashes of Napoleon.

On the 15th of December, 1840, as soon as day dawned, and in spite of the intense cold—the thermometer registered fourteen degrees of frost—the whole of Paris was rushing on foot towards the Champs Elysées and the Esplanade des Invalides; it looked as though the city were pouring itself out on one side "like fluid in a tilted vessel"—the Prince de Joinville was bringing the ashes of Napoleon to the capital. Towards midday the winter mist lifted and the sun began to shine—"it might have been the month of Austerlitz"—and there could be seen slowly advancing, surrounded by dignitaries in gold-lace and sailors in dark uniforms, a huge chariot, an enormous gilt mass, "the stages of which rose like a pyramid above the four great wheels that supported it." Before the gate of the Invalides the chariot came to a standstill and the sailors carried the coffin on their shoulders beneath the dome. "Sire," said Joinville to the King, "I present you with the body of Napoleon."—"I accept it in the name of France," replied Louis-Philippe; and a salvo of artillery announced that the ceremony was over.

Among the spectators there were some who were disappointed. "The return of the ashes," said Hugo, "was a sort of disappearance trick. The Government was terrified of the phantom they had conjured up—they seemed to be trying to show Napoleon and hide him at the same time. They merged the imperial procession into the military procession, the army into the National Guard, and they conjured the coffin into the cenotaph." And X. Doudan added, "The ceremony was cold both literally and figuratively. The lavish display of gilt paper used in the ceremony did not make any very great appeal to the imagination."

But these were the opinions of a poet and a chronicler. As a matter of fact the people seem to have been profoundly moved, especially at the moment when the funeral car stopped beneath the Arc de Triomphe. The people sang:

> "Napoléon aimait la guerre
> Et son peuple comme Jésus. . . ."[1]

[1] "Napoleon loved war and his people like Jesus. . . ."

and the beggars in the crowd demanded alms, not for love of God, but in the name of Napoleon. In other cases, it is true, this sumptuous display revived feelings of hatred, and as the King and his Ministers passed, there were some cries of "Down with the traitors!" They could not forgive them for having avoided war.

Thus ended the parliamentary agitation which had lasted for four years. Above the crumbling of parties, the miserable intrigues, plots and coalitions, one sentiment remained alive—the cult of Napoleon. "A thousand cannon," said Heine, "lie sleeping in that name as they do in the colonne Vendôme."

BIBLIOGRAPHY. Chassin, *Edgar Quinet. Sa Vie et ses Œuvres* (1859). D. Cochin, *Louis-Philippe* (unpublished documents) (1918). G. Delahache, *L'Insurrection de Strasbourg* (*Revue Alsacienne Illustrée*, 1913). X. Doudan, *Mélanges et Lettres* (4 vols., 1876–77). Dupin (the elder), *Mémoires* (4 vols., 1855–61). Elias Regnault, *Histoire de Huit Ans* (sequel to Louis Blanc) (3 vols., 1851). de Falloux, *Mémoirs d'un Royaliste* (2 vols., 1885) (Vol. I). Fermé, *Les Grands Procès Politiques*. I. *Strasbourg*. II. *Boulogne* (1868). de Flers, *Le Roi Louis-Philippe. Vie Anecdotique* (1891). G. Geffroy, *l'Enfermé* (Blanqui) (1897). A. Laity, *Le Prince Napoléon à Strasbourg* (1838). Vicomte de Launay (Madame A. de Girardin) *Lettres Parisiennes* (4 vols., 1853). G. Lenôtre, *Vieilles Maisons, Vieux Papiers* (5th series) (1924). Nougués, *Une Condamnation de Mai* 1839 (1850). Sencier, *Le Babouvisme Après Babeuf* (1912). Taschereau, *Revue Rétrospective ou Archives Secrètes du Dernier Gouvernement* (1848).

CHAPTER V

THE CONQUEST OF ALGERIA (1830–1848)

Uncertainty of French policy after the capture of Algiers. The army blockaded in Algiers; attempt to escape. The appearance of Abd-el-Kader; his tactics with regard to France. General Desmichels deceived by the Emir; will France abandon Algeria? Clausel saves the situation but fails before Constantine. The restricted occupation. Bugeaud and the Treaty of la Tafna. Capture of Constantine. General Valée organises the conquered territory. The expedition of the Iron Gates. The Emir hurls himself upon the Mitidja. The new French method of warfare; the *razzia*. Tremendous activity of La Moricière. Changarnier. The African army. Capture of the *smala* by the Duc d'Aumale. The Emir seeks refuge in Morocco. Difficulties with England. The victory of Isly. Methods of colonisation. Battle of Sidi-Brahim. Bugeaud asks to be recalled. Surrender of Abd-el-Kader.

The French in Algeria.

THOUGH bellicose passions may have been suppressed in France, they found a wide field of action in Algeria, where for ten years a stubborn struggle had been carried on, the fortunes of which alternated between victory and defeat, and which was made all the more difficult by the insufficient knowledge of the country, the inhabitants and the native customs possessed by the French.

Although legally under the suzerainty of Turkey, Algeria was in practice a free State, governed by a sort of military aristocracy, "the divan," which delegated its powers to the Bey of Algiers, to whom the three Beys of Oran, Constantine and Titteri (Medea) were theoretically in subjection. There was no political or even religious cohesion among the population, consisting of Arabs and Berbers, tribes, like the Kabyles, who recognised no central power, officials, like the imams and the muftis, who were at once priests and judges; and last but not least religious confraternities who blindly obeyed the orders of their marabouts. Among them all there was only one clear distinction—that of the Government officials (the *maghzen*), on the one hand, and the subjects, or *raias*, on the other—" the devourers and the devoured."

France possessed only the foggiest ideas about this semi-inorganic state of affairs so different from her own. She marched forward on the adventure and felt her way, and it was only by means of experience dearly bought that she at last learnt an efficient method of ruling the country.

Charles X had decided upon the conquest of Algeria as a point of honour, and also in order to create a diversion from difficulties at home. But the expedition, as we know, was not popular, and after the revolution of 1830 the public mind was much more concerned with the revision of the Charter than with the consequences of the French victory in Africa. Nevertheless the July Monarchy kept the French troops in Algiers; Bourmont was replaced by General Clausel, who set sail in a foreign vessel and to the salute of a few guns, " taking with him, as the reward of his courage, only the heart of his son, who had been killed in battle."

Clausel, who had served under the Empire, arrived full of confidence—all that was required to make Algeria a French possession was to occupy the country and come to some agreement with the Mussulman chiefs. And as a matter of fact he seized Medea, where he established a new Bey, and was making preparations for similar action with regard to Oran and Constantine, when his optimism received a rude rebuff—the garrison of Medea, surrounded by the Arabs and without food, were begging for help. The Government, anxious at the turn of affairs in Belgium, recalled 10,000 men and disavowed Clausel, who had embarked upon imprudent negotiations with the Bey of Tunis, with the result that Medea had to be evacuated. In short, in February 1831 the French army was blockaded in Algiers and the period of difficulties had set in.

The French Blockaded in Algiers.

Having learnt by experience, the successors of Clausel acted with extreme caution and refrained from embarking upon any undertaking on a large scale. Berthezène confined himself to safeguarding Algiers; Savary, Napoleon's old confidant, " the executioner of the Duc d'Enghien " as the Legitimists called him, tried a policy of intimidation, and treated the natives as the Turks would have done, though without success. Voirol, who was wiser, carried out important works, and sent detachments to Oran, Arzeu and Mostaganem; while an expedition despatched from Toulon occupied the port of Bougie; and thus a series of bases was formed, separated from each other, it is true, but which it was hoped would be of use when it came to penetrating inland. At the same time Captain La Moricière, who was better acquainted than anyone else at the time with the language and habits of the natives, took over the management of the Arab offices—that is to say, of an organisation at once military and civil, established for the administration of the conquered territories. Hope had just been rekindled, when all of a sudden Abd-el-Kader appeared.

Abd-el-Kader.

He was an Arab from the neighbourhood of Mascara, in the province of Oran, a member of a family of marabouts, the Hachem, and was said to be descended from the Prophet. Young—he was twenty-four in 1833—with regular features, pale, smooth skin, a pointed beard, blue eyes, thin, nervous hands and extremely small feet, he cast an extraordinary spell over all with whom he came in contact. He was known to be extremely brave and extremely religious, and when he spoke in his grave and sonorous voice the audience was overcome with admiration. He had already won his laurels as a soldier, and as he had never been wounded even in the thick of a fight, he was regarded as invulnerable. The neighbouring tribes of Mascara offered him the title of Sultan; but, out of respect for the Sultan of Morocco, he would accept only that of Emir, thus at one stroke proving himself to be a real leader of men.

His Tactics.

His plan, which he carried out with astonishing determination, consisted in making the Arabs forget their differences, in restoring order among them by stimulating religious feeling to the extent of frenzy at the expense of national sentiment, and in organising a sacred war against the foreigner. But the hostility of rival confraternities against him constituted a formidable obstacle, and in order to maintain his prestige, he was forced to fight and convince the French that he was a real ruler and not a sovereign in name alone. Now Abd-el-Kader was endowed not only with military gifts, but also with administrative capacity; in the midst of this inchoate conglomeration of tribes, in a country without roads or means of transport, he nevertheless succeeded in creating an army which he fed by means of requisitions and ruled by means of prayer; in short, he gave the impression of being the only leader the Arabs possessed at the time, and he was recognised as such.

General Desmichels, who was commanding the Oran division at the time, thought it would be more politic to parley with the Emir than to fight him, and the latter was clever enough to consent—for, after all, did this not mean the recognition of his power? And thus, as Thureau-Dangin put it, " barbarian astuteness got the better of civilised ignorance." In a note drawn up in Arabic which accompanied the treaty (26th of February, 1834) the Emir reserved to himself the right of all traffic in powder and arms. The General did not examine his demand too closely, being satisfied that Abd-el-Kader should acknowledge the suzerainty of France and pay tribute to her. The Government, little interested in the texts of treaties, gave its consent to everything, and the public immediately jumped to the conclusion that the Emir sincerely desired an alliance; civilisation, it was maintained, had got the better of the heroic nomad who was now dreaming of introducing into his country the benefits of French industry and commerce and, in order to give tangible proof of his submission, was aspiring to the hand of a Frenchwoman! In Paris everybody was talking of embassies and presents of welcome.

Desmichels Deceived.

But it was all an African mirage of which France was the dupe. It soon became evident that General Desmichels, who had but little knowledge of Mussulman ways, had fallen into a trap and added to the prestige of Abd-el-Kader at the expense of his own country. The question was then raised as to whether it was worth while to face further mortifications of the kind or whether it would not be better to abandon Algeria. The Duc de Broglie replied, " Algiers is a box at the Opera. France is rich enough to have a box at the Opera, but this one is too dear." Others, still a prey to the fever of 1815, added, " I would willingly give

Possibility of Abandoning Algeria.

the whole of Algiers in exchange for a hamlet on the Rhine." Whilst the politicians were of opinion that a really democratic system was unsuited for colonisation, the merchants maintained that the trade with Algeria was prejudicial to their business, and in short that the adventure cost 40 millions a year. To this Clausel and his supporters objected that it was imperative for France to rebuild her colonial empire if she wished to free herself from the economic bondage in which she was held by England. A decision had to be reached, and a commission of inquiry was appointed, which, though acknowledging the precarious nature of the French occupation, yet came to the conclusion that it would be better to keep Algeria. The Government accepted its findings, and old General Drouet d'Erlon was made Governor of the French possessions in North Africa.

A young and active general would have been a better choice. Abd-el-Kader, recognised by France, was occupied in founding an Arab nation. Certain of his power, he crossed the Chélif in April 1835, and the tribes in the provinces of Medea and Algiers immediately recognised him as chief. Drouet d'Erlon remonstrated with him, but it was only waste of time, for at that very moment General Trézel, General Desmichel's successor in Oran, met with a defeat in the defile of Macta near Arzeu which, owing to the accompanying circumstances, produced a profound impression.

His column, caught between two fires, was forced to fight in torrid heat; it was the month of June. The convoy got into difficulties, the wounded were abandoned, and the massacre began; the survivors, shut in between the mountains, without access to the plain, circled round and round; some of them, overcome with delirium, took off their clothes, and giving vent to incoherent cries, or laughing in a blood-curdling way, hurled themselves upon the Arabs; others, blinded by the sun, threw themselves into the river. . . . The remains of the column reached Arzeu after meeting with innumerable difficulties. Trézel had lost 300 men.

It was clear that with a fighter like the Emir negotiations were not enough. The Government recalled Drouet d'Erlon, and once again placed its confidence in Clausel. The latter soon put matters right; he saw that he must attack Abd-el-Kader at the centre of his power, at Mascara. The town, which had already been destroyed by the Arabs, was occupied by French troops, who, without evacuating the place, pushed forward to Tlemcen, and the Emir, "pursued for many miles by an officer of the Spahis, owed his escape only to the swiftness of his horse. At night, absolutely alone, without a tent, food or fire, he was reduced to sleeping on the bare ground by the side of his horse" (January 1836). Thenceforward he was apparently no longer to be feared.

Clausel defeated at Constantine.

With peace established on the side of Mascara, Clausel returned to his idea of occupying Constantine. The expedition was hastily prepared, insufficiently provided with artillery, and without siege materials of any kind; the army arrived in November 1836 beneath the walls of the town. The cold was terrible and reminded the veterans of the worst days of the Russian campaign; the troops were demoralised. Nevertheless during the night of November the 23rd they attacked the two gates of El-Kantara and Coudiat-Aty. Repulsed at all points, they were obliged to fall back. The retreat was terrible; the army, harassed by the enemy's cavalry, moved with the greatest difficulty, gradually abandoning its baggage and wagons. Nevertheless it was saved through the cool-headedness of Clausel and the courage of Changarnier. The latter, who was in command of the rearguard, made his battalion form square, and pointing to the Arab horsemen with the utmost unconcern, said, "My friends, look at those men. They are 6000 and you are 300, you see that you are evenly matched. *Vive le Roi!* and do as I tell you!" On the 1st of December all that remained of the expedition reached Bone.

Restricted Occupation.

Clausel's defeat put an end to the policy of conquest which he had endeavoured to apply. Although it was no longer a question, as it had been in 1834, of the complete evacuation of Algeria, it was necessary to have recourse to half measures, to what was known as restricted occupation. General Damrémont, the successor of Clausel, supported by a civil commissioner, was given instructions which may be summed up as follows: "The Regency is to be subjected neither to absolute dominion nor to effective occupation. What France has more especially in view is her settlement along the coast, the security and increase of her trade and the extension of her influence in the Mediterranean. Her main object is to be mistress of the coast. The chief points to be occupied are Algiers, Bone and Oran, with the surrounding territory; the rest may be left to the native chiefs."

But before the new idea of colonisation, which seemed to meet with the approval of the wiser heads, could be applied, it was necessary to hold out against the Emir, who, after his defeat at Tlemcen, had roused Morocco and had appeared again in the province of Oran. No reverse daunted this Protean warrior; defeated, openly abandoned by his followers, he would disappear, and then suddenly return to the fight again with fresh forces. How was it possible to get the better of him? The Government, having adopted the system of restricted occupation, hoped to find in it the basis of an understanding with Abd-el-Kader, and General Bugeaud, who was appointed to Oran, was endowed with full powers to negotiate with him.

Bugeaud was a man of extraordinary appearance and of frank and determined character. Tall and young-looking in spite of his grey hair, his face discoloured and pitted by small-pox, this old officer of the Empire, who had won his spurs in Spain and had returned to active service in 1830, had a certain curious bluntness of manner which never descended to coarseness. Passionately fond of agriculture, the founder of various agricultural societies, and a landowner in Périgord, he was a happy blend of the peasant and the man of the world, "weather-beaten and full of good cheer," he had a light touch and was frequently witty.

Bugeaud.

This was not his first experience of Algeria. In July 1836 he had defeated the Emir's infantry at the Sickack; but on this occasion he had no bellicose intentions. Devoted to the July Monarchy, sick of politics and a resolute advocate of the golden mean, he had long been opposed to the occupation of Algiers. In 1833, when he was taking back his old prisoner, the Duchesse de Berry, to Palermo, on the frigate *l'Agathe*, he remarked, as he pointed out the African coast, the outlines of which could be seen on the horizon, "If the Restoration thought they were pleasing us by making us a present, I think they were mistaken. It will cost us something to keep that barren soil." His opinion had not changed since—a good treaty seemed to him preferable to a disastrous war. Placed face to face with the Emir, what sort of figure was he going to cut?

Treaty of la Tafna.

The Treaty was signed at la Tafna (30th of May, 1837). France gave Abd-el-Kader possession of the Provinces of Algiers, Oran and the Medea, with the exception of certain stretches of land and a few towns—Algiers, Oran, Mostaganem, Arzeu and Mazagran . . . in return for which he recognised French suzerainty in Africa. After the treaty had been signed an interview took place between Abd-el-Kader and Bugeaud. The latter went out to meet his old enemy, but could not find him. His aides-de-camp told him that he was venturing too far, but the General replied, "It is too late to go back," and they went on. Suddenly, on the slopes of the hills which surrounded them like an amphitheatre, the whole Arab army, consisting of about 10,000 horsemen, appeared; in the centre was a group of chiefs magnificently attired, and in front of them, wrapped in a coarse burnous, but mounted on a magnificent black charger, was the Emir. Bugeaud and his scanty escort looked as though they had come to do him homage. The Emir dismounted from his horse and sat down, and Bugeaud followed suit. The music was making such a noise that it was impossible to hear anything else. Whereupon Bugeaud got up, and as Abd-el-Kader remained seated, he said to him, "You ought to get up when I do." Then, as the Emir appeared to be in no hurry, he took him by the hand and pulled him up from the ground, thinking to himself, "He is not very heavy."

Not very heavy, it is true—Abd-el-Kader was a small man—but certainly no fool. In this diplomatic encounter Bugeaud had been made a laughing-stock, and an officer in the African army wrote at the time: "France descended a little bit too low in consenting to treat with a miserable little marabout, and the interview of General Bugeaud with Abd-el-Kader represented nothing great or honourable for our arms. It might even be called a mystification of the representative of the French nation. General Bugeaud has been fooled!"

The Treaty of la Tafna, which, but for a few modifications,

repeated the mistake made by the French in 1833, was followed by a truce, which General Damrémont turned to account in order to organise a fresh expedition against Constantine to avenge the defeat of the preceding year. On this occasion every precaution was taken, but the bad weather set in, with glacial rains and storms; the horses succumbed, while fever and dysentery raged among the troops. Nevertheless on the 11th of October, 1837, it was decided to attack by the Coudiat-Aty, "a sort of isthmus by which the rocky peak of Constantine is joined to the surrounding plateaux."

Capture of Constantine.

A howitzer fired by General Valée made a breach in the walls, whereupon Damrémont suggested to the besieged that they should capitulate, but received the following reply: "If the Christians are short of powder, we will send them some; if they have no more biscuits, we will share ours with them; but as long as a single man of us remains alive they shall not take Constantine."—"There are brave people for you!" exclaimed Damrémont. "Ah well! the affair will be all the more glorious for us!"

And so it turned out. On the following day Damrémont was killed by a shell as he was examining the works in company with the Duc de Nemours. Valée took his place, and on the 13th of October the Zouaves, under the leadership of La Moricière, launched the assault, shouting, "Down with Mahomet! Jesus Christ to the rescue!" The struggle was terrific, it was a hand-to-hand fight, furious and pitiless; the houses became so many crenellated fortresses which had to be captured one by one; there was fighting in the streets, through the loopholes and on the roofs. . . . Suddenly a powder magazine blew up; the assailants wavered and hesitated, but Colonel Combes pushed on with the 47th regiment of light infantry across the barricades and renewed the fight. He was hit by two bullets, and went to report to General Valée and the Duc de Nemours, whereupon, cool and collected, he returned to the bivouac, and lay down and died.

Nevertheless the enemy still held out. "It was the most terrible thing in the world, even in the opinion of old soldiers, who had fought under the Empire!" wrote an eye-witness, the future Marshal Saint Arnaud. "The resistance was admirable—men who had to be killed twice over, and a town taken at the point of the bayonet under deadly fire." The massacre lasted from three o'clock onwards; the maddened inhabitants tried to flee by way of the Rummel ravine which surrounds the town. "They pushed each other over . . . and fell in a terrible human cascade to the bottom of the chasm; over 200 bodies were heaped up in it. . . ." At last Constantine capitulated. On the following day the Prince de Joinville, who had taken part in the siege, said to General Valée, "But, General, if the assault had failed, what would you have done?"—"We would have begun again!" And so saying Valée pursed his lips with an expression of extraordinary hardness which, in conjunction with his diminutive stature, won him in the Army the name of Little Louis XI.

After the capture of Constantine relative peace reigned in Algeria for almost two years. Valée, who was made a Marshal and Governor of the Province, revived the Roman tradition and aimed at organising the conquered territory by building roads. But method and confidence were both lacking. The idea of colonising by calling upon Frenchmen to come and live there seemed extravagant in those days, and it was only by chance that a few more adventurous souls came to settle down in the neighbourhood of Algiers, where some sort of security might be expected. But they received no encouragement. In Bugeaud's opinion this African business always remained "a dreary sort of gift," and his loyalty to the King made him fear that it would prove for the July Monarchy what Spain had been to the Empire—one of the reasons of its downfall. Most of the officers shared this view. "Africa will cost us very dear," wrote one of them, "and we shall never get a farthing out of it, in spite of all our friends the economists, with their sheaves of theories and plans, may say. . . . Just let them come and drag their emaciated carcases over that desert ground. If they succeed in finding a lentil or a dwarf-pea they will be clever indeed." Nevertheless those who were endowed with the spirit of adventure

Valée Organises the Conquered Territory.

allowed themselves to be tempted, and in 1840 there were about 30,000 Frenchmen or other Europeans settled in Algeria.

But whilst the civil administration and the army were constantly at loggerheads with each other, peace became more and more difficult to maintain, and far-sighted men, like Major Cavaignac, the brother of the Republican, regarded a rupture as inevitable—the existence of a peaceful French colony side by side with an Arab Empire which lived by war was impossible.

This was recognised at the end of 1839. Contrary to the Treaty of la Tafna, the Emir approached the province of Constantine, and by the gradual infiltration of his supporters threatened to cut the French communications between Algiers and this province. It became necessary to stop him at all costs, and this was the object of the expedition of the Iron Gates. This was the name given to a gorge in the Jurjura range, nearly four miles long, barely twenty yards wide, enclosed between two mountain walls with peaks 300 to 600 feet high, "providing as it were a natural cover for guns." To engage in battle at this spot meant running great risks; nevertheless Valée placed the Duc d'Orléans in command of 2500 men, who left Mila, near Constantine, on the 18th of October, and arrived a fortnight later at Algiers without having been seriously interfered with. The whole of France applauded this brilliant feat of arms and believed that the war was over.

Expedition of the Iron Gates.

It broke out again, however. Abd-el-Kader had never regarded the Treaty of la Tafna as putting an end to the struggle against the foreigner. "Peace with the infidel," he said, "should be regarded by Mussulmans as a sort of truce during which they must prepare for war." And in saying this he was only obeying the true doctrine of the Koran—faith saves, the first of all religious duties is blind obedience to the Prophet, and the Holy War is the first of all good works. When he heard of the expedition of the Iron Gates, he exclaimed, "Praise be to God! The infidel has taken it upon himself to break the peace; it is for us to show him that we do not fear war!"

There was an outburst of fanaticism, a unanimous upheaval among the Arabs. "We shall soon drive the French out of Algiers," they sang in that extraordinary war poem quoted by Monsieur Charléty. "Yea, we shall cross the sea in ships.

We shall take Paris and gather together therein. Then we shall conquer the other nations and teach them the unity of the true God." At the same time Abd-el-Kader flung down the gauntlet: "Let the Duc d'Orléans come on to the field of battle. I too will come. If he succeeds in overcoming me, the land shall be yours!" At the end of November 1839 he hurled his troops against French Mitidja.

The Emir Attacks the Mitidja.

The suddenness of the attack, and the all-too-obvious failure of the methods hitherto adopted, led to a drastic change in the colonial policy of France. "Restricted occupation is impossible," wrote the Duc d'Orléans to Thiers; "it may be unfortunate, but it is the truth." And Tocqueville, who was well versed in Algerian affairs, added, "There is no half-way house between complete evacuation and full dominion." There was no longer any question of evacuation; the national honour was at stake. But in order to secure dominion, what system was to be adopted? La Moricière, the oldest of those who had fought in Africa, and after him Bugeaud, who had taken the place of Valée in 1841, supplied the answer.

The *Razzia*.

In future no attempt would be made to conquer in pitched battle an enemy who vanished into thin air; he would be attacked in his lair and starved out, and the whole country as far as the desert reduced to subjection. "A vigorous offensive by means of several extremely mobile small columns; untiring pursuit of the Emir and a *razzia* against the tribes that remained faithful to him; the occupation of a few posts chosen not to serve as barriers against the enemy, but in order to advance the base of operations" —such was the plan outlined by Bugeaud, who, fortified by the experience he had won in Spain, and still smarting under the humiliation to which he had been exposed at la Tafna, took command of the operations. He had received reinforcements and explained to his men, "The war we are about to wage is not one that can be carried on by means of musket-fire. It is only by depriving the Arabs of the resources with which the land provides them that we shall succeed in making an end of them. So go out and cut down their corn and barley!"

This inaugurated an entirely new phase in the history of the conquest. As soon as night fell, the soldiers—light infantry, Zouaves and Zephyrs—lightly equipped and driving in front of them donkeys carrying the field-mills (two small grindstones turning on an iron axle) used to set out. A rebel tribe is sighted in the neighbourhood. "As soon as the ground occupied by the tribe has been reconnoitred, they all rush forward and scatter in all directions, falling upon the tents, from which the inmates struggle higgledy-piggledy with their flocks, their wives and their children. The whole crowd flee hither and thither; the men, women and children are soon surrounded; the cattle, sheep, goats and horses swiftly collected together. . . . One man catches a sheep, kills it and cuts it up—it is the work of a moment. Another runs after a calf and tumbles to the bottom of a ravine with it; the others burst into the tents, where they lay hands on the booty, each man emerging laden with rugs, pots of butter, chickens and arms. . . . Whereupon everything that cannot be carried away is set on fire, and the animals and people conducted to the convoy to the accompaniment of cries, bleating and braying—an ear-splitting noise." The position is left, and then the shooting begins. The horsemen, who at first took flight, come back as soon as they see the column marching away; they harass the rearguard, who retaliate; the latter drive them off, and as soon as they reach a halting-place, the soldiers, turned bakers, set to work to grind the corn.

La Moricière.

For more than two years similar *razzias* were repeated, especially in the district of Mascara, the stronghold of the Emir, where La Moricière was in command. The latter really accomplished miracles during the severe winter of 1841–42. "Glory to General La Moricière, glory to him alone!" exclaimed one of his subordinates. "He has solved the knotty problem of how to support the soldier in Africa. . . . He can never stand too high in public estimation." And indeed the young General aroused the enthusiasm of his little army by his decision and his almost mad activity; he got them to make incredible efforts, never leaving the enemy a day's respite, setting out through storm and snow, making surprise attacks and administering blow after blow. "The two months' occupation of Mascara," declared his admirers, "did more than eleven years' occupation of Africa."

But La Moricière was not the only one; there was also Changarnier, the terror of the Arabs, who trembled at the name of Changarlo—Changarnier, "the man of universal gifts, indispensable in all African affairs," who was just as good at organising a *razzia* as "fixing up telegraphic communication in the clouds."

Changarnier.

The French army in Africa was really an extraordinary organisation for the period. "Imagine," says one of the men who went through this war, "a crowd of great big devils, dressed in rags patched with cloth, bits of woollen material of every colour under the sun, and pieces of goat or sheep skin, some of them wearing on their heads a cap, others a fez, others huge sombreros made of palm a foot and a half high and finishing in a point, their extremities for want of shoes wrapped in sheep or bullock's skins with the hair still on." They were the most experienced and, in spite of all, the best disciplined troops the French had had for a long time. "One can go anywhere with those fellows," declared one of their leaders, "and scour Africa in all directions." The Duc d'Orléans was well aware of this improvement when he wrote, "In France the army exists only in name, here we have it in spirit. They are rough soldiers who are upholding the French flag in Africa. . . . But there are also heroes among them. One learns endurance and nobility by rubbing shoulders with them."

The African Army.

By the beginning of 1843 the Emir had lost almost all his strongholds; Bugeaud had even founded a French town, Orléansville, on the site of his citadel of Ouarsenis, while every day he saw tribes that had been loyal to him abandoning him. Hunted down, he wandered from place to place, dragging about with him his *smala*—his family, his flocks and herds, and his treasure.

On the 16th of May, 1843, the Duc d'Aumale, the King's son, was leaving Boghar at the head of a column consisting of 1300 infantry, 560 mounted troops and a contingent of 300 natives, when Colonel Yusuf, who was in command of the advanced guard, saw an Arab scout galloping towards them at full speed. "Fly!" he cried, "If they see you, you are lost! They are 60,000 strong, and even with sticks alone they will kill you like hunted hares."

Capture of the *Smala*.

The Duc d'Aumale was consulted. " By your father's head," begged the *agha* of the native contingent, " do not do anything rash ! " But without a moment's hesitation the prince replied, " My family never retreats ! "

Behind the crest of a small hill the *smala* was encamped. It looked like a colossal ant-hill—women, children and animals—this city on the march and for the time being at rest, made a deafening buzz. It was impossible to surround the whole crowd all at once. The Duc d'Aumale, in a moment of youthful impulse, resolved to break through the *smala* from one end to the other, and cut it in half.

The light cavalry charged at full gallop, overturning and cutting down everything in their path—the victory was instantaneous. The *smala* was broken up, nobody dreamt of defence, and the confusion was terrible. . . . It was indeed a magnificent *razzia*—at the end of an hour, when the infantry arrived on the scene, all was over.

Only one prisoner was lacking—Abd-el-Kader. He had escaped from the massacre, and accompanied by a few faithful followers, he was still trying to harass the column, but the latter, under its young leader, would allow no one to approach. " I was there myself," the Emir told the Duc d'Aumale later on, " I watched you and kept in touch with you for twenty-four hours. . . ." But all in vain ! The French had learnt African methods of warfare.

Nevertheless Bugeaud was not satisfied, and wanted to settle once and for all with this enemy who had made mock of him—it was a question of wounded vanity. The old General could no longer contain himself; he exaggerated the bulletins of victory in a most unprecedented manner, which seemed outrageous even in the eyes of his own troops. But he had a very definite object—the Emir had taken refuge in Morocco for the second time, and he was going to follow him.

The Emir in Morocco.

Whereupon Europe, bribed by England, appeared once more upon the scene. Louis-Philippe looked favourably upon the war in Africa; a pacifist everywhere else, he was bellicose only with regard to Africa. His sons would win glory there, and he argued, " What do

Difficulties with England.

a hundred thousand musket-shots over there matter? Europe cannot hear them." But when it became a question of attacking the Emir on Moroccan territory, England immediately raised a protest: "If France fires a single shot in Morocco, it will mean war." Louis-Philippe immediately became frightened.

Nevertheless the opportunity was favourable. The Arabs' pæan of victory had changed to a dirge; "the complete Jugurtha," mentioned by Bugeaud, saw his troops melting away, whilst the "ulemas" in Mecca, by a subtle interpretation of the Koran, accepted the domination of the Christian, provided religious liberty were safeguarded—the Emir was losing even his religious prestige. But fear of a European war—Louis-Philippe at this time had not the strength of mind of Charles X—counselled prudence. Nevertheless Bugeaud felt confident of victory; he had become popular in the army and had exchanged his large round hat trimmed with a feather for a double-peaked cap; in the evening he would receive his officers in a cotton cap, posing as a bourgeois in the field; and as he was known to be brave and intelligent he was well loved, and his men would have followed him anywhere. The General had set himself the task of conquering Abd-el-Kader, and this delay on the frontier of Morocco, this hesitation, annoyed him.

At last France made up her mind, and declared that the Emir could not be allowed to make Morocco an inviolable retreat from which acts of aggression could be committed, and on the 6th of August, 1844, the Prince de Joinville bombarded Tangier, in spite of the protestations of England. This news delighted Bugeaud—the time for action had come at last! On the 12th of August the officers of the army had gathered together in camp in order to give a welcome to comrades who had just arrived from France; they were feasting in a grove of oleanders, when Bugeaud made his appearance. He was greeted with cheers, and with his characteristic military and at the same time rustic accent, the General said, "The day after to-morrow will be a great day, I warrant you. With my little army I am going to attack the army of the Moroccan prince, which consists of 60,000 horsemen." (This was an exaggeration, the Emir had only 40,000 men.) "I should like the number to be double or treble; for the more

Victory of Isly.

there are the greater will be their rout and the disaster that will overtake them. I have an army; he has only a rabble. . . . I shall form my little army in the shape of a boar's head. Do you understand? The tusk on the left is Bedeau; the snout is Pélissier, and as for me, I am between the two ears. Who will be able to stop our advance? Ah, my friends, we shall cut into the Moroccan host like a knife into butter!" And this was the victory of Isly.

Bugeaud drove in the Arab cavalry; it tried to re-form, but he attacked it with infantry and guns, and drove it back along the road to Fez, where there was no water for thirty miles. Whereupon he brought his troops back into camp. The Sultan of Morocco made Abd-el-Kader an outlaw.

This time everything seemed definitely at an end, and Bugeaud was able to turn his attention to the matter which lay nearest his heart—"his hobby," colonisation by the army. The soldiers, set free from their labours, were to be settled in Algeria and found families there; they were to be supplied with agricultural implements, and gradually on the conquered territory innumerable military villages were to spring up. This grand project was a failure. Civilian colonists were then tried; but the men who were sent were booksellers, ushers, and down-at-heel business men, and Bugeaud was in despair. "It is labourers we want!" he cried. Nevertheless, in spite of these unfortunate experiments, Algeria was gradually populated—in 1846 more than 100,000 Europeans were settled there. There was now a civil sphere and a military sphere, each with a separate administration. Land was granted for a small sum to those who proved that they possessed the means of cultivating it, and the example set by the Trappists made a good impression.

Colonisation.

The latter had been recommended to Bugeaud by Monsieur de Corcelle, a deputy, who had written to him: "Try my Trappists; I beg you to introduce this drop of sanctity into the African den." Although the Trappists were not soldiers or armed colonists, Bugeaud gave them a concession of land in the district of Sahel—a far from attractive neighbourhood, for it was uncultivated and unhealthy, and a hot-bed of fever. But the monks, under the guidance of Don François Régis, an energetic, courageous and cheerful man, set to work. Two years after they arrived they had cleared and drained the land, laid out plantations and constructed buildings, and when Bugeaud came to pay them a visit he declared that "the new marabouts" had transformed the aspect of the country.

Thus the work of colonisation was gradually being carried out, when, in the month of September 1845, the news of the disaster of Sidi-Brahim was received. A body of 360 infantry and 60 hussars, under the command of Lieutenant-Colonel de Montagnac, who were reconnoitring on the Moroccan frontier, fell into an ambush. The Arab horsemen were commanded by Abd-el-Kader in person. The French soldiers, collecting on a slight elevation, formed square and refused to surrender. In their midst Montagnac, mortally wounded, cried out to them, "Courage, my children! Try to reach the marabout of Sidi-Brahim!" Some of the troops succeeded in getting there and barricaded themselves in. Their only response to the summons of the Emir was to hoist a flag made up of bits of their clothes. An officer, who had been taken prisoner, advanced to present them with a fresh summons from Abd-el-Kader. "Soldiers," he said, "they are going to cut off my head if you do not lay down your arms; and I have come to tell you to die to the last man rather than surrender!" The officer was beheaded. The resistance lasted for three days, when at last, dying of hunger, the survivors attempted a sortie and were massacred. Twelve men alone escaped.

Disaster of Sidi-Brahim.

This episode, followed shortly afterwards by the capitulation of a column at Ain-Temouchent, assumed the magnitude of a disaster in France. Bugeaud, who was away at the time, returned in hot haste. In his opinion there was but one solution —to pursue the Emir into the interior of Morocco. But the Government absolutely forbade him to cross the Mouloya, which marked the frontier. Once again Bugeaud had to mark time. The Arabs, encouraged by their successes, became more aggressive; and the agitator Bou-Maza roused tribes that were thought to have been pacified. But Bugeaud, ever indefatigable, again drove the Emir back to Morocco and begged to be allowed to complete his victory. He was met by a flat refusal.

In the month of August 1846, Abd-el-Kader had 280 French prisoners massacred, giving as his excuse that his request to have them exchanged for the same number of Arab prisoners had been refused. Whereupon public opinion turned against Bugeaud; he was blamed—how unjustly!—for not having ended this terrible war, and for persisting with his system of military colonisation. The General, who had been made a Marshal and Duc d'Isly, was not the man to submit meekly to criticism; he was tired "of perpetually struggling against the mad ideas with which the public, and above all the Press, were infatuated." Furious at seeing his qualities as an administrator misunderstood and at being hampered in his direction of operations, he demanded his recall (June 1847).

Recall of Bugeaud.

Why did he not wait a few months longer? He would at last have tasted the fruits of triumph.

The position of Abd-el-Kader was at this time extremely critical. Repulsed by the Sultan of Morocco, deprived of his title, under the ban of a sort of religious excommunication, abandoned by his troops, and harassed by La Moricière, he resigned himself to laying down his arms. On the 23rd of December, 1847, on the very plateau of Sidi-Brahim where, two years previously, Colonel de Montagnac's heroic soldiers had perished, he came and delivered himself up to the Duc d'Aumale, who had succeeded Bugeaud. "God's will be done," he said to the latter. "I put myself in your hands." On the following day, as a sign of submission, he led his horse by the bridle to the door of the Duke's tent. "I offer you my horse, the last one I rode; I hope he may bring you good luck."—"I accept it," replied the Prince, "as a token of homage to France, whose protection shall safeguard you in future and as a token that the past is forgotten." A few hours later the Emir was put on board ship for Toulon.

Surrender of Abd-el-Kader.

The surrender of Abd-el-Kader marked the end of an epoch which had lasted nearly eighteen years. To the clash of two civilisations France had "served her apprenticeship" in the art of colonisation.

Bibliography. Colonel Azan, *l'Emir Abd-el-Kader*, 1925. Duc d'Aumale, *Campagnes en Afrique*, 1843–44 (no date). Général du Barail, *Mes Souvenirs* (3 vols., 1894) (Vol. I). Bellemare, *Histoire d'Abd-el-Kader* (1863). Marshal Bugeaud, *Lettres Inédites* (publ. by Captain

Tattet) (1923). Marshal Canrobert, *Souvenirs d'un Siècle* (publ. by G. Bapst) (5 vols.). Daumas, *La Société Arabe* (1844). Gaffarel, *La Conquête de l'Algérie Jusqu'à la Prise de Constantine* (1890). d'Ideville, *Le Maréchal Bugeaud* (3 vols., 1862, new ed.) (1 vol., 1885). de Montagnac, *Lettres d'un Soldat* (1885). Duc d'Orléans, *Campagnes d'Afrique de 1835 à 1839* (1870). L. Roches, *Dix Ans à Travers l'Islam*, 1834–44 (1904). C. Rousset, *La Conquête de l'Algérie* (2 vols., 1889). Marshal de Saint Arnaud, *Lettres* (2 vols., 1855) (Vol. I). Thureau-Dangin, *Histoire de la Monarchie de Juillet* (7th ed., 7 vols., 1914). Tocqueville, *Œuvres et Correspondance Inédites* (2 vols., 1861). Wahl, *l'Algérie* (1903). Yusuf, *La Guerre d'Afrique* (1851).

CHAPTER VI

GUIZOT "THE KING'S MOUTHPIECE"

Guizot governs in conjunction with the King. Peace and order. Settlement of the Eastern Question. The Convention of the Straits. Antagonism with England; the right of search. Attacks on the personal policy of the King. Quénisset's crime. Election of Ledru-Rollin. Lamartine in opposition; "the milestone Ministry." Death of the Duc d'Orléans. The Regency. "The system of corruption." The pilgrimage to Belgrave Square and the discussion about its condemnation. Consolidation of the Conservative majority; *entente cordiale* with England. Colonial policy and the Pritchard incident. The Spanish marriages. Collapse of the *entente cordiale*. Triumph of Guizot. Fresh attempts on the King's life. His safety. Isolation of the monarchy.

EVER since 1839 Guizot had been a convert to Conservative ideas; he had seen the danger of "immoral coalitions" and witnessed the fairly decisive downfall of his old friend Thiers. Nothing further was required to turn him into a Government man cut on the King's pattern.

Guizot.

When he returned from his mission to England, everybody said, "Here is the saviour of the day," and Louis-Philippe, believing that he was ready to undertake the direction of affairs, summoned him to the Ministry.

Thin and puny, with a pale complexion and almost emaciated features, a delicately outlined mouth, and eyes as it were veiled with melancholy, Guizot did not give the impression of being a man who could sway the mob. A certain foreigner, who was fairly broad-minded in his outlook, described him as "a cross between a professor of French and an old actor pensioned off by the theatrical management"; and indeed he seemed to be cut out for some University appointment.

But on the rostrum, when he became animated, and with eyes shining emphasised his speech with peremptory gestures, and laid down the law with the disdainful manner characteristic of him, his hearers, forgetting his commonplace appearance, felt themselves dominated by his severe and commanding attitude, which stirred them by its dry and rigid manner. The actress Rachel, as she one day left the Palais Bourbon, where she had heard Guizot speak, exclaimed, "I should like to act in tragedy with that man!" The contrast with Thiers was striking—Guizot, cold and direct, Thiers, excited and familiar, "Mirabeau turned insect" as Madame de Girardin called him.

The understanding between Guizot and the King was complete from the very first days. Both of them masterful men, they were pursuing the same object. According to Guizot, "there were two things indispensable for government—reason and guns"; Louis-Philippe was of the same opinion and was in entire agreement with his Minister. "He is my mouthpiece," he used to declare.

Peace and Order.

Their common programme might be summed up as follows—at home, order; since the political organisation of France was admirably adapted to the needs of the country, nothing required to be added to it or taken from it; it was merely a question of keeping it as it was by securing to the "legal country"—that is to say, to those whom the law recognised as electors—the wherewithal for the prosperity of their concerns. If Guizot did not pronounce the famous maxim, "Get rich," he certainly thought it. Abroad, a similar policy—peace everywhere and always, as the only means of securing the growth of general prosperity; hence no tempestuous demonstrations or military adventures.

For nearly eight years, Guizot, in complete accord with the King, carried out this programme to the letter.

He was not President of the Council, a post which was given to Marshal Soult, the illustrious sword, according to some, "the illustrious scabbard," according to others; but although Guizot had not the title, he alone possessed the real power. On his arrival he found the Eastern Question still unsettled, and his first care was to decide it in the best interests of France and of the national honour, but without compromising peace.

He set to work in the first place to undo the effect produced by the Treaty of London, by showing that there had been no intention of isolating France, there had merely been a certain lack of consideration with regard to her—was she going to war for the sake of lack of consideration? To which Thiers, who was still smarting from his fall, retorted that France had been well and thoroughly humiliated by the coalition of the Powers; and the polemics began again. Quinet persisted in seeing in recent events the proof that France was still the vanquished nation of 1815. "We thought that the Revolution was going to pick up her sword again in 1830, but her mighty wounded body could only raise itself on one knee. . . . And so for five-and-twenty years we have been bowed beneath the Caudine Forks, endeavouring to put a cheerful face on things and to gild our chain."

Whereupon, in order to give a sop to public opinion, Guizot promised that the Pasha should be given the hereditary pashalik of Egypt—Syria was no longer mentioned—but he was confronted by the uncompromising attitude of Palmerston, who, proud of his success, intended to enjoy the full benefits of it. The situation remained strained, and, like Thiers, who a few months previously had declared, "We are still where we were in 1792," Guizot was obliged to keep the army on a war footing and continue the fortifications of Paris. It was no easy task—the Opposition regarded the construction of these circumvallations and detached forts as a menace to liberty. They still had in mind the suppression of the Lyons insurrection, and were afraid that all this warlike preparation was directed much more against the adversaries of the established system than against any foreign foe. Louis-Philippe, on the other hand, regarded the function of these works from quite a different point of view. "Napoleon," he said, "was obliged to make war in order to keep his army in check; I have to be everlastingly slaving in order to keep the heroes, who are persuaded that I owe my position to them, in check. The fortifications will occupy them for at least ten years, which is longer than I can hope to reign." In vain did the Opposition maintain their point of view, they could not prevent the supplies demanded by the Government from being voted.

The negotiations which, for better or worse, were being carried on with England and the Sultan, at last ended in an agreement being reached—Mehemet was given Egypt, and the Powers invited France to sign the Convention known as the "Straits Convention" at the same time as they did. By this Convention all warships were forbidden to enter the Bosphorus and the Dardanelles (14th of July, 1841). Thus the Treaty of Unkiar-Skelessi was swept away; Russia lost the supremacy she had arrogated to herself in Turkey, while the latter once more came under the control of Europe. As for the Russian fleet, it was doomed to be shut up in the Black Sea. The Eastern Question was solved for the time being, and France resumed her place in the concert of Europe. But public opinion still harboured feelings of violent resentment against Palmerston and the three Powers on account of this diplomatic struggle which had almost led to tragedy.

Settlement of the Eastern Question.

The antagonism between England and France soon broke out afresh in connection with the "right of search." The Congress of Vienna having forbidden the slave-trade, England in 1831 signed a treaty with France by which each nation recognised the right of the other to stop and search their respective merchant vessels when the latter were suspected of carrying slaves. Until 1840 no difficulty occurred, but at this juncture a new Bill for a convention was introduced in the Parliament, widening the scope for the right of search by the inclusion of other States.

Antagonism with England.

The Right of Search.

Whereupon the ship-owners protested, maintaining that the convention gave to England the right of harassing French shipping in the name of philanthropy, and this argument was immediately brought to bear on the Chamber. The latter, not content with throwing out the Bill, expressed the desire that the previous treaties should cease to be observed. In the face of this almost unanimous demonstration all that Guizot could do was to insist upon the King's right to abide loyally by the engagements he had made; and the matter remained in suspense until the signature of a fresh convention in 1845.

In inflicting this defeat upon the Government, the majority in the Chamber were aiming much less at Guizot than at the

King, whose personal power was becoming more and more a reality. New and particularly insidious attacks were made upon the citizen-King. An adventuress, named Ida de Saint-Elme, who had lived on intimate terms with certain generals under the Empire, sold to two Legitimist papers letters, which were probably forgeries, in which Louis-Philippe declared himself in favour of the evacuation of Algeria, boasted of having participated in the crushing of Poland, and confessed that the fortifications of Paris were directed against "the enemy at home." The publication of these letters in the newspaper called *La France* caused a scandal, and in spite of their doubtful authenticity the King's prestige suffered.

Attacks on the King's Power.

At the same time, financial difficulties and the revision of the land tax, which menaced town and country folk alike, kept alive a spirit of hostility, and in September 1841 it seemed as if the worst days had been revived. As the Duc d'Aumale, just returned from Algeria, was passing through the Faubourg Saint Antoine at the head of his regiment, the 17th light horse, accompanied by his brothers, the Duc d'Orléans and the Duc de Nemours, and the people were saluting him respectfully, suddenly a shot rang out at the corner of the Rue Traversière, and the horse of an officer just in front of the Duc d'Aumale dropped dead. The assassin, who was caught by the crowd as he shouted, "This way, friends!" was a sawyer named Quénisset, a member of a communistic society, the *Égalitaires*. He did not possess the determination of Alibaud, but begged protection for his family and was pardoned.

Quénisset.

This deed of mercy, however, did nothing towards diminishing the unpopularity of the King. The election of Ledru-Rollin had already proved how hostile the electorate was to the new Government. Ledru-Rollin was a lawyer, tall, broad-shouldered and loud-voiced, who when he made a speech with his head thrown back, accompanied by the solemn and grandiloquent gestures of a tribune of the people, made a great impression on his audience—he had the physical and spiritual gifts for the part. Believing that the hour had

Ledru-Rollin.

come, he withdrew his support from the old programmes and demanded that every citizen should have the vote—the system of the Radicals (the party retained the name) which terrified the Tuileries. And indeed for the first time the minority had a formula which rallied all the malcontents to their side. The Government thought proper to prosecute Ledru-Rollin, which was a mistake; he was acquitted and became famous.

But men who were not merely politicians, men imbued with lofty and disinterested motives, also declared themselves against the Government. For a long time Lamartine had been wanting "to free himself from that taste for poetry which he dragged about with him like the tattered crimson robe which a stage king drags behind him as he descends from the platform among the gaping crowd in a public place." In the end he gave up poetry altogether for politics; but his genius remained. With the unfailing instinct of the prophet, he had proclaimed, as far back as the Molé Ministry, the disease from which France was suffering: "1830," he remarked at that time, "has not succeeded in marking out a line of action or finding its inspiration. . . . It must not be imagined, because we are tired of the great movements which have convulsed our century and ourselves, that all the world is as tired as we are and terrified of the smallest stir. The generations that are growing up behind us are not tired; they want to act and grow weary in their turn. What line of action have you given them? France is a nation that is bored."

Lamartine.

Thus the poet condemned the golden mean, the bourgeois torpor. On the advent of Guizot and of the system of peace at any price, he adopted an even more definite attitude, denouncing the flabby policy "hostile to all improvement," and ended his diatribe with the following words: "If that were all the genius required of a statesman charged with the direction of affairs, there would be no need for statesmen—a milestone would do as well." The word met with huge success, and from that day forward "the milestone" meant Guizot in the newspaper controversies.

The "Milestone Ministry."

Supported by the writers and orators, the agitation revived once more, and Heine predicted that the curtain would ring down on the bourgeois comedy to the accompaniment of hoots and hisses, and that it would be followed by an epilogue entitled "The reign of the Communists." All this crowd were anxious to be rid of "schoolmaster Guizot."

The latter, turning a deaf ear to the clamour, and convinced of the validity of his own standpoint, decided to dissolve the Chamber in order to secure a less unreliable majority; he believed in the electoral system as it stood, but his hopes were disappointed. The new Chamber was in no way different from the old, and a tragic accident occurred which added strength to the Opposition.

Death of the Duc d'Orléans.

On the 13th of July, 1842, the Duc d'Orléans was driving to Neuilly when, near the Porte Maillot on the Route de la Révolte, both the horses ran away; the postilion obviously had no control over them. The Prince jumped with his feet together out of the carriage and fell on to the pavement. He was picked up senseless, and a few hours later he died in a grocer's shop without having recovered consciousness.

The Duke, who had won his spurs in Algeria, was, according to a writer who could not be suspected of having any tenderness for the House of Orleans, "one of the noblest and most magnificent human flowers that ever bloomed on the soil of that fair garden known as France." He was admired for his Liberal views and his clear understanding of events; and his will, when it was published, only confirmed this opinion of him. In this document the Duke, with anxious forethought, wondered whether his little son, the Comte de Paris, would prove himself to be "one of the artificers of that social regeneration, glimpses of which might be seen only across great obstacles and possible streams of blood," or whether "he was merely one of those instruments which are broken before they are used." Prophetic fears, which aroused astonishment at the time by their profound sincerity! Hitherto nobody had dared to praise the Crown Prince, the heir to the throne, for fear of being accused of servility; but when he was dead, he was regretted even among the masses, and Hugo pointed out, not without a certain melancholy, that since the time of Louis XIV no son of a King had succeeded to the throne. "Six times running," he said, "human forethought designated a certain head from among the whole nation to wear the Crown, and it was precisely that head that was destined never to wear it!"

The mourning for the Prince was deep and sincere; the widow and the orphan alike were objects of compassion. But politics quickly assumed the upper hand of sentiment. The death of the Duc d'Orléans swept away the only obstacle between the monarchy and the republic. Louis-Philippe was seventy, his grandson four years old—if the King were to die, what would happen? Would there be a Regency? But who would be invested with the powers of Regent? The Government saw the danger, and introduced a Bill passing over the Duchesse d'Orléans, who had the reputation of being a Liberal and hostile to Guizot, and arranging that "the Prince who stood nearest to the throne in the order fixed by the Charter"—that is to say, the Duc de Nemours, who was known to have Conservative opinions—should be made Regent. This Bill, moreover, was in conformity with the wishes expressed by the Duc d'Orléans himself in his will.

The Regency.

The debate was extremely animated. Lamartine supported the candidature of the Duchess. "Do not let it be said by France, by Europe and by history, who are watching us in the performance of this great act of building up our new monarchy, that in order to confirm and perpetuate it, it was necessary to drive this mother and all mothers, if not from the cradle, at least from the steps of a son's throne, and banish the last remnants of the right of election from our institutions!" This was greeted with applause by the Left; but even Thiers himself defended the attitude of the Government, which he regarded as inevitable. Guizot made a haughty speech, in which he pointed out the dangers of applying the elective system to a monarchy. Then, following the lead of the Opposition, and on his own ground now, strong in his historical knowledge, he reminded his hearers that although women might have acted as Regents in absolutist States, no democratic society had ever made use of their services. The Government won the day, and the system, which for a moment was menaced, seemed to have been consolidated once and for all.

A period of extraordinary peace followed, which Guizot turned to account in order to attach the majority to him. It was a strange spectacle—this man whose austerity of life and severity of manner, as Louis Blanc pointed out, made him stand out conspicuously in the midst of the frivolous society that surrounded him, this Protestant "whose haughtiness was monotonous," this upright and scrupulous politician not only tolerated abuses about him but was actually guilty of them himself. In order to secure himself in power, which he regarded as vital for the monarchy, he bought the votes of the electors in the colleges, and of the deputies in the Parliament, not for ready money, it is true, but by means of favours and appointments—tobacconists' shops and scholarships for the humbler folk; offices, contracts for public works or agencies for Government supplies for the greedier and more important. This traffic was euphemistically called "winning people to the cause," but the minority, who had their own reasons for being frank, corrected this and called it—corruption. Royer-Collard dubbed Guizot "an austere wire-puller."

Corruption.

In this state of parliamentary debility, demoralisation gradually set in, though without being too obvious. In vain did Thiers, supported by Odilon Barrot, conduct a campaign against the Government; he was met only by the ill-will of the majority, who were fully determined not to upset anything, but to continue this peaceful and profitable state of affairs as long as possible. "Heaven save us from innovating Governments!" wrote the *Journal des Débats*.

Nevertheless, on the apparently unruffled surface of the Parliament, a storm would occasionally burst forth.

Ever since the death of Charles X, his grandson, the Duc de Bordeaux—the Comte de Chambord, as he was called, after an estate with which he had been presented under the Restoration—had been working for the revival of the Legitimist Party. In 1843 he went to England, and Louis-Philippe, who was alarmed, obtained from Queen Victoria the promise that she would not receive him. But the old *Ultras* were not bound to exercise any such precaution, and about a thousand of them presented themselves

The Comte de Chambord.

in London with Chateaubriand at their head. It was a regular pilgrimage of honour to Belgrave Square, where the Count was living. This homage having been rendered to royalty, it was Chateaubriand who became the hero of the festival; in him royalty of intellect was saluted, and this old man of genius, who, in spite of many a misfortune and inconsistency on his part, had remained loyal, confessed—as he himself tells us—that in the midst of all this adulation and worship "he cried like a child."

Louis-Philippe, however, took a tragic view of the matter. He refused to countenance the participation of peers and deputies in the pilgrimage to Belgrave Square, and demanded their condemnation by the Chamber. In the draft of the Address which was being debated at the moment, the following words occurred: "The public conscience utterly condemns guilty demonstrations." But some regarded the expression as too hard, and suggested that it should be changed for the more academic word—disapproves; and over this question of the shade of meaning the conflict raged. In 1815 Guizot had made the journey to Ghent in order to join Louis XVIII, and the Opposition were not slow to remind him of it.

When he mounted the rostrum in order to defend himself, he was met with shouts of fury and insults which reached him even from the public galleries. For a long while he could not make himself heard; every time he opened his mouth he was interrupted by cries of "Traitor! Treason!" It was like a "pack of butcher's dogs howling round a malefactor." Their tactics were carefully planned. "If we cannot conquer Guizot," said one of the deputies, "we must tire him out." But Guizot was not a man to give in; with his head thrown back and an expression of unswerving disdain, he remained on the rostrum, and as soon as the opportunity offered, shot out words of defiance. "You can exhaust my strength," he exclaimed, "but I have the honour to assure you that you will never exhaust my courage." For an hour and a half he was on his feet, and nothing could move him; in the end it was the Opposition that grew tired. Whereupon Guizot opened his defence—he had the country with him; the Left had never created either a power or a liberty. "And as for insults, calumnies and superficial outbursts of fury, you may repeat them and heap them up to your hearts' content, they will never rise to the level of my contempt."

Utterly exhausted, the Chamber postponed its vote. As for Guizot, he went home and slept the clock round. On the following day the Address, including the words "utterly condemn," was passed by the majority, and one of the deputies, named Sauzet, summed up the situation in the following bad pun: "*Voilà bien du bruit pour un petit ouragan* (*tour à Gand*)."[1]

The Conservatives Consolidated.

In July 1846 Guizot, having got the better of the Radical and Legitimist Opposition, considered himself strong enough to dissolve the Chamber again. The event proved him right, and the Government at last had a resolutely Conservative majority.

In complete accord with the King, Guizot carried out his programme—order at home and the maintenance of the *status quo*. But he was far too clever not to perceive the precarious situation of France with regard to foreign nations. If it was not a position of isolation it was something very much like it.

Entente Cordiale with England.

Even after the compromise which had temporarily settled the Eastern Question, Austria and Russia remained aloof, whilst Prussia was frankly hostile. In vain did the King keep up a correspondence with Metternich; the latter seemed in no hurry to make engagements. Just at this juncture the Liberal Government in England was turned out and the Conservatives came into power. Whereupon Guizot thought that he might come to some understanding with Lord Aberdeen, the successor of the enemy of France, Lord Palmerston. He hoped that the monarchy, which found it impossible to exist in complete isolation, would thus consolidate its position by an alliance with the English Conservatives, and by returning with fresh men and fresh ideas to the policy followed during the early years of the reign.

In 1843 the news suddenly reached Paris that Queen Victoria and her husband were going to pay a visit to Louis-Philippe, who at the time was in residence at the Château d'Eu. It was

[1] Literally "What a fuss about a little storm! (journey to Ghent)." It is impossible to render in English the pun, which depends upon liaison between *petit* and *ouragan*.

a great event! Since 1830 no foreign sovereign had set foot on French soil, and the citizen-King, regarded as suspect, had never received a crowned head. The Royal Family were quick to see the opportunity offered, and they organised a magnificent reception. "Behold," said X. Doudan, "the little Queen with blue eyes and fair hair, and her little husband with fair hair and blue eyes, are coming to visit our funny country. It is the Queen of Sheba coming to visit Solomon, and Solomon will strain every nerve. All the war material that was made ready for war against England three years ago will be used for decking another Field of the Cloth of Gold, and the guns that Monsieur Thiers had cast will boom out in honour of a purely pacific festival." And so it was; while Louis-Philippe was all gracious attention to the Queen, who declared that "the gaiety and vivacity of the King charmed and amused her," Guizot conversed amicably with Lord Aberdeen—both trying to find the means of avoiding friction between the two countries and of laying the foundations of a sure and lasting peace. At the end of five days an agreement had been reached between them (September 1843).

Thus the *entente cordiale*, or "a good understanding" as the English Minister called it, came into being, and so great was the satisfaction of Guizot that at one moment he thought of retiring on his laurels. "I am not like Joan of Arc," he wrote, "for she drove the English out of France, while I have secured peace between England and France. But truly this day has been for me what the coronation in Rheims was to Joan of Arc." And thus in the eyes of the Minister for Foreign Affairs, Louis-Philippe assumed the features of Charles VII. The idea was somewhat fantastic.

Goodwill, however, and the intentions, even though honest, of statesmen could avail nothing against the clash of interests and economic rivalry. Both on the Continent and outside it, wherever French influence came into play, France found England on her path.

Colonial Policy.

It seemed as though the colonial work of the July Monarchy might be summed up in the one word—Algeria. As a matter of fact the Government of Louis-Philippe established the foundations, and as Monsieur Christian Schéfer expressed it, laid the trail of the French Empire in Africa. First of all, at the repeated request of certain Bordeaux merchants, it founded establishments on the coast of Guinea, ordered the exploration of Benin and Gabon, and signed treaties with the native chieftains; on the northern coast of Senegal the same policy was adopted. In the Indian Ocean, where France had only one possession left—the Island of Bourbon—the Governor, who at that time was Rear-Admiral de Hell, tried to lay hands on Madagascar. He negotiated with the Hovas with the object of pitting them against the English, and reconnoitred the neighbourhood of Diego-Suarez, which appeared to him the best point of disembarkation. In 1841, Nossi-Bé was occupied, and the Sultan of Mayotta announced that he had ceded his country to France—this was the first step towards the conquest of Madagascar.

In the Pacific Ocean France had several reasons for intervening and not allowing herself to be outdistanced by England, as she had been in the case of New Zealand—the commercial interests of the traders and whalers, and the military considerations which made a station on the Pacific route a necessity for France, and lastly the protection of the Catholic missionaries, who ever since the Restoration had been carrying on their work in Oceania in rivalry with the Protestant missions supported by England.

The Pritchard Incident.

It was here that the conflict which hitherto had been latent broke out with the new ally of France. In 1838 Admiral Dupetit-Thouars had landed on the island of Tahiti and obtained from Queen Pomare certain privileges, including freedom for the Catholic religion for the French settlers there. But Pritchard, the English representative, who was at once an apothecary, consul and missionary, and had been established on the island since 1824, refused to accept this curtailment of his influence, and rousing up the natives against the French, ended by persuading Pomare to repudiate the French protectorate. Dupetit-Thouars was obliged to return to Tahiti, but on this occasion he proclaimed the deposition of Pomare and the annexation of the island to France. Pritchard, who regarded himself as all-powerful, immediately called upon the natives to rebel; but he failed and was arrested and shut up in a redoubt, " where his food was passed to him through a hole in the roof," after which he was expelled (March 1844).

On his arrival in London a storm of indignation broke out against France, and Pritchard, " a British citizen," became the unfortunate victim of the French policy of conquest. Difficulties with regard to Algeria and Morocco had already raised the possibility of war; was the trifling incident of Tahiti to make it inevitable? At one moment this seemed likely. Nearly everybody in England declared they were ready to open hostilities, " even at the cost of an income tax of two shillings in the pound "; and the Tsar had a meeting with Queen Victoria; in short, the state of mind existing at the time of the Treaty of London in 1840 was revived. But Guizot, faithful to his system—peace always and everywhere—made concessions. He repudiated the action of Dupetit-Thouars, which amounted to being content with a protectorate, and proposed to give Pritchard compensation.

It was then the turn of French public opinion to protest—the country would be humiliated and abased if they gave up the annexation of the island and before the whole of Europe offered compensation to Pritchard, who had caused the massacre of French soldiers! But Louis-Philippe was as determined as his Minister not to turn " a trifle into a *casus belli*." Guizot defended his policy on the rostrum, and with considerable difficulty secured its acceptance; England had helped him by saying she would be satisfied with an apology and the offer of compensation—which, as a matter of fact, was never paid.

For two years, thanks to the efforts of Guizot and Lord Aberdeen, the *entente cordiale* managed, more or less successfully, to survive diplomatic setbacks, and the difficulties which arose in Africa and the Pacific, when a new blow shattered it once and for all.

The Spanish Marriages.

The Chancelleries of Europe were at this time very much excited over the marriage of Queen Isabella of Spain, who had been declared heir to the throne by Ferdinand VII. The English had their aspirant, Prince Leopold of Saxe-Coburg, who was allied to their own Royal Family. But Louis-Philippe could not accept such a candidate. The marriage of a sovereign was a very serious matter "at a time when provinces were still regarded as dowries or portions of a heritage, and were added to each other like private fortunes." The King—and to anyone who knew him this was no cause for surprise—had never abandoned this standpoint or these old-established customs. England having put a ban on any prince of French blood, he retaliated by saying that he would refuse to recognise the accession to the throne of Spain of any prince who was not a member of the House of Bourbon, and put forward the candidature of the Duke of Cadiz, a nephew of Ferdinand VII, at the same time negotiating for the marriage of the Duc de Montpensier, one of his sons, with the Infanta, the sister of the Queen of Spain. Would this twofold union suit England? In 1843 Guizot and Lord Aberdeen had come to an understanding on this point, by agreeing to postpone the marriage of the Infanta with the Duc de Montpensier until Queen Isabella had a child and the succession to the throne had been secured in the direct line.

But in 1846 Palmerston returned to power, and forthwith repudiated the policy of Lord Aberdeen, whom he accused of "having allowed himself to be completely dominated by the ascendancy of Guizot." At his command, Lord Bulwer, the English Ambassador at Madrid, revived the candidature of the Coburg prince and tried to rush the marriage. But Guizot, who was informed, regarded himself as released from his engagements, and turning the friendly attitude of the Regent Christina towards France to account, clinched the matter. In the month of September 1846 the news reached London that the marriage of Queen Isabella with the Duke of Cadiz and of the Infanta with the Duc de Montpensier had been arranged, and a month later the weddings took place.

This was a rude rebuff for England, and for France a revenge for the humiliation she had suffered through the Treaty of London. Lamartine wrote: "The imprudent marriage of the Duc de Montpensier with the sister of the King of Spain, arranged by intrigue, suddenly discovered like a trap, and finally proclaimed like a victory, has given grave offence to England." And, indeed, Palmerston did not hide his fury; in his opinion it was the most flagrant act of political ambition and aggrandisement that Europe had seen since the Empire, the result of base intrigues; and he invoked the Treaty of Utrecht to support him in maintaining that the marriage was impossible. Queen Victoria gave expression to similar sentiments; though but a little while previously she had succumbed to the charm of Louis-Philippe, she now inveighed against the old man for embarking on such an enterprise, whilst with regard to Guizot she was still more outspoken. "His conduct," she said, "surpasses in ignominy anything one could possibly have believed. He is guilty of infamous behaviour."

Collapse of the *Entente Cordiale*.

But was this really so? Had not Palmerston, in once again supporting the candidature of the Coburg prince, released France from her undertaking? In whatever way the blame for this tragi-comedy of the Spanish Marriages might be apportioned, one fact was evident to the whole world—the *entente cordiale* was at an end.

In France the Opposition tried to exploit this change in her foreign policy, and through an Italian refugee in England named Panizzi, Thiers put himself in touch with Palmerston, and advised him to take a high hand. "The King is a coward," he said, "and Guizot a traitor and a liar." The English Minister, only too pleased to hear such sentiments and to act on such advice, endeavoured to set the Powers against France, and to attack Louis-Philippe himself by addressing to the Chancelleries of Europe a note in which the citizen-King was presented in a very bad light—in 1809 he would have regarded himself "as the vilest of perjurers if he ever accepted the Crown." But these far from tactful methods of conducting international controversies aroused no enthusiasm in Europe, and Palmerston got the worst of the bargain.

Triumph of Guizot.

Guizot was triumphant. The Spanish Marriages meant the liberation of the July Monarchy, the hall-mark of its power, "the only great thing which France has accomplished alone, quite alone, in Europe since 1830," he declared on the rostrum. He felt that he had behind him the majority, who had only unwillingly acquiesced in the *entente* with England. Had not the latter just created fresh difficulties for France in Syria, where she was supporting the Mussulman Druses against the Christian Maronites, who were French *protégés*? The Chamber was almost unanimous in its support of Guizot (February 1847). Times seemed to have changed considerably since the Pritchard affair.

In Government circles, in the Chamber and among the bourgeoisie, everybody was saying, "Guizot is master of the situation, he is the only man." The lasting peace, the merging of parties, who were on the whole agreed to regard Government by the middle classes, and by the middle classes alone, as inevitable, and the increase in public wealth, all augured well for the future; and Guizot, at last master of a docile majority, contemplated his work with satisfaction and repeated, "Conservative policy alone can secure progress."

Nevertheless there were still some disquieting features. On the 16th of April, 1846, on his return from a walk in the forest of Fontainebleau, the King almost fell a victim to another attempt upon his life; Lecomte, who had once been a forester, shot at him with a gun, but missed him. On the following 29th of July, the anniversary of the revolution, Louis-Philippe was saluting the crowd from the balcony of the Tuileries when two pistol shots rang out in his direction. A fellow who had been hiding behind a statue was arrested; he was a man named Henri who had been a manufacturer, but had fallen on evil days. These repeated attempts at assassination, though it is true they had no political significance—Lecomte and Henri were not members of any secret society—proved how extraordinarily tenacious was the spirit of hatred, not so much against the monarchy as against the monarch "who reigned and governed." Nevertheless Louis-Philippe remained calm, and humorously observed, "It is only in hunting me that there is no close season." Although he had moments of weariness, in which he confessed to Guizot that in spite of their combined efforts "they would never found anything in France," his behaviour was, as a rule, full of confidence.

Attempts on the King's Life.

In vain did Bugeaud advise him to fight the Press, which was again becoming violent. "As for newspapers," replied Louis-Philippe, "I never read them."—"But your subjects read them."—"They will be worn down by the good sense of the nation."—" Yes, as granite is worn down by being rubbed against the soft clay from which the mass of your subjects are moulded." But the King would not allow himself to be convinced, and nothing seemed to trouble his philosophic serenity.

There was only one subject that made him lose his temper—the charge of being a usurper; and the anecdote related by the Ambassador, Sainte-Aulaire, in this connection is significant. In 1842, at the Château d'Eu, Sainte-Aulaire was conversing with the King and Queen in a room next to the Galerie des Guises, in which the orderly officers were sitting; the doors were wide open. Suddenly the King got up, and raising his voice said to the Queen, who was sewing at the other end of the room, " There are some people who regard me as a usurper; but you know, don't you, that I am not a usurper ! " The Queen, her eyes full of tears, passed silently behind the King and went to shut the door leading into the orderly-room. The Queen's silence, her emotion and this simple precaution, aroused the King's ire, and although he was generally so tender and respectful to his wife, he opened the two wings of the door again with some difficulty, and exclaimed at the top of his voice, " And why do you not wish me to say in front of X— that I am not a usurper? I insist upon saying it, and I insist upon everybody hearing me. No, I am not a usurper ! " The Queen burst into sobs. . . .

Possibly Louis-Philippe was right in his indignation. When Charles X went into exile, the Lieutenant-General of the Kingdom, it was said, sent an emissary, an officer of the British Embassy, to ask the old fugitive King to hand over the young Duc de Bordeaux to him, and the latter's mother, the Duchesse de Berry, refused. If the tale is true, Louis-Philippe could with some show of right on his side maintain that he was not a usurper.

At all events he knew that he had kept the letter of the agreement made in July 1830 not to infringe the constitution, and through his ability had mastered anarchy and kept the peace. All this was a matter of some pride to him. " I feel," he observed to Hugo, " that Europe turns on me."

But was this scrupulous respect for the law sufficient? Did the law itself, as it was established by that minority known as the "legal country," really express the wishes of the nation? Was there any real and cordial understanding between the King and his subjects, and did the popular clamour reach the foot of the throne? "Power," said Béranger, "is a bell which prevents those who set it pealing from hearing any other sound."

Bibliography. D'Alton-Shée, *Mes Mémoires* (2 vols., 1869). V. de Balabine, *Journal* (publ. by E. Daudet) (Vol. I, 1914). E. Daudet, *La Reine Victoria en France* (*Revue des Deux Mondes*, 1902). Debidour, *Histoire Diplomatique de l'Europe* (1814–78) (3 vols., 1890). Guizot, *Mémoires* (Vols. VI to VIII) (1864–67). *Lettres à sa Famille et à ses Amis* (1884). Lamartine, *La France Parlementaire* (4 vols., 1864–65). M. Levaillant, *Lamartine* (1925). Quentin-Bauchard, *Lamartine Homme Politique* (1903). L. de Ronchaud, *La Politique de Lamartine* (1878). C. Schéfer, *La Monarchie de Juillet et l'Expansion Coloniale* (*Revue des Deux Mondes*, 1912). Cl. Tillier, *Pamphlets* (ed. Gérin) (1906).

CHAPTER VII

MENTAL AND MATERIAL PROGRESS

The new society. The political salons. The literary salons; a *soirée* at Madame de Girardin's. The evolution of the bourgeoisie; influence of foreigners, and of George Sand. The lioness. Paris of the period; amusements. The provinces. Religious ideas; the Church of France. The tragedy of Lamennais. Lacordaire at Notre Dame. Ozanam and the Society of Saint Vincent de Paul. Montalembert and free education. Diversion against the Jesuits; Michelet and Quinet at the *Collège de France*. Literature; Romanticism becomes a sect. Renaissance of classicism. Pansard. Influence of Rachel. The Press and industrial literature. The genius of Balzac. Evolution in art. Théophile Gautier. Slowness of economic progress; the cause of this. Prejudice against railways. The law of 1842; the impetus is given. The people. Misery of the industrial workers. Timid attempts at intervention on the part of the State. Impotence of Companionship. The history of Saint-Simonism; its initial success; its inadequacy and decay. It adjusts itself to capitalism. Fourier, the doctrinaire of individualism. The organisation of the work of Louis Blanc. The advocates of violence; the Communists. Proudhon as critic. Social uneasiness.

THE rise of the bourgeoisie, that triumphant bourgeoisie whom Ingres symbolised once and for all in his *Bertin l'ainé*, who, firmly installed, seems to defy the universe, profoundly modified the society established by the Restoration. The latter had succeeded in founding a hierarchy modelled upon that of the *ancien régime*, though modified by a few concessions made to the middle classes, but it found itself suddenly overthrown by the July Revolution. The conquerors, turned into aspirants for office, made a shameless assault upon the Government posts; and there was a fine scramble in which everybody pushed and shoved to secure a place. When the scuffle was over, what had French society become, and more particularly that portion of it that set the tone—Paris society?

The old aristocrats, the unrepentant Legitimists, remained confined in the Faubourg Saint Germain. The Charter of 1814 had been but little to their liking, far less therefore the revised Charter of "the King of the barricades." They pretended to be ruined, and read with delight all the pamphlets directed against the ruling House; that Louis-Philippe, as one brochure entitled *L'Histoire de Maria Stella* maintained, was not only a usurper, but a common child surreptitiously smuggled into a princely family, seemed to them by no means improbable, since it flattered their passion. But gradually these "die-hards," divided by the sorry adventure of the Duchesse de Berry, left the capital and spent almost the whole year at their country seats, saying with Madame de Gouvello, "Even the bread I eat in Paris lies heavy on my conscience." And soon a few women "*aux rubans verts*"—the Legitimist colours—and fervent adorers of Henry V, sulking in their corner, were all that remained of them.

The Old Aristocrats.

The political, literary or purely social salons had undergone a complete change. As Guizot remarked, they were no longer the centres of social life or characterised by that variety and amenity of intercourse, those interesting but pointless, animated but amicable discussions, which for so long made French society the original and pleasant institution it was. The gatherings of the old days, charming by reason of their heterogeneity, were replaced by coteries each of which had its own peculiar tone "and was like a page torn out of the great volume of national history"; and indeed each circle had its representative, the celebrity about whom all the members gathered.

The Salons.

At the house of Princess Liéven, a Russian who had connections with Berlin and whom Thiers suspected of being a spy, it was Guizot who held sway. Bound to the Princess by the ties of a loyal and tender affection, he was surrounded by the flower of the diplomatic world of the day and foreigners of note.

The opposition salon was that of the Comtesse de Castellane, whose hero was Molé. Here the tone was at once refined, witty and serious. Whilst those who believed in "balanced systems" and belonged to the intermediate section met at Madame de Chastenay's, where a certain eclecticism prevailed—

Orleanists like Barante, Mignet or Salvandy (the author of the famous expression " We are dancing on a volcano ") hob-nobbed in the most friendly way with Legitimists like Bauffremont or Maillé.

But in addition to these purely political salons there were many others the atmosphere of which was frequently delightfully original! At Madame de Rauzan's, for instance, the guests would listen with somewhat stupefied admiration to the *Symphonie fantastique* of Berlioz. There was also the salon of the Princesse de Belgiojoso, the Egeria of Augustin Thierry, who had gone blind, " a pale gaunt woman with flashing eyes, who dabbled in spectres and phantoms " and received her friends in a room entirely draped with white satin, in which a turbaned negro-boy circled round and round. Then there was Madame de Castris, the Duchesse de Duras . . . and many others. On Saturdays, all the artistic world of Paris would meet at Lamartine's, where their host would greet them with the affability of an English aristocrat. But this threshold was never crossed by Guizot after the master of the house had veered towards revolution : " the honourable member who spoke last " had become in the Minister's mouth " the honourable renegade." Lastly there were circles in which piety was the rule, under the leadership of " the matrons of the Church," as Abbé Deguerry, the *curé* of la Madeleine, put it, where the deepest problems of religious metaphysics were discussed.

But the most flourishing of the salons was undoubtedly that of Madame de Girardin, or " Delphine," the wife of the founder of *la Presse*.

Madame de Girardin.

Imagine a vast room draped with sea-green woollen damask, in the middle of the room a platform and a table on which two tall candelabra are burning. The poetess Delphine advances, clad in a robe of black velvet, and reads a tragedy of her own composition. On either side of her, two rotund personages are seated, " the two chubbiest and ruddiest faces in the literary world "—Balzac and Jules Janin. The audience, at the end of each act, expresses its admiration; with his hand on his heart and his eyes turned to heaven, a man of short stature but with a magnificent brow declares emphatically, " Extremely fine ! " Hugo, to whom the "part of romantic luminary" has already become second nature, says no more. But Balzac waxes enthusiastic and shows his crooked teeth. With clothes that are too skimpy for his enormous frame, his untidy waistcoat, and shoes that sink into the carpet, there is very little of the man of the world about him; he looks more like a school-boy on holiday who has grown too fast during the year and is bursting out of his clothes. Nevertheless there is "the man who alone is worth a whole library of his century."

Such was the usual programme at the *soirées* of "the Muse," as Madame de Girardin was called. In the dining-room three seats were invariably reserved—one for Hugo, one for Balzac and one for Lamartine, "little places laid for the kings without subjects." But beneath these lofty altitudes there was many another name that appeals to our imagination, and on which time has but shed added lustre! Théophile Gautier, the good Theo, so obliging in spite of the work that weighs him down, whom Delphine calls "her elephant," and who—a rare phenomenon—does not squabble with his friends; Alexandre Dumas, "the King of humbugs," according to Lamartine, but at all events a jolly giant, who when asked whether he is bored, replies with charming frankness, "I am never bored in my own company"; and, in his dark corner, Vigny the aristocrat, Vigny the imperturbable, the philosopher of abnegation and of resignation, with whom no one can boast of being intimate and who, in the presence of the inspired Muse, improvises splendid verses, which seem dedicated, not to Delphine, but to the very spirit of Poetry:

> "Lorsqu'on voyait encor grandir ta svelte taille
> Et la Muse germer dans tes regards d'azur. . . ."[1]

It was a unique meeting-place for talent and genius, as it were the second stage, the blossoming of the intellectual festivals founded in the old days by Charles Nodier in the *salon de l'Arsenal*. No description of it, however, would be complete without mention in their places of Musset, "that young man with such a beautiful past," who, in a quarter of an hour, composed in Delphine's garden his retort heaping vengeance on

[1] "When they saw thy slim form growing ever taller and the Muse coming to life in thine azure eyes. . . ."

the head of Becker for his *German Rhine*; of musicians like Chopin and Liszt, and of novelists like Eugène Sue, so resplendent in his sea-green suit, but disconsolate because he has a snub nose, " a vulgar nose," which is detrimental to his dandyism as the future popular writer.

" Those were fine times ! " Gustave Claudin, who was present at these festivals, afterwards wrote. People were fond of intellectual pursuits and Paris society indulged whole-heartedly and even with a certain ingenuousness in literary distractions.

The Bourgeoisie.

The bourgeoisie of the " golden mean " had no salons properly so called, though they entertained in their own way—that is to say, they went in for amusement pure and simple —according to the Romanticists an extremely dull form of amusement. They sang ditties, and they danced. But the victors of yesterday felt they were strong; they had their political opinions dictated to them by the *Journal des Débats* and satisfied their literary curiosity in the columns of the *Revue des Deux Mondes*, founded by " that clever and witty curmudgeon " called Buloz. With regard to the King they maintained an attitude of respect mingled with suspicion, displeased with him for no longer being the hail-fellow-well-met King of the early days and for his lavish expenditure on the restoration of Versailles and the museums and the furnishing of the palaces. " The King, the head of a nation that has become an industrial country, and of a peaceful bourgeoisie," they declared bitterly, " is surrounded only by men girt with swords and clinking their spurs." It passed their comprehension.

Foreign Influences.

Before the end of Louis-Philippe's reign there appeared in these various circles, much as they differed from each other, the same symptom of disintegration. In the first place there was foreign influence; the entirely political salon of Madame de Liéven, and the apparently entirely intellectual salon of Madame Swetchine, had already introduced habits that were not French, an unaccustomed way of looking at things; there was intellect and loftiness of mind there, no doubt, but they were not native to the French genius.

Gradually intellectual circles acquired a taste for everything bizarre and out of the way; and in this connection the fortune made by Dr. Koreff, a German doctor, mesmerist, occultist, quasi-encyclopædist, and into the bargain a spy in the pay of Germany, is exceedingly significant. This "small, thick-lipped man, with his blinking eyes and childish wig, made partly of dog-grass and partly of hemp," had a phenomenal success—Paris was mad about him; and for fifteen years the public followed his career, and, what was worse, made use of his medical prescriptions. He had introduced Hoffmann into France, and revived interests which had thrilled the aristocracy of the end of the eighteenth century. Lastly, he too had his salon, a cage lined with books written in every language—for he was a great polyglot—into which two or three hundred people used to squeeze themselves.

But, in addition to these foreigners, there was George Sand, whose triumph was more complete and direct. *Indiana* in 1832, followed by *Valentine* and *Lélia*, had the effect of a revolution. Madame de Staël's *Corinne* was very old-fashioned, and France welcomed the advent of the truly lyric novel. Her attack on social shackles—against the *fait social* already denounced by Stendhal—her veiled though unmistakable apotheosis of free love, "that cry of a society in its death agony," filled everybody with astonishment and rapture. What a fresh source of inspiration for the writers! But the women, not satisfied with fiction, adopted free-and-easy manners and acted George Sand literally—and, protesting against "the conventions held in honour by the Faubourg Saint Germain" *the lioness* made her bow. She affected to despise feminine graces; dressed like a man, with a cigar in her mouth, booted and spurred; talking about clubs and sport—words that were new in those days—she hoped to impress the world by her audacity and extravagances. And she succeeded. Daniel Stern, whose real name was Madame d'Agoult, declared that "there was a gap in the place the lioness had occupied, and that no one came forward to fill it."

George Sand.

The Lioness.

And thus the old framework was broken up. Among the upstart bourgeoisie, even the lioness won a place. And at the same time the Legitimists, tired of fruitless opposition, compounded with the new *régime*—their younger sons were sent to the royal colleges, went to fight in Africa and occasionally acted as aides-de-camp to the "usurper." Gradually a sort of levelling of classes took place, a fusion which, in the eyes of those who belonged to the Restoration, seemed outrageous and scandalous. Everybody was now bent on paying homage to the modern deity, of whom Balzac was the immortal historian—Mammon!

Paris.

From the salon let us turn to the street. Paris at this time was divided into twelve *arrondissements* and had a population of one million, crowded within a narrow compass; Belleville, Auteuil, Montmartre and Montrouge were villages outside the barriers; the Champs-Élysées was a badly kept wood, where there were underground cabarets like those described by Eugène Sue in *Les Mystères de Paris*; the Madeleine towered aloft amid sheds and waste land, while just beyond the Trinité the country began. The heart of the capital was no longer, as it had once been, the Palais Royal with its restaurants and cafés—the *Frères Provençaux*, *Véry*, *Lamblin* and the *Café du Sauvage*, for in 1837 the Government had forbidden public gaming, with the result that the traditional fame of the quarter was immediately destroyed.

Those who wanted to know the real Paris, and see the celebrities of the day, now frequented the Boulevard des Italiens, which only a little while before was still called the Boulevard de Gant. It was here, between the Rue Drouot and the new Opera, that the people of fashion used to congregate; on the pavement there were two rows of chairs, and the fine ladies and gentlemen used to walk up and down beneath the admiring gaze of the crowd. Here the latest fashions could be seen. The ladies had their hair dressed *à la girafe* with bows, ringlets and kiss-curls; they wore huge hats with veils in front and streamers behind; their dresses had elaborate leg-o'-mutton sleeves and were short enough to show their buskin shoes. Everything had to come from the best houses—it was no good if the dress were not by Palmyre, the hats by Simon, and the shoes by Gelot. But in course of time this sartorial romanticism became toned down like romanticism itself.

Villemessant.

As for the *lion*, the following is his own description of himself: "I was wearing," said H. de Villemessant, who was then in the flower of his youth, "a white hat of angora skin, a suit of shot pink and blue, the fashionable shade, covered by a nut-brown frock-coat called a *balayeuse*, the skirt of which falling in organ-pipe folds, swayed with every movement and, when I lifted it on either side like a fan, looked like a pair of bats' wings. My waistcoat, which was extremely short, was of red cloth embroidered in black silk, and barely reached a pair of nigger-coloured trousers, cut out above the boot and finished off with brass curbs, passing under the feet, which as they hit up against plaques of the same metal, with which my heels were lined, made a clinking sound which delighted me. I pushed refinement to the point of putting the finishing touch to this dandyish get-up by carrying a riding-whip, an article of parade which reminds me of Jule Janin's pretty joke: 'He wore spurs although he had a horse.'"

And whilst the smart set promenaded about or regaled themselves in the Café de Paris, brandishing thick canes with gold knobs, and with square monocles in their eyes, ogling the passers-by, the boulevard was filled with the rattle of omnibuses. They were of every shape and form—*dames blanches*, *citadines*, *trycilles*, and *Orléanaises*, carrying from twenty to twenty-five passengers, who for six sous (3*d.*) secured a comfortable conveyance. On the box was a fine coachman in livery, under the box a chest containing five or six horns, which the coachman blew as he drove along, while at the back of the vehicle or on the steps a jolly postilion helped the passengers to mount.

For those who wanted amusement there was *embarras du choix*—in addition to the theatres there were the Tivoli, with its orchestra, in the Rue Saint Lazare, the Boulevard du Temple, with its perennial fair, where Bobèche and Galimafré played the fool, Madame Saqui danced and performed acrobatic tricks, and the Petit-Lazari, the Funambules and the Olympic Circus of the Franconi Brothers were always on view. On Sunday evenings there was a ball at the opera frequented by the great Chicard, who on a week-day was a worthy business man and an officer in the National Guard, but on Sundays would get into outlandish clothes and lead unspeakable farandoles, to the accompaniment of breaking chairs and pistol shots, keeping time to Musard's famous orchestra; Gavarni, the draughtsman, was also there, tall and fair and "extremely fashionable in his attire, with something English

Amusements.

about it," making lightning sketches of various movements in the *cachucha*, the fashionable dance popularised by Lola Montez. Here too was the eccentric Mylord l'Arsouille, who was mistakenly said to be an English nobleman, but who only appeared in all his fine feathers on Ash Wednesday, the day of the *Descente de la Courtille.*

After dining at Belleville, at Hainsselain's or Dunoyer's, Mylord and his companions—the Comte d'Alton-Shée, a peer of the realm, and Romieu, who had not his equal for mystifications—would take the head of the procession and return to the centre of Paris by the Faubourg du Temple; there would be a crowd of 100,000 spectators, and a line of 2000 carriages from which, says an eye-witness, " sugar-plums, flowers, sweets and filthy jokes, which were always loudly applauded," would fall.

On the left bank there was the charming life of the *quartier Latin*, adorned by Mimi Pinson and the younger sisters of Béranger's Lisette. Here Schaunard, Colline and the heroes of Murger, wearing tasselled caps and smoking chibouks, had created a new, sentimental and romantic world, where the exquisite sensitiveness of Gérard de Nerval brushed shoulders with the sinister musings of Petrus Borel and the " social imaginings " of Latouche.

To foreigners, life in Paris seemed extremely expensive. " It is impossible to satisfy even quite a small appetite for less than 5 or 6 francs. Bread, 25 centimes; wine, 2 francs; beefsteak and potatoes, 1 franc 25; fried sole, 1 franc 75 to 2 francs; coffee, 40 centimes; total 5 francs, with a further 25 centimes for the tip. And after a dinner like this one is hungry again by nine or ten o'clock in the evening." Such at all events was the opinion of the petty bourgeois, who lived very thriftily, and took far more interest in the crime of Lacenaire, the La Roncière case, or the trial of Madame Lafarge, than in politics, and by way of amusement would take a walk to Romainville. " By way of Belleville," wrote Paul de Kock, their favourite author, " they would take the road through the Parc Saint Farjean, where the country lay directly in front of them, with fields of barley and corn intersected by clumps of gooseberry and black-currant bushes. Here in the autumn furtive little halts would be called, under the shade of plum and walnut trees, from which a little fruit would be surreptitiously borrowed. . . . At last they reached the wood, on the edge of which, before allowing them to wander further, a good village inn, at once clean and simple, the *Poule Russe,* invited all comers to partake of refreshment. Here there was *petit vin de Bagnolet* and *picton* at four sous (2*d.*) the bottle."

The Provinces.

The provinces copied the example set by Paris, though slowly and cautiously. The manners of the Restoration had survived there almost unchanged, and evening gatherings represented the principal if not the only distraction. People went to their neighbours with pattens on their feet and by the light of a lantern, and in the old drawing-room there would be games of cards, whist and *bouillotte.* Between the games the daughter of the house would hand round cakes and pour out sugar water or beer. On feast days and at carnival time there would be a ball, after which everything would return to its old rut and the hum-drum existence that brought no surprises.

Nevertheless since the passing of the law of 1831, the bourgeoisie, who had been given the vote and could even become deputies, owing to the lowering of the tax-qualification, had begun to play a more active part in politics. They used to visit headquarters, and began to realise their new importance. After going to Paris and hoarding up their savings, they made large fortunes in industrial or commercial concerns, so that gradually an aristocracy of wealth sprang up in opposition to the aristocracy of birth.

Such, as regards externals, was French society during the time of Louis-Philippe. We must now endeavour beneath this outer covering to discern the movement of ideas and the direction of thought. How were the religious, literary and political aspirations of the generation of 1830 realised, modified or transformed?

The Church of France.

The need for reform and the opposition to the clergy under the Restoration gave rise in 1831 to a sort of schism in miniature—the creation of "the Church of France." Abbé Châtel, maintaining that the Catholic liturgy was old-fashioned and incomprehensible to the people, substituted a French liturgy; he administered the sacraments for nothing, and recognised no impediments to marriage except such as were laid down by the civil law; in short, he republicanised public worship; the children to whom he administered communion wore tricoloured ribbons.

The innovation met with a certain measure of success. The enemies of the monarchy attended the new church, a nomadic church which was constantly changing its habitation, leaving the Rue des Sept Voies to take anchor in the Rue du Bac, and Abbé Châtel openly proclaimed himself Primate of all Gaul. But he was a Primate who had some difficulty in finding his clergy. Nevertheless, he refused to make any concessions to the established Church, and his flock imitated his heterodoxy like sheep, one of them on a certain occasion protesting against the continued use of the Latin word *Amen* in the liturgy. "Monsieur," one of those present gravely replied, "the word *Amen* is not Latin, it is a Greek word." Whereupon, on the strength of this assurance, *Amen* was retained.

This rationalism, mingled with pantheism, the main object of which was to translate the liturgy into French, failed to find any solid support in France, and the Church of Abbé Châtel was really only a minute offshoot from the Catholic tree, and soon degenerated into a revolutionary chapel, where services were held in memory of the regicides "who had died to stamp out the infamous monarchy."

By the side of Châtel, Lamennais was a grand figure, and his failure possesses all the beauty of a spiritual tragedy.

Tragedy of Lamennais.

The doctrine of *l'Avenir*—God and Liberty—and the ardent claims of its founders disquieted the Bishops, who, weakened as they were, by the separation between Church and State and by the rescinding of grants for public worship, banned the paper. The effect produced was far-reaching—timid Catholics and even Liberals deserted Lamennais. "It is not my courage that I am losing," observed the latter, "but my voice." Whereupon, he unhesitatingly stopped the publication of his paper and went to Rome in order to make his defence. But Pope Gregory XVI, not wishing either to discourage this generous soul, or to approve doctrines that were contrary to Catholic tradition, refused to enter into any discussion, or at all events temporised.

Meanwhile, at the gates of the Vatican, Lamennais lost patience; this diplomatic caution, this care never to hurry matters, seemed to the reformer the height of cowardice. And the man who had arrived in Rome full of confidence, the convinced Ultramontane, whose aim it had been to regenerate the world under the ægis of the Pope, suddenly turned to the opposite extreme and became an opponent of Rome and of the Pope. Rome in his eyes was now nothing but a vast tomb filled with worms and bones, or rather "the most infamous sink of iniquity that ever defiled the eye of man"; and, seeing the destruction of all his hopes, he returned in a rage to France. Whereupon, Rome opened her mouth, and without mentioning Lamennais and his writings, the encyclical *Mirari vos* (12th of August, 1832), formally condemned the Liberal doctrines of *l'Avenir* and its propagandist spirit among the nations.

Up to this moment Lacordaire had been a follower of Lamennais, and he still remained with him on his return from Italy in the solitude of la Chênaie. But "though the woods still had their same silent depths and the same tempests raged through them, though the sky of Armorica had not changed, the same could not be said of the heart of the Master." He could not forgive his judges; his grief and the violence of his resentment against Rome terrified his disciple, who, for his part, was ready to recognise that *l'Avenir* had been guilty of mistakes and had verged on "exaggerated ideas by means of exaggerated language." On the 11th of December, 1832, not daring to face a farewell scene, Lacordaire fled from la Chênaie, leaving in his room a letter "written with a broken heart" breaking off his relations with Lamennais. And the latter remained all alone amid the ruins of his life-work.

A picture of him at this time has been drawn by George Sand. He was small, emaciated and sick, but what a light shone from his soul! His eyes darted flames, his straight brow, furrowed with vertical lines, was an index to the ardour of his will. And everything about him, his simple manners, his sharp movements, his awkward attitude, his frank gaiety, his passionate obstinacy, his sudden good cheer, "everything down to his coarse but clean clothes and his blue stockings, was reminiscent of the Breton *cloarek*." He commanded respect and affection by the courage and candour of his soul.

This Lamennais was no longer the man who wrote the *Essai sur l'Indifférence*, but the author of *Les Paroles d'un Croyant*, a book "which preached pure Jacobinism beneath a veil of mysticism." Ultramontanism and Gallicism were lost causes! Henceforward the regeneration of the world would be brought about without the help of the Pope, by the people themselves, the people in arms, and by revolution based upon religion. As for the old political and ecclesiastical hierarchies, "they would pass away together, like two spectres embracing in the tomb." When Renduel, the publisher, was having *Les Paroles d'un Croyant* printed, somebody said to him, "Apparently you are publishing a book the letters of which burn the fingers of your compositors."—"Yes," replied Renduel, "they jump for joy as they set up one after the other the letters of a book which will make the sovereigns of the world tremble on their tottering thrones!" Thus, from an "absolutist Catholic" Lamennais became a herald of revolution; but he no longer had any followers.

The latter had gone over to the Conservative Party. The bourgeoisie, frightened by the insurrections and the extremes to which ideas had gone, were now seeking protection in Catholicism. Although they had been far from friendly to this creed after 1830, they had come to see that it represented a capacity for resistance, a social brake which deserved support. The clergy, deprived of their political power, were no longer to be feared, and the hostility against them cooled down and gradually gave place to a kind of tolerance, which eventually developed into sympathy, and inaugurated a renaissance of religious belief.

Lacordaire.

Lacordaire and Montalembert, separated from Lamennais, knew how to exploit this state of mind. After the condemnation of Rome, which they accepted, they stripped the Catholic programme of its political articles, and renouncing all idea of demanding important social reforms, confined this programme within the bounds of the reformed Charter. "Let us practise religion," wrote Montalembert to his friend Cornudet, "that will be the best way of securing liberty for the future." It is true that they left far behind them the magnificent aspirations and sublime schemes of Lamennais; but was not propaganda by means of deeds, preaching and teaching, a method that was both practical and expedient? Just at this time the taste for historical studies and a better understanding of history was spreading among the people, and "the revival of this feeling led to a clearer conception of the Christian faith." It was at this juncture that Lacordaire appeared in the limelight.

He preached in the pulpit of Notre Dame, and his success was stupendous—a crowd of 5000 young men pressed about him, whilst in the middle of the cathedral that same Archbishop of Paris whose palace had been looted and destroyed four years previously sat in all his pontifical vestments. These were no longer the days when "the Church, teaching the catechism to a society in its infancy, put both the question and the answer"; Lacordaire had taken as his thesis "Faith cometh of God, reason of the Devil," and he conjured up the Middle Ages to confront latter-day doubt. Guessing what the objections of his hearers would be, he did not adopt the tone of authority; he did not address them as "Brethren," but as "Gentlemen," and his discourse showed that "he felt no hostility or contempt for the age to which these young men were proud to belong."

This presented quite a novel spectacle, due to the preacher's intelligent eloquence and his fresh, straightforward way of attacking spiritual problems. "It is a pleasure," wrote Madame de Girardin, "to see the youth of France coming of their own accord, independent and generous, to seek guidance, bearing their beliefs to the foot of those same altars where in the old days one saw only officials trembling in ecstasy before an invisible inquisition, only Court penitents and Government Pharisees."

Those days were far away when in *Rolla* Musset sounded the knell of Catholicism:

> "Ta gloire est morte, O Christ! et sur nos croix d'ébène,
> Ton cadavre céleste en poussière est tombé. . . ."[1]

The people "returned in the good old French fashion to

[1] "Thy glory is dead, O Christ! and upon our ebony crosses Thy celestial body has crumbled to dust. . . ."

their Pater Nosters," and from the highest to the lowest the movement spread. A certain student of Lyons, who had grown

Ozanam.

up in the Catholic environment of the Restoration, the learned, gentle and courageous Ozanam, once more taught his contemporaries the value of charity and preached by example the efficacy of good works. He founded the Society of Saint Vincent de Paul, which soon spread its branches all through the provinces and even reached foreign countries, and with the discreet assistance of the clergy became a real power. In 1833 Dom Guéranger settled at Solesmes and revived the Benedictine tradition. And finally Lacordaire, after having gone into retirement for a time "before his own weakness and before God," set out for Rome, and, purified by silence, donned the monk's frock and worked for the restoration in France of the Dominican Order.

Tolerance became the order of the day; there was no longer any spirit of violence against the clergy, but a lofty and upright impartiality prevailed, the influence of which could be seen in the law on elementary education. Catholic periodicals, and literary or scientific publications, animated by the same spirit, increased—*l'Univers*, a journal founded by Abbé Migne, and *la Patrologie* by the same writer, *Les Annales de Philosophie Chrétienne* by Bonnetty, *La Revue de l'Université Catholique* by Abbé de Salinis. This religious revival, which the monarchy took care not to oppose in any way, for it saw in it an instrument of order, was a source of astonishment and satisfaction to Rome. "I could not be better pleased with France and with her King," observed Gregory XVI to Montalembert. "I wish all the Kings of Europe were like Louis-Philippe."

Strong in the sympathy of public opinion and in the good will of the Government, the Catholic Party embarked upon the conquest of a form of freedom which was of peculiar value to it—free education.

Free Education.

As regards elementary education, their object had already been attained; but the University still had the monopoly of secondary education, and it was this monopoly that the Catholics were anxious to destroy. The campaign opened in 1840, and was conducted with brutal energy. Abbé Rohrbacher attacked the State schools, "pestilential schools," and the University, "a sink of iniquity." But the violence of his tone was surpassed by a gifted pamphleteer, Louis Veuillot, who had become director of the old *Univers* founded by Abbé Migne, and whose invectives, whose "human and inhuman vulgarities," flattered the passions of the petty clergy, who found the Catholic Press of the day extremely dull and colourless.

Victor Cousin, at the head of the University representatives, gave back blow for blow—his life's work was at stake. For he was the inventor of the philosophy of the reign—eclecticism, a doctrine made up of the amalgamation of various systems, a compromise which was admirably adapted to that other compromise consisting of a semi-legitimate monarchy; eclecticism was the official truth, regularly taught at the same hour in all the colleges throughout France, and Cousin marched at the head of his regiment like a soldier. He was known as "the little Pope of philosophy."

The Government tried to hold the scales evenly between the two parties, and Guizot even openly pronounced himself against the State monopoly, invoking the rights of fathers of families. But the plans suggested did not satisfy the Catholics. In their name Montalembert demanded absolute liberty, complete equality between the University and the clergy, and this he did with an eloquence and a nobility of outlook that brought over to his side not only the Bishops, but also a certain section of the Parliament. He did not suggest restoring the France of the period between Clovis and Louis XIV, or of putting the clock back, but insisted upon the rights of the new Catholics, "who are Catholics," he said, "above all and not after all," adding, "We are not conspirators, neither are we satisfied with the present system; we have been neither to Ghent nor to Belgrave Square, our pilgrimages have been only to the tombs of the Apostles, the Popes and the Martyrs. We are the children of the Crusades, and we shall not fall back before the children of Voltaire."

This was an extremely strong position; it led to "the conquest of religious liberty beneath the colours of civil liberty"; but the entry of the Jesuit body, which was still under a legal ban, into the conflict modified matters. Benjamin Constant once remarked that an Opposition which lacked arms could always create an opportune diversion against the Jesuits. "Like a valet who is rung for, they always come in reply." And thus it was in 1842—the University had discovered a ground for defence.

Michelet, whom Heinrich Heine had called "the sweet and peaceful Michelet, whose nature was as placid as moonlight," and Quinet, his more vehement friend, hurled their invectives from the *Collège de France* against the Jesuits. It was a regular intellectual upheaval, a tourney of ideas; young men gathered together from every quarter, from Paris and the suburbs, and marched in groups, singing as they went, to the Montagne Sainte Geneviève, where they acclaimed the two orators. "We adored these two men," said one of the fanatics, "we idolised them." And they all shouted, "Down with the Royalists, down with the Jesuits!" The governor of the *Collège de France* was frightened by their violence, and confided to a friend that he did not know whether by the evening there would be a stone of the College left.

Michelet and Quinet.

In the Press a similar hostility was displayed. Eugène Sue, quick to turn currents of public opinion to account, published in the *Constitutionnel* his serial *Le Juif Errant*, which the public swallowed with avidity. Thus the problem was completely changed—it was no longer a matter of pronouncing for or against the monopoly held by the University, but of deciding for or against the Jesuits.

The Jesuits.

Louis-Philippe had held himself aloof from these disputes, which he called "a quarrel between vulgar pedants and beadles." Nevertheless, he had no desire to risk his Crown for the sake of the Jesuits, for whose doctrines he had but little liking, being of opinion that in their institutions they displayed over-much zeal in teaching the children the verse in the *Magnificat: Deposuit potentes de sede.* He accordingly sent Rossi, the Professor of Law, to Rome as his envoy, charged with the mission of securing the dispersion of the Jesuits. In his heart of hearts, the Pope was not favourably disposed towards Montalembert's new party, which Rossi called "*la coda di* Lamennais," and he complied with the King's request. But, as a matter of fact, the Jesuits did not leave France, but merely retired into obscurity. Peace was restored, though the question of freedom of education still remained in suspense. When it was settled in 1850, Louis-Philippe was no longer King.

Since the beginning of the reign there had been a revolution in literary standards. Chateaubriand, filled with mortal disgust with the men of his age, and having lost confidence in the monarchy, felt himself forgotten and was threatened with a species of hypochondria. "You know that Chateaubriand is getting deaf?" said some. "Bah! it is only since people have stopped talking about him," was the reply. Nevertheless, when in 1834, at Madame Récamier's at Abbaye-aux-Bois, he gave a reading to a few privileged persons of extracts from his *Mémoires d'Outre Tombe*, it was a great event; the papers and the critics were full of the last masterpiece of the ageing René, and these scraps of thought from the pen of a man of genius became all the rage. Nevertheless the younger generation, who had lost their bump of reverence, and penetrated into the Holy of Holies, declared that he stank of the tomb.

Chateaubriand.

Beneath Chateaubriand, outside the decaying *oppidum* of early romanticism, anarchy reigned. "The ordered good sense and moral varnish of the Restoration had disappeared," and apparently there was nothing to take their place. What had become of the hopes to which Lamartine had given expression in 1830? "A studious and pure generation of young people," he said at that time, "are advancing into life with grave deliberation; the great events which met their infant eyes have ripened them before their time—it seems as though a century separated them from the generations that preceded them. They feel the dignity of man's destiny." Would these young people, despising outworn institutions that were crumbling to bits, really be filled with a breath of new life and set to work to build a fresh structure on the basis of romanticism and, to quote Lamartine once more, "weave a new cable"?

Certainly not! Romanticism had sunk into a coterie; it was no longer a corporate movement, but was made up of scattered, sterile and frequently ridiculous efforts. In the realm of fiction, "the reader is tempted only by a hook baited with a small decaying corpse"; such is the confession of Gautier, a romantic above suspicion. The

Romanticism.

theatre still followed the formula laid down by Merimée in *Clara Gazul:* "Tap! Tap! Tap!—The three knocks.—The curtain rises.—Laughter, pain, tears, and death.—He is killed, she is dead.—The End." And still the bourgeoisie continue to wax indignant—Hugo's *Le Roi s'amuse* is, in their opinion, Paillasse after Racine, and they leave the theatre "as though they were waking out of a nightmare, with a bad headache."

And thus the romantic revolution, begun in 1827, dragged on; but the rank and file no longer followed a leader. "What has become of those friends of the same age," sighed Sainte Beuve, "those brethren of poetry who grew up side by side, united, though still obscure, all of whom seemed destined to glory?" They had all gone off in different directions, accepting office, circumscribing and watering down the glorious enthusiasm of yore; and the critic who had been everywhere and tried everything—romanticism, Christian democracy, Saint-Simonism—without any support from the established powers such as his old friends of the *Globe* had received, concluded, "The literary movement of the Restoration was broken up and as it were disbanded while it was still in full swing and at the most brilliant heights of its enthusiasm, by the July Revolution."

Nevertheless in the long run romanticism learnt wisdom. Though it still retained a certain Byronic frenzy and a mania for antitheses, of which it never quite rid itself, it ceased to ponder on the disease of the age, and adopted a less vagabond air, whilst those who remained true to the excesses of the early days were considered ridiculous by Gautier himself, the historian of "Young France."

Ponsard.

The success of Ponsard, a classicist with a touch of the romantic about him, who revived admiration for the old tragic subjects, was a clear proof of the change that had taken place in public taste (*Lucrèce*, 1843). In spite of the condemnation of the romantics of the old school, he enjoyed a stubborn success; he had a regard for order and for style, and the bourgeoisie were grateful to him for it. At

Rachel.

the same time Rachel, the frail weakling daughter of a Jewish pedlar and a secondhand clothes dealer, gave a fresh lease of life to the classic repertory. When in January 1843 she acted *Phèdre* in the Théâtre Français, the audience raved about her. Never had Racine's heroine been played with such fire and animation! The enthusiasm which greeted Rachel showed the distance that had been traversed since the day when, in the same theatre, the art students howled in chorus, "Racine is done for! Wigs are done for!"

But literature at this time was undergoing a still greater change, coming on this occasion not from within, but from without.

The Press.

In 1836, Emile de Girardin, a writer of but little culture, though gifted with audacity, who knew the most efficacious manner of using his energy, a business man rather than a man of letters, revived the idea first created by an unknown individual named Dutacq, and founded a cheap newspaper—the subscription to it was 40 francs a year. It was an astounding innovation—the number of subscribers to Paris papers, which in 1835 was 70,000, rose to 200,000 in 1846, and with a wave of the wand the whole Press was transformed. In order to feed it, the directors made use of publicity—puff paragraphs and advertisements; and in order to attract readers offered them, higgledy-piggledy, articles on politics, art and literature.

Jasmin, a Gascon poet, the author of *Papillotes*, who in 1842 paid a visit to Paris, was astonished to find that literature had become a regular business. "There are firms of agents," he said, "which supply all kinds of articles, comic operas, melodramas and novels." And there was indeed a medley of styles in the new commercial enterprise, a confusion which had an immediate effect upon the position of writers. The man of letters had already become a politician, and *vice versâ*; Lamennais and Thiers, for instance. By this means they both reached a wider public, and used the newspaper as a platform "from which they addressed the passers-by in the street." But the idea materialised by Girardin had graver consequences—the man of letters found out, a thing of which he had been hardly aware hitherto, that a livelihood could be earned with the pen, and that writing was a profession like any other. Whereupon commercial literature made its appearance.

Under the appellation of *roman-feuilleton* (serial story) it has had a long career, which is not yet ended. The elder Dumas regularly and painstakingly fed several papers, making their fortune at the same time as his own, and astonishing the masses by his mechanical production, timed to the moment. But he was dethroned by Eugène Sue, whose *Mystères de Paris*, published in the *Débats* from 1843 onwards, held " master and man, ambassador and secretary, the Duke and peer of the realm and the grocer's wife " breathless. It was in vain that Gérard de Nerval, a charming and delicate writer, expressed his contempt of such inartistic productions, saying, " All that was done on the boulevards ten years ago "; the public did not share his opinion. They found in this novel and others like it a fresh atmosphere—a picture of the way of life and nature of that obscure and miserable world where revolution lies hid, a tendency to portray things as they really are—at least, so they believed—with a picturesqueness of expression and a disregard for convention which at first came as a shock, but afterwards proved attractive, in short, a story with a social significance.

Balzac.

Balzac had long before set the example, boasting of " probing with the eager scalpel of the nineteenth century into those recesses of the heart that the modesty of preceding centuries had respected." And he applied his maxim literally—his heroines have nothing in common with Velléda and Elvire; it is the women of his day, embellished or vilified according to his fantasy, that he presents to us; it is a whole world taken from everyday life, with its feet firmly planted on mother earth, but rearranged and moulded by his genius, which he sets before us in the pages of that prodigious microcosm, *la Comédie Humaine*; and through his power of creation, realism gradually crept into romanticism.

Art.

Like literature, the fine arts learnt wisdom almost at the same time. In 1834 Delacroix paid a visit to Africa, and the bourgeoisie allowed themselves to be won over when he exhibited " Women of Algiers in their home "; seven years later they waxed enthusiastic over " The Crusaders at Constantinople." As a matter of fact Delacroix did not shock them, for in a certain sense he paid homage to the antique, " the source of all." With the shy smile that gave him a strange resemblance to Talleyrand, he observed to

Berryer, "I study purity of line, and more especially the mastery of drawing in the great works of the past; I soak myself in them and admire them! And thus I keep in check the tendency my palette has to run away with me." Nevertheless he did not desert his old faith, and, as Gautier points out, he interpreted antiquity, not as David, but as Shakespeare did.

The war in Africa opened up fresh horizons for painters at this time, and orientalism assumed a prominent place in Art; the popular subjects, the interiors, the large desert landscapes treated by Decamps, Delacroix and in a more classic style by Vernet, were immediately accepted by the public, and thus the old forms were once again revived.

Sculpture, however, became ever more and more daring in its development. On the pediment of the Panthéon, David d'Angers presented his figures in modern dress, which ten years previously would have been regarded as an outrage on common sense. But the man who at this period really gave a fresh impetus to the art of sculpture was Rude, an old pupil of David, the painter—Rude, who was movement, passion and grandeur turned into marble, the author of the *Marseillaise* (1836).

Sculpture.

In music, on the other hand, there was a renaissance of the Italian style (*Les Huguenots*, 1836), whilst comic opera consisted almost exclusively of Scribe and Auber, "just as a drop of water consists of oxygen and hydrogen." Berlioz, who was as yet accepted only by the *élite*, inveighed against these melodies, which made him feel sick, and in the pit of the Opera he astonished his neighbours by the fury with which he shook "his huge umbrella of hair, which was like a loose canopy shading his vulture's beak of a nose."

Thus, on the whole, romanticism seemed to have reached its final development. Hugo, who had been made a peer of the realm, was apparently silent, Lamartine confined himself to politics, George Sand had launched out into social propaganda, Sainte Beuve had abandoned fiction for criticism pure and simple, whilst the work of Musset was more or less finished. In this quasi-silence that prevailed after 1840, there was one man who began to stand out—Gautier, who had

Gautier.

preserved his romantic faith unsullied, and his absolute devotion to art for art's sake, and who, when he was asked, "What is the purpose of it?" replied, "Its purpose is to be beautiful."

Slow Economic Progress.

From the economic point of view the triumph of the bourgeoisie in 1830 did not lead to any very great change from the system in vogue during the Restoration. The Conservatives, when they were in power, remained true to the principle of Protection, in spite of the fact that it led to a constant rise in the price of articles of prime necessity, and, as Monsieur Charléty points out, novelties, and the reductions of duties which took the place of absolute prohibition—the duty on cotton, for instance—were only accepted owing to pressure of circumstances.

An attempt at a Customs Union with Belgium failed on account of protestations from England; smuggling was rampant, but ended by being winked at, since it was a necessity for certain of the French industries. Meanwhile production increased, there were changes in the means of transport, and a new spirit came into being throughout the country. Hence a state of instability, of legal maladaptation to circumstances which hindered progress.

Iron in France cost about 12*s*. a hundredweight, in England it was 6*s*.; coal was about 4*s*. a sack, in England about 6*d*.; and this difference in price, due to Protection, weighed heavy on the French industrial system. The use of steam and electricity was adopted very slowly; France was still constructing wooden vessels at a time when her neighbours had long since possessed iron ones. In vain did Free Traders, like Michel Chevalier and Dunoyer, taking Sir Robert Peel's reforms in England as their model, advocate the abolition of duties on iron; they were told that this would mean a lowering of wages. In vain did Bastiat, in his pamphlets, point out by means of well-chosen and easily accessible examples, how great were the inconveniences of Protection; nobody would listen to him. The Free Trade of Peel and Cobden was regarded as an English importation, and that was quite enough to condemn it in the eyes of the majority.

This wilful inferiority from the economic point of view, and these deep-rooted prejudices, made the development of railways particularly difficult. The public, even the most enlightened among them, were suspicious of the innovation — Thiers merely shrugged his shoulders when their future was mentioned, whilst Arago, a man of science, was afraid that transport in railway carriages "would make the army effeminate, and that the Saint Cloud tunnel would give coughs and colds to the passengers." As for the old aristocrats, they unhesitatingly declared, "It is a cursed invention, a fashion which will last only a little while. In fifty years people will be tired of it, and they will be right." Owing to this scant encouragement France, on the 31st of December, 1840, had about 270 miles of railway working, whilst England had 1200.

The Railways.

In the end the Government decided to make a move, but it still hesitated as to the best methods to be adopted for the building and improvement of railways. Ought they to be run entirely by the State, or ought they, on the contrary, to be handed over to private initiative and concessions made for their construction? The claims of the State were defended by Lamartine, who regarded large companies as a menace to liberty and pointed out the danger of handing over territory to moneyed powers. At last a compromise was reached—the State was to buy the land, and to build the permanent ways, the stations and outbuildings, whilst the rolling-stock was to be provided by companies. Such was the object of the law of 1842, which led to an immediate rush of speculation. Whilst in the Chamber "local feeling" ran high—every deputy wanted the railway to run through his own *arrondissement*—in financial and business circles there was feverish excitement reminiscent of the days of the Regency and the Rue Quincampoix. All the talk was of concessions, safeguarding of interests and subsidies; indifference gave way to passionate concern.

Nevertheless on the 8th of May, 1842, a terrible tragedy had occurred at Versailles. One holiday—the day of the Fountain Display—owing to an accident, fifty people, and among them the famous Admiral Dumont d'Urville, had been killed in the compartments of a train the doors of which, according to regulation, were locked. A furious mob had collected in front of the Gare Montparnasse with the intention of setting fire to it. . . . But in spite of tragedies and disappointments, the idea gained ground. Between 1841 and 1847 the number of passengers was doubled, whilst the goods traffic was trebled. The impetus had been given.

In time industrial activity took the place of political interests and men's ideals descended to the sphere of business. Foreign trade, which was carried on chiefly by sea, had increased by one third since 1830, and that in spite of the inadequacy of the French merchant service. Paris had become the great market for Government securities, of which 198 were quoted on the Stock Exchange in 1847. Capital was gradually unlocked, thanks to the development of the credit system, although bank notes, paper money and cheques, etc., had not yet come into common use. Large shops, like *Le Bonhomme Richard*, came into being, whilst exhibitions brought to the notice of the public scientific inventions, such as steam, electric and photographic appliances which were assuming ever greater international importance. In Paris, the Prefect Rambuteau was responsible for the laying of pavements, the levelling of the boulevards and the rebuilding of the quays; he also inaugurated the installation of gas lighting.

Whilst over the ancient land, once so peaceful and still, there ran as it were a shudder, what was happening to the inhabitants?

The People.

In 1846 France had a population of about 35½ millions; it had risen everywhere, though the increase was already lower than it had been in the rest of Europe. Agriculture was still the principal source of wealth. Cereals, effectively protected by the system of "the sliding-scale," which raised or lowered Customs duties according to whether the harvest had been good or bad in France, assured the bourgeois or peasant proprietors a fairly steady income; and although the land, in contradistinction to its present share, bore the burden of half the taxation of the country, the lot of the rural populations was nevertheless quite tolerable.

Misery of the Poor.

The same cannot be said of industry. Since the Restoration there had been a tendency for wages to fall, and Monsieur Fournière estimates that calculated on the basis of a working year of 260 days, the average daily earnings of a family were 1 franc 38 (about 1*s*.).

In Alsace a spinner earned 2 francs (about 1*s.* 8*d.*) a day; in Lyons a weaver earned from 2 to 2 francs 50. If these figures are correct—though there is a lack of reliable documents—it cannot be a matter of surprise that the number of foundlings rose to 130,000 in 1840, and that in Lyons 100,000 people out of 150,000 were destitute. It is true that savings banks increased in number, but they did not reach the working classes, who remained miserably poor, living huddled on the top of each other in wretched underground cellars such as those described by Hugo:

Caves de Lille! on meurt sous vos plafonds de pierre.[1]

The increase in crime was terrific, and in the end old offenders formed from year to year an ever-growing "army of crime." This plague was a source of anxiety to the politicians and writers, who brought forward suggestions for reformatories for the regeneration of the criminal. The idea of State intervention—an idea formerly repudiated in the name of liberty—began to gain ground, and was even embodied, though tentatively, in a law of 1841 which forbade the employment of children under eight years of age, and between the ages of eight and twelve limited their working day to eight hours.

The fall in wages, the agricultural crises that occurred more especially in 1846–47, the increasing use of machinery, which supplanted manual labour "and resulted in mass production," the inadequacy of the legal regulations, all conduced to the development of the movement for social reform which had started under the Restoration. Would Companionship, which had fallen from its pristine glory, but of which Agricole Perdiguier was at this time writing the history and which George Sand was treating in fiction, have been able to ameliorate the lot of the working-man, and result in the organisation of the proletariat? It was a society animated by a sincerely religious spirit, whose object was to give apprentices facilities for making the tour of France, but divided, as it was, into three rites or "duties" which were conflicting, and unable to adapt itself to the new economic conditions with which it was incapable of dealing, it had no real power.

[1] Cellars of Lille! People are dying beneath your stone ceilings. . . .

After 1830 it was believed that Saint-Simonism would provide the system, at once practical and theoretical, which, according to its inventor's writings, would secure the happiness of the greater number; and Olinde Rodrigues, Enfantin and Bazard, the pupils of the master, were agreed as regards the following principles: the creation of a world-wide league of nations, hence the abolition of competition; the distribution of wealth on the maxim of "to each man according to his capacity, to each capacity according to his works," hence abolition of the hereditary principle; the international organisation of industry, hence the abolition of war. Society was to be a family in which each member had his share of responsibility; the exploitation of man by man was to cease; work was to be the modern religion patronised and encouraged by the State.

Saint-Simonism.

With a programme to bind them together, the Saint-Simonians displayed great activity. In the Rue Monsigny they had their organ, the *Globe*, in which they proclaimed the new morality; in the Rue Taitbout and the Place de la Sorbonne they had their assembly rooms, where they taught their disciples and gave various courses of instruction, some public, others reserved for the members of certain professions. In the midst of the somewhat sceptical and scoffing society of the day it was a curious spectacle to see Père Enfantin preaching, and the eloquent Barraud describing the misery of the people and making his brethren feel ashamed of their indifference. Whole days were spent in discussion, and nights as well; some would fall into a trance and prophesy; others, believing they had the Holy Spirit within them, would be seized with convulsions; the words of Holy Script made their way into the vocabulary of these reformers, Enfantin crying out against a recalcitrant disciple, "Thou wouldst crucify me. My son hath soiled my countenance!"

This eccentricity gave both offence and amusement, though it cannot be denied that these men were absolutely sincere; a real love of humanity, a fervent desire to improve the lot of their fellow men uplifted them, but they lost their heads in the clouds, attempting to found a new religion on a moral basis alone, and when they saw that dogma was indispensable, that the mere outward and visible signs of religion were not sufficient, they disagreed among themselves. Enfantin held beliefs on the subject of marriage and the resurrection of the body which seemed scandalous to Bazard, who was married; the *Globe* ceased to be published (April 1832), and the Saint-Simonian family was broken up.

Prosecuted on an absurd charge of swindling, Enfantin appeared in court with a red cap on his head, and wearing a blue jerkin, and white trousers fastened by a patent leather belt. On his chest the words *Le Père* were inscribed. His hair was long and his beard trimmed in oriental fashion, while, convinced of what Montaigne called " the appeal of the body," he tried the magic power of his eye upon his hearers. He was acquitted, and followed by a few faithful disciples—about forty—he returned to Menilmontant, where the remnants of the family had sought refuge and where manual labour and the work of the house were done to the accompaniment of melodies by " son " Félicien David.

Saint-Simonism, " that romanticism of sociology," had an extraordinary career. Most of its disciples, men of sterling worth, turned their energies to industrial enterprises and public works, and soon won important positions in these fields; it will be sufficient in this connection to mention the cutting of the Suez Canal. Thus from social reform the Saint-Simonians suddenly went over to capitalism in its most blatant form—the height of irony, which drove Cournot to exclaim, " Apparently these men of the spirit did not altogether believe in their apostolic mission." And indeed Enfantin subsequently confessed that there were times when he had felt he was a little bit mad. But in 1846 there were no longer any signs of this, and a stranger who met him at the time thought " that he looked like a gentleman connected with the railways and bore the stamp of his calling."

Nevertheless the doctrines of Saint-Simon did not die out; they were revived by Buchez, an old Carbonaro, who in 1840 founded *l'Atelier*, a paper edited and run by working men, who earned their livelihood by the sweat of their brow, and the aim of which was to bring about the reform of society in a perfectly peaceful and Christian way. It was afterwards run by Leroux, "a philosophic Capuchin and the spiritual director of George Sand," who enveloped the doctrines in a veil of metaphysic.

Fourier.

All these systems, including that of Auguste Comte, another Saint-Simonian whose influence during his own lifetime was almost negligible, rested on the authority and guidance of the State. As a reaction against this, Fourier aimed at transforming the world through the individual, and through liberty. He showed his originality at the age of seven, when "he swore the oath that Hannibal swore against Rome, vowing eternal hatred against commerce," the cause of all our ills, and imagining he could change the face of society by satisfying the passions and making corporate work attractive. A kind of Rousseau mellowed by playing a practical part in business, he hoped to find happiness for mankind by means of vocational careers; the State was to be done away with and its place taken by the phalanstery, a series of cells acting independently in providential harmony. The system of Fourier enjoyed a period of success among certain sections of the bourgeoisie, whom his ideas did not frighten, and even among the masses; it survived Saint-Simonism, and after the death of its founder in 1837, Victor Considérant carried on his master's teaching so successfully that it became famous even abroad. Nevertheless in the end the phalansterian venture perished of inanition.

Louis Blanc.

Whereupon reformers set forth in search of practical solutions within the framework of society as it already existed, and in 1839 Louis Blanc brought out his *l'Organisation du travail.* This is not the chief work of this remarkable historian, "with his smooth face, his clear, piping voice and childlike appearance, who was so small that when he was over twenty people thought he was barely twelve or thirteen." But the book contains an interesting suggestion that competition should be stopped through the intervention of the State as the supreme organiser of production, the banker of the poor, and by the creation of communal workshops. Nevertheless later on, when it was a matter of applying his system, Louis Blanc met with serious disappointments, and it became apparent that the solution based on State intervention was possibly not the best that could be devised.

These theories, supported by politicians, economists, socialists and metaphysicians, all had one point in common—they made no appeal to revolutionary methods. The latter, however, were adopted by another school of reformers, of whom the most famous was Blanqui, men who, correctly speaking, had no precise doctrine, but who had a common source of inspiration in Babouvistic Communism. Through the instrumentality of Buonarrotti, whose influence was already being felt in the Young Italy movement under Mazzini, Communism took root in France, where it was modified according to the nature of different men's minds—some, like Cabet, constructing an ideal city, Icaria, in Texas, an experiment which met with dismal failure; others, like Pecqueur, reconciling Communism with Christianity and suggesting a socialistic interpretation of the Gospel. Lamennais himself, who had plunged into solitude and apocalyptic reveries, caught the disease, and in *Le Livre du Peuple* (1838) preached that all things should be shared in common; whereupon, astonished at his own audacity, he retired into the background.

Communism.

All these were merely theories, conflicting systems which led to no grave consequences. But the men of action learnt something else from Communism—namely, method and realisation by means of violence—and they acted upon the masses. "The elements of this universal language," said Heine with regard to egalitarian doctrines, "are as simple as hunger, envy and death. They are easily learnt." The Communist army was recruited from the ranks of the poor and discontented; Darmès, as we know, was taught in this school, as well as Quénisset. Papers, clandestinely published, like *l'Homme Libre,* and revolutionary catechisms kept alive in the hearts of the faithful the creed once taught by the secret societies; they had no programme beyond a declaration of war upon the rich and the noble, the exaltation of the "Sublime Committee of Public Safety," which was the religion of the regicides—the heroic Morey and the fierce Alibaud. This army, which was believed to have been extinct ever since the insurrection of the *Saisons* in 1839, came into being again unnoticed, and was destined to show renewed activity during the revolution of February 1848.

In distinction to the writers who were remaking the world

on paper, and a stranger to all egalitarian dreams, though in spite of this he wished to preserve liberty, Proudhon occupies a place apart. His dictum "Property is burglary" made his fortune, but his work was essentially that of a critic, and bears the stamp of a "one man conspiracy." The son of a working man and a country servant, he was proud of his fourteen quarters of rusticity—"Can you boast the same number of quarters of nobility?" he one day demanded of a Legitimist—and belonged to no party, to no school. As for the deputies of the Opposition, he would have liked to see them thrown into the Seine with a millstone about their necks. Fourierism? "The last nightmare of delirious debauchery." Communism? "A system which binds men like oysters, side by side, devoid of either activity or feeling, upon the rock of fraternity." He attacked recognised principles with a force of dialectic and a torrent of "passionate and deadly" invective which choke the reader, and the echo of which may be found again in the genial forcefulness of a Charles Péguy. But in spite of all he was good-natured, free from rancour and bitterness, and uplifted by some strange impetus of joy.

Proudhon.

The destructive criticism of Proudhon—his constructive work was only outlined before 1848—plainly proved the instability of the monarchy and the uneasiness from which society was suffering; on the one hand, a victorious bourgeois minority, oblivious of the misery by which it was surrounded; on the other, a plebeian majority which felt competent to play a part and have its say in the government of the country, and which, deprived of the legal power to act, nursed its rancour.

The conflict appeared menacing, and rare indeed were those who, like the charitable Ozanam, hoped to avoid it by obtaining alms in abundance from the rich and resignation in abundance from the poor.

Short Bibliography. L. Abensour, *Le Féminisme sous le Règne de Louis-Philippe et en* 1848 (1913). Bastiat, *Sophismes Économiques* (1834). A. Bellessort, *Balzac et son Œuvre* (1924). Blaze de Bury, *Alexandre Dumas* (1885). M. Bouteron, *Les Muses Romantiques* (*Rev. Hebdomadaire*, March–April 1926). H. Bremond, *Pour le Romanticisme* (1914). M. du Camp, *Souvenirs Littéraires* (2 vols., 1892) (Vol. I). S. Charléty, *La Monarchie de Juillet* (Book III) (with the bibliography); *Histoire du Saint-Simonisme* (1896). G. Claudin, *Mes Souvenirs* (1884). L. Curnier, *La*

Jeunesse de France. Ozanam (1890). E. Daudet, *La Princesse de Liéven* (1903). Fournière, *Le Règne de Louis-Philippe* (A Socialist History) (1905). Th. Gautier, *Histoire du Romanticisme* (new ed., no date). V. Hugo, *Douze Discours* (1851). Madame Jaubert, *Souvenirs* (no date) (Hetzel's edition). W. Karenine, *G. Sand, sa Vie et ses Œuvres* (4 vols., 1899–1926). P. de Kock, *Mémoires* (1873). Lacordaire, *Fr. Ozanam* (1856). Lamartine, *Souvenirs et Portraits* (3 vols., 1872). Lecanuet, *Montalembert* (3 vols., 1895–1902). Legouvé, *Soixante Ans de Souvenirs* (4 vols., 12th ed., no date) (Hetzel's edition). H. Malo, *Une Muse et sa Mère* (1924); *La Gloire du Vicomte de Launay* (1925) (an excellent bibliography). Marie, *Gérard de Nerval* (1914). M. Martin, *Le Docteur Koreff* (1925). J. Marsan, *La Bataille Romantique* (2nd series, no date) (Hachette's edition). Michelet and Quinet, *Des Jésuites* (1843). Montalembert, *Le Père Lacordaire* (1861). M. de Montrond, *Frédéric Ozanam* (1869). E. Mouton, *Le XIXe Siècle Vécu par Deux Français* (no date). D. Nisard, *Souvenirs et Notes Bibliographiques* (2 vols., 1888). M. L. Pailleron, *La Vie Littéraire Sous Louis-Philippe* (no date). A. Picard, *Les Chemins de Fer Français* (1884). G. Planche, *Portraits Littéraires* (2 vols., 1838). Sainte-Beuve, *Portraits Contemporains* (Vol. I, 1846) (article on literature as a trade). G. Sand, *Histoire de ma Vie* (10 vols., 1856). *Correspondance* (1883–84). E. Seillière, *G. Sand, Mystique de la Passion, de la Politique et de l'Art* (1920). J. Simon, *Victor Cousin* (1887). G. Augustin Thierry, *Augustin Thierry d'après sa Correspondance et ses Papiers de Famille* (1922). L. Veuillot, *Mélanges* (1857). H. de Villemessant, *Mémoires d'un Journaliste* (1867). Werdet, *Souvenirs de ma Vie Littéraire* (1879). Weill, *Un Précurseur du Socialisme : Saint-Simon et son Œuvre* (1894).

CHAPTER VIII

THE REVOLUTION OF 1848

The progressive Conservatives in favour of reform. Their defeat. Liberal agitation in Europe. Pius IX and Italy. Revolutionary education. Lamartine, Michelet, Louis Blanc. The scandals of corruption. The Teste-Cubières trial. Assassination of the Duchesse de Praslin. Signs of revolt. The campaign of the banquets: Louis-Philippe and Guizot insist on refusing reform. The banquet of the 12th legion cancelled. The days of the 22nd and 23rd of February. By summoning the National Guard the Government increases the disturbances. Guizot dismissed. The Republicans at the head of the movement. The massacre of the Boulevard des Capucines. Thiers Minister, Bugeaud Commander-in-Chief. The 24th of February. Bedeau's column checked. Parleys. Order to cease fire. Bugeaud's illusions. The Tuileries menaced. Louis-Philippe reviews his troops. Attack on the guard-house of the Château d'Eau. Abdication of the King. His flight. Looting of the Tuileries. The Duchesse d'Orléans in the Chamber. Rising of the people. Lamartine and the provisional Government. Louis-Philippe crosses to England. Causes of his downfall. The achievements of the July Monarchy.

ON the 27th of April, 1847, on the rostrum in the Chamber, an almost unknown deputy summed up the work of the Guizot Ministry in the following words: "Behold, gentlemen, the whole system of Government. Nothing! Nothing! Nothing!" This was said with apparent simplicity, and a bow first to the Left, then to the Right, and lastly to the Centre. And these words, which denounced the emptiness of the system, so exactly expressed the feelings of the Opposition that from this moment Desmousseaux de Givré became famous. His expression was snapped up and adopted by the Press and had the honour of being used as a rallying cry by all the enemies of the Government.

Givré.

Guizot, calm and imperturbable, refused to introduce any change, however innocuous. When it was suggested that postal rates, which had hitherto varied in different localities, should be made uniform, and thus do away with the prejudice against pre-payment which had been in use only with tradespeople—in the case of private people it would have been out of keeping—Guizot met it with a blank and sharp refusal. He was sincerely convinced that the system had reached the apex of perfection and that any imprudent meddling would only mar it.

The Progressive Conservatives.

But those deputies who, owing to the Government's long tenure of office, had been immured in opposition, disliked this marking of time and apathy on the part of the Ministry—for it is a well-known fact that nothing makes people more clear-sighted than the lust for power. Thus for some time there had been in existence a new group consisting of men of worth—from the intellectual point of view they were perhaps the best in the country—who called themselves progressive Conservatives. They saw the necessity, if not of satisfying, at least of giving a sop to the malcontents, of pacifying "the popular lion," and of disarming Communism by giving to the masses the hope of having a share in the Government. Tocqueville, full of the experience he had won on a visit to America, maintained that the organisation of democracy was urgent; while Duvergier de Hauranne was of opinion that a truce should be declared between the parties and that they should agree to an extension of the right of suffrage. To meet claims half-way and transform them into laws while there was yet time (a policy afterwards adopted by Bismarck in Germany) constituted their programme, which they put into practice by reviving two proposals which were by no means new—electoral reform and parliamentary reform.

Duvergier's scheme was as follows—every Frenchman who paid 100 francs in taxes was to be given the vote, while certain categories of citizens, teachers, officers on half pay, lawyers, doctors—"men of ability" in fact—were to enjoy the same privilege; this would increase the electorate by about 200,000 voters.

At the same time Rémusat proposed to prohibit deputies from holding public office, more especially that of attaché in the royal household. This was aimed at the devoted servants of Louis-Philippe, his aides-de-camp, who, when a session was in full swing, used to convey their master's commands to the deputies.

These proposals were very sound—possibly they might have put a stop to the movement which grew stronger every year in favour of an extension of the suffrage. Whilst they flattered the vanity of tradespeople, of the National Guard, and of the carping petty bourgeois, who would at last have been given the vote, the withholding of which had been a sore grievance, they also met the demands of the intellectuals and the charges of corruption. The monarchy could only have gained by their acceptance.

But Louis-Philippe remained suspicious; he thought that an increase in the number of electors would lead to disorder and undermine the Charter, and he turned a deaf ear to the respectful warnings of his sons, the Prince de Joinville and the Duc d'Aumale. In discussing reform he observed, " It would be a clip of the scissors into taut material. The whole piece would give way." Guizot was of the same opinion. In the Chamber he replied to his adversaries that he acknowledged only one sovereign power in the land, that of the King in conjunction with the Parliament, only one category of rights, those recognised by law. And when Garnier-Pagès, a republican deputy, exclaimed, " The day of universal suffrage will come," he retorted drily, " There will be no day of universal suffrage." The proposals were thrown out, and the King, releasing the shadow, replaced Soult by Guizot as President of the Council, a title which he had not yet enjoyed (September 1847).

The failure to carry this double reform alienated from the monarchy all those who had hoped to get the vote, and who, feeling that they were henceforward freed from any obligation towards the system that persisted in ignoring them, went to swell the ranks of the minority. A fresh campaign of abuse broke out against the Government. " It is no longer, as in 1830, violence that menaces them," said Duvergier, " it is the fact that they are riddled by corruption." The bourgeoisie took a delight in upholding the elective against the hereditary principle, the sovereignty of assemblies against that of the

Crown; and as the financial situation was far from flourishing, and corn was dear owing to bad harvests, the "milestone Government" was blamed and was accused of being incapable of guiding the destinies of the country, in addition to being obstructive of all progress.

Just at this juncture foreign affairs provided the Opposition with fresh arguments. Ever since 1846 Liberal ideas had been gaining ground in Europe—the King of Prussia had granted a constitution to his subjects, and found his intentions being exceeded by the deputies, who meditated nothing less than the formation of a federated State in place of the existing federation of States. The Radical cantons of Switzerland were imitating the French Republicans, and adopting a hostile attitude towards the Catholic cantons, which were united by a League known as the *Sonderbund*; and having the majority, they decided upon the expulsion of the Jesuits. Guizot protested, but found himself confronted by England, where Palmerston had returned to power and was posing as the champion of Liberalism.

Foreign Affairs.

But it was above all in Italy that Conservatism had been put to a severe test—in the month of June 1846 Pius IX had succeeded Gregory XVI. The new Pope, in order to celebrate his accession, granted a wide amnesty, a *perdono*, to political prisoners, and showed himself favourable towards social reform; whereupon there was an outburst of enthusiasm such as may occasionally be witnessed among southern peoples. When one summer's night Pius IX appeared on the balcony of his palace clad in a white cassock and scarlet hood, his face lit up by torches, the crowd, delirious with joy, shouted, "Courage, Holy Father! Courage!" a cry in which all their hatred of Austria, the Power which was stifling the liberty of the Italian people, was summed up.

Italy.

Hugo remarked at the time, in the prophetic tone that had become familiar to him, "The Pope who embraces the French Revolution and turns it into a Christian revolution, the Pope who is capable of this extraordinary and sublime action is not a mere man—he is an event!" And indeed the Liberal idea, introduced by men who were no longer conspirators, but writers and politicians like Gioberti, Balbo and Massimo d'Azeglio, and supported by the power regarded as most hostile to all change, was spreading throughout Italy. The Duke of Tuscany followed the example of Pius IX, whilst Charles Albert, King of Sardinia, confided to d'Azeglio that he would spend his last farthing in the cause of Italy—that is to say, that he would fight with all the forces at his command against Austria.

The latter immediately asserted her rights and drove the Papal forces out of Ferrara. Italy felt she had been attacked and ranged herself solidly behind Pius IX when he denounced this violation of the right of nations. "Holy Father," wrote the revolutionary Mazzini to him, "I am watching your movements with great hope. Be confident, and trust in us!" A new day seemed to be dawning over the old, downtrodden country; the people were awaking in the light of liberty. The Italians, with that magnificent and dramatic feeling which is their peculiar gift, called the phenomenon "*il Risorgimento*."

But this ideology did not appeal to Guizot. Reforms or disturbances—it was all one to him. He represented stability, and supporting the system of Metternich, refused, in spite of all the appeals of public opinion, to intervene against Austria. "It is only with the help of France," he said, "that the revolutionary spirit can be successfully combated." And he was not the only one to hold this opinion. "With the exercise of a little patience," wrote X. Doudans at the time, "Italy in a few years time would have been well fed and housed and free in her movements, well governed and sure of herself for some time to come. But she had to dance the carmagnole—such is the fantasy of every people when they are set free."

But Guizot had not the smallest intention of "dancing the carmagnole." In vain did Italy inveigh against France, the chosen home of liberty, who was making common cause with the Austrian despot; Guizot turned a deaf ear. But when the Pope, who was himself surprised at the passions he had aroused, felt himself menaced, Guizot immediately went to his assistance. Having done so, however, he remained true to his unvarying policy of peace and order. And it must be confessed that this attitude, by its very persistence, was not lacking in a certain grandeur; it was like a pale reflection of Casimir Périer.

In France it seemed as though the heroic days of boundless enthusiasm for Poland and the emancipation of the nations had returned; but the years had gone by, and the new movement was of a different calibre, less ingenuous and instinctive, more calculated and conscious—the rising generation had learnt their lesson, and the writers, almost all of them guided by political considerations, undertook to complete their education.

Lamartine.

As early as 1828 Lamartine had said of himself, " I have the mass instinct. I feel what they feel and what they are going to do, even when they are silent." Since then he had boasted of being the rallying point in France of every idea, every fancy and noble sentiment: " I have the women and young men on my side, I can do without the rest." But this apparent detachment was not strong enough to resist the course of events. Lamartine wanted to reach the crowd, and between March and June 1847, he published the eight volumes of his *Histoire des Girondins*, one after the other.

The enthusiasm they aroused was enormous and almost unanimous. The one topic of conversation, alike in the streets and the salons, was Vergniaud, Buzot and Madame Rolland; the heart of the public had been directly stirred. Thiers and Mignet, it is true, had already told the same tale, the one with the fluency of the orator, the other with an almost scientific severity and the impartiality of a judge. Lamartine's work belonged to another category—never had the figures of the past been thus clothed " in words of purple and gold," never before had their lives been lived in the pages of a book. And, as a matter of fact, the author had drawn his information from the last survivors of the revolutionary period. He wrote with a generous transport and a poetic fervour—" here is the matter for half a million poems," observed a certain Orleanist—a young and lively faith, and an extraordinary ardour for vindication. At first glance the *Histoire des Girondins* might be taken for the romance of a soul, " Lamartine playing a part in his own work," admiring the Girondins, only to end in an apotheosis of Robespierre. But these inconsistencies did not affect the public, and even those who did not share the ideas of the poet-historian admired " his magnificent rapture."

Lamartine was not the only writer to remind the people of their ancestors, and to be the heraldist to draw up their patent of nobility—in short, to undertake the task of revolutionary apologist. In February 1847 Michelet and Louis Blanc added their stones to the monument raised to the glory of 1789, the former endowed with the intuition of the visionary, and the capacity for placing men and events in a dazzling light by imparting to them the irresistible charm of life; the other having a somewhat superstitious respect, though a finer sense of the requirements of politics and parliamentary difficulties.

Michelet and Louis Blanc.

Thus, through the medium of the historians, the revolutionary cult, which hitherto had been celebrated in obscurity in the conventicles of the secret societies, invaded the streets. Put into poetical form and magnified, it fed the popular passion; France, as represented by Michelet, seemed a living and active being, pouring out her blood for the liberty and happiness of humanity—Louis-Philippe and Guizot, with their policy of prudence, seemed insignificant by comparison.

As if Fate were taking a delight in irrevocably undermining the monarchy, one scandal followed close on the heels of another, thus revealing to the light of day the hidden and, at that period, still rare sores of corruption. The head of the army bakeries had speculated in corn with Government funds; the director of a light opera theatre had secured the renewal of his contract on payment of a large sum to a Government paper; another journal had become a centre for the sale of the Cross of the Legion of Honour; but it was the Teste trial that showed up the immorality of the system in its most glaring colours.

Corruption.

Teste, Marshal Soult's parliamentary advocate, enjoyed such a dubious reputation that he was kept out of the Cabinet—he had at one time been a Minister—but he had been compensated for this disgrace by being given the post of President of the *Cour de Cassation*. In May 1847 he was accused of having received, through the instrumentality of General Cubières, an ex-Minister of War, the sum of 94,000 francs for granting to a third party the concession for a salt

Teste.

mine. Before the Court of Peers the accused put a bold face on the matter. "It is incredible," people exclaimed. "Such impudence and cynicism in the way they sell themselves!" Yet there was no possibility of doubt—Teste tried to commit suicide; he failed, and together with Cubières was condemned to loss of civic rights and three years imprisonment. From the opening of the trial Louis-Philippe had been unable to control himself, and burst out in reproaches against President Pasquier: "What! You could not be satisfied with one of my old Ministers! You had to have a second! And so after it has taken me seventeen years to restore authority in France, in a single day, a single hour, you have overthrown it again!"

This was only too true. But a few days after the condemnation of the dishonest Ministers another scandal occurred. The Duc de Choiseul-Praslin, a peer of the realm, under the influence of his children's governess, brutally murdered his wife, the only daughter of Marshal Sébastiani (18th of August, 1847). The mob rushed in a body to the house where the murder had been committed and mounted guard over it in order to prevent the escape of the criminal. It was not that they wanted to see justice done to the victim, they merely wished to make certain of seeing "the head of a duke and a peer roll from his body, and noble blood flowing." Revolutionary memories had regained all their power. But the popular fury was disappointed, for the Duke poisoned himself by means of arsenic. But in order to placate public opinion a posthumous trial was held—a mediæval proceeding which only showed the pitch of excitement that had been reached.

Murder of the Duchesse de Praslin.

The King was in despair. "What a muddle," he exclaimed with his head in his hands, "a machine which is always going wrong!" And indeed, as Hugo pointed out, the army had been hit through General Cubières, the magistracy through President Teste, and now it was the turn of the old nobility in the person of the Duc de Praslin. Whereupon, to crown all, Prince d'Eckmühl stabbed one of his mistresses with a knife, whilst Comte Mortier, in a fit of madness, tried to kill his children. . . . What an opportunity for the people, who were ever on the watch for the shortcomings of the aristocracy!

Every day the system became more and more discredited. When the Duc de Montpensier drove to Vincennes in a sumptuous coach he was greeted with shouts of "Down with the robbers!" whilst street loafers would stop in front of placards bearing some such words as the following: "Wanted! Out-of-work women to clean a yard and two rooms." Yet Guizot remained imperturbable. Without knowing it, he had, during his long tenure of power, become isolated from the nation, even from the "legal country" of whom he imagined himself the mouthpiece, but with whom he now communicated only through his officials—the deputies who were his creatures. Perfectly content with "the electoral aristocracy" by whom he was surrounded, he imagined he was master of the situation. It was here that the danger lay. Conservative ideas may possibly have commanded a majority in the country, but as soon as self-interest and vanity came into play, the question became very different, and "the slightest disinterested affection would have been more reassuring." This was abundantly proved when the campaign of the banquets was inaugurated.

Campaign of the Banquets.

The banquet was an old instrument of propaganda. It had been employed after 1830, though it had subsequently fallen into disuse; but the Opposition revived it, for they had at their disposal men who were extremely gifted in all that was required of these popular love-feasts. Ledru-Rollin, with his fine figure and his beautiful white hands stroking his ruffle beard, always charmed his hearers, whilst Thiers remarked of his friend O. Barrot, "He is the man for such functions!" As Guizot had a clear majority in the Parliament, there was only one alternative left—to open the window, as Lamartine put it, to address the street and appeal to the people.

On the 9th of July, 1847, 1200 guests met at the Château-Rouge, where they demanded reform and sang the *Marseillaise*, while in their speeches the orators compared the times in which they lived to the evil days that marked the fall of the Restoration, likening Guizot to Polignac. The provinces followed suit. At Mâcon, Lamartine, who was a past-master in providing the Opposition with striking phrases, held forth to the accompaniment of a storm of thunder and lightning. "If royalty continues to act as it has been doing," he exclaimed, " you will find that instead of revolutions of liberty followed by counter-revolutions of glory you will have the revolution of the public conscience and the revolution of contempt ! " These last words from the lips of the " Moses of democracy " re-echoed all through France.

Nevertheless the organisers of the movement, the Orleanists Thiers and Odilon Barrot, had not the slightest intention of overthrowing the monarchy. But they met with the same experience as La Fayette had done—they were outdistanced by their followers. The advanced Radicals and Republicans occupied an ever more important place in the agitation for reform, whilst the competition of oratory and platform rhetoric bore fruit. When the meeting, at which the campaign of banquets had been decided upon, broke up, Garnier-Pagès remarked to one of his friends, " You see that tree? Well, cut into its bark the date of to-day—what we have just decided means revolution."

When the Chambers met in January 1848 the gravity of the situation was patent to all. The Government received warning after warning. " At home," said Montalembert, " you have an element that did not exist either in 1831 or in 1834—the increasingly open and avowed public sympathy for the Convention and the Montagne." Thiers, who felt the time had come for him to pose as a Liberal, adopted Jacobin airs, and whilst hoping that the revolutionary Government would remain in the hands of the moderates, declared that if his hopes were not fulfilled he would still support the revolution. Guizot listened to everything with perfect equanimity; when he was called upon to pronounce either for or against reform he gave evasive replies, and such was his ascendancy, and so habitual had the servility of the Chamber become, that he secured the majority. But a vote was not sufficient. The matter was getting beyond the parliamentary horizon; public opinion had been stirred, and the fact that the Government was not overthrown settled nothing.

The King, for his part, adopted an attitude out of which nothing would shake him. " All these people," he declared of the Opposition, " are bullies who are trying to intimidate the Government." He refused to be impressed by them, and repeated that there would be no reforms: "I do not want them. If the Chamber of Deputies votes in favour of them, I have the Chamber of Peers to throw them out. And even if the Chamber of Peers were to sanction them, there still remains my veto." His stubbornness was extraordinary and showed a strange misunderstanding of the circumstances—was the monarchy to risk its existence by refusing the vote to 200,000 more citizens and keeping its officials and salaried servants out of office? But neither Guizot nor Louis-Philippe would listen to reason in this connection. In vain did the Prince de Joinville, who was becoming anxious, write to his brother that their father was violating the constitution, and that "everything hung upon him," which was a grave menace to the system. It was labour lost. The Tuileries remained firm, and it was an apparently trivial incident that provoked the tumult.

Banquet of the 12th Legion.

The officers of the 12th legion of the National Guard, almost all of them Radicals, had arranged to give a banquet, to which they invited the deputies of the Left, but the latter, feeling they were outnumbered, refused. Was Guizot going to take advantage of this misunderstanding? Far from it! He prohibited the banquet (14th of January, 1848), whereupon his adversaries were immediately reconciled, and uniting solidly against him, made up their minds that the banquet should take place. Moreover, it was not to be a mere demonstration, as its predecessors had been; there was to be a procession through the streets in which the students, the National Guard and the working classes were to take part—a demand on the part of the people for reform and liberty. The date fixed was the 22nd of February.

But the deputies were not unanimous, some among them regarding this great act of legal resistance as dangerous. "If we are ready for a revolution," said one of the dissentients, "give your banquet; if we are not ready, it will mean a disturbance, and I do not want a disturbance." It was patent to everybody that the people were exasperated. Timid souls who had sharp ears declared that they could hear a dull rumble in the depths; philosophers like Tocqueville, terrified by the moral condition of the country, maintained that if they were not actually on the eve of a revolution, it was certainly thus that revolutions were prepared. Shrewd men, like X. Doudan, after examining the situation in Europe from the beginning of 1848, came to the conclusion that if the powder did not catch, they would regard "those who held the universe in their tiny hands as exceedingly clever people"; even the Republicans hesitated. They were of opinion that the secret societies were breaking up, and one of them observed, "In the present state of mind and morals, if I had the Republic in my hand I should take care not to let go of it." As for Thiers, he did not believe in the possibility of revolution, and remarked to Falloux, who had confided his fears to him, "A revolution! It is quite clear that you do not know the Government and are ignorant of their power. I know them; they have ten times more strength than any disturbance that could possibly break out." In short, prudence prevailed, and the Opposition negotiated with Guizot on the following basis—the banquet was to take place, but as soon as the guests had assembled a police commissioner would enter the hall and declare the assembly dissolved by order of the Prefect and draw up a report. Barrot would make a show of protesting, but would advise submission to the law; the guests would disperse, and when the case was brought to court it would be decided whether or not the Government had exceeded its powers.

It was a subtle expedient, a legal device which satisfied only the advocates of half-measures. "Are you going to take part in the farce that is going to be acted?" the deputies asked each other. But the question of the banquet really became of secondary importance. The thing that was arousing a passionate interest in Paris—and with the system of centralisation, Paris represented France—was the solemn and peaceful procession in which Armand Marrast, Carrel's successor on the *National*, had summoned the people to take part on the 22nd of February.

Guizot immediately retaliated by prohibiting both the banquet and the procession. The plan had failed, and hostilities were opened.

Louis-Philippe was firmly decided to hold out to the end: "It is I, I personally, whom the banquets are aimed against. We shall see who is the strongest." And this clarity disconcerted the Opposition. One section among the deputies saw clearly that although the Government might have violated liberty by prohibiting the banquet, they were perfectly entitled on the other hand to prevent riotous gatherings in the streets. Were they going to infringe the law and abandon the domain of legality in order to launch out into the unknown? Their attitude was reminiscent of that of the Liberals in 1830, who, having brought about the downfall of Charles X, were terrified by their own success.

On the matter being discussed, the wiser heads carried the day, and the banquet was postponed. But in order to disguise this retreat, it was decided to propose the indictment of the Ministers. The Republicans, on their side, most of whom "repudiated the idea of an attack as madness or an evil inspiration," set to work to appease their followers, and cancelled the procession that had been announced. Everything seemed to have been satisfactorily settled, and Louis-Philippe in great good cheer observed to Salvandy, who had expressed pessimism, "Well! You told us that we were sitting on a volcano! It was a fine volcano! They have given up the banquet, my dear fellow. Didn't I tell you that it would all end in smoke? It is a regular April Fool's Day."

This April Fool's Day was destined to have a sequel that the King was far from suspecting. But had he not received from Delessert, the Prefect of Police, the assurance that the Government was in a position to deal with the situation? Whilst General Jacqueminot, the commandant of the National Guard, repeated at the Tuileries that there was no cause for anxiety; and to make assurance doubly sure the garrison had been confined to barracks.

On the 22nd of February it was raining. Nevertheless in the neighbourhood of the Madeleine and of the Place de la Concorde groups of people gathered, "smocks and threadbare coats," guttersnipes shouting "Down with Guizot!" and singing the Girondin refrain which Lamartine had made fashionable. It was clear that in spite of the advice that had been given, the people refused to obey their leaders any longer, but were marching forward and insisting at all costs upon holding their demonstration.

Beginning of the Revolution.

Just at this moment there emerged from the Palais Bourbon a column of students, whom the troops dispersed without trouble, but as soon as the Municipal Guard, whom the people hated, showed themselves, the demonstration threatened to degenerate into a disturbance—the Guards were met by a volley of stones. . . . When darkness fell there was fighting in the Champs Élysées—a fairly harmless battle it is true, for the people confined themselves chiefly to the burning of chairs and benches and the pulling down of gas lamps. An armourer's shop was looted, an attempt made to set up a few barricades, and some bourgeois were mobbed; after which all was quiet. "It is all over," said Thiers; while even those who were in favour of insurrection, like Caussidière, for instance, who was destined subsequently to play a part as Prefect of Police, remarked regretfully that "it would not come to shots." During the night the troops bivouacked round bonfires in the rain, but at one o'clock in the morning, as everything was still quiet, they returned to barracks, and Louis-Philippe laughingly remarked to his friends that the people of Paris were not accustomed to making revolutions in the winter.

The National Guard.

On the 23rd the weather was still bad—heavy showers with intervals of sunshine. The troops had returned to their positions and the insurrection seemed to have fizzled out. And it would have done so had the Government not been foolish enough to call out the National Guard. The latter, the majority, if not all, of whom were hostile to Guizot, met to the cry of "*Vive la réforme!*" and the aspect of affairs changed from that moment.

The legions from each *arrondissement*, as they left their *mairie* for the position allotted to them, made loud demonstrations; the third legion prevented the cuirassiers from clearing the Place des Victoires, that had been invaded by the mob; the fourth made preparations to present at the Palais Bourbon a petition demanding the immediate trial of the Ministers; the twelfth, which was the most revolutionary of them all, belonging to the Panthéon, shouted, "*Vive la République!*" Maintain order? Not a single one of these men dreamt of doing any such thing.

What could have come over the citizen militia, "the bulwark

of the system," whose uniform the King donned on holidays, whom he regarded as his chattels, his creation, and for whom he reserved all his favours? Had the moderate members of the National Guard remained at home? It is possible; and the Prefect of Police boasted of having forced them to come out into the street by frightening them "and allowing fifty shops to be looted." But it was too late; at midday the Government saw that it had resuscitated the moribund insurrection, and that the defenders of public order had been transformed into insurgents. Louis-Philippe was overwhelmed—the unprecedented and unexpected disloyalty of the Guard cut him to the heart. Already weakened by old age—he was seventy-four—and distressed by the recent death of his sister, Madame Adelaide, whom he loved dearly, and to whom he had been accustomed to turn for support and advice, the King, whose shrewd features seemed to say, "I am cleverer than you, and I know the cards you all hold," was apparently overcome with terror, and all of a sudden his decrepitude became obvious. To make the troops fire upon the National Guard, the bourgeoisie—he thrust the idea from him in horror. "I have seen too much blood!" he exclaimed. His mind was made up; without further ado he dismissed Guizot and his colleagues, observing to them in accents of peculiar bitterness, "You are more fortunate than I am, all of you!"

Fall of Guizot.

It was half-past one. The Chamber was sitting at the Palais Bourbon. Suddenly Guizot entered, more haughty than ever, "his head thrown back so that there might be no excuse for thinking it was drooping." He mounted the rostrum and announced that he had resigned. Tumult reigned. The Left applauded with all the enthusiasm of victors; the majority, overcome with fury, exclaimed, "It is outrageous! We have been betrayed!" and they proceeded to heap abuse upon the head of the ex-President of the Council, whilst Thiers, ever sardonic, and doubtless thinking of the King, sneered, "Ah! *he* is frightened!" Outside, Guizot's resignation was greeted with a transport of joy—what a success for the National Guard! It was they who had overthrown the corrupt Government, and that by their presence alone, without violence and merely by asserting their will to power. Whereupon the legions in the streets, with their shakos stuck on the ends of their muskets, marched triumphantly past, shouting, "*Vive la réforme!*"

From that moment the success of the revolution was assured. By capitulating not to an insurrection, but to a demonstration, and by granting in a moment of depression all that he had hitherto refused, Louis-Philippe had laid down his arms. He offered the Government to Molé, who accepted with great reluctance and set to work to find colleagues. But while the politicians were wasting time in palavers, events moved on apace.

The departure of Guizot was not enough for the Republicans, who were gradually beginning to take the lead in the movement.

The Republicans.

When, on the Place de la Concorde, Tocqueville announced the fall of the Government, a working man, a short, thick-set fellow, replied, "We know that," and then pointing to the Tuileries, he added, "We want something more than that!" The victory seemed to have been won; the National Guard, already seeing themselves electors, continued to shout aloud their joy all over Paris; but in the suburbs and in the students' quarters, the members of the secret societies, the Socialists and Communists, all those who were thought to have disappeared since the disturbances of 1839, but whose revolutionary faith had on the contrary only been strengthened in solitude, met together, and plucking up their spirits, prepared for the real insurrection, the popular, plebeian insurrection, which was to be grafted upon the innocent bourgeois disturbance, and in the end dominate it. This subterranean activity, this taking in hand of the moribund agitation, escaped the notice of the police and even of the Opposition.

On the 23rd of February, at nightfall, there were outbreaks here and there; the Municipal Guard drove back the demonstrators and there was no fighting.

Massacre of the Capucines.

The houses were lighted up, and groups marched along singing the *Marseillaise* and demanding the death of Guizot. About nine o'clock a body that had set out from the Faubourg Saint Antoine made for the Ministry of Foreign Affairs, on the Boulevard des Capucines, where they found themselves face to face with the 14th line regiment, which was protecting the building. They tried to get past, and endeavoured to force a way through the ranks, but the troops stepped back and crossed bayonets. Whereupon the mob became exasperated, and the more enraged among them defied the soldiers by holding flaming torches under their faces. Suddenly a report was heard—did it come from the troops or from the insurgents? It was impossible to say. Was it a certain Republican, named Lagrange, who, eager to open the fight, had fired the first shot? Or, on the other hand, was it a sergeant, who, seeing his Colonel threatened, tried to defend him? The fact remains that the isolated report was followed by shooting on all sides. . . .

The mob fell back, the troops dispersed, and in the empty space lay the dead and wounded. . . . When the moment of terror was over, the mob returned, shouting, "Vengeance! they are murdering the people!" Stopping a passing vehicle, they heaped up the victims, sixteen dead, and promenaded them through Paris, howling and roaring in the rain, and coming to a standstill under the windows of the *National*, demanded reprisals in ever more threatening tones. This lugubrious procession ended only at half-past two in the morning, before the *mairie* of the fourth *arrondissement*, where the bodies were deposited.

The news of the massacre of the Place des Capucines plunged the Tuileries into confusion. It reached there at ten o'clock, and the King wavered between the contradictory counsels with which he was overwhelmed. Molé had very prudently resigned his office, the massacre providing too good an excuse for him not to rid himself of a difficult task. Thiers remained. He believed himself to be the Messiah of the moment, just as Guizot had been in 1840, but he needed friends to support him, colleagues as deeply immersed as himself in the reform movement. "Barrot is indispensable for the suppression of the insurrection," he informed the King, to which the latter replied, "You are merely repeating the gossip of the cafés!" It was not a time for argument: Barrot could be Minister, but at the same time the King placed Bugeaud in command of the troops—Barrot stood for reform; Bugeaud for repression. "The King held out his right hand and shook his left fist."

Thiers Minister.

Bugeaud might save the situation. About one o'clock in the morning, while the mob were still exhibiting the victims in the streets, he arrived at the Tuileries, and putting his watch down on the table, said, "By four o'clock we must have opened the attack everywhere. I have never known defeat, and I count upon not losing my reputation to-day." As he remembered the siege of Saragossa, he ordered free bullets to be placed in the muzzles of the guns, and in the declamatory tones which he had been accustomed to use since his African campaigns, he gave his orders to his subordinates, Tiburce Sébastiani and Bedeau—there were to be four columns, one directed towards the Hôtel de Ville, the second to the Bastille, the third manœuvring between the first two, and the fourth to the Panthéon. But in all the arrangements no mention was made of the National Guard.

Bugeaud.

The morning of the 24th of February dawned; it was still pouring in torrents. The columns began to move at six o'clock in the morning, but the insurgents had not been idle during the night, and General Bedeau's regiment was pulled up by a solidly constructed barricade across the Boulevard Bonne-Nouvelle. What was he to do? Instead of attacking, Bedeau held a parley; he was advised to be lenient—everything could be arranged. And the old African veteran, powerless and inexperienced in the face of civil war, decided to send an envoy to Bugeaud.

Bedeau.

The latter, "a brave and worthy soldier," as Morny called him, "but a regular old washerwoman in politics," had not yet got over the manner of his departure from Algeria, and wanted to have his revenge. He had already written confidentially to Thiers, "I have always thought that you and I would be called upon to save the monarchy," and had let it be understood that he would be willing to enter the new Government. But could he do so with blood on his hands? Deafened by well-meaning advisers and groaning bourgeois—"They sent me silly like themselves," he afterwards remarked—he gave the order to cease fire everywhere. Bedeau's column fell back on the Tuileries.

It seemed as though everybody had lost their heads and, as Cournot declared, were vying with each other "in stupidity and cowardice." But the Republicans knew what they wanted

—during the course of his retreat Bedeau found the barricades erected once more. Negotiations were again opened. The troops, demoralised, and sick of prolonged operations in mud, ended by making common cause with the insurgents, and with muskets reversed disorderly bands of soldiers might be seen marching arm in arm with workmen. At this juncture Bugeaud came to the conclusion that one or two concessions and the announcement of the Thiers Ministry would restore order.

Parleys.

On the Place de la Concorde a struggle ensued between the motley crowd which were descending the boulevards and the Municipal Guard, who had remained loyal. It ended in the defeat of the latter, who were torn to pieces and massacred. Whereupon the Opposition tried to show its head—Barrot, encouraged by Thiers, who accused Bugeaud of being responsible for all the misfortunes of the day, came out into the street and urged the mob to be quiet. But the tribune was no longer speaking in the atmosphere of popular meetings, and was received with cries of " Down with the sycophants ! We don't want Thiers ! We don't want Barrot ! The people are masters ! " And when General La Moricière was detailed to appease the mob, he met with no better success.

About half-past ten, as the King was quietly having his breakfast, Monsieur de Laubespin, an officer on the staff, arrived, and with his face all distraught, asked to speak to Rémusat, who happened to be among the guests, and in two words informed him of the situation—the Place de la Concorde was threatened and the Royal Family in danger. " What is Moniseur de Laubespin telling you ? " the King asked aloud. " Sire, he has very grave news." Louis-Philippe remained cool and collected. At the instance of Thiers and his friends, he consented to dissolve the Chamber and, in order to restore his rapidly vanishing popularity, decided to review the National Guard and the troops who were protecting the Tuileries.

At eleven o'clock he mounted his horse, and followed by his two sons, Nemours and Montpensier, together with Bugeaud and La Moricière, he rode along the front of the troops drawn up in the Carrousel. A few soldiers shouted "*Vive le roi!*" but

The King Reviews his Troops.

the majority exclaimed "*Vive la réforme!* Down with the Ministers!" Suddenly Louis-Philippe turned his horse's head, and returning to the castle, sank silent and motionless into his chair—this last failure had taken away all his courage.

At the Tuileries the scene resembled a market-place—messengers, people offering advice and politicians with eleventh-hour suggestions. "All is lost," exclaimed Thiers, "I am done for!"—"I have known that for a long time, sir," replied the King. Nobody, not even Bugeaud, seemed to remember that the monarchy still had 8,000 or 10,000 men at its disposal, and that order might be restored if a little determination were shown. But just at this moment the sound of firing was heard—the insurgents were attacking the guard-house of the Château-d'Eau, which was only two hundreds yards away from the Tuileries in the direction of the Palais Royal. La Moricière galloping off towards the sound, tried to intervene and put a stop to the fight; but he was met by Republicans, who were determined not to come to terms, and in discouragement he retraced his steps.

The King Abdicates.

In the King's cabinet his abdication was now being discussed. Louis-Philippe himself was the first to mention the word: "My abdication! They will only get my abdication with my life!" Suddenly Emile de Girardin appeared upon the scene, his eyes aflame, declaring that immediate abdication was necessary. The King hesitated, but the Queen intervened: "You must not sign, you must not abdicate. We must die here!" Every fresh arrival shouted his opinion, whether he were a member of the National Guard or an official; the tumult was terrible, and for a moment drowned the noise of the shooting outside. Louis-Philippe, still sitting in his arm-chair near the window, then addressed his generals, Soult, Gérard, and Sébastiani, who were gathered round him: "Is defence possible?" Absolute silence reigned; nobody answered, nobody expressed an opinion. "I will abdicate," said the King; and in spite of the protests of the Queen, he slowly and deliberately wrote the following lines: "I abdicate in favour of my grandson, the Comte de Paris, the Crown which the will of the people called upon me to wear. May he succeed in the great task which falls to his lot to-day."

Some of those present suggested that if the Duchesse d'Orléans were made Regent the people would be better pleased, but the King, pulling himself up, exclaimed in determined tones, "I shall never sign that. I would rather die! It is against the law!"

About half-past twelve, a lawyer named Crémieux rushed in breathless and panting and with his clothes all disarranged: "The people are coming, in a few minutes they will be here. . . . Sire, you must go." Louis-Philippe stared fixedly at him, then he took off his general's hat and his uniform with its wide epaulettes, and without leaving his chair, said, "A round hat and an overcoat!" When these garments were brought to him, he added, "My keys!" Through the Tuileries, the King and the Queen, followed by the Duc de Montpensier and his wife, together with a few faithful followers, made for the gate leading to the Pont-Tournant. Louis-Philippe was calm; the Queen extremely excited was murmuring: "Treason! Treason!" At the gate there were a few moments of agonising delay—the carriages were not there. . . . At last two broughams and a cabriolet drew up. The fugitives crowded into them, and Crémieux, taking from the hands of a footman a large green portfolio, stuffed it with his fist into the royal carriage.

Flight of the King.

The mob, already masters of the Hôtel de Ville, found the Tuileries deserted; the troops who had been defending it had fallen back on to the Place de la Concorde. Whereupon the orgy began—in the royal apartments everything was broken up, looted and pillaged, the furniture was thrown out of the windows and the King's bed fouled; on the stairs wild women might be seen dressed up in robes trimmed with silver and gold, and guttersnipes in brilliant uniforms. The cellars were forced and the casks broken open, with the result that the wine flowed in such quantities that some of the insurgents, already drunk, were drowned. Meanwhile, in the Throne Room, the Republican Lagrange, who had just been handed the deed of abdication, mounted the platform and shouted "*Vive la République!*"

Looting of the Tuileries.

At the Palais Bourbon, the Chamber was sitting, protected by a brigade of troops. Thiers, who was still legally Minister, put in an appearance, but he was so dazed by the rapidity with which events had moved that he could only keep repeating, " The flood is rising ! The flood is rising ! " Whereupon he made his way home by back streets, and in front of his house found his liveried servants working at the construction of a barricade.

The Duchesse d'Orléans in the Chamber.

The Duc de Nemours and the Duchesse d'Orléans alone kept their heads. Leading her two sons, the elder of whom was the Comte de Paris by the hand, the Duchess presented herself in the Chamber, where she was greeted with cheers. Dupin, supported by Barrot, announced the establishment of the Regency, and it seemed as if the dynasty had been saved, when a Republican, named Marie, moved the adjournment of the House in order to allow the Duchess to leave. The latter refused, whereupon Marie demanded the formation of a Provisional Government, and the debate rambled on. Suddenly one of the doors of the hall was violently burst open and a mob of armed men rushed into the arena—the troops and the generals, outnumbered and at their wits' end, had allowed the insurgents to break through.

Lamartine.

Lamartine was sitting silent in his seat, his head buried in his hands, lost in thought. Tocqueville went up to him : " You are the only man that will be listened to. Speak or we are done for ! " Slim and erect, his eyes " fixed and vacant," Lamartine replied, "I refuse to speak as long as that woman and that child are here." And he relapsed into meditation. One orator succeeded another in the hubbub, but they were hardly heeded. . . . Suddenly Lamartine rose, slowly mounted the steps of the rostrum, and after saying a few words on " one of the most touching sights it was possible to see in the annals of the human race—a proud princess defending herself together with her innocent son," he declared himself in favour of a provisional Government.

The Duc de Nemours had been right when, in giving orders for the Chamber to be defended at all costs, he added, " The safety of the country depends on it, and cost what it may the debate must be carried on to the end." But now the insurrection had forced its way; in successive waves it had invaded the Chamber to the cry of " *Vive la République !* " After that all idea of a regency was out of the question, and the Duchess made her escape through the President's house in the direction of the

Invalides. At one moment she was separated from her sons, and cried out in heart-rending tones, "My children! My children!" and the Comte de Paris, passed along from the arms of one to another, and let down out of a window, at last rejoined his mother.

In the debating hall the disorder had reached its height; almost at haphazard, the mob acclaimed the names of the members of the provisional Government as they were pronounced from the rostrum—Arago, Lamartine, Garnier-Pagès, Ledru-Rollin and Marie. . . . But the voice of an actor named Bocage rose above the tumult: "To the Hôtel de Ville! Lamartine at the head!" Whereupon, as though they were obeying an order, the triumphant insurgents immediately left the Palais Bourbon and made for the Hôtel de Ville, the traditional citadel of the Paris insurrections. It was about four o'clock.

Meanwhile, in a little dark blue bourgeois brougham drawn by one black horse, the King and Queen made their way towards Saint Cloud; the Queen calm and silently weeping, the King downcast and demoralised. That night the fugitives slept at Dreux, where they heard the news of the proclamation of the Republic. The next day, avoiding the main roads, they skirted Evreux, and in a farmer's gig made for the coast of Normandy, and reached the neighbourhood of Honfleur, where they hoped to embark secretly for England.

But no boat could be put at their disposal and the sea was very rough. Under an assumed name the King then left for Trouville, where he entered into negotiations with the owner of a fishing-smack. But in the little town the people were beginning to get suspicious of a certain Monsieur Lebrun who bore an extraordinary resemblance to the fallen monarch. Whereupon the latter moved on again during the night and returned to Honfleur, where he rejoined the Queen. Eventually the English vice-consul at Le Havre, by permission of his Government, placed a vessel at the disposal of the King, and on the evening of the 2nd of March, Louis-Philippe set sail for Newhaven on board the passenger steamer the *Express*.

The King Crosses to England.

He was destined to live another two years, in exile at Claremont, a mansion lent to him by the King of the Belgians. At first he was so poor that Lord Aberdeen, taking pity on him, slipped £1000 into the hand of one of his companions. Guizot, who during February had hidden with friends, soon joined him in England. And in this foreign land these two men, who thought they had once and for all established the bourgeois monarchy in France, were able to ponder over the mistakes they had made and the way in which they had helped each other to commit suicide.

It is said that on his flight, when they were changing horses at the Trianon, Louis-Philippe, overcome with fatigue, leant against a tree and murmured, "Worse, worse than Charles X! A hundred times worse than Charles X!" And he was right. What a difference between this precipitate disorderly flight, denuded of all honour and even of seemliness, and the exodus of Charles X, that slow and peaceful exodus, that was still as it were illumined by a reflection of majesty! What a difference too in the days immediately preceding the fall of the two dynasties, that of the elder branch of the Bourbons and that of the House of Orleans! The revolution of 1848, it has been said, was a result without a cause; but Falloux quite rightly corrected this somewhat sweeping assertion—it was, as a matter of fact, a result out of all proportion to its cause. There was no tyranny to be shaken, no provocation to be met, it was a power that had always respected the law, while there was not the smallest suspicion of a *coup d'état*, nothing reminiscent of the ordinances. What then was the reason for this "saturnalia," as Cournot called it, this revolt that cost the lives of 72 soldiers and 289 insurgents, and overthrew the dynasty?

Alfred de Vigny in *Les Destinées*, referring to the King under the name of Ulysses, wrote:

> "Ulysse avait connu les hommes et les villes,
> Sondé le lac de sang des révolutions,
> Des saints et des héros les cœurs faux et serviles,
> Et le sable mouvant des constitutions. . . .
> Et pourtant, un matin, des royales demeures,
> Comme un autre en trois jours, il tombait en trois heures." [1]

[1] "Ulysses had known men and cities, he had fathomed the bloody waters of revolution, the false and servile hearts of saints and heroes, and the shifting sands of constitutions. . . . Nevertheless, one morning, from the royal palaces, as another had done in three days, he fell in three hours. . . ."

And indeed what explanation was there to offer for the fact that the King, in the twinkling of an eye, had been forsaken by all?

Causes of his Downfall.

The trouble was to be found at the very root of the system—those who had profited by the revolution of 1830 were not those who had made it; the men of July, the bourgeoisie, were not the combatants of July, the proletariat. The latter had never assented to the compromise presented by the semi-legitimate dynasty, "the juggling away of the revolution"; and the attempts at assassination that occurred throughout the reign of Louis-Philippe, afforded sufficient proof of the strength of their resentment. When in February 1848 the insurrection was triumphant, the bourgeois of the Opposition were not prepared, as the Liberals had been in 1830—they had no programme, no leaders; and the Republicans, seeing that there was no Government, boldly took the task of ruling on their own shoulders.

Moreover the policy of the King and of Guizot was calculated to please only the possessing class, the rich bourgeoisie, "the satisfied," who constituted a mere minority. This deliberate stagnation and this dogma of immobility offended the majority—at home they were denied the vote, abroad the Government refused to wipe out the disgrace of 1815 and fight for liberty. "They are humiliating the country," was the constant reproach of the Opposition for almost eighteen years. And gradually the people, who in spite of everything had remained faithful to the memory of Napoleon, confounding the Emperor and Liberty in a common worship, became alienated from a dynasty that brought them no glory. To these general reasons, others, possibly more trivial but none the less decisive, must be added. There was a certain similarity between the crisis of 1830 and that of 1848—just as the hostile rivalry between Villèle and Chateaubriand had contributed to the fall of Charles X, so the rivalry based upon dislike between Thiers and Guizot was conducive to the overthrow of the bourgeois monarchy. In both cases a similar chain of intrigues and appeals to public opinion undermined the system.

And Louis-Philippe himself also had his share of responsibility for his own fall. In spite of all his cleverness and experience, he was unable to see and arrest the movement of disloyalty which was growing every day; rightly convinced of his own worth, he wanted to establish personal rule once and for all, and hurt the feelings of the petty bourgeoisie and the National Guard, who were his most devoted adherents. Lacking the support of popular assent to his rule as well as the right of legitimacy, relying on the Charter and nothing but the Charter, and convinced that universal suffrage amounted to anarchy, he gradually lost all touch with the country. That Guizot should have a majority was enough for him; he did not want to make "any sacrifice in advance," and from year to year, without his being aware of it, his isolation became more and more manifest.

Nevertheless, if in 1848 he had still been the man he was in 1830, everything might have been different. But weakened by age, he lacked firmness as well as foresight. The attitude of the National Guard and its disorderly demonstrations in favour of reform left him stupefied, disarmed and powerless. "In the case of a moral insurrection," he declared, "it is impossible to take either the offensive or the defensive," and after making one concession after another he descended to the rank of a fugitive.

But to regard the July Monarchy only from the political angle would be to take a narrow, unjust and one-sided view. It must

Achievements of the July Monarchy.

not be forgotten that between 1830 and 1848, the principles of liberty and of "free scope for the individual," which had been germinating under the Restoration, had developed, and that Louis-Philippe left France richer and more prosperous than she had been under Charles X; in spite of a few passing crises and the persistence of certain prejudices, the country, at the time of his downfall, was on the full tide of economic expansion and quite ready to take a prominent place in Europe. As for the policy of peace at any price for which he has been so much blamed, did it have any disastrous results for France? And would it be fair to leave out of account the conquest of Algeria and the proclamation of Belgian neutrality, that neutrality which but yesterday formed one of the mainstays of European equilibrium?

BIBLIOGRAPHY. Apponyi, *Journal* (Vol. IV, 1926). L. Blanc, *Histoire de la Révolution de* 1848 (2 vols., new ed.) (1880, Vol. I). M. du Camp,

Souvenirs de l'Année 1848 (1876). A. Crémieux, *La Révolution de Février* (1912) (with bibliography). Garnier-Pagès, *Histoire de la Révolution de* 1848 (5 vols., 1861). La Hodde, *La Naissance de la République en Février* 1848 (1850). Lamartine, *Histoire de la Révolution de* 1848 (2 vols., 1849). Lemoine, *Abdication de Louis-Philippe Racontée par Lui-Même* (1851). Princesse de Ligne, *Souvenirs* (Brussels, 1923). L. Ménard, *Prologue d'une Révolution* (1849). de Normanby, *Une Année de Révolution* (2 vols., 1859). E. Pelletan, *Histoire des Trois Journées* (1848). Proudhon, *Correspondance* (4 vols., 1875) (Vol. II). Saint-René Taillandier, *Les Souvenirs du Conseiller de la Reine Victoria* (*Revue des Deux Mondes*, 1877). D. Stern, *Histoire de la Révolution de* 1848 (3 vols., new ed., 1878, Vol. I). Tocqueville, *Souvenirs* (1893); *An Englishman in Paris* (French translation by Hercé) (2 vols., 1893). Véron, *Mémoires d'un Bourgeois de Paris* (6 vols., 1853–55 (Vol. V).

INDEX

INDEX

INDEX

INDEX

INDEX

INDEX

INDEX

INDEX

INDEX

INDEX

INDEX

INDEX

PRINTED IN GREAT BRITAIN BY
RICHARD CLAY & SONS, LIMITED,
BUNGAY, SUFFOLK.